THE 100 GREATEST
CONSOLE VIDEO GAMES
1977–1987

BRETT WEISS

FOREWORD BY WALTER DAY

Schiffer Publishing Ltd

4880 Lower Valley Road • Atglen, PA 19310

DEDICATION

This book is dedicated to the late, great Bill "The Game Doctor" Kunkel, one of the cofounders of video game journalism. As a teenager, I devoured every issue of *Electronic Games*, the magazine he helped establish with Arnie Katz and Joyce Worley. I finally had to throw away the original copies because I had read them to pieces.

When Bill and his wife Laurie bought my first book at the Classic Gaming Expo in 2007, you could have knocked me over with a cathode ray. When he enthusiastically agreed to write the foreword to my second book, I was humbled and honored more than words can say.

The video game industry misses you, Bill.

Copyright © 2014 by Brett Weiss

Library of Congress Control Number: 2014939715

All rights reserved. No part of this work may be reproduced or used in any form or by any means—graphic, electronic, or mechanical, including photocopying or information storage and retrieval systems—without written permission from the publisher.

The scanning, uploading, and distribution of this book or any part thereof via the Internet or via any other means without the permission of the publisher is illegal and punishable by law. Please purchase only authorized editions and do not participate in or encourage the electronic piracy of copyrighted materials.
"Schiffer," "Schiffer Publishing, Ltd. & Design," and the "Design of pen and inkwell" are registered trademarks of Schiffer Publishing, Ltd.

Designed by Molly Shields
Type set in Square721 BdEx BT/Garamond

ISBN: 978-0-7643-4618-7
Printed in China

Published by Schiffer Publishing, Ltd.
4880 Lower Valley Road
Atglen, PA 19310
Phone: (610) 593-1777; Fax: (610) 593-2002
E-mail: Info@schifferbooks.com

For our complete selection of fine books on this and related subjects, please visit our website at www.schifferbooks.com. You may also write for a free catalog.

This book may be purchased from the publisher. Please try your bookstore first.

We are always looking for people to write books on new and related subjects. If you have an idea for a book, please contact us at proposals@schifferbooks.com

Schiffer Publishing's titles are available at special discounts for bulk purchases for sales promotions or premiums. Special editions, including personalized covers, corporate imprints, and excerpts can be created in large quantities for special needs. For more information, contact the publisher.

CONTENTS

Foreword by Walter Day...5
Preface..6
1. *Adventure* (Atari 2600)...8
2. *Air-Sea Battle* (Atari 2600)......................................11
3. *Antarctic Adventure* (ColecoVision)........................13
4. *Arkanoid* (NES)..15
5. *Artillery Duel* (ColecoVision, Astrocade).................17
6. *Asteroids* (Atari 2600, Atari 7800)...........................19
7. *Atlantis* (Intellivision)...22
8. *Attack of the Timelord!* (Odyssey2).......................25
9. *Balloon Fight* (NES)...27
10. *Beauty & the Beast* (Intellivision)..........................29
11. *Berzerk* (Atari 5200)..31
12. *Boulder Dash* (ColecoVision)................................33
13. *Bounty Bob Strikes Back* (Atari 5200)...................35
14. *Bump 'n' Jump* (ColecoVision, Intellivision).........37
15. *BurgerTime* (ColecoVision, Intellivision)..............39
16. *Carnival* (ColecoVision).......................................42
17. *Castlevania* (NES)...44
18. *Cat Trax* (Arcadia 2001).......................................46
19. *Centipede* (Atari 5200, Atari 7800, ColecoVision)....48
20. *Choplifter* (Master System)...................................51
21. *Circus* Atari (Atari 2600).......................................53
22. *Combat* (Atari 2600)..55
23. *Communist Mutants from Space* (Atari 2600).......57
24. *Defender* (Atari 5200, ColecoVision)....................59
25. *Demon Attack* (Atari 2600)...................................62
26. *Dig Dug* (Atari 7800)...64
27. *Diner* (Intellivision)...66
28. *Dodge 'Em* (Atari 2600)...68
29. *Donkey Kong* (ColecoVision, NES).......................70
30. *Donkey Kong Jr.* (NES)...73
31. *Donkey Kong 3* (NES)..75
32. *DragonStomper* (Atari 2600).................................77
33. *Escape from the MindMaster* (Atari 2600)............79
34. *Fantasy Zone, Fantasy Zone II* (Sega Master System)......81
35. *Food Fight* (Atari 7800)...84
36. *Fortress of Narzod* (Vectrex).................................86
37. *Freeway* (Atari 2600)...88
38. *Frenzy* (ColecoVision)...90
39. *Frogger* (ColecoVision), *The Official Frogger* (Atari 2600).......92
40. *Galaga* (Atari 7800)...95
41. *Galaxian* (ColecoVision).......................................97
42. *Ghosts 'n Goblins* (NES).....................................100
43. *Gradius* (NES)...102
44. *Gremlins* (Atari 5200)...105
45. *H.E.R.O.* (Atari 2600, ColecoVision)..................108
46. *The Incredible Wizard* (Astrocade).....................110
47. *Indy 500* (Atari 2600)..112
48. *Jawbreaker* (Atari 2600).....................................114
49. *Joust* (Atari 7800)..116
50. *Jr. Pac-Man* (Atari 2600).....................................118
51. *K.C. Munchkin!, K.C.'s Krazy Chase!* (Odyssey2)......120
52. *Kaboom!* (Atari 2600)..123
53. *Killer Bees!* (Odyssey2).......................................125
54. *Lady Bug* (ColecoVision)....................................127
55. *The Legend of Zelda* (NES).................................129
56. *Mario Bros.* (NES)...132
57. *Mega Man* (NES)...134
58. *Metroid* (NES)..136
59. *Miner 2049er* (ColecoVision)..............................138
60. *MineStorm/MineStorm II* (Vectrex)....................140
61. *Missile Command* (Atari 2600, Atari 5200).......142
62. *Moon Patrol* (Atari 5200)....................................145
63. *Mouse Trap* (ColecoVision)................................147
64. *Mr. Do!* (ColecoVision).......................................149
65. *Mr. Do!'s Castle* (Atari 5200, ColecoVision)......152
66. *Ms. Pac-Man* (Atari 7800)..................................154
67. *Pac-Man* (NES)..156
68. *PBA Bowling* (Intellivision).................................158
69. *Pengo* (Atari 5200)..160
70. *Pepper II* (ColecoVision)....................................162
71. *Phoenix* (Atari 2600)...164
72. *Pick Axe Pete!* (Odyssey2)..................................167
73. *Pitfall!* (Atari 2600, ColecoVision).....................169
74. *Pitfall II: Lost Caverns* (Atari 2600, Atari 5200)....172
75. *Popeye* (NES)..174
76. *Qix* (Atari 5200)...176
77. *Rambo: First Blood Part II* (Master System).......178
78. *River Raid* (Atari 2600, Atari 5200, ColecoVision)......180
79. *Robotron: 2084* (Atari 5200)...............................183
80. *Scramble* (Vectrex)..185
81. *Shark! Shark!* (Intellivision)................................187
82. *Slither* (ColecoVision)...189
83. *Solar Fox* (Atari 2600)...191
84. *Space Dungeon* (Atari 5200)...............................193
85. *Space Invaders* (Atari 2600)...............................195
86. *Spy Hunter* (ColecoVision).................................198
87. *Stampede* (Atari 2600, Intellivision)...................200
88. *Star Castle* (Vectrex)..202
89. *Super Breakout* (Atari 2600)...............................204
90. *Super Mario Bros.* (NES).....................................207
91. *Turbo* (ColecoVision)..209
92. *Turmoil* (Atari 2600)..212
93. *Turtles!* (Odyssey2)..214
94. *Tutankham* (ColecoVision).................................216
95. *Video Olympics* (Atari 2600)..............................218
96. *Warlords* (Atari 2600)...220
97. *Web Wars* (Vectrex)...222
98. *Worm Whomper* (Intellivision)...........................224
99. *Yars' Revenge* (Atari 2600).................................226
100. *Zaxxon* (ColecoVision)......................................228
Appendix: The Next 100..230
Bibliography..235
Index..236

ACKNOWLEDGMENTS

Special thanks to my beautiful wife, Charis, for her love, support, and mad computer skills, and to our awesome teenagers, Ryan and Katie, who help make life fun.

Special thanks also to my parents, who gave me life, a roof over my head, three squares, and half of a ColecoVision.

I'd also like to give a shout out to: Al Backiel, Syd Bolton, Van Burnham, Chris Cavanaugh, Jeff Cooper, Walter Day, Rob Dire, Marty Goldberg, Earl Green, Jesse Hardesty, Leonard Herman, David Kaelin, Arnie Katz, Rick Kelsey, Adam King, Scott Alan Marriott, Skyler Miller, Dave Mrozek, Russ Perry Jr., Tien Phan, Joe Santulli, Holt Slack, Geoffrey Douglas Smith, Brandon and Rebekah Staggs, Sean Stewart, Darren Sulfridge, Jonathan Sutyak, Michael Thomasson, Kurt Vendel, Joyce Worley, Albert Yarusso, Julie Bryant, Matt Miller, and Tom Zjaba.

Certain images courtesy of Bryan C. Smith, Joe Santulli (Digital Press), and Albert Yarusso (AtariAge).

FOREWORD

BY WALTER DAY

On behalf of the one billion gamers who have enjoyed playing video games since the early 1970s, I would like to thank Brett Weiss for boldly taking up the task of creating his landmark books on classic video games, including *The 100 Greatest Console Video Games: 1977–1987*. Though we are all pioneers—yes, the first generation to pioneer the video game age—it's a very rare individual who puts their money, time, and energy on the line to create books on the subject that will pass our legacy on to future generations. Brett Weiss is such a man. And, thanks to Weiss 'inspired work, the gamers of the future will be able to better appreciate the remarkable heritage we have created for them.

But, our work is not yet finished. I believe that Brett's books are like the lightning rod that attracts the storm. I believe that it is our duty to turn over every stone in order to unearth every last bit of historical information on the birth of the video game age—and document it, just like Brett is doing. Brett has inspired us by showing us what needs to be done. Now, it is time to support Brett in his scholarly efforts by finding any data he can use for his upcoming books or by making sure that his books make it onto the reference book shelves of the world. After all, he is not only telling the story of history's greatest games, he is telling our story. Because we were history's first gamers. *We were the Golden Age.*

A highly respected industry figure, **Walter Day** founded the legendary Twin Galaxies arcade in Ottumwa, Iowa, in 1981. He's a world-renowned video game scorekeeper, having contributed to the *Guinness Book of World Records* and created *The Official Video Game & Pinball Book of World Records*. Mr. Day also publishes the *Twin Galaxies Video Game Trading Cards* and, wearing his patented referee shirt, has been featured in such films as *Chasing Ghosts: Beyond the Arcade* (2007) and *The King of Kong: A Fistful of Quarters* (2007).

PREFACE

Throughout the relatively short history of video games, a number of "best-of" and "top-100" lists have appeared in print and online. Since lists of this type have been done before, what's the point of this book?

For starters, to my knowledge there has never been a "100 Greatest" video games *book* of any type, just articles and magazine features. Further, most previous top-whatever video game lists offer a couple of sentences or maybe a paragraph or two about each title. This book, on the other hand, covers each game in exhaustive detail, featuring such content as production histories, sequels, remakes, ports for current consoles, anecdotes, creator info, collector pricing, comparisons to similar games, comparisons to lesser versions of the game, and, most interestingly (at least to me), quotes from industry professionals (both recent and from older publications).

In addition, most endeavors of this type cover too narrow or, conversely, too broad of a category, focusing on either a single system—best 100 NES games, for example—or the industry as a whole, lumping together console, handheld, computer, and arcade games from all eras. By comparison, this book zeroes in on those console titles released during a singular, highly crucial, fondly remembered decade—one marked by the introduction of the indispensable Atari 2600, Odyssey2, and Intellivision, the unleashing of the underrated Vectrex, the mind-blowing debut of the next-gen ColecoVision and Atari 5200, and the rebirth of the industry through Nintendo's legendary juggernaut, the NES.

To the very best of my ability, which is informed by 40 years of playing video games and more than 15 years of writing about them professionally, I've boiled the hundreds of console games released from 1977–1987 down to the 100 greatest titles. I'm sure I excluded some cartridges that many gamers—including you, constant reader—hold in particularly high regard, and for that I don't apologize.

Rather, I hope my perceived oversight makes your blood boil (or at least simmer), forcing you to fire up the respective classic console, plug in that old favorite that I neglected to include, and extol the virtues of that game to anyone who will listen online or in person. Like movies, paintings, and novels, video games are an art form, and it's okay to be passionate about them.

But before you get too angry, check the back of the book for "The Next 100" appendix, which catalogs 100 more great games—honorable mentions, if you will—many of which just barely missed the main section.

One of the primary goals I hope to achieve is to introduce casual and hardcore gamers alike to games they've never played before, or games they've only played once or twice, and then blown them off without really giving them a fair shake. You'll find obvious selections listed, such as *Space Invaders* for the Atari 2600 and *Super Mario Bros.* for the Nintendo NES, but you'll also find obscure gems such as *Killer Bees!* for the Odyssey2 and such drastically underrated games as *Donkey Kong 3* for the NES.

While preparing this book, playing and replaying countless old favorites, I made sure to include only those games that have held up well over time and are still fun to play today. A game like *Superman* for the Atari 2600 or *Utopia* for the Intellivision may be more important historically than *Frenzy* for the ColecoVision, but the latter game is more fun (at least to me), so it made the list, while the other two, quality titles though they are, remain relegated to more straightforward video game history books.

Narrowing the list down to 100 games was tough; there are just too many great games from the era to include them all. *Alien*, *Boxing*, and *Worm War I* for the Atari 2600 barely missed "The Next 100" appendix at the back of the book, for example, as did a number of excellent ColecoVision, Intellivision, and Vectrex titles. If you are disappointed that some of your favorites didn't make the list, believe me, so am I.

For certain entries in this book I "cheated," such as when I lumped the Atari 2600 and 7800 versions of *Asteroids* into one entry, and when I did the same with *K.C. Munchkin!* and *K.C.'s Crazy Chase!* for the Odyssey2. Allowing these "cheats" helped give the book more cohesion, and it let me sneak in a few extra titles that otherwise would have remained on the cutting room floor.

One thing to keep in mind as you read is that I wrote the book in such a way as not to be redundant. For example, *Centipede* for the Atari 2600 is an entertaining game that probably deserves to be in "The Next 100" appendix, but *Centipede* for the Atari 5200 and ColecoVision are listed in the main section of the book, where I also detail the 2600 version. Since 2600 *Centipede* isn't the best (or tied for the best) *Centipede* port, and since it's already covered in the 5200/ColecoVision chapter, it doesn't get its own entry.

Another thing to keep in mind is that, even though video games are my area of expertise, my opinions are just that—opinions. I've got a considerable amount of gaming experience, of course, so I can compare and contrast with the best of them, but a lot of the book simply comes down to my specific tastes, which is one reason I included numerous quotes from other prominent gamers. (I did so for historical purposes as well.)

A key inspiration for this work was my love of heavily opinionated reference books, including such indispensable tomes as *Science Fiction: The 100 Best Novels* (1985, Carroll & Graf) by David Pringle and *The 100: A Ranking of the Most Influential Persons in History* (2000, Citadel Press) by Michael H. Hart. These types of books rarely gather dust on my shelves, as I flip through them again and again.

More precisely, the idea for this book came to me while I was reading Bill Warren's *Keep Watching the Skies!* (2010, McFarland Publishers), which is a massive (not to mention massively entertaining) tome chronicling American science fiction movies of the 1950s (and up through 1962). Warren's book isn't a best-of volume, but, with its production histories, quotes from other sources, coverage of a specific era, and the like, it did get me thinking along the lines of the book you are holding in your hands.

Though games listed in this book are, obviously, decades old, they remain timeless and relevant, having influenced generations of games to follow. Many are available as downloads for current consoles, some have been remade for smart phones and tablets, most have been emulated via personal computers, and all show up on eBay from time to time (some way more often than others). Keeping this in mind, there's no excuse not to treat yourself (and your friends and family) to some old-school gaming.

I hope you are able to use this book as a guide to what games are worth your time and money. Just be sure to let me know what games I should have included, and which ones I should have left out.

You can reach me at brettw105@sbcglobal.net.

As always, thanks for reading!

~Brett Weiss

CHAPTER 1

ADVENTURE

ATARI 2600
GENRE: ADVENTURE
PUBLISHER: ATARI
DEVELOPER: ATARI
1 PLAYER
1979

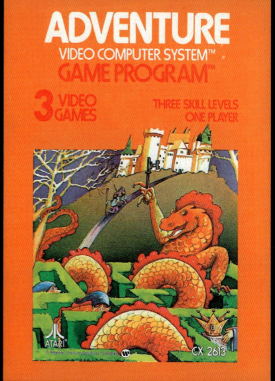

Adventure for the Atari 2600, complete in box. $27.

"BOTH CHARMINGLY SIMPLE AND DAUNTINGLY DIFFICULT."

Although extremely dated in appearance, *Adventure* for the Atari 2600 is such an influential and continually endearing game that I simply had to include it in this book. Not only is it a fun game in its own right, it paved the way for countless adventure quests to follow, including such favorites as *The Legend of Zelda*, *Final Fantasy*, and *Tomb Raider*.

Created by Warren Robinett, *Adventure* has players trying to retrieve an enchanted chalice that was stolen by an Evil Magician and hidden somewhere in a labyrinthine Kingdom. Said chalice must be returned to the Golden Castle where it belongs. Making this task difficult are three dragons created by the Evil Magician: Yorgle, the mean yellow dragon; Grundle, the mean and ferocious green dragon; and Rhindle, the fastest, most ferocious red dragon.

There are three castles in the Kingdom for players to explore: Black, Gold, and White. Each castle contains a gate over its entrance that must be opened with a color-coded key. Castles are separated by labyrinths, pathways, and rooms, and there are items scattered about these areas that will help the player in his or her quest. In addition to keys, players can find a bridge for passing through barriers, a magnet for moving objects and removing stuck and out-of-reach objects, and a sword for slaying the dragons.

Each dragon guards specific items. In addition, there's a pesky black bat that tries to switch out items with the player, such as—God forbid—an enemy dragon in exchange for the fabled chalice.

Adventure offers three skill levels, the hardest and most tantalizing of which finds the objects and dragons placed randomly within the Kingdom. Further, when the left difficulty switch is set in the "B" position, the dragons hesitate before they attack the player, making them a little easier to dodge.

Robinett got the idea for *Adventure* from a computer game, as he revealed in an interview published on www.dadgum.com. "I played the original text adventure, written by Don Woods and Willy Crowther, at the Stanford Artificial Intelligence Lab in 1978," he said. "This was while I was working on *Slot Racers*. Then it was time to do another game, and I thought that doing *Adventure* as a video game would be really cool."

Creating such a game with graphics created some "tricky problems," as Robinett explained: "Text adventures used verbal commands like 'Go North' or 'Take Wand' or 'Wave Wand.' My idea was to use the joystick for the North/

South/East/West commands, the button for picking up and dropping objects, and touching graphical objects together on the screen for all the other miscellaneous actions…instead of describing each room in text, I would show it on the screen, one room at a time…driving off the edge of the screen was the analog of 'Go North' or east or whatever. This allowed the game to have a much larger playing space than a single screen, which was a big change in the feel of a video game."

The "character" players control in *Adventure* has the appearance of a simple square, and the dragons look like ducks you might find in a shooting gallery. The castles are comprised of squares and rectangles, and the mazes consist of the type of crude outlines found in such early Atari titles as *Slot Racers* and *Maze Craze*. The sparse sound effects are a meager collection of bleeps and bloops.

In a recent interview with Chris DeLeon (hobbygamedev. com), Robinett talked about working on *Adventure* and the special challenges of programming for the 8-bit console. "The Atari 2600 has so many limitations that it's hard to do anything," he said. "If I had more resources I might have represented it [the graphics in *Adventure*] differently, but it worked."

When Robinett was developing *Adventure*, Atari didn't pay royalties to programmers, nor did they publish creator credits, as he related in *High Score! The Illustrated History of Electronic Games* (2002, Osborne/McGraw-Hill). "When I first went to Atari, I thought I'd died and gone to heaven," he said. "I was being paid to design games. But then, after about a year and a half, it started to dawn on me that Atari was making hundreds of millions of dollars and keeping us all anonymous. They didn't even give you a pizza if you designed a good game. There was no incentive at all. Nothing. That's when I had the idea of hiding my name in the game."

As any retro gamer worth his thumbs knows, Robinett created a secret room in *Adventure* "that could only be accessible by selecting a single gray dot on a gray wall," a major violation of company policy. "I could have been fired if anyone had discovered it, so I kept it secret for a year," he said. "The game code would have been very easy for Atari to change if they had known about the secret room. But after 300,000 *Adventure* cartridges had been made and shipped around the world, it was too late."

For years, Robinett's name in *Adventure* was thought to be the first "Easter egg"—a term coined by Arnie Katz, Joyce Worley, and Bill Kunkel of *Electronic Games* magazine—in a video game. However, in 2004, a programmer and collector named Sean Riddle found an Easter egg—programmer Bradley Reid-Selth's surname—in *Videocart-20: Video Whizball* (featured in "The Next 100" appendix at the back of this book) for the Fairchild Channel F system. *Video Whizball* was released to stores in 1978.

According to *Before the Crash: Early Video Game History* (2012, Wayne State University Press), however, the exact historical timeline of Easter eggs in video games is muddled. Contributor Zach Whalen wrote, "… some confusion may yet exist over which programmer deserves credit, since Reid-Selth claims to have gotten the idea because of reports that programmers at Atari were already doing it, and Robinett had completed at least some of the code for *Adventure* as early as 1978."

Regardless of who invented the video game Easter egg, everyone agrees that Robinett popularized the idea, and

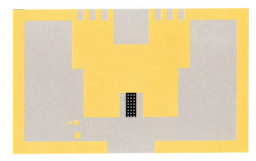

The entrance to the Gold Castle in *Adventure*. Courtesy of AtariAge.com.

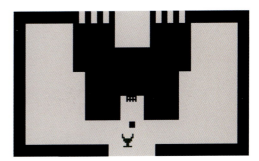

The entrance to the Black Castle in *Adventure*. Courtesy of AtariAge.com.

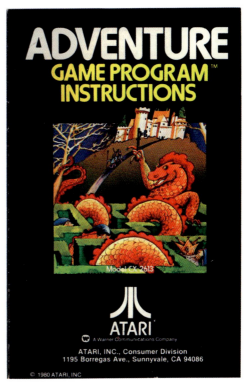

Adventure instruction manual. $5.

most everyone agrees that *Adventure* is a great title, despite its primitive audio/visuals.

"Rich gameplay more than makes up for the game's rudimentary graphics and sounds," said Chris Cavanaugh of the All Game Guide (allgame.com). Jeff Rovin, in *The Complete Guide to Conquering Video Games* (1982, Collier Books), called the game "absorbing" and said that "if you like surprises [and] enjoy seat-of-the-pants play mixed with ingenuity and bravado, *Adventure* is your cup of hemlock."

In a review published in issue #7 (June, 1984) of the British publication *TV Gamer*, the writer said, "*Adventure* is one of the most enthralling games you can buy for the Atari 2600 and any adventure enthusiast should not be without it."

In the "Digital Press Presents: Our 99 Favorite Classics" feature published in issue #33 (Sept./Oct., 1997) of the *Digital Press* fanzine, the contributors had predictably high praise for *Adventure*, calling it "a longtime favorite…arguably the most replayable adventure game because of its random skill setting on game 3…the perfect example of the video gaming spirit."

In *Classic Gamer Magazine* #3 (spring, 2000), Kyle Snyder said *Adventure* is "both charmingly simple and dauntingly difficult. It speaks to the inner child in all of us. Those of us who saw it brand new when we were six were blown away at all the things you could do. Whether you were busy searching catacombs, collecting objects, or slaying dragons, there was so much to interact with." (Snyder was apparently a child prodigy—*Adventure* would have confused me silly as a six-year-old.)

In *Ken Uston's Buying and Beating the Home Video Games* (1982), the noted gamer and gambler made a prescient prediction about *Adventure*: "I have a feeling that this cartridge…is going to be the wave of the future."

With countless fantasy adventure video games following in its wake, *Adventure*, which sold more than a million copies, did nothing less than change the industry forever. Not only did it create the fantasy adventure genre for consoles, it predicted an industry in which "entire games would be built around hidden surprises" (2001, *The Ultimate History of Video Games: From Pong to Pokemon—The Story Behind the Craze That Touched Our Lives and Changed the World*).

A timeless classic, *Adventure* has been reissued for modern systems on such compilation discs as *Atari Anthology!* (2004, PS2, Xbox) and *Atari Classics: Evolved* (2007, PSP). It's also built into Atari Flashback consoles 1–3. In 2010, Microsoft made *Adventure* available as a downloadable title for the Xbox 360 Game Room service.

Atari announced a sequel to *Adventure* in 1982, but it devolved into the ill-fated *Swordquest* series. In 2005, Curt Vendel created a true sequel, *Adventure II*, for the Atari Flashback 2. In 2007, AtariAge also released a game called *Adventure II*, this one a homebrew sequel on the Atari 5200. *Epic Adventure*, an AtariAge homebrew for the Atari 2600, followed in 2011.

FUN FACT:
Adventure is parodied in "Cannot Be Erased, So Sorry," a 2009 episode of *Robot Chicken* (a stop-motion animated show produced by Seth Green).

WHY IT MADE THE LIST:
"Possibly the greatest game ever written for the Atari 2600 platform" (*Time Magazine*, Nov. 15, 2012), *Adventure* not only created a new console gaming genre, it is still widely played today.

CHAPTER 2

AIR-SEA BATTLE

ATARI 2600
GENRE: NON-SCROLLING SHOOTER
PUBLISHER: ATARI
DEVELOPER: ATARI
1 OR 2 PLAYERS (SIMULTANEOUS)
1977

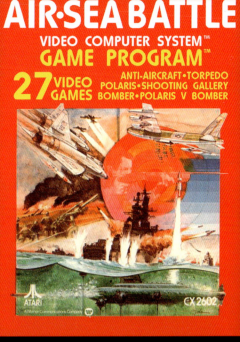

Air-Sea Battle for the Atari 2600, complete in box. $10.

"AIR-SEA BATTLE IS A TRUE TEST OF SKILL—THE BETTER PLAYER USUALLY WINS."

A favorite of the late, great Bill "The Game Doctor" Kunkel, *Air-Sea Battle* was released the same day the Atari VCS (later called the Atari 2600) hit store shelves. With its pitch-perfect two-player simultaneous action and pick-up-and-play mentality, it was an excellent choice for a launch title and still holds up extremely well today.

Sporting 27 play variations, *Air-Sea Battle* consists of six different types of games, all of which involve aiming and shooting, and all of which are highly entertaining: Anti-Aircraft, Torpedo, Shooting Gallery, Polaris, Bomber, and Polaris vs Bomber.

In Anti-Aircraft games, each player points and shoots a ground-based gun at small jets, large jets, and helicopters flying horizontally overhead. Observation Blimps (a shape with the letter "A" inside) flying randomly across the bottom of the playfield yield no points when shot, but they do obstruct the players' line of fire.

Torpedo games are similar to Anti-Aircraft games, but instead of a gun that can be angled, players control a submarine that fires straight upward at PT boats, aircraft carriers, pirate ships, and freighters that move horizontally along the water up above. Unlike the gun base, the submarine can move right and left along the bottom of the screen.

Shooting Gallery variations are a cross of sorts between Anti-Aircraft games and Torpedo games. Players can adjust the angle of the gun (as in Anti-Aircraft) and they can maneuver the gun base back and forth (similar to the subs in Torpedo). The targets include rabbits, ducks, and clowns.

Keeping the formula firmly intact, Polaris games have each player guiding a ship that travels across the bottom of the screen, shooting at small jets, large jets, and helicopters. Bomber variations change things up a bit by putting players at the helm of a plane flying across the top of the screen, dropping bombs on PT boats, aircraft carriers, pirate ships, and freighters.

In both Polaris and Bomber, players compete to shoot the most enemies; games end after 2 minutes, 16 seconds of play, or after either player scores 99 points. In Polaris vs Bomber, it's pure head-to-head nirvana, with one player flying a bomb-dropping plane across the top of the screen while the other controls a missile-equipped ship along the bottom of the playfield. Depending on the option selected, mines can obstruct players' lines of fire.

As with *Combat*, *Pong*, and other pure, undiluted, two-player simultaneous games, *Air-Sea Battle* is a true test of skill—the better player usually wins. To handicap the action, gamers can toggle the difficulty switches on the Atari console: in position "A," the missiles players fire are one-fourth the size of those in position "B." Another cool feature is that gamers can opt for guided missiles and bombs, which are maneuverable after they've been fired.

Like all early Atari 2600 titles, *Air-Sea Battle* has primitive graphics. However, the airborne vehicles and boats are recognizable as such, and the blue background, which is dark at the top and gradually gets lighter toward the bottom, looks pretty neat for a game that came out in 1977.

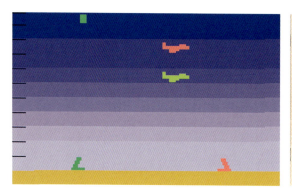
Anti-Aircraft Game in *Air-Sea Battle* for the Atari 2600. Courtesy of AtariAge.com.

Air-Sea Battle instruction manual. $2.

Air-Sea Battle game cartridge. $5.

To put the game into some historical perspective, consider the comments from the "Programmable Parade" section of *Electronic Games* magazine #1 (winter, 1981), written by Kunkel and Frank Laney Jr.:

> One of the earliest cartridges offered for the VCS became an instant classic when it was released and is still a remarkably fine video game today. Its introduction heralded the dawn of the age of true programmability because it was the first title that departed from the ball-and-paddle contests that ruled the roost back in 1978…*Air-Sea Battle* may be one of the oldest VCS cartridges, but it certainly hasn't dated. It has, rather, aged gracefully and is still one of Atari's outstanding software selections.

On a far less positive note, Walter Lowe, Jr., author of *Playboy's Guide to Rating the Video Games* (1982, PBJ Books), wrote that, "Children may play it for hours, but adults will get bored with it pretty quickly." However, he contradicted himself a short time later when he called the guided-missile variations "good party games" and said that "if you want to introduce a date to video games, this is a fun one to start with."

In an interview conducted by Scott Stilphen published on www.digitpress.com, *Air-Sea Battle* programmer Larry Kaplan (*Kaboom!*, *Super Breakout*) revealed how he came up with the idea for the game: "*Air-Sea Battle* was based on an Atari coin-op called *Anti-Aircraft* [1975]," he said. "In those days, we just ripped off anything we could make work."

In that same interview, Kaplan shared some of the difficulties he had in designing *Air-Sea Battle*. "The development process was a nightmare in the beginning," he said. "We had a time share service we reached via a teletype to do our editing and assembling. Then we downloaded to a development kit that had only a display and some address switches. Extremely primitive and difficult to use, it made game programming even more difficult."

In *Atari, Inc.—Business is Fun* (2012, Syzygy Company Press), Kaplan further discussed the creation of the game. "I discovered early that it was possible to reposition player objects during a screen (which is a frame of the TV picture), though that was not a consideration of the original design specs," he said. "So by designing *Air-Sea Battle*, which had used horizontal bands of player objects, this programming technique was used as a cornerstone extensively with many VCS games. Without that single strobe, H-move, the VCS would have failed as a game platform very quickly."

As fans of the cartridge well know, if you've only played *Air-Sea Battle* against the computer, you haven't truly played *Air-Sea Battle*.

Dave "The Video Game Critic" Mrozek (videogamecritic.com) summed up the two-player appeal of the game thusly: "It may not be much to look at, but *Air-Sea Battle* is an unadulterated head-to-head shooting game. In some ways it's only as good as the people at the controls. Playing it casually against a friend (or the ultra-lame CPU) just isn't going to cut it. It's only properly played between two enraged, testosterone-laden males willing to put everything on the line! As the trash talk begins to flow, *Air-Sea Battle* really comes into its own."

If you don't have an Atari 2600, you can play *Air-Sea Battle* on such compilation discs as *Atari Anthology!* (2004, PS2, Xbox) and *Atari Classics: Evolved* (2007, PSP). It's also built into Atari Flashback consoles 1 and 3. In 2010, Microsoft made *Air-Sea Battle* available as a downloadable title for the Xbox 360 Game Room service.

FUN FACT:
With the title changed to *Target Fun*, *Air-Sea Battle* was the original pack-in game with the Sears Tele-Games version of the Atari 2600 console.

WHY IT MADE THE LIST:
Like *Combat* and *Video Olympics*, *Air-Sea Battle* offers fair, competitive, two-player action that never gets old.

CHAPTER 3

ANTARCTIC ADVENTURE

COLECOVISION
GENRE: CHARACTER RACING
PUBLISHER: COLECO
DEVELOPER: KONAMI
1 PLAYER
1984

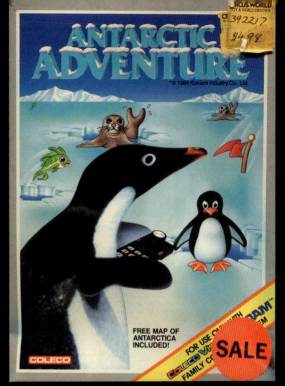

Antarctic Adventure for the ColecoVision, complete in box. Courtesy of Bryan C. Smith. $50.

> "EVERYTHING ABOUT THIS GAME IS GOOD. THE MUSIC IS PERFECT. THE GRAPHICS ARE SMOOTH, DETAILED, AND COLORFUL."

Hardcore gamers and macho joystick jockeys alike may wonder why I would include a cutesy penguin racing game in a book called *The 100 Greatest Console Video Games: 1977–1987*. The answer, my testosterone-fueled, troglodytic friends, is simple: because it *is* one of the greatest games of the Golden Age.

You don't race penguins in *Antarctic Adventure*. Rather, you *are* a penguin (unnamed in this game, later called Penta), sliding and gliding down twisting, turning, ice-covered pathways to the tune of Émile Waldteufel's "The Skaters' Waltz," which plays in an endless loop. I've heard some gamers complain that this music gets old after extended play, but it's never bothered me in the least. In fact, I like it quite a bit. It's an upbeat, catchy, circus-like song that fits the action very well.

The view in *Antarctic Adventure* evokes a slower *Pole Position*, with players watching the action from behind the penguin (as opposed to behind a formula-one racer). Pressing up on the joystick makes the penguin go faster while pressing down slows the flightless fowl. The penguin can also jump, which sets the game apart from most racers.

As the penguin skates his way to his destination, obstacles in the form of small ice puddles and wide ice crevasses appear on the track. Seals intermittently pop out of puddles, adding to the challenge. If the penguin hits a puddle or a seal, he'll skitter to the side, wasting precious seconds. If he falls in a crevasse, you must help him climb out.

As you approach the aforementioned holes in the ice, they appear to get larger, and part of the challenge is determining whether you should skate around or jump over them, and when it's necessary to slow down. If you slow down too often (by purposely skating slower or by hitting too many obstacles), time will run out and you won't reach your goal, bringing the game to an abrupt end (you only get one life).

So, what is your goal in this game, you may be wondering? The track in *Antarctic Adventure* circles the South Pole and is comprised of 10 sections (some much longer than others), each of which ends in a quick stay in front of an Antarctic ice station. When the penguin reaches a station, he turns around and waves his little flipper, and a flag will go up on the station building. After this brief, but charming, intermission, it's off to the races again. If you manage to circle the South Pole (i.e., make it to the last station) the cycle repeats itself, but at a more difficult pace.

As I alluded to earlier, keeping a fast pace is important to staying alive, especially deep into the game. Skating fast

Antarctic Adventure game cartridge. $15.

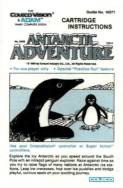
Antarctic Adventure instruction manual. $5.

Antarctic Adventure foldout poster. *Courtesy of Digital Press (digitpress.com).* $12.

also racks up big points. Other ways to make your score soar include capturing green flags as they appear along the pathways and catching flying red fish as they leap up from holes in the ice. However, you should be careful not to let these goodies distract you from the primary goal: to reach the station before the timer runs out. Stations, in order, are as follows: Australia, Australia, France, New Zealand, South Pole, U.S.A., U.S.A., Argentina, United Kingdom, and Japan.

The original *Antarctic Adventure* was released by Konami in Japan in 1983 for the MSX computer. I've never played *Kekkyoku Nankyoku Daibōken* (as it was called), but I can tell you that after watching a YouTube video of the MSX game in action, the ColecoVision cartridge is an excellent, extremely faithful port. The crisp, cute graphics—stark white and rich hues of blue, complemented by playful penguin animations—are fully intact, as is the memorable music. More importantly, gameplay appears to be the same.

In issue #27 (Sept./Oct., 1995) of the *Digital Press* fanzine, longtime gaming enthusiast Jeff Cooper said, "Everything about this game is good. The music is perfect. The graphics are smooth, detailed, and colorful. *Antarctic Adventure* helps cement the ColecoVision's reputation as the very best of the classic video game systems."

In the seventh edition of the *Digital Press Collector's Guide* (2002), Joe Santulli said the game is "a top 10 for the ColecoVision" and that it has "the best graphics the system ever saw and a quality (albeit repetitive) soundtrack."

In 1985, Konami released *Antarctic Adventure* for the Famicom, which is the Japanese equivalent of the Nintendo NES. The music's not as good in this version, but it does have an interesting addition in the form of flashing flags. If the penguin grabs a flashing flag, a beanie with a propeller will appear on his head, letting him fly for a limited time. In addition, the Famicom game has different flag colors—green, red, and blue (as well as flashing)—and two colors of fish: red and green.

In 1986, Konami released *Penguin Adventure*, a Japan-only sequel for the MSX. Designed by Ryouhei Shogaki and Hideo Kojima (*Metal Gear*, *Metal Gear Solid*), *Penguin Adventure* added numerous elements to the formula, including boss fights, mini-games, purchasable items (including a gun), different environments (forest, caves, outer space, water), multiple endings, and multiple pathways.

Ever since I got my ColecoVision console in the Christmas of 1982, I've had a ColecoVision hooked up to my television set (I've gone through four units). As such, I've logged many an hour on *Antarctic Adventure*. My kids have enjoyed it as well, especially when they were in elementary school and called it "The Penguin Game."

Antarctic Adventure starts off easy (unlike most ColecoVision titles, there is no difficulty level selection screen), but it does present a challenge later on as more seals and more holes appear. It's especially tough to reach all 10 stations more than once, a goal I always shoot for when I play the game.

I'm a big fan of such hardcore classic racers as *Pole Position*, *Turbo*, and *Bump 'n' Jump*, and I've thoroughly enjoyed such slickly modern racing titles as *Gran Turismo*, *Rage Racer*, and *Burnout*, but *Antarctic Adventure*, an unlikely character game starring a perky little penguin, will always get some play time at the Weiss household.

FUN FACT:

When *Antarctic Adventure* for the ColecoVision was released in stores, it came packaged with a foldout map poster, which is difficult to find in today's collector's market.

WHY IT MADE THE LIST:

Challenging, fun, and irresistibly cute, *Antarctic Adventure* appeals to gamers of all stripes, from young kids to grizzled racing fans willing to give it a chance.

CHAPTER 4

ARKANOID

NINTENDO NES
GENRE: BALL-AND-PADDLE
PUBLISHER: TAITO
DEVELOPER: TAITO
1 OR 2 PLAYERS (ALTERNATING)
1987

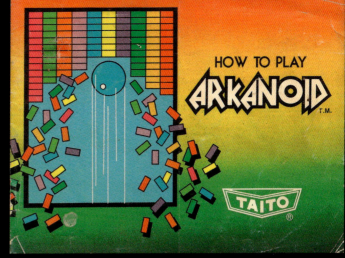

Arkanoid instruction manual. $5.

> "ARKANOID'S SIMPLICITY IS ITS GREATEST STRENGTH, AND THE BREAKOUT FORMULA REMAINS SOLIDLY PLAYABLE TO THIS DAY."

In 1977, when I was 10 years old, my life changed forever. Okay, that's a bit hyperbolic, but the year did have significance in terms of how I perceived video games. I was a huge pinball fan at the time, and I still love the silver ball to this day. However, when Atari's *Breakout* (1976) showed up at my local arcade, I suddenly realized that pinball might have to take a backseat to video games.

I had previously played and enjoyed *Pong* (Atari, 1972), *Gun Fight* (Midway, 1975), and a number of other arcade cabs, but *Breakout* was my breakout video game (so to speak)—I simply loved it. It took the basic idea of *Pong* and mixed it with something altogether new: the addictive and challenging notion of clearing groupings of similar items from the screen, a gameplay conceit that would be repeated again and again with the likes of *Space Invaders*, *Asteroids*, *Tetris*, and too many other titles to mention.

In 1986, Taito upped the ante with *Arkanoid*, a coin-op game that has players guiding a paddle (called a "Vaus spacecraft") along the bottom of the screen, keeping a bouncing ball in play by rebounding it off said paddle so it will hit and eliminate bricks that are the building blocks of space walls. If the ball gets past the paddle, the player loses a "life." The objective is to eliminate all the bricks. Programmed by Akira Fujita, *Arkanoid* adds dramatically to the *Breakout* formula by incorporating such elements as levels, power-ups, a boss named Doh, and a sci-fi storyline.

Arkanoid for the NES is a near-perfect port of the coin-op game, boasting 35 different block formations and a 36th screen featuring the aforementioned boss (the manual mistakenly claims there are only 33 rounds of play, probably because that's how many are in the arcade version), which is a large face that must be hit 16 times to be destroyed. Once the boss has been vanquished, the game will end. It's a shame the action doesn't start over again at a more challenging pace, but this is a small gripe, as only the most skilled players will make it that far.

One thing to keep in mind is that gold bricks are indestructible. Also, floating obstacles frequently appear onscreen and will change the trajectory of the ball when hit. Certain bricks in the space walls contain color-coded power-ups, which fall when released and can be captured. Colors include orange (slows movement of ball), yellow/green (players can catch the ball and release it), light blue (splits ball into three balls), pink (opens warp escape to advance to next round), red (lets players shoot lasers at the bricks), gray (awards players with an extra paddle), and dark blue/purple (widens the paddle).

The power-ups and level progression add immeasurably to the already fun *Breakout* formula. Even more important is the fact that the home version of *Arkanoid* originally came packaged in an oversized box with a special controller featuring a rotary control knob. The knob is small, especially when compared to the paddle controllers used for playing *Breakout* on the Atari 2600, but it works flawlessly, giving players

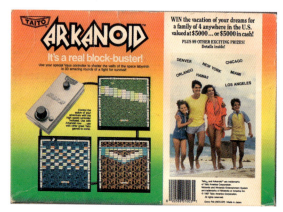

The back of the *Arkanoid* box.

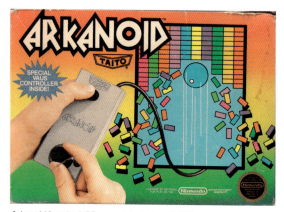

Arkanoid for the NES, complete in box. $125.

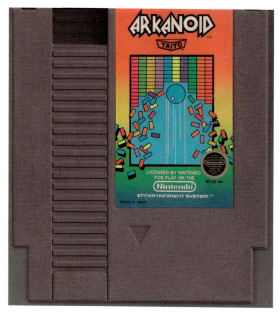

Arkanoid game cartridge. $10.

precise, quick, and smooth control over the Vaus spacecraft. Unfortunately, it's hard to find the controller nowadays (the cartridge shows up for sale way more often than the controller), and the manual and box are pretty darned scarce as well.

Like all ball-and-paddle games, *Arkanoid* is less impressive from an audio/visual standpoint than the average platformer or adventure title, but it's a good looking and sounding game nevertheless. The bricks making up the space walls are crisply drawn, the backgrounds aren't distracting, and the shimmering effect when a gold brick is hit is a nice touch. The musical intro is inviting, as is the pinging sound the ball makes when it hits a brick or the paddle.

In *The Video Games Guide* by Matt Fox (2006, Boxtree), the author underrated the game a bit, giving it three out of five stars. However, he did say that "*Arkanoid*'s simplicity is its greatest strength, and the *Breakout* formula remains solidly playable to this day."

Eric Bailey, writing for www.examiner.com, called *Arkanoid* a "fantastic action puzzler that blends mind-bending puzzle strategy with tense on-screen action elements." He also said it's a "true classic, a worthy battle…a game that will be fondly remembered for a long time."

Two arcade sequels were produced in 1987: *Tournament Arkanoid* and *Arkanoid: Revenge of Doh*. These games were followed in 1997 by *Arkanoid: Doh it Again* for the Super Nintendo. Unfortunately, *Doh it Again* lacked rotary control, making the NES game far superior.

Arkanoid Returns, released to the arcades in 1997, only appeared in Japan.

In 2008, *Arkanoid DS* (2008) was released for the Nintendo DS. In 2009, two downloadable titles were produced: *Arkanoid Live!* for the Xbox 360 (via XBLA) and *Arkanoid Plus* for the Nintendo Wii (via WiiWare). In 2009, *Arkanoid* made it to the iPhone.

Classic console games similar to *Arkanoid* include *Breakaway* (Arcadia 2001), *Blockout!/Breakdown!* (Odyssey2), *Clowns/Brickyard* (Astrocade), *Flipper Slipper* (ColecoVision), and *Super Breakout* (Atari 2600).

FUN FACT:

Arkanoid was reviewed in issue #144 of the RPG magazine, *Dragon* (Oct., 1986), earning five out of five stars.

WHY IT MADE THE LIST:

Smooth rotary control, crisp graphics and sounds, and a slick updating of the *Breakout* formula make *Arkanoid* an A+ title for ball-and-paddle fans.

CHAPTER 5

ARTILLERY DUEL

COLECOVISION
GENRE: TURN-BASED STRATEGY
PUBLISHER: XONOX
DEVELOPER: XONOX
2 PLAYERS (SIMULTANEOUS)
1983

ASTROCADE
GENRE: TURN-BASED STRATEGY
PUBLISHER: ASTROCADE
DEVELOPER: ASTROCADE
2 PLAYERS (SIMULTANEOUS)
1982

Artillery Duel for the ColecoVision, complete in box. $115.

"GOOD, OLD-FASHIONED FUN [IN A] KILL-OR-BE-KILLED FORMAT."

They say that every dog has its day, and that is certainly true of Xonox, publisher of such dreck as the virtually unplayable *Tomarc the Barbarian* (Atari 2600, ColecoVision) and the laughably bad *It's Only Rock 'n' Roll* (ColecoVision). Xonox's bright and shining moment was *Artillery Duel* for the ColecoVision, a masterful turn-based strategy game that isn't terribly original (more on that later), but is a blast to play.

As the game begins, players are treated to the opening strains of "The William Tell Overture," with an automatic paint program of sorts drawing randomly placed hills and trees on the screen, along with clouds overhead and snow-capped mountains in the background. Then artillery guns pop out of the ground (as if by magic), one on the left side of the playfield (player one) and the other on the right (player two).

The artillery guns face one another, and players must take turns lobbing shots back and forth to try and take out the opposing gun. During the aiming process, the player positions the angle of the barrel of the gun. It is preset to 60, but players can maneuver it between 90, which shoots straight up, and 00, which fires straight toward your opponent.

Gamers should also consider toggling the powder charge (between 00 and 99—70 is the default setting), which determines the strength of the shot. Wind plays an important role; arcaders are advised to take the strength (indicated by a wind speed indicator) and direction (indicated by moving clouds) of the wind into account when readying the artillery gun to fire.

Another key aspect of the game is the level of difficulty selected: Corporal gives you 59 seconds to adjust and fire your shot; Captain gives you 30 seconds; and General provides only 15 seconds. Unlike most ColecoVision games, *Artillery Duel* lets each player choose their own difficulty level, giving less skilled gamers a fighting chance.

Artillery Duel moves slowly, which may annoy certain players. In addition to waiting for the other player to fire, you must watch as each bullet moves slowly toward its destination. For me, this only builds the excitement and anticipation of the possible impact of each shot fired, so I don't mind the relaxed pace.

If you miss the target, your shot will hit a tree or part of a hill, destroying it incrementally. Sometimes you have to shoot through terrain to reach the enemy artillery gun. One

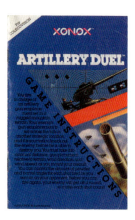

Artillery Duel instruction manual for the ColecoVision. $12.

Artillery Duel for the ColecoVision game cartridge. $15.

Artillery Duel for the Astrocade instruction manual. $5.

direct hit will destroy that gun and start another round of play, with the loser getting to shoot first. The first person to score five kills wins the game.

I don't necessarily recommend drinking alcohol while playing video games—it tends to slow your reaction time and inhibit your eye/hand coordination, among other potential problems—but one of the most enjoyable times I've ever had playing a two-player title was when my brother and I polished off a bottle of tequila during an extended session of *Artillery Duel* sometime during the late 1980s. I had just gotten back from Mexico, and, other than a sleeveless Acapulco T-shirt, the tequila was the only souvenir I had bought.

My brother was a great *Frogger* and pinball player in the arcades, but he rarely played any of my home systems. I don't remember why we decided to play *Artillery Duel* that day (or drink all that tequila—neither one of us were big drinkers), but I do know that we had a lot of laughs (and, as the day wore on, missed a lot of shots).

Whether played sober or drunk, *Artillery Duel* is a great cartridge. In a review published on www.consoleclassix.com, someone going by the name of "brumburger" showed that he clearly understood the appeal of the game, calling it "excellent head-to-head competition" and "good, old-fashioned fun [in a] kill-or-be-killed format."

Artillery Duel does indeed offer terrific two-player action, but the game didn't exactly create a new genre. It is similar to *Artillery* (1980) for the Apple II, in which players adjust the barrel of a tank and the power of their shot to destroy one another. Further, *Artillery* itself owes a huge debt of gratitude to earlier text-based games, such as Mike Forman's BASIC program, *Artillery*, published in *Creative Computing* magazine in 1976.

Artillery Duel was produced as a standard cartridge for the ColecoVision, but it was also released as part of a "double ender" with *Chuck Norris Superkicks* (a licensed karate game that was flawed, but ahead of its time). Other Xonox double enders for the ColecoVision include *Sir Lancelot/Robin Hood* and *Tomarc the Barbarian/Motocross Racer*. (A double ender is a long cartridge with two sides you can plug into the console.)

The year before *Artillery Duel* hit the ColecoVision, Astrocade released it for their Bally Astrocade console. That version, programmed by John Perkins, lacks clouds and background mountains, but it's an excellent game as well, earning a place in this book.

The Atari 2600 rendition, which came out the same year as the ColecoVision cartridge, has blocky graphics and is missing the classical theme song, but it's also entertaining (though not quite worthy of inclusion).

Odyssey2 owners with a fondness for *Artillery Duel* can enjoy the similarly great *Smithereens!*, which is listed in "The Next 100" near the back of this book. Players, competing simultaneously, use a catapult to fire boulders across a lake to destroy the opposing tower. There's no terrain or wind factor in this medieval contest, but fast-paced gameplay and excellent controls—holding the joystick longer makes the boulder travel farther—help make up for these absences. In addition, those fortunate enough to own The Voice speech module can enjoy such verbal taunts as "That's easy!" and "You blew it!"

For those wanting a one-player game that uses roughly the same type of gameplay mechanics as *Artillery Duel* (actually, it has more in common with the simpler *Smithereens!*), you've probably already got it on your smart phone or tablet—that would be the ubiquitous and addicting *Angry Birds*.

FUN FACT:

In the March, 1984 issue of *Video Games* magazine, Mickey Elfenbein of Xonox expressed interest in creating a *Thundarr the Barbarian* video game. Unfortunately, this never came to pass. Instead, we got the dreadful *Tomarc the Barbarian*.

WHY IT MADE THE LIST:

Artillery Duel offers some of the best strategic (though not overly complicated) two-player action from the Golden Age of video games.

CHAPTER 6

ASTEROIDS

ATARI 2600
NON-SCROLLING SHOOTER
PUBLISHER: ATARI
DEVELOPER: ATARI
1 OR 2 PLAYERS (ALTERNATING)
1981

ATARI 7800
NON-SCROLLING SHOOTER
PUBLISHER: ATARI
DEVELOPER: GENERAL COMPUTER CORP.
1 OR 2 PLAYERS (SIMULTANEOUS)
1986

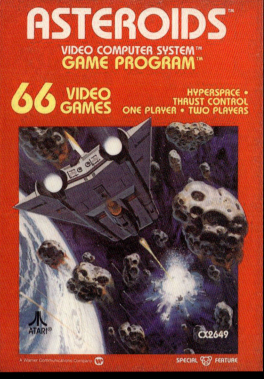

Asteroids for the Atari 2600, complete in box. *Courtesy of AtariAge.com. $10.*

"…OVERLOOK THE COSMETIC DIFFERENCES TO THIS SHOOT-'EM-UP AND ENJOY…"

Programmed by Ed Logg (from an idea by Lyle Rains), mastermind of such megahits as *Centipede* (1980) and *Gauntlet* (1985), the original arcade version of *Asteroids* (1979) was a mammoth success, moving more than 70,000 cabinets and grossing more than a billion dollars' worth of quarters. Not only did *Asteroids* supplant *Space Invaders* (1978) as *the* game of choice amongst arcade enthusiasts of its day, it spawned a trio of sequels—*Asteroids Deluxe* (1980), *Space Duel* (1982), and *Blasteroids* (1987)—and a number of remakes, including *Asteroids* (1998) for the PlayStation and *Asteroids Hyper 64* (1999) for the Nintendo 64.

More importantly for the purposes of this book, Atari's arcade juggernaut begat two very nicely programmed console ports, one for the Atari 2600 and one for the Atari 7800.

Atari 2600 *Asteroids* faced a dilemma from the get-go. According to the second issue of *Electronic Games* magazine (March, 1982), technological limitations meant a delay in the game's release.

"Making a home version of this coin-op smash proved to be a vastly complicated process," wrote Bill Kunkel and Frank Laney Jr. "The original *Asteroids* uses an intelligent Quadrascan monitor that allows hi-res images to be drawn anywhere on the screen. This permits the machine to vary the speed and direction of each chunk of space debris. It is impossible to simulate the unique Quadrascan output on a traditional rasterscan screen such as television sets employ."

The 2600 space rocks are colorful—filled-in pastels replace the white outlines found in the arcade game—but they flicker when too many are onscreen at once. In addition, they don't change speed when shot, and they move primarily vertically, helping make the game easier than its quarter-gobbling counterpart. The ship in the 2600 version can only shoot two bullets in succession (as opposed to four), but the arcade classic is still a tougher challenge.

In terms of controls, the 2600 version of *Asteroids* has a significant drawback. While the arcade game boasts five

Asteroids for the Atari 7800 instruction manual. $2.

Asteroids for the Atari 7800 game cartridge. $5.

Asteroids for the Atari 2600 in action. *Courtesy of AtariAge.com.*

control buttons—one apiece for rotating right, rotating left, firing, thrusting, and engaging hyperspace (which makes your ship disappear and reappear in a random spot on the screen)—the 2600 controller consists of a joystick and a single fire button.

Naturally, the fire button is used for firing, but the joystick is forced into service as thrust (press forward), hyperspace (press back), clockwise movement (press left), and counterclockwise movement (press right).

All things considered, this setup works pretty well (kudos to programmer Brad Stewart), but hardcore *Asteroids* fans will want to hunt down a Starplex Deluxe Videogame Controller (which I bought at the Digital Press booth at the 2007 Classic Gaming Expo), a wonderful third-party control panel with five buttons.

Despite the aforementioned flaws, 2600 *Asteroids* is a great game, thanks in no small part to the brilliance of the arcade original, in which players guide a triangular ship around the screen, shooting space rocks that break into smaller pieces when hit. Unlike *Space Invaders* before it, *Asteroids* doesn't confine the player to the bottom part of the screen. Rather, players can rotate their ship 360 degrees and maneuver it in all directions.

Periodically, flying saucers will appear, and these can be shot for extra points. The large, slow-moving saucers are less accurate when firing at the player than the small, quicker saucers. According to Steven L. Kent, author of *The Ultimate History of Video Games* (2010, Three Rivers Press), these saucers were known around the Atari offices back in the day as Bill and Sluggo (from the *Saturday Night Live* claymation series of skits) until lawyers for NBC took exception and sent Atari a cease-and-desist order.

The *Asteroids* gameplay mechanic wasn't entirely unprecedented—the ship movement had its origins in the groundbreaking computer game, *Spacewar* (1962)—but the fast, workmanlike quality of blasting asteroids was revelatory, giving the player a sense of blue-collar satisfaction combined with an odds-be-damned struggle to survive for as long as possible in hostile, unpredictable, anarchic outer space.

Likewise, the vector visuals weren't an arcade first—that honor belongs to the early flight sim, *Lunar Lander* (1979)—but the crisp, minimalist graphics are definitely a part of the game's appeal. As with most classic arcade cabs, you can't flat-out beat *Asteroids*, since it can theoretically last forever. However, you can enter your initials on the high score screen, which was an arcade first.

Unlike the original arcade game, *Asteroids* for the 2600 includes 66 game variations, which is down from 112 for *Space Invaders*, but still offering plenty of variety. Certain variations allow for shields (a la *Asteroids Deluxe*), which surround the ship with protection for up to two seconds (exceeding two seconds makes the ship explode). In addition, there's a special feature that lets players flip the spaceship around 180 degrees, instantly aiming it in the opposite direction. This is useful for attacking asteroids that quickly come from behind. For beginners, there are modes of play in which the asteroids move very slowly.

Regarding the masterful Atari 7800 release of *Asteroids*, Atari removed such variations as shields and flip, but the game trumps the competition by including a pair of highly entertaining two-player simultaneous modes, in which each player takes the helm of his or her own ship. In Competition Asteroids, each ship is vulnerable to the other player's shots. In Team Asteroids, shots pass harmlessly through the other player's ship. In both games, the player with the highest score wins. *Centipede* for the 7800 employs a similar technique, but it's a shame that more classic arcade ports weren't given this type of two-player simultaneous treatment.

Visually, 7800 *Asteroids* has richer, more detailed graphics than its 2600 counterpart, giving it more than a passing resemblance to the 1987 arcade sequel, *Blasteroids* (the textured space rocks appear to spin as they cross the screen). There is no children's mode, but there are four difficulty levels from which to choose: novice, intermediate, expert, and advanced. The controls function like those in the 2600 game, despite the 7800 controller's extra fire button.

Getting back to the original arcade *Asteroids*, certain players back in the day developed a strategy unofficially called "lurking," in which they would leave one asteroid onscreen—preferably a slower one—and fly around avoiding it, taking pot shots at flying saucers as soon as they would appear. This method could rack up points with relative ease, potentially earning the enterprising player vast quantities of extra ships (a bonus ship is awarded with every 10,000 points scored).

As a teenager, I used that formula quite well. Once, at a convenience store near my house, I played a single game of *Asteroids* on one quarter for more than four hours. The only reason I quit was because the store was closing for the night. During that session, an onlooker paid me 50 cents to play the game for a while. He lost a bunch of ships during his stretch at the controls, but by that time I had already accumulated a couple of rows of them, so it was no big deal.

Years later, at the 2003 Classic Gaming Expo, I discussed my four-hour-plus feat with arcade champion Brian Kuh, who frowned and told me that I had "violated the spirit of the game." Those of you who have seen *The King of Kong: A Fistful of Quarters* (2007) will remember Kuh as the guy walking around Funspot arcade telling other players that Steve Wiebe was about to reach the final "kill screen" of *Donkey Kong*.

Lurking is doable to some degree in the Atari 2600 and 7800 versions of *Asteroids*, but playing the game the more traditional way is more enjoyable, so I rarely "lurk" at home.

The arcade version of *Asteroids* remains a Golden Age favorite. In *The Video Games Guide* (2006, Boxtree), author Matt Fox called the game "an undisputed classic…the greatest of all the greats …:" In Van Burnham's *Supercade: A Visual History of the Videogame Age, 1971–1984* (2003, MIT Press), contributor Tom Vanderbilt said, "There was an almost spiritual sense of purpose to breaking the rocks down into smaller and smaller rocks, and then into nothingness…"

The 2600 and 7800 versions of *Asteroids* maintain a strong following as well. The Video Game Critic (www.videogamecritic.com) gave the 2600 version an "A-" and the 7800 rendition an "A." Writing for The Atari Times (www.ataritimes.com), Darryl Brundage's advice regarding the 2600 port is to "…overlook the cosmetic differences to this shoot-'em-up and enjoy…" Rob Dire, in his Digital Press (www.digitalpress.com) review, claimed that "if you're looking for the gameplay that the arcade offered, *Asteroids* [for the 2600] delivers in spades—and then some."

Regarding *Asteroids* at home and in the arcades, Walter Low, Jr., author of *Playboy's Guide to Rating the Video Games* (1982, PBJ Books), espoused the following: "There's something about the basic theme of the game that makes it easy to become addicted to, sort of like eating salted peanuts. Children, women, and men all like this game once they've learned to manipulate the rocket."

My all-time favorite version of *Asteroids* is the Atari 7800 port, thanks in large part to the raucously enjoyable two-player modes. But I still crank up the 2600 version from time to time, making sure to always use the Starplex Deluxe Videogame Controller.

The Atari 2600 version of *Asteroids* has been re-released on various compilation discs for modern systems, including *Atari Anthology!* (2004) for the PlayStation 2 and Xbox. In 2010, the game was made available as a downloadable title for the Xbox 360 Game Room service. In terms of dedicated consoles, *Asteroids* for the 2600 was built into Atari Flashback 3 (2011), while the Atari 7800 port was included as part of the first Atari Flashback (2004).

FUN FACT:

Asteroids was one of the most successful coin-op games ever produced, selling more than 70,000 units to arcade operators and other buyers.

WHY IT MADE THE LIST:

Whether played on the 2600 or 7800, Asteroids is one of the all-time greats; blasting space rocks into smaller and smaller bits and then into oblivion is still cathartically enjoyable.

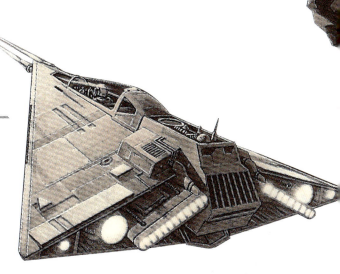

CHAPTER 7

ATLANTIS

INTELLIVISION
GENRE: NON-SCROLLING SHOOTER
PUBLISHER: IMAGIC
DEVELOPER: IMAGIC
1 OR 2 PLAYERS (ALTERNATING)
1982

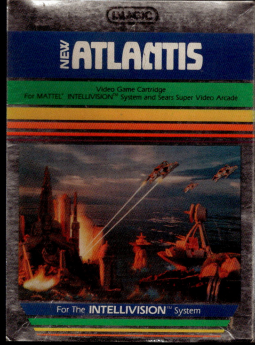

Atlantis for the Intellivision, complete in box. $10.

"OUTSTANDING VISUALS AND SURPRISINGLY RICH GAMEPLAY."

The fabled underwater city of Atlantis is under fire in this deep, beautifully rendered shooter, which screams "high production values" every step of the way.

Packaged in a typical (for Imagic) shiny silver box, *Atlantis* comes with a full color, well laid out instruction manual that includes a nicely painted centerfold battle scene and tells a simple, but urgent story: the hated Gorgons have assembled their fleet and are on the attack, spurring General Tarrick to cry out, "Defend Atlantis—before it becomes a watery grave!"

To defend Atlantis, you must protect several sectors of the city, including the Domed Palace, the Imperial Quarter, and two Acropolis Command Posts. You are armed with three weapons: a Sentinel Saucer and two anti-aircraft guns—one on the left and one on the right—meaning most of the gunshots you fire will travel diagonally through the sky.

To aim an anti-aircraft gun, you must guide a cross-hair sight around the screen. Pressing either top side button on the controller fires the left anti-aircraft gun, while either bottom side button fires the right anti-aircraft gun. Shots fired from the anti-aircraft guns go straight toward the sight and explode upon contact with said sight, destroying any enemy ship within the explosion cloud. This gameplay element is similar to another great and deep shooter, *Missile Command*, which also has you protecting buildings that are positioned down below.

The Sentinel Saucer sits atop an underwater mountain in the center of the city. Pressing a button on the keypad launches the Saucer into play and makes the cross-hair sight disappear. You guide the Saucer around the sky, shooting right and left. The Saucer is a powerful weapon that makes destroying enemies easier (aiming is less difficult), but it has a fuel gauge that acts as a timer.

The fuel gauge counts down unit by unit at regular intervals, and crashing into an enemy deducts 10 units. A buzzing sound will emit when only five fuel units remain. However, you can refuel by returning the Saucer to its launch pad. When parked at the pad, the Saucer's fuel level will increase incrementally to a maximum of 90 units. If you run out of fuel, the Saucer will explode and won't appear again until dawn of the next day (more on the day/night transition later).

The Gorgon Fleet consists of nine types of ships: Squid Bomber, Rocket Rally, Spar Module, Bandit Bomber, Bi-Winged Bullet, Spider Fighter (not to be confused with the Atari 2600 game of the same name), Recon Rocket, Astro Orbiter, and Cosmic Crawler. Some enemies fly in straight lines while others move in unpredictable patterns.

The ships begin their attack high above Atlantis and make four passes from the right to the left, descending a bit with each pass (vaguely similar, at least in concept, to *Space Invaders*, but more akin to the targets in *Carnival*). In its fourth

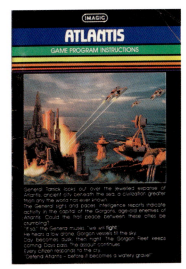 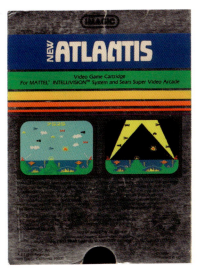 

Atlantis instruction manual: $2.   The back of the *Atlantis* box.   *Atlantis* game cartridge. $4.

and final pass, an enemy ship will fire a "deathray" at one of your city installations, so you should definitely destroy the ships before they get that low. Once all your city sectors have been destroyed, it's "game over."

As I alluded to earlier, *Atlantis* is a gorgeous game, highlighted by the detail, layout, and vibrancy of the titular city. The domed skylines, rotating sentry posts, pulsating generators, and other details make the game fun to simply sit back and watch. The city seems alive with activity, as do the enemy ships.

Like *Enduro* (1983) for the Atari 2600 and *Subroc* (1983) for the ColecoVision, *Atlantis* transitions from day to night and back again, and it does so beautifully. During the day, the sky is light blue with a few clouds. At night, the sky turns pitch black, with two searchlights cutting bright yellow swaths so you can get glimpses of the Gorgon fleets passing by. The night scenes not only add aesthetic value, but also a higher degree of difficulty.

Atlantis offers three skill levels: easy, medium (which I usually play), and hard. Two players can alternate turns, but, unfortunately, they cannot play at the same time as they can in the otherwise inferior Atari 2600 version. In the 2600 game, which came out first, one gamer controls the anti-aircraft gun (called a "sentry post" in the 2600 manual) on the left while the other player fires the one on the right.

The Atari 2600 version of *Atlantis* was designed by Dennis Koble, who once told *Omni* magazine (Oct., 1982 issue) that he made the game simple because manufacturers have "consistently overestimated the intelligence of the player and consistently underestimated his dexterity."

While 2600 *Atlantis* is good for some mindless fun, it's decidedly less enjoyable than the more complex Intellivision cart. There's no cross-hair sight to maneuver, nor is there a Sentinel Saucer to pilot. Players simply fire diagonal shots from the sentry posts and shoot straight upward from a centrally located "Acropolis Command Post."

Atlantis for the 2600 does have some historical importance, however, as it's one of the first 2600 shooters to have a storybook-style ending (it also has nicely drawn, rainbow-colored enemy ships). After aliens destroy the city, a flying saucer escapes. That flying saucer appears again in *Cosmic Ark* (1982), making *Atlantis* the first Atari 2600 game not based on a coin-op title to spawn a sequel.

Atlantis was also released for the Odyssey2, one of only two U.S.-released third-party titles for the system (Imagic's own *Demon Attack* was the other). The Odyssey2 version, which was designed by Jeff Ronnie, is similar to the 2600 game, but was graphically simplified and lacks the Acropolis Command Post. What it does have, though, is one "blitz bomb" per level that can destroy all onscreen enemies.

Getting back to the superior Intellivision cartridge, it was programmed by 26-year-old Pat Ransil (with sound by Dave Durran), who was the Senior Systems Engineer at Imagic. In an interview published in *Blip* #6 (July, 1983), Ransil described the types of games he enjoys:

> I personally like quick-reaction games rather than those that rely on complicated strategy. Success in *Atlantis* depends on your ability to react fast and manipulate the controls accordingly. You have to act *now*! That's the type of game I like.

In that same interview, Ransil spoke about the game's graphics. "It opens in mid-day, goes through the evening hours, and then nighttime comes and the sky is black," he said. "You see the enemy only by means of searchlights. Lighting the sky in that manner was the idea of Mike Becker, one of our graphics specialists. That's the way games get created. It's a team effort."

Ransil also talked about his love of creating video games:

> Designing games gives me a great deal of satisfaction, much more satisfaction than I get from designing the standard computer program…with a video game, you get the graphical presentation of the program onscreen; you get something that is pleasing to the eye…you see kids playing it and having fun…it gives you a good feeling to know you have created something that can give enjoyment to others.

In *TV Gamer* #1 (summer, 1983), a staff reviewer called *Atlantis* for the Intellivision an "exciting game" that "combines interesting graphics and good sound effects." On his website, The Video Game Critic (videogamecritic.com) called the cartridge a "showcase title," praising its "outstanding visuals and surprisingly rich gameplay."

Sadly, *Atlantis* never received a proper sequel. There was *Atlantis II* for the Atari 2600, but it was part of a contest and was only sent to 10 people who achieved a particularly high score in the game. As such, it's exceedingly valuable, selling at auction for as much as $18,000.

According to Skyler Miller of the All Game Guide (allgame.com), "*Atlantis II* is virtually the same as *Atlantis*. The cartridge and box are identical to the packaging of the original game, with the only discerning exterior feature being a typewritten label on the box that reads '*Atlantis II*.' The game itself is essentially a more difficult version of *Atlantis*, with a faster pace and different scoring system."

FUN FACT:

Imagic's "Destination Atlantis" high score competition was a victim of The Great Video Game Crash of 1983. The four top players were to be sent to Bermuda to compete in a contest to win a $10,000 chest of gold, but that never happened.

WHY IT MADE THE LIST:

From its gorgeous graphics to its deep, yet fast-paced shooting action, *Atlantis* exudes quality.

CHAPTER 8

ATTACK OF THE TIMELORD!

ODYSSEY2
GENRE: SLIDE-AND-SHOOT
PUBLISHER: NAP
DEVELOPER: NAP
1 PLAYER
1982

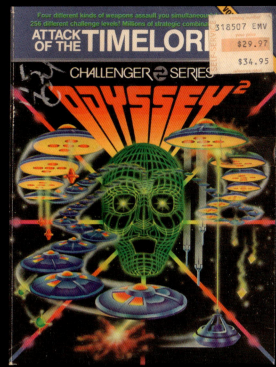

Attack of the Timelord! for the Odyssey2, complete in box. $18.

"FAST-PACED AND FUN…ONE OF THE BEST ODYSSEY2 GAMES."

The Odyssey2 has some really bad games—*Bowling!/Basketball!* and *Thunderball!* come to mind—but it's got some terrific cartridges as well. One such jewel in the O2's crown is *Attack of the Timelord!*, a sterling example of the slide-and-shoot genre that was so popular during the early 1980s and is all but dead today.

As with many games of this type, players guide a laser cannon (actually, the player's triangular ship is purported to be a Time Machine mounted with a laser cannon) along the bottom of the screen, firing at swarming enemies. The baddies in question are the Timelord's fleet of Timeships, which move quickly in intricate, snakelike patterns, firing four types of weapons: missiles, antimatter mines, annihilators (which home in on the player), and nucleonic time killers (which are "piloted by expendable robots programmed to anticipate human reactions").

The enemies exhibit relatively intelligent A.I. and are fun and challenging to avoid and kill. One entertaining aspect of the game is that you can shoot down the missiles and other projectiles the enemies unleash. Another is the appearance between levels of a skull-like creature called Spyrus the Deathless—Time Lord of Chaos. Unfortunately, you never get to battle this pseudo-boss, but he is a striking visual, and if you play the game with The Voice speech module hooked up, he'll spout such dialogue as "Attack and destroy," "Kill the human," "Conquer the Earth," and "Your planet is doomed."

Like most Odyssey2 games, *Attack of the Timelord!* gives players only one life (*Turtles!* is a noteworthy exception to this rule), which is unfortunate, since the game boasts a whopping 256 levels—it's a formidable challenge to simply get past the sixth or seventh round. There's no onscreen level indicator, but the high score remains displayed as long as the game hasn't been reset, which is a good thing, since you'll likely try to increase your high score again and again.

Attack of the Timelord! was developed by the prolific Ed Averett under the working title of "Snake Ships from Sirius." According to various sources, Averett, not wanting his computer scientist wife to feel left out, gave her programming credit for the game as well. Unfortunately, this tactic reportedly backfired, as she was angry for being credited for something she didn't create.

Attack of the Timelord! was highly touted when it was new, especially in the pages of *Electronic Games* magazine. In issue #14 (April, 1983), in the "Programmable Parade" section, the reviewer called it "an absolute mind-bender…challenging but compulsive…a tremendous technological achievement…one of the best new programmable video games on store shelves today."

The back of the *Attack of the Timelord!* box.

Attack of the Timelord! game cartridge. $8.

Attack of the Timelord! advertisement.

In *JoyStik* magazine #5 (April, 1983), Jim Gorzelany called *Attack of the Timelord!* "engrossing," "colorful," "addictive," and "truly blistering." He also said that, along with such titles as *Freedom Fighters!* and *K.C.'s Krazy Chase!*, the "Odyssey2's manufacturers have [finally] proven that they can produce games that play as good as—if not better than—anyone else's."

In recent years, *Attack of the Timelord!* has received accolades as well. William Cassidy of the All Game Guide (www.allgame.com) called the cartridge "fast-paced and fun…one of the best Odyssey2 games." On The Odyssey2 Home Page, www.the-nextlevel.com, Cassidy said *Attack of the Time Lord!* was "one of the fastest games produced for the Odyssey2 and features some of the best graphics and sound on the system. The fact that you only have one life—a problem that handicaps so many other Odyssey2 games—is perhaps the only flaw in this superb game."

Earl Green, who oversees the pop culture site www.thelogbook.com, referred to *Attack of the Time Lord!* as a "gem of an addictive shooting gallery," a "blast," and a "thrilling little game." In *Classic Gamer Magazine* #5 (fall, 2000), he called it "a great tip of the hat to *Galaga*, incorporating a fleet of enemy ships that would bob, weave, and drop all kinds of weaponry on my head with alarming regularity."

Not everyone agrees with these positive assessments, however. Perry Greenberg, writing in *Video Games* #5 (Feb., 1983), said the game is "really not that much fun" and that the graphics are "flat, stilted and dull." (Greenberg referred to the game as *Timelord* instead of *Attack of the Timelord!*, which makes me a little suspicious about the reliability of the review.)

Perry's opinion notwithstanding, *Attack of the Timelord!* is a sensational game.

When my cousin received an Odyssey2 for Christmas during the early '80s, the only cartridges she ever got for the system were *Baseball!*, *Speedway!/Spin-Out!/Crypto-Logic!* (the pack-in cart with the console), and *Invaders from Hyperspace!*, the latter of which was all but unplayable, since she had her system hooked up to a black-and-white television set.

My cousin and I played plenty of *Baseball!* and *Speedway!*, but we would've killed for an electrifying game like *Attack of the Timelord!* Even the box art crackles with excitement.

FUN FACT:

For the European release of *Attack of the Timelord!*, the title, box art, and storyline were changed to fit Gerry Anderson's *Terrahawks* TV series. In addition, the graphics were spruced up a little to include the Earth and Moon in the background.

WHY IT MADE THE LIST:

Thanks to nice graphics and killer shooting action, *Attack of the Timelord!* is one of the most exciting games in the Odyssey2 library.

CHAPTER 9
BALLOON FIGHT

NINTENDO NES
GENRE: NON-SCROLLING PLATFORMER
PUBLISHER: NINTENDO
DEVELOPER: NINTENDO
1 OR 2 PLAYERS (SIMULTANEOUS)
1986

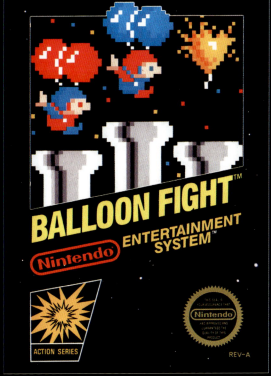

Balloon Fight for the Nintendo NES, complete in box. $175.

"…GREAT FUN ALONE OR WITH A PARTNER, WITH SOMETHING TO OFFER ALL AGES AND SKILL LEVELS."

Before I wax eloquent (or at least hammer out some scribblings) about the attributes and gameplay of *Balloon Fight*, a disclaimer is in order. The game, designed by Yoshio Sakamoto (*Metroid*), is very similar to *Joust*—an arm-flapping balloon fighter simply replaces the knight-mounted ostrich—which would disqualify it from this list in some gamers' eyes.

I don't begrudge that opinion, and I definitely value originality (*Killer Bees!* anyone?), but I also appreciate a copycat title when it's done right and adds some new features. If not, I would have had to disqualify such great games as *K.C. Munchkin!* and *Mr. Do!*, which heavily borrow from *Pac-Man* and *Dig Dug*, respectively.

Now, upward and onward (so to speak).

In *Balloon Fight*, which is a very nice port of the 1984 Nintendo Vs. System arcade game, players use the NES control pad to move a balloonist up, down, right, and left on a series of non-scrolling screens, each populated with enemies that are also held aloft by balloons. As in *Joust*, each screen has several platforms to land on. Also like *Joust*, players repeatedly press buttons to remain in flight: the "A" button flaps the balloon fighter's arms once while the "B" button flaps his arms continuously.

To thwart an enemy, players must bump him from at least slightly above (another *Joust*-like component) in order to pop his balloon. When an enemy's balloon pops, the enemy will float down using a parachute. To make the enemy drop into the water below and disappear, players must bump the enemy again. When the enemy sinks underwater, a bubble will float up that can be popped for extra points.

If the parachuting enemy reaches land, he will blow up another balloon and become airborne again, this time in stronger form. If the player's balloon fighter gets too close to the water, a fish can rise up to eat him (similar to The Troll of the Lava Pits in *Joust*).

One key gameplay element that separates *Balloon Fight* from *Joust* is the fact that the player begins the game with a safety shield of sorts in the manner of two balloons. If an enemy pops one balloon, the player can still fly, but it will be harder. If both balloons get popped, the balloon fighter falls into the water and the player loses a life. If a particular screen lasts too long, a thunder and lightning storm will occur, forcing players to dodge lightning bolts, so there is a time factor involved.

After three screens, the game enters an enemy-free bonus round—another aspect separating the game from *Joust*—in

The back of the *Balloon Fight* box.   *Balloon Fight* title screen.   *Balloon Fight* game cartridge: $15

which balloons waft upward from ground-based pipes, with players flying around trying to pop as many as possible.

No game like this would be complete without a raucous two-player mode, in which contestants can agree to either team up against the enemies or sabotage one another, and you better believe that *Balloon Fight* is a blast to play with a friend (who may very well become your enemy after a few competitive rounds).

In addition to the standard one- and two-player versions of *Balloon Fight*, the cartridge offers a fun, but difficult Balloon Trip mode, in which gamers, flying solo, traverse a forced-scrolling playfield, avoiding lightning while popping as many balloons as possible. There are no platforms to land on, and getting too close to the water can result in the balloon fighter becoming fish food. During the action, the player's ranking (from 1–50), which goes up with progress, appears at the top right corner of the screen.

While critical reaction to *Balloon Fight*, which was #36 on GameSpy's "50 Favorite Console Games of the '80s," isn't 100% positive (Corbie Dillard, reviewing the WiiWare release for www.nintendolife.com, called the game a "rather bland and repetitive arcade experience"), most retro gamers, including me, agree that it is a highly entertaining action title, especially for those of us who enjoy such NES non-scrolling platformers as *Mario Bros.*, *Popeye*, *Donkey Kong*, and, of course, *Joust* (which came out in 1988, making it ineligible for inclusion in this book).

In the expanded edition of Jeff Rovin's *How to Win at Nintendo Games* (1989, St. Martin's Press), the author said that *Balloon Fight* is "similar to the old arcade game *Joust* but improves on the theme with the bouncing balloons, self-repairing enemy balloonists, lightning, fish, propellers and so forth…Great fun alone or with a partner, with something to offer all ages and skill levels."

In 1990, Nintendo released a sequel for the Game Boy called *Balloon Kid*. In this game, players control Alice, who, in addition to keeping aloft with balloons (by waving her arms), can remove the balloons, walk along the ground, and jump. If her balloons are popped, but she lands safely, she can inflate new balloons and get airborne again. As in the Balloon Trip mode of *Balloon Fight*, the action scrolls.

Alice's objective in *Balloon Kid* is to make her way through "Pencilvania" (the buildings look like pencils) and a variety of unnamed locations, including a forest, an ocean, an icy mountain, and an industrial building. There are balloons to collect, bosses to destroy (by detaching the balloons and bouncing on them, and by simply jumping on them), and Alice's brother to rescue. Some of the standard *Balloon Kid* enemies come from *Balloon Fight*, including the Balloon Birds and the fish that grabs you if you get too close to the water. In two-player mode, Alice battles it out with her friend and rival Samm as they compete to gather the most balloons.

In 2002, Nintendo re-released *Balloon Fight* (as *Balloon Fight-e*) on the Game Boy Advance e-Reader. *Balloon Fight* was also released for the Supervision (1992) handheld system, the Wii Virtual Console (2007), the 3DS Virtual Console (2013), and the Wii U Virtual Console (2013).

In 2011, Nintendo re-released the sequel, *Balloon Kid*, on the 3DS Virtual Console.

FUN FACT:

Balloon Fight is available as a playable game in *Animal Crossing* (2002) for the GameCube.

WHY IT MADE THE LIST:

Balloon Fight is similar to *Joust* (1982), one of the all-time great arcade games, but it adds a few new wrinkles to make it a fun and challenging game in its own right.

CHAPTER **10**

BEAUTY & THE BEAST

INTELLIVISION
GENRE: CLIMBING/NON-SCROLLING PLATFORMER
PUBLISHER: IMAGIC
DEVELOPER: IMAGIC
1 PLAYER
1982

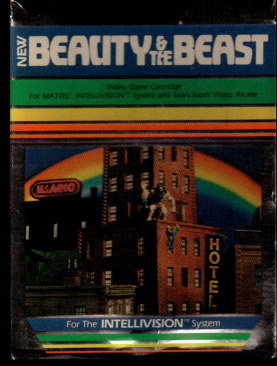

Beauty & the Beast for the Intellivision, complete in box. $7.

"A VERY GOOD GAME AND PROOF THAT IMAGIC WAS THE BEST REASON TO OWN AN INTELLIVISION."

Imagic's *Beauty & the Beast*, programmed by Wendell Brown (*Nova Blast*), may not be a "tale as old as time," but it did come out way back in 1982, during the height of the Golden Age of home video games, when such ubiquitous climbing titles as *Donkey Kong*, *Miner 2049er*, and *Popeye* were entertaining gamers across the country.

Oozing with arcade-style excellence, *Beauty & the Beast* is an Intellivision exclusive, but it does share elements with the aforementioned games. Players guide Bashful Buford as he scales the side of a skyscraper (called the Mutton Building), running across ledges and quickly climbing up windows that open and close randomly. As in *Crazy Climber* (1980), the very first climbing video game, Buford can only climb up a window when it is open. If a window closes while Buford is climbing on it, he will fall. The objective on each screen is to reach the top.

While Buford scales the building, his girlfriend, Tiny Mabel, who is being held captive by an ape-like Bully named Horrible Hank, will float down hearts for Buford to catch (a la *Popeye*). When Buford catches a heart, it will temporarily make him invincible (unlike *Popeye*) and able to turn the tables on his enemies (as in *Miner 2049er*), which include birds, rats, and boulders. Buford can also jump over enemies. In addition to thwarting (or avoiding) enemies, Buford should be careful not to step off either side of the building, or he'll plummet to the bottom.

Reaching the very top of the building, which happens after climbing to the top of several screens, rewards players with a screen-shaking, *King Kong*-like finale in which the "camera" fades back to show Horrible Hank falling to his "death." This is followed by a helicopter picking up Bashful and Tiny and then Bashful beginning once again at the bottom of the building, this time with amped up difficulty.

The controls for *Beauty & the Beast* are as good as those for any game for the system. Pressing the much-maligned control disk maneuvers Buford with the greatest of ease, with him rarely going in a direction you didn't intend. The climbing, jumping, obstacle-avoiding action has a smooth level of difficulty, and it's great fun to try grabbing a heart at just the right time to be able to zip up a window or two with impunity, regardless of where the enemies are positioned.

Beauty & the Beast is a good looking and sounding game as well. The music, programmed by Dave Durran (*Atlantis*, *Fathom*), is peppy, even when your game ends, and the only visual shortcoming is blue (upper torso and head) and black (pants and shoes) Mabel, who is far from beautiful, but does look quite beastly (not to mention blocky).

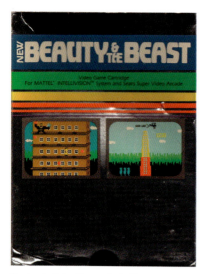 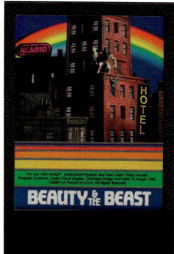 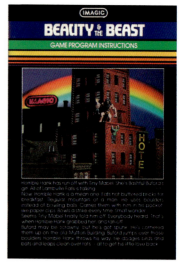

The back of the *Beauty & the Beast* box. | *Beauty & the Beast* game cartridge. $3. | *Beauty & the Beast* instruction manual. $1.

Randi Hacker, senior editor of *Electronic Fun with Computers & Games*, writing in issue #2 (Dec., 1982), underrated the game somewhat, giving it three out of four joysticks (stars), but she did say: "The running, dodging and evasive action, as well as the burning curiosity to know just what awaits you on the next level, definitely maintain the interest level."

In issue #1 (summer, 1983) of the British publication, *TV Gamer*, the writer underrated the game as well, saying it only has a "slight edge over the Coleco version of *Donkey Kong* for Intellivision." If you've ever played Intellivision *Donkey Kong*, with its ugly graphics and sluggish controls, you know this is faint praise indeed.

Tom Zjaba of Tomorrow's Hero's (www.tomheroes.com) gave *Beauty & the Beast* a "B+", calling it "a very good game and proof that Imagic was the best reason to own an Intellivision." The Video Game Critic (videogamecritic.com) bumped it up a grade to an "A-", calling it "an entertaining platformer" with "quality graphics and exciting gameplay…a showcase for the system."

Despite its greatness, *Beauty & the Beast* never received a true sequel. However, in an interview with Scott Stilphen published on www.2600connection.com, *Tropical Trouble* programmer Steve DeFrisco called his side-scroller "sort of a sequel to Wendell Brown's game *Beauty & the Beast*. The same basic premise—the Beast steals your girl and you've got to get her back."

FUN FACT:

In addition to programming *Beauty & the Beast* and *Nova Blast* for the Intellivision, Wendell Brown (with Michael Becker) developed *Moonsweeper* for the ColecoVision (featured in "The Next 100" appendix near the back of this book). He's also a prolific entrepreneur, scientist, and inventor. According to www.crunchbase.com, Brown has "more than 120 U.S. and international patent applications issued or pending in the fields of telecommunications, virtual workforce services, electric car technology, mobile phone peripherals, LED lighting, insurance, 3D cameras, biodiesel processing, food packaging, and online music distribution."

WHY IT MADE THE LIST:

A great cartridge for those of us who mourn the climbing genre, *Beauty & the Beast* is one of the most arcade-like games in the Intellivision library.

CHAPTER 11

BERZERK

ATARI 5200
GENRE: MAZE SHOOTER
PUBLISHER: ATARI
DEVELOPER: ATARI
1 OR 2 PLAYERS (ALTERNATING)
1983

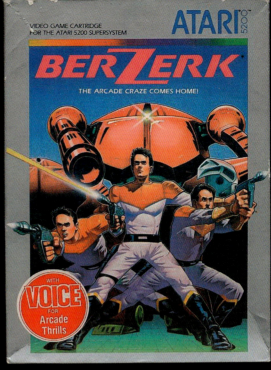

Berzerk for the Atari 5200, complete in box. $15.

"AS CLOSE AS YOU CAN GET TO THE ARCADES."

You can't talk about *Berzerk* for the Atari 5200 without mentioning the remarkable voice effects, which were achieved without using a voice emulator (the system never had one). Sounding like Cylons from the original *Battlestar Galactica*, the game taunts and tantalizes players with "Humanoid must not escape!", "Chicken! Fight like a robot!", and "Intruder Alert! Intruder Alert!"

In addition to nicely emulated voice effects, the game is a stellar port in the gameplay and graphics department as well, offering up an almost note-for-note rendition of Stern's 1980 coin-op classic, despite the absence of "Coin detected in pocket," a line spoken during the arcade game's attract mode. (Of course, this line wouldn't make much sense in the context of a home console title.)

In *Berzerk*, the player guides a relatively slow stick-figure humanoid through a series of simple mazes, shooting (in eight directions) at robots while avoiding getting shot. Running into maze walls—which produces a cool electrifying sound effect—is deadly, as is making contact with the robots or their gunfire.

Avoiding bullets can be difficult, especially at point-blank range; but, luckily, robots lend a helping hand by being clumsy—they tend to collide, shoot one another, and run into the electrified walls. Seasoned players can employ a bit of strategy by predicting the robots' movements and by tricking them into killing themselves.

If the player stays in a maze too long, an indestructible, panic-inducing smiley face named Evil Otto appears, bouncing quickly toward the humanoid and acting as a time limit of sorts. Exiting a maze without killing all the robots prevents the player from earning that screen's bonus points. Once Otto appears, a gripping race to the exit frequently ensues. When the player exits, he or she enters a maze of a different design.

By pressing the * key in the 5200 game, players can toggle through eleven difficulty levels, but even the easiest mode of play is a steep challenge.

Despite (or because of) its high level of difficulty, *Berzerk* is widely regarded as a top-notch title. In issue #34 (Nov./Dec., 1997) of the *Digital Press* fanzine, Joe Santulli called *Berzerk* a "favorite of mine because there's no way a game can go on longer than about 10 minutes." He also referred to Evil Otto as the "coolest" villain in video game history.

Jonathan Rose of The Atari Times (www.ataritimes.com) called *Berzerk* "pure gold" and a "must-own." Tom

The back of the *Berzerk* box.

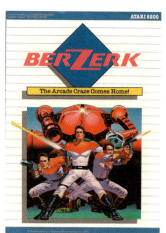

Berzerk instruction manual. $2.

Berzerk for the Atari 5200 in action. *Courtesy of AtariAge.com.*

Zjaba of Tomorrow's Heroes (www.tomheroes.com) said the game is a good reason to "put up with" the Atari 5200.

When *Berzerk* was new in stores, Charles Ardai, writing in *Electronic Fun with Computers & Games* Vol. 2 #2 (Dec., 1983), said the game was "as close as you can get to the arcades" and that "every graphic detail is perfect." Ardai was especially appreciative of the game's audio, saying that "*Berzek* without the voice is like *Donkey Kong* without the girl: it's playable, but most of the motivation is gone."

The manual for the Atari 2600 version of *Berzerk* includes a sci-fi storyline (the player, as a space explorer, is marooned on planet Mazeon), something the 5200 rendition leaves out. Other than this extremely slight advantage, the 2600 cart, though a perfectly respectable port for the console, comes up lacking in comparison; specifically, it lacks voice effects and robots that can fire diagonally.

The original arcade version of *Berzerk* (1980), which was one of the earliest maze shooters, has an interesting backstory. The game's programmer, Alan McNeil, working at Universal Research Laboratories (a division of Stern Electronics), got the idea for the coin-op from a dream in which he was battling robots. This, combined with inspiration from a BASIC game called *Robots* (*Daleks* in the UK), inspired McNeil to create *Berzerk*. He titled the game after SF author Fred Saberhagen's *Berserker* series of novels and short stories.

According to Good Deal Games owner Michael Thomasson, McNeil named Evil Otto after Dave Otto, "a sadistic security chief that tormented McNeil." Apparently, Otto, while working with McNeil at Dave Nutting Associates, would smile when he chewed out his coworkers.

Thomasson also explained that *Berzerk* was originally going to have monochrome visuals, but "Stern changed their display format to use a color overlay board" to compete with Williams' recently released *Defender* (1980). Regarding the voice effects, they were created for approximately $1,000 per word via a National Speech microchip.

At 37,620 arcade cabinets produced, *Berzerk* was a huge success for Stern. The game gained further notoriety in *Chasing Ghosts: Beyond the Arcade* (2007), a documentary chronicling competitive gaming from the early 1980s. (Two years before that, the 2600 version of *Berzerk* was immortalized in an episode of *My Name is Earl* called "Crabman," in which Earl's pal plays the game and pins a Polaroid photograph of his score to the wall.)

As with many coin-op classics, *Berzerk* spawned a sequel, in this case *Frenzy* (1982), a great game that was ported to the ColecoVision (but not the 5200) in 1983. Lesser known among the general public than *Berzerk*, *Frenzy* added such elements as shots that reflect off solid walls, walls comprised of dots that can be destroyed, and the ability for players to kill Evil Otto.

FUN FACT:

A huge inspiration for such games as *Robotron: 2084* (1982), *Wolfenstein 3D* (1992), and *DOOM* (1993), *Berzerk* was also ported to the Vectrex, but, like the 2600 game, that rendition lacks voice effects.

WHY IT MADE THE LIST:

Imbued with arcade-like voice effects, *Berzerk* for the 5200 is a slow (in a good way), methodical maze shooter that is as fun as it is challenging—a great way to kill a few minutes while you are waiting to go somewhere.

CHAPTER 12
BOULDER DASH

COLECOVISION
GENRE: MAZE
PUBLISHER: TELEGAMES
DEVELOPER: MICRO LAB
1 PLAYER
1984

Boulder Dash for the ColecoVision, complete in box. Courtesy of Bryan C. Smith. $350.

"BOULDER DASH IS ABOUT AS STRATEGICALLY RICH AS ANY ACTION-ORIENTED GAME YOU CAN FIND."

There are undoubtedly numerous ColecoVision fans who have never played *Boulder Dash*, an obscure cartridge published late in the life of the console. More common iterations of the game exist, such as the original Atari 8-bit computer classic (1984) and the rock solid Nintendo NES version (1990), but the ColecoVision game was rarely seen when it came out and is very tough to find today.

In this ingenious game, players guide a thin, big-headed, odd-looking fellow named Rockford as he tunnels through scrolling, underground caves, digging pathways to collect jewels. Digging under one of the many boulders in each cave causes it to drop, and Rockford should be careful to move out of the way so he's not crushed.

As the manual states, "The rocks will fall whenever gravity dictates. They will fall straight down if unsupported or they will topple off underlying objects if there is nothing to block their way."

In order to complete a cave, Rockford must collect the required number of jewels. Many jewels are obvious and immediately available, but you can also create jewels by dropping boulders on butterflies. Other ways to create jewels include suffocating amoebas by surrounding them with boulders and dropping boulders through an enchanted wall. Enchanted walls look like regular walls, but vibrate briefly when hit by a falling boulder—while an enchanted wall is vibrating, boulders that drop through it are turned into jewels.

If you rush Rockford through the caves too quickly, it's easy for him to get crushed by boulders, especially when he unleashes an avalanche. Another hazard is fireflies that "glide about in the tunnels." Fireflies come in handy strategically because, when you drop a boulder on one, it will explode, potentially demolishing a wall and giving you access to jewels (unlike butterflies, fireflies don't turn into jewels when they explode).

Surrounding the exterior of each maze is an indestructible titanium wall. The only way for Rockford to exit a cave and go on to the next cave is to guide him to the exit, which will appear after the required amount of jewels have been collected (a similar form of exiting is found in *Bomberman*, which was originally released in Japan in 1983). Once the exit is revealed, you can try to grab more jewels or go ahead and exit for extra time bonus points. You should work quickly to try and beat each level, but not haphazardly.

The manual for *Boulder Dash* says there are 16 caves (each of them different in design and color scheme), but there are actually 20 when you take the bonus levels into account, which are caves 5, 10, 15, and 20.

In Coleco-produced ColecoVision games, the manuals have a THE FUN OF DISCOVERY section where it states:

This instruction guide provides the basic information you'll need to start playing [insert game name here], but it is only the beginning! You'll find that

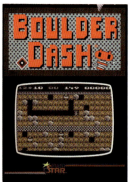

The back of the *Boulder Dash* box (ColecoVision). *Courtesy of Bryan C. Smith.*

Boulder Dash for the Atari 5200, complete in box. $100.

ColecoVision video game console. $100.

this cartridge contains special features that make this game exciting every time you play. Experiment with different techniques—and enjoy the game!

Since *Boulder Dash* wasn't published by Coleco, there is no THE FUN OF DISCOVERY text in the manual. However, the sentiment applies to *Boulder Dash* as much as it does any ColecoVision game. With 20 different caves, varying strategies for locating and creating jewels, and virtually limitless pathways to create by digging tunnels, *Boulder Dash* is about as strategically rich as any action-oriented game you can find, which is remarkable considering the simple four-way controls.

The original Atari computer version of *Boulder Dash*, published by First Star Software and designed by Peter Liepa and Chris Gray, was clearly inspired by *Dig Dug* and *Mr. Do!*, and by a lesser-known 1982 arcade game called *The Pit*.

The ColecoVision cart, programmed by Apple II veteran Chris Oberth, is an excellent conversion, but for one thing: the scrolling isn't very smooth. It's not as rough as the otherwise excellent *Tutankham*, but it is noticeable. One nice touch Oberth added is Rockford tapping his foot if he stands still for a second or two while facing the screen (possibly an inspiration for Sonic the Hedgehog looking at you and tapping his foot when he gets impatient?).

Oberth also programmed *One-on-One* for the ColecoVision, a widely derided rendition of the computer classic noteworthy for excising such features as replays, demos, and slow motion. In an interview by Alan Hewston published in *Retrogaming Times Monthly* #24 (May, 2006), Oberth explained why *Boulder Dash* was a much better conversion than *One-on-One*, saying he had more time to work on *Boulder Dash* and that he had "access to the original source code, which was very helpful."

Personally, my first experience playing *Boulder Dash* was the Nintendo NES port, published in 1990 by JVC and developed by Data East. In a review of the NES version appearing in issue #11 (Aug., 1991) of the UK magazine, *Mean Machines*, the writer said: "Data East have improved the graphics and added a neat front end [referring to an overworld map screen], but have retained the same maps [referring to level design] and gameplay that made the C64 version one of the classic games of all time. It's massively addicting, calling on arcade skills and fiendish puzzle-solving in a way that draws you totally into the game. You shout with frustration as a wrong move results in Rockford being buried under a pile of boulders, then yell victoriously when you work out how to get those last few diamonds and finish the screen."

Boulder Dash was released through various other avenues, including the arcade (1984, Exidy), Game Boy (1990), Nintendo Wii (2009, via the Virtual Console), and more.

In September of 2006, Atari2600.com began taking pre-orders for an Atari 5200 version of *Boulder Dash*, releasing it in limited numbers in four different box colors (pink, red, black, and yellow) at the 2007 Classic Gaming Expo. According to Atari2600.com owner Joe Cody, quoted on www.digitpress.com, "The original Atari computer code was modified for use on an Atari 5200 with the permission and direction of the copyright owner, First Star Software Inc."

In 2012, Andrew Davie and Thomas Jentzsch created a homebrew version of *Boulder Dash* for the Atari 2600. In 2014, Elektronite developed *Boulder Dash* for the Intellivision.

Boulder Dash sequels and remakes include *Boulder Dash EX* (2002, GBA), *Boulder Dash-XL* (2011, Xbox 360 via XBLA), and *Boulder Dash-XL 3D* (2012, 3DS), among others.

NES owners can play a similar game in *Crystal Mines* (1989) while Atari Lynx fans can tunnel underground on the go with *Crystal Mines II* (1990). *Boulder Dash* fans should enjoy both titles.

SAD FACT:
While researching this book, I read in the July 16, 2012 edition of the *Chicago Tribune* that Chris Oberth passed away at the age of 59. The short piece said the programmer was "passionate about playing and making games."

WHY IT MADE THE LIST:
Like the legendary maze titles *Dig Dug* and *Mr. Do!*, *Boulder Dash* is a tunnel-digging game loaded with challenges and strategic opportunities.

CHAPTER 13

BOUNTY BOB STRIKES BACK

ATARI 5200
GENRE: CLIMBING/NON-SCROLLING PLAT-
FORMER
PUBLISHER: BIG FIVE SOFTWARE
DEVELOPER: BIG FIVE SOFTWARE
1 OR 2 PLAYERS (ALTERNATING)
1984

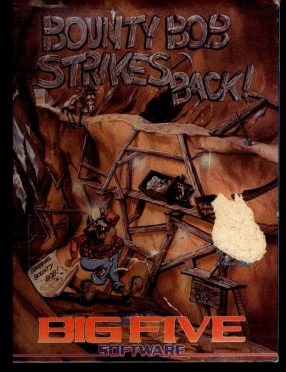

Bounty Bob Strikes Back for the Atari 5200, complete in box. $800.

"A SEQUEL THAT'S BETTER THAN THE ORIGINAL."

In 1982, Big Five Software, the company that would release *Bounty Bob Strikes Back* a couple of years later, was on top of the world. *Miner 2049er* was a big hit, and Big Five founders Bill Hogue and Jeff Konyu were young superstars in their field, promoting their company on ABC's *Good Morning America*.

The dynamic duo was also featured in an issue of *The National Enquirer* in an article entitled "Computer Whiz Kids Turn Fun and Games Into Million-Dollar Business." The piece referred to their youthfulness (Hogue was 20, Konyu was a high school junior), their "flashy $10,000 Pontiac Trans Am cars," their humble beginnings (Hogue borrowed $500 from his mother for blank cassettes and magazine ads), and their projected sales of $1.5 to $2 million for the year.

Unfortunately, The Great Video Game Crash of 1983 eventually derailed the company, as Hogue explained: "The game market started to collapse for us after the release of *Bounty Bob Strikes Back*. We started scaling back our company operations as the orders slowly stopped coming in. Our office lease ran out and we decided just to run the company out of my house. Ultimately everyone moved on to other things and I closed the company down."

One of the greatest, most impressively programmed home video games of the 1980s, *Bounty Bob Strikes Back* is also one of the hardest to find, meaning most retro enthusiasts have never even held the cartridge in their hands, much less played the game. The box and foldout map/poster/manual are especially tough to come by.

Bounty Bob, which was designed by Hogue, Curtis Mikolyski (graphics), and Jeff Zinn (music), is the sequel to Big Five's critically acclaimed megahit *Miner 2049er*, but is even better, thanks in part to the game's whopping 25 levels of play (as opposed to 10 in *Miner* or 11 in the ColecoVision version of *Miner*).

Players guide Bounty Bob as he tries to "claim every section of the framework in each mine cavern." To complete a screen, he must walk over each section of framework (platform), which fills it in with color.

In addition to walking on platforms, Bob will climb up and down ladders, ride a grain elevator, slide down slides, jump over gaps and enemies, eat super energy food bars (for longer jumps), ride hydraulic lifts, travel via suction tubes, dodge acid rain, get shot from a cannon, get transported

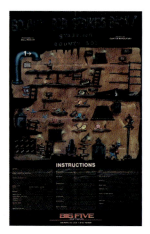

Bounty Bob Strikes Back foldout poster manual. $125.

The back of the *Bounty Bob Strikes Back* box.

Bounty Bob Strikes Back game cartridge. $350.

via transporters, maneuver on a utility hoist, avoid getting pulverized by pulverizers, negotiate moving platforms, avoid mutant organisms, and eat yummy treats, the latter of which irradiate Bob, letting him chase the mutants *Pac-Man* style.

Clearly, *Bounty Bob Strikes Back* is loaded with variety, but it's even more noteworthy for its high degree of challenge. To make it through each screen, players must plan a good, strategically sound route, maneuver very carefully, and maintain a high level of concentration. Visually, like *Miner 2049er*, the game is fairly pedestrian, but it does have some nice flourishes, such as an animated title screen, titles for each level, and a new pseudo-3D look for the platforms.

Bounty Bob Strikes Back offers four difficulty levels: easy, in which "filled-in framework remains filled-in and dead mutants remain from one life to the next"; medium, in which the enemies move a little faster; hard, in which "filled-in framework resets and dead mutants resurrect from one life to the next"; and c'mon, in which the game begins with 1000 less on the bonus counter.

If Bounty Bob gets stuck in an area where there's no escape (not even death), the player can enter 8187826861 (Big Five's phone number back in the day) via the controller keypad for emergency help. Otherwise, you have to wait until the bonus timer counts all the way down to zero.

Most gamers who have actually played *Bounty Bob Strikes Back* love it.

In the seventh edition of the *Digital Press Collector's Guide* (2002), a contributor claimed that *Bounty Bob* is "a sequel that's better than the original" and that it "could be the most enjoyable game ever made."

Doug Jackson, on the Digital Press website (digitpress. com), called the game "well-rounded," "wonderful" and full of "depth," but warned that each stage is "very hard and requires a lot of fast thinking to beat the timer."

In a "Top 10 Gaming Grails" feature on www.gamespy. com, William Cassidy said *Bounty Bob Strikes Back* "outshone the original [*Miner 2049er*] in almost every way…the lucky few who have played it consider it to be one of the most enjoyable games ever made…Extreme rarity coupled with extreme enjoyment leads to extreme collectability."

FUN FACT:

According to an interview with Bill Hogue published on www.armchairempire.com, Hogue dismissed an earlier idea he had about producing a combination cartridge for the 5200 that would include *Bounty Bob Strikes Back* and *Miner 2049er*. "I decided it wouldn't be profitable so I shelved it," he said.

WHY IT MADE THE LIST:

With 25 levels of outstanding gameplay, *Bounty Bob Strikes Back* is nothing less than one of the greatest games of the 1980s.

CHAPTER 14

BUMP 'N' JUMP

INTELLIVISION
GENRE: DEMOLITION/COMBAT RACING
PUBLISHER: MATTEL
DEVELOPER: TECHNOLOGY ASSOCIATES
1 OR 2 PLAYERS (ALTERNATING)
1983

COLECOVISION
GENRE: DEMOLITION/COMBAT RACING
PUBLISHER: COLECO
DEVELOPER: COLECO
1 OR 2 PLAYERS (ALTERNATING)
1984

Bump 'n' Jump for the Intellivision, complete in box. $30.

"THE GAMEPLAY EVOKES THE SPIRIT OF THE ARCADE CAB."

Bump 'n' Jump is the best racing game for the Intellivision and, along with *BurgerTime*, one of the console's most accurate coin-op conversions.

The top-down, vertical scrolling action has players driving up straightaways and curving roads in a red racecar, battling it out against 10 different types of vehicles. You can bump enemy vehicles off the road or jump on top of them, both thoroughly entertaining maneuvers. Jumping also comes into play when you go airborne to make it across various bodies of water. If you land on an island, you get bonus points.

One thing to keep in mind is that you can only jump while going 100 miles-per-hour or more, which keeps the game moving along at a fast pace (almost always a good thing for a racer). When a body of water is just ahead, a beeping noise will sound (accompanied by an onscreen exclamation point), letting you know to get ready to jump.

Enemy vehicle types include: tractor (heavy, slow, drives straight ahead), cycle (light, drives at medium speed, weaves back and forth frequently), skull car (light and fast, frequently drives straight toward you), racecar (light and fast, frequently zigzags), dump truck (fast, dumps debris on the road, explodes when you bump it), white car (light, frequently drives straight toward you), yellow truck (heavy, frequently weaves back and forth), green car (light, frequently zigzags), blue car (light and fast, frequently weaves back and forth), and brown car (light, frequently zigzags).

The lighter the vehicle, the further you can bump it. If you bump an enemy into a pile of dirt, a rock, a causeway wall, or other obstacle, it will crash. Be careful, though, because enemy vehicles can bump you as well. As in the 1982 arcade original, which was manufactured by Bally/Midway and developed by Data East, if you manage to complete a roadway without bumping another car, you'll score 50,000 bonus points, a feature also seen in the ColecoVision port.

Speaking of the ColecoVision game, the dump trucks are absent, and the cars tend to flicker, but it's an excellent

Bump 'n' Jump advertisement (Intellivision).

Bump 'n' Jump game cartridge (ColecoVision). $15.

Bump 'n' Jump instruction manual (ColecoVision). $5.

translation as well. One benefit of the ColecoVision port is compatibility with Expansion Module #2, a.k.a. the steering wheel/gas pedal driving controller. You may be surprised to know that the arcade game was *not* equipped with a steering wheel or gas pedal— just a simple joystick and button.

Getting back to the Intellivision version, which has mono-colored enemy cars, it was programmed by Joe Jacobs and Dennis Clark of Technology Consultants. According to intellivisionlives.com:

> One day, Mattel Electronics was contacted by a couple of guys from New Jersey, Joe Jacobs and Dennis Clark, with startling information: they had hooked up a PlayCable unit to a personal computer and made their own Intellivision development system. They demonstrated that they had figured out how to program Intellivision games quite well, and they wanted to offer their services to Mattel before going to some other company. Ah, blackmail is such an ugly word...
>
> To keep them away from the competition, Mattel contracted with them to program the Intellivision version of the arcade game *Bump 'n' Jump*. They, under the name Technology Associates, were paid $24,000 for the conversion.
>
> David Warhol (*Mind Strike*) served as liaison, giving technical assistance as needed. Except for the title screen graphics by Daisy Nguyen, all the work was done in New Jersey, in one of the programmer's basements; they weren't invited to Mattel headquarters.

Nguyen's misleading (if visually impressive) title screen graphics, depicting a *Pole Position*-style view of the car with pine trees lining the roadway, is not found in the arcade or ColecoVision game, but the two home ports lack the instructional attract mode of the coin-op classic. The arcade game and Intellivision cartridge each boast 32 courses, while the ColecoVision version has just 20. Enemy vehicles are randomly placed on each course, making for a different challenge each time.

As the ColecoVision manual states, "Each pattern begins on the roadway and ends at the gas pump, where you refuel before the next leg of the race." (The car automatically refuels, meaning fuel concerns don't come into play for the gamer.)

In a review of the Intellivision game published on www.digitpress.com, Matt Paprocki admits that he's not much of a classic gamer, but he tells a little story about the greatness of *Bump 'n' Jump*. While testing an Intellivision II he found at a garage sale, he quickly became addicted to the game. Instead of selling the console on eBay, he decided to keep it, based strictly on the enjoyment he derived from a few hours with *Bump 'n' Jump*.

Now that's a ringing endorsement if I've ever heard one.

Bump 'n' Jump was also ported to the Atari 2600 and the NES. The graphics were simplified for the 2600, of course, but the dump trucks were included, and the gameplay evokes the spirit of the arcade cab. The NES version of the game, released in 1988 (making it ineligible for inclusion in this book), is fantastic, going so far as to add an extra element that complicates matters somewhat: power barrels to grab for energy and fuel. The NES game also has an emergency brake and an instruction manual storyline.

FUN FACT:

In Japan, the arcade version of *Bump 'n' Jump* is called *Burnin' Rubber*. In 2010, *Burnin' Rubber* was ported to the Wii via *Data East Arcade Classics*.

WHY IT MADE THE LIST:

If you like crashing into and jumping on top of other cars instead of just racing them, you'll love *Bump 'n' jump*, a great arcade game that spawned several beautifully programmed console ports.

CHAPTER 15

BURGERTIME

INTELLIVISION
GENRE: CLIMBING
PUBLISHER: MATTEL ELECTRONICS
DEVELOPER: MATTEL ELECTRONICS
1 OR 2 PLAYERS (ALTERNATING)
1983

COLECOVISION
GENRE: CLIMBING
PUBLISHER: COLECO
DEVELOPER: COLECO
1 OR 2 PLAYERS (ALTERNATING)
1984

Flyer for the original arcade version of *BurgerTime*.

"...IT'S SUCH A WONDERFUL GAME, YOU'LL EVEN START FEELING BENEVOLENT TOWARD THE CONTROLLERS."

In *Video Games* #13 (Oct., 1983), reviewer Perry Greenberg said that the original coin-op *BurgerTime* "didn't generate the following it deserved in the arcades when it was first released by Data East and then licensed by Bally/Midway. It was a clever, entertaining maze chase with the kind of excellent sound effects, graphics, and playability that should have insured it becoming a major hit."

Greenberg blamed the odd theme of the game, which puts players in the role of Chef Peter Pepper, building giant burgers. The individual hamburger ingredients—buns, meat patties, tomatoes, cheese slices—are situated vertically on horizontal platforms. Peter must climb ladders and walk over the food items. When he walks the length of an item, it will drop one level. If an ingredient falls on another ingredient, the latter will drop a level. To complete a burger, all the parts in a vertical alignment must be dropped to a plate situated below. Completing all the burgers advances the game to the next screen.

While Peter is busy building burgers, he'll be chased by frankfurters, eggs, and pickle slices, i.e. Mr. Hot Dog, Mr. Egg, and Mr. Pickle. The enemies should be avoided, of course, but Peter can eliminate his stalkers by dropping burger ingredients on them, or by dropping an ingredient while the enemy is on it. Peter can also temporarily stun the bad guys with a shake of pepper. To earn extra pepper, Peter can eat bonus ice cream cones, coffee, and French fries that appear periodically on the playfield. Pepper is crucial for getting out of tight spots, so it should be used judiciously and grabbed whenever possible.

Like the original 1982 coin-op classic, *BurgerTime* for the ColecoVision has six screens. The graphics flicker, but the characters are cute, and the platforms and burger

BurgerTime instruction manual (ColecoVision): $3

BurgerTime for the Intellivision, complete in box. $15.

BurgerTime instruction manual (Intellivision): $3

BurgerTime advertisement (Intellivision).

parts look great. The Intellivision version, developed by Ray Kaestner (program), Karen Nugent (graphics), and Bill Goodrich (sound), is a terrific port as well. In fact, it trumps the ColecoVision version (and, in some respects, the arcade original) with an extra game screen, an animated title sequence, and an extra pepper-granting item: ketchup. One thing the Intellivision game lacks is cheese slices, but this is no big loss. Both ports have excellent music that mimics the arcade game beautifully.

According to intellivisionlives.com, Ray Kaestner created the Intellivision *BurgerTime* port under duress, which is surprising considering the extra screen. Ray had returned from vacation in August of 1982, assuming he was going to be doing the *Loco-Motion* conversion. Instead, he was given *BurgerTime*. He was going to get married in December, so he was determined to finish the game in three months, clearing his schedule for wedding preparations.

"Three months was a tight schedule," the website says. "Ray did it in two, a record for an Intellivision game in the Hawthorne office. The extra month gave him a chance to tinker with the timing of the game to get it just the way he wanted." The site also says Kaestner's groomsmen were playing the game while waiting for his wedding reception to begin.

No doubt Kaestner was pleased with the reception—no pun intended—his game received. In *Electronic Fun with Computers & Games* #8 (June, 1983), Randi Hacker said *BurgerTime* "may be Intellivision's finest hour so far" and that it's "unerringly faithful to its arcade predecessor, right down to the tiny temper tantrum the chef throws when he's been outsmarted by the enemy…the music, graphics, and gameplay are outstanding…It's such a wonderful game, you'll even start feeling benevolent toward the controllers."

In *JoyStik* Vol. 2 #1 (Sept., 1983), the reviewer called the Intellivision version of *BurgerTime* slow, but "extremely good," touting its sound—"better on this version than it was at the arcade"—and its "stable, non-blinking and very clear" graphics.

The ColecoVision version of *BurgerTime* is highly regarded among the video game elite as well. "Oh, yeah, this one is a winner," The Video Game Critic (videogamecritic.com) said, giving the game an "A" rating. "[It is] easily the best home version I've played, and it even gives the arcade a run for the money. With its meticulously detailed graphics and arcade-perfect gameplay, I really can't find any flaws with this one."

The Video Game Critic also pointed out a subtle characteristic of the ColecoVision game that is key from a strategic viewpoint. "Unlike some lesser versions," he said, "in this game the pepper is 'contagious' between bad guys, which is a good thing."

BurgerTime is loaded with strategies experienced arcaders like to employ. As with such great games as *Space Panic* and *Mr. Do!'s Castle*, players can kill several enemies at once, scoring extra points and, perhaps more importantly, helping clear space on the screen.

The Intellivision version's manual offers the following advice: "For maximum points, lead the nasties on a chase and get them to meet at corners. If they meet and head in the same direction (and you're lucky), they will stick together. Get as many stuck together as you can and give them a ride on a falling bun or other ingredient."

I've always been a *BurgerTime* fan, especially when the home ports started appearing, but I've never really been able to pinpoint exactly what it is that makes the game transcendent. I love the climbing genre, but *BurgerTime* has a certain tangible something I couldn't quite identify, at least until very recently, when I was reading an e-book that I had downloaded to my phone.

In Doug McCoy's *Arcadian* (2012, Amazon Kindle), the author articulates the appeal of the coin-op classic in masterful fashion. "The best arcade games were not just seen and heard but also felt," he writes. "There was a palpability to their gameplay. *BurgerTime* had that. When Chef Pepper ran over a hamburger ingredient, you could feel it sag under his weight. When that ingredient dropped, you felt it hit and settle on the next platform or hamburger stack. If it crushed a hot dog on the way or took an egg with it, you felt that as well. It didn't seem like you were merely putting a computer program through its paces or simply shifting pixels across a screen. It felt like you were doing something, like you were physically dropping that huge hamburger ingredient."

BurgerTime was also released for the Atari 2600 (1983) and Nintendo NES (1987). The NES version looks and sounds fine, but the ColecoVision and Intellivision versions have better controls. The 2600 version, which only has five screens, suffers from simplified graphics (bread sticks have replaced Mr. Pickle, for example) and mediocre sound.

The original coin-op *BurgerTime* spawned a fairly obscure arcade sequel, *Peter Pepper's Ice Cream Factory* (1984), along with a Japanese arcade sequel, *Super BurgerTime* (1990). There's also a console sequel, *Diner* (1987), which is an Intellivision exclusive you'll find featured in this book.

Portable sequels include *BurgerTime Deluxe* (1991) for the original Game Boy and *The Flintstones: BurgerTime in Bedrock* (2001) for the Game Boy Color. Downloadable sequels, each released in 2011, include *BurgerTime Deluxe* (3DS) and *BurgerTime World Tour* (PS3, Xbox 360, Wii).

In the world of homebrews, Ken Siders created a *BurgerTime* clone called *Beef Drop* for the Atari 5200. He also programmed a 7800 version called *Beef Drop VE*. Both were released by AtariAge in 2004.

FUN FACT:

BurgerTime was the first Intellivision title not released as part of a game "Network." In addition, it was the subject of the first non-George Plimpton television commercial focusing on a single Intellivision cartridge.

WHY IT MADE THE LIST:

One of the better entries in the climbing genre, *BurgerTime* was translated extremely well to both the ColecoVision and the Intellivision—building burgers has never been more fun.

CHAPTER 16

CARNIVAL

COLECOVISION
GENRE: SLIDE-AND-SHOOT
PUBLISHER: COLECO
DEVELOPER: COLECO
1 OR 2 PLAYERS (ALTERNATING)
1982

Carnival for the ColecoVision, complete in box. $15.

"A LETTER-PERFECT RECREATION OF THE ARCADE ORIGINAL THAT IS NOT TO BE MISSED."

Carnival is unusual in that it's one of relatively few slide-and-shoot games not set in outer space. Rather, it's a target shooter with a traditional theme, sporting such targets as rabbits, owls, and ducks.

Gamers guide a gun right and left along the bottom of the playfield, firing upward at the aforementioned animals, which move horizontally in three rows and descend one row each time they pass. If a duck gets to the bottom row and isn't shot, it will come to life, leave the pack, and fly downward. If the player doesn't kill the duck in short order, it will continue on to the bottom of the screen and eat several of the player's bullets, which are lined up below the gun.

Ammunition plays a big role in *Carnival*, so players should aim well and not waste bullets. Targets marked "5" and "10" appear in the rows and should be shot for extra ammo. In addition, a box at the top/left portion of the screen can also be shot for extra bullets (or extra points). Be warned, though, because shooting that box when a negative symbol is showing will decrease the bullet supply (or point total).

Carnival is one of the most strategic shooters of the Golden Age. As play begins, gamers should shoot each of the eight rotating clay pipes near the top/center of the playfield.

A screen can't be beaten until all the pipes are gone, and their point value goes down the longer you wait to shoot them, so it's a good idea to go ahead and get rid of them early. Rabbits and other targets shot on higher rows are worth more points than those shot on lower rows, adding to the game's myriad strategic opportunities.

Another strategy is to shoot letter targets spelling out BONUS to get extra points, but you should do so in the correct order. If a letter is shot out of turn, the bonus point indicator (at the top/right of the playfield) goes away, taking the potential for extra points with it.

Once all of the targets have been cleared away (more and more appear from the top/left side of the screen as the game progresses and gets more difficult), gamers get to play a fun, between-level bonus round in which a bear with a target on its side walks back and forth, turning in the opposite direction and increasing in speed each time it is shot. After several passes, the bear will get too fast to hit and leave the screen. A second and then a third bear appear onscreen in later levels.

Like many ColecoVision games, such as *Lady Bug* and *Mouse Trap*, *Carnival* is based on a semi-obscure coin-op classic. It's an excellent port of the Gremlin/Sega arcade

  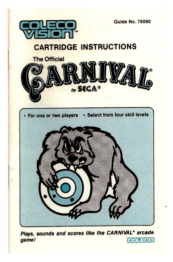

Carnival catalog advertisement.   *Carnival* game cartridge. $5.   *Carnival* instruction manual. $4.

cab from 1980, which was the first video game to include a bonus round (the aforementioned bear screens).

And, like many ColecoVision ports, it is a highly regarded game, both now and back in the day.

The Electronic Games Software Encyclopedia (1983) called *Carnival* the "definitive video shooting gallery," extolling its terrific gameplay and excellent graphics and sounds. In the May, 1983 issue of *Electronic Games*, Arnie Katz and Bill Kunkel referred to the game as "a letter-perfect recreation of the arcade original that is not to be missed."

In *Electronic Fun with Computers & Games* #6 (April, 1983), Raymond Dimetrosky said *Carnival* is an "outstanding" translation and that it "includes all the charm of the arcade game." He also said the "graphics are excellent" and the "sound effects are outstanding."

More recently, Dave "The Video Game Critic" Mrozek (videogamecritic.com) said that *Carnival* is "a heck of a lot of fun" and that he "even likes the old-fashioned carnival music." The music Mrozek is referring to is a looping version of "Sobre las Olas" (a.k.a. "Over the Waves") by Juventino Rosas, a Mexican composer from the late 1800s.

One thing to remember when plugging *Carnival* into your ColecoVision—something you should do on a regular basis—is to not let the cute theme, charming graphics, and delightful music fool you: this is one hardcore shooter. It has a smooth degree of difficulty, but when it amps up in later rounds, it really kicks into gear, releasing lots of ducks on the unsuspecting gamer and making bullets more of a premium than ever. Even experienced players may want to use skill level one (of four) in order to make the game last a good long while.

Coleco also released *Carnival* for the Atari 2600. Programmed by Steve Kitchen (of Activision fame), it was a solid port, but lacked music and bonus rounds. And, of course, the graphics were simplified. The Intellivision version of *Carnival* retains the music and bonus rounds, but doesn't hold up in terms of audio/visuals when placed side-by-side with the ColecoVision game.

Indispensable for the classic gamer wanting a cute, strategic, challenging shooter with a lighthearted theme, *Carnival* for the ColecoVision gets an "A+" in my book (so to speak).

FUN FACT:

To turn off the music in *Carnival*, players can shoot a box containing a musical note positioned on the right side of the screen.

WHY IT MADE THE LIST:

Imbued with a variety of strategic opportunities for the skilled player to score extra points, *Carnival* is a cute, but deadly shooter that hardcore "shmup" (shoot-'em-up) fans should embrace.

CHAPTER 17

CASTLEVANIA

NINTENDO NES
GENRE: SIDE-SCROLLING PLATFORMER
PUBLISHER: KONAMI
DEVELOPER: KONAMI
1 OR 2 PLAYERS (ALTERNATING)
1987

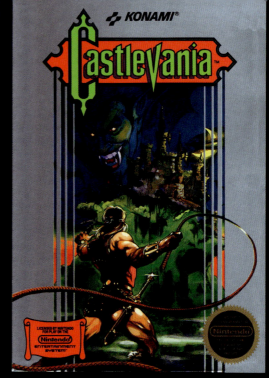

Castlevania for the Nintendo NES, complete in box. $85.

"INCREDIBLE ATMOSPHERE AND MEMORABLE MONSTERS, AS WELL AS A CHILLING MUSICAL SCORE."

While *Castlevania* has its background in 1986 releases for the Japanese Family Computer Disk System and the MSX 2 computer (in Europe and Brazil, the MSX 2 version was known as *Vampire Killer*), most Americans first learned of *Castlevania* through the NES cartridge (1987), or, less likely, the Nintendo Vs. System arcade game (1986).

A cross of sorts between *Super Mario Bros.* (the secrets and surprises), Indiana Jones (the whip and the adventure), and classic Universal and Hammer horror films (the creepy creatures and gothic setting), *Castlevania* puts players in the role of Simon Belmont, whose mission is to "destroy forever the Curse of the Evil Count."

To reach Count Dracula, players must walk, jump, and climb stairs through six three-stage floors of a huge castle, using a magic whip to battle knights, skeletons, ghosts, hunchbacks, axe-men, skele-dragons, zombies, vampire bats, fish men, and other malevolent monsters, including such famed fear mongers as Medusa, the Hunchback, the Grim Reaper, the Mummy (called Mummy Man), and the Frankenstein monster (with Igor). Each type of beast moves differently, from hopping to flying to walking, making for fun and challenging enemies to kill.

Belmont, who would go on to appear in the *Captain N: The Game Master* cartoon series (NBC, 1989-1991), begins the game armed only with a short whip, but he can hit candles, bricks, and creatures to uncover such hidden items as morning stars (increases power and length of whip), crosses (smart bombs), invisibility potion, money bags (for extra points), pork chops (partially restores health), and magic crystals (completely restores health).

In addition, Belmont can keep one special weapon in inventory: a watch, a dagger, an axe, a fire bomb, or a boomerang. All but the watch, which freezes enemies, are projectiles. Special weapons are hidden throughout the levels, as are small and large hearts that act as ammo for said weaponry. Small hearts add one "shot" while large hearts add five.

Although it was far from the first horror-themed console game (that honor belongs to 1972's *Haunted House* for the original Odyssey, not to be confused with the Atari 2600 game of the same name), *Castlevania* set new standards for the genre with its macabre mood, tone, and graphical detail. Plus, it's got an atmospheric soundtrack equal to the terror-filled task. More importantly, it's a blast to play—killing the creatures and completing the levels is enormously satisfying.

The back of the *Castlevania* box (NES).

Castlevania spawned numerous sequels, including the terrific *Castlevania III* (NES). Pictured complète in box. $85.

Castlevania was re-released on the Game Boy Advance in 2004. Pictured complete in box. $30.

Castlevania is an excellent game, but many consider it imperfect, such as The Video Game Critic (videogamecritic.com), who explained: "*Castlevania*'s simple, arcade-style gameplay is compelling, but slightly tainted by its preponderance of cheap hits. Being touched by a little bat can send you plunging into the nearest abyss, and many traps spell instant death…but despite its rough edges, *Castlevania* is a fun game that has stood the test of time."

There's no doubting that *Castlevania*, like many other NES games of the era, is difficult (Belmont can't change direction in mid-air, and yes, cheap hits do rear their ugly head), but it is beatable. Shortly after *Castlevania* hit Toys "R" Us, I picked up a copy of the game (having heard it was great) and played the heck out of it. As was customary at the time, there was no save system (though passwords and battery backup were introduced for the NES the same year), so I had to replay the game many times to finally defeat Count Dracula, but it was well worth the effort.

In the revised edition of *How to Win at Nintendo Games* (1989, St. Martin's Press), author Jeff Rovin said he wished *Castlevania* had "creaky sound effects," but loved that the game was "fraught with things to explore and discover" and that it had "incredible atmosphere and memorable monsters, as well as a chilling musical score."

Adam King, writing for the NES Times (nestimes.net), described the appeal of the game quite well, especially from a "looking back" point of view. "There's no denying that the main gameplay in *Castlevania* is straight-up arcade action," he said. "It doesn't have the multiple paths, playable characters, passwords, and other features you find in the later chapters of the series, but despite its simplicity, the action has held up well over the years. There's a certain charm to this game that makes it fun and addicting to play through."

As King alluded to, *Castlevania* was followed by a slew of sequels, including: *Castlevania II: Simon's Quest* for the NES (which befuddled some with its non-linear approach); *Castlevania III: Dracula's Curse* for the NES (my favorite game in the series); *Super Castlevania IV* for the Super Nintendo (one of the first SNES games that I beat); *Castlevania: Bloodlines* for the Genesis (one of the best games for the console); *Castlevania: Symphony of the Night* for the PlayStation (the most widely praised game in the series); *Castlevania* for the Nintendo 64 (which unwisely changed the action to 3D); and many more.

The latest release (as of this writing) is *Castlevania: Lords of Shadow—Mirror of Fate*, which hit the Nintendo 3DS in March of 2013.

If you want to play the NES version of *Castlevania* on a more modern system, the game was re-released in 2004 for the Game Boy Advance ("Classic NES Series"), in 2007 for the Nintendo Wii (via the Virtual Console), and in 2013 for the Nintendo 3DS (via the Virtual Console).

FUN FACT:
After you beat *Castlevania*, altered names of such Hollywood horror legends as Christopher Lee (Christopher Bee), Bela Lugosi (Belo Lugosi), Lon Chaney (Love Chaney), and Boris Karloff (Boris Karloffice) appear among the credits.

WHY IT MADE THE LIST:
Other than the cheap hits, most every aspect of the creepily cool *Castlevania* is enjoyable, from climbing the castle stairs to whipping the evil monsters to using the projectile weaponry.

CHAPTER 18

CAT TRAX

ARCADIA 2001
GENRE: MAZE
PUBLISHER: EMERSON
DEVELOPER: UA LIMITED
1 PLAYER
1982

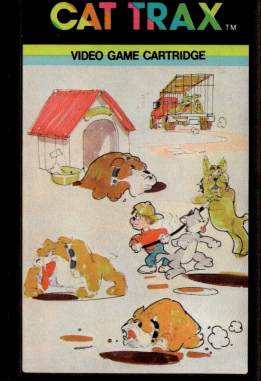

Cat Trax game cartridge. $8.

"CAT TRAX HAS A FRIENDLY ARCADE QUALITY THAT MAKES YOU WANT TO PLAY, AND ENOUGH DEPTH TO KEEP YOU PLAYING."

Cat Trax for the Arcadia 2001 began life overseas as a *Pac-Man* look-a-like called *Crazy Gobbler*. For the American release, the Pac-Man sprite was changed to a cat and the ghost sprites were changed to dogs. According to Moby Games (www.mobygames.com), this was done to "avoid the kind of legal problems which were brought by official home licensee Atari upon Philips/Magnavox for its *K.C. Munchkin!* game."

To play this quality cart, gamers guide a cat around a maze, eating catnip (dots) while avoiding a trio of nicely programmed dogs that move around the maze in such a way as to ensure plenty of close calls. This constant threat helps create dynamic tension and ample challenges, making for a game that fans of the genre will return to again and again in hopes of increasing their high score.

Like the similarly themed *Mouse Trap*, there are gates to open and close (in *Mouse Trap*, they're called doors). However, instead of three color-coded buttons as in the arcade, ColecoVision, and Intellivision versions of *Mouse Trap*, there are two general purpose buttons: one for opening gates, which is good for escaping pursuit; and one for closing gates, which can block the dogs.

Cat Trax has no *Pac-Man*-style power pellets, but it has something similar: a fish that randomly appears in the middle of the screen for a set period of time. Eating the fish will temporarily turn the cat into a dog-catching truck that can chase the canine enemies. Barely making it to the fish in time to kill dogs that are in hot pursuit can be very exciting.

As in most dot-eating maze games, the enemies in *Cat Trax* don't actually die. Rather, they get sent to the doghouse at the top of the screen (by comparison, the enemies in *Pac-Man* and *Lady Bug* reset to the center of the playfield). The doghouse contains a timer that counts down the time (approximately 15, 20, 25, or 30 seconds, depending on the level) for the dogs to reenter the maze and the truck to turn back into a cat.

One annoying aspect of the game is that when the cat turns into a truck, the cat disappears and the truck appears to slowly rise out of the ground. During this time, the truck, frustratingly and pointlessly, cannot move (though it will

Atari 2600 version of *Cat Trax* in action.

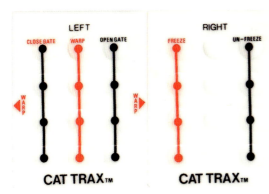

Cat Trax keypad overlays. $2.

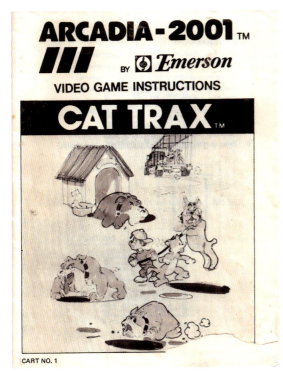

Cat Trax instruction manual. $2.

eliminate dogs that touch it). On a more positive note, the cat walks slowly, but the truck is fairly quick, making for a nice contrast between the two protagonists.

In addition to catnip and fish, the cat can gobble an apple that appears randomly at the bottom of the screen. Eating an apple scores bonus points, but doing so also uses up a warp. That's right, a warp. Unlike *Pac-Man* and most other maze games, *Cat Trax* lets you get out of tight spots by pressing a button to instantly appear in another part of the maze. (In *Mouse Trap*, you can warp by entering the IN box in the center of the playfield.)

Unfortunately, the warp element is not used to good effect since you can never use the warps on later, more challenging screens, which is when you really need them. The game begins with a set number of apples, and after an apple appears within the playfield, it will be gone forever, whether you eat it or let it simply disappear. Once all the apples are gone, which is fairly early in the game, you can no longer warp. This is a shame—those warps would really come in handy deep into the game when the enemies get tougher to dodge.

Warp issues aside, *Cat Trax* is a bright, colorful maze title with enough going for it to warrant a high recommendation. It hasn't gotten a whole lot of press over the years, but in *Electronic Games* magazine #9 (Nov., 1982), Henry Cohen, in an evaluation of the Arcadia 2001 system, called *Cat Trax* "clever" and "almost as much fun as" *Pac-Man*.

More recently, The Video Game Critic said, "*Cat Trax* has a friendly arcade quality that makes you want to play, and enough depth to *keep* you playing."

Some gamers may fault me for putting *Cat Trax* in this book. It's not terribly original, and the maze genre is already ably (not to mention heavily) represented by such all-time greats as *Jr. Pac-Man*, *Lady Bug*, *Mouse Trap*, and *Ms. Pac-Man*.

Well, I really, really like maze games, the strategies of which are perfectly suited for home gaming. Further, the better maze games, including *Cat Trax*, never seem to get old, no matter how many times you play them.

Cat Trax was also programmed for the Atari 2600 during the early 1980s, but that version didn't see the light of day until Atari Age released it in 2003, complete with professionally printed box, manual, and cartridge label. The game released alongside two other lost Atari 2600 titles: *Funky Fish* and *Pleiades*.

FUN FACT:
According to Moby Games (mobygames.com), although *Cat Trax* wasn't released for the Atari 2600 during the early 1980s, it "did appear on a European multi-cart under the name *Cat N Mouse*."

WHY IT MADE THE LIST:
Despite its lack of originality and the waste of perfectly good warps, *Cat Trax* is one of the more enjoyable maze games produced for any console.

CHAPTER 19

CENTIPEDE

ATARI 5200
GENRE: NON-SCROLLING SHOOTER
PUBLISHER: ATARI
DEVELOPER: ATARI
1 OR 2 PLAYERS (ALTERNATING)
1982

COLECOVISION
GENRE: NON-SCROLLING SHOOTER
PUBLISHER: ATARISOFT
DEVELOPER: ATARISOFT
1 OR 2 PLAYERS (ALTERNATING)
1983

ATARI 7800
GENRE: NON-SCROLLING SHOOTER
PUBLISHER: ATARI
DEVELOPER: GENERAL COMPUTER CORP.
1 OR 2 PLAYERS (ALTERNATING, SIMULTANEOUS)
1987

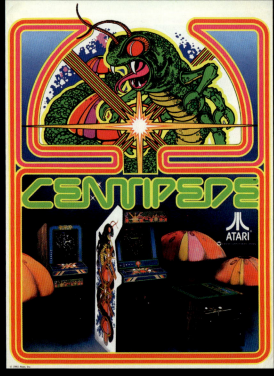

Centipede arcade flyer.

"RELENTLESS AND ADDICTING."

One of the greatest games in the history of the arcades, Atari's *Centipede* (1980) is often referred to as the first shooter to appeal to women (in fact, it's my wife's favorite arcade game of all time). Designed by Dona Bailey (in collaboration with Ed Logg), one of the few females in the industry at the time, the game eschews such masculine precepts as asteroids, spaceships, lasers, and alien invaders in favor of a field of psychedelic mushrooms infested with colorful creatures.

In 2007, Bailey spoke to Gamasutra (gamasutra.com) about being a female in a male-dominated industry. "It was the closest to being in a frat that I'll ever be," she said. "I was hired as the only software engineer who was a female. It was a ratio of 30 to 1! And by the time I left, it was about 120 to 1."

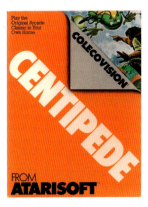

Centipede advertisement (Atari 5200).

Centipede instruction manual (Atari 5200). $2.

Centipede for the ColecoVision, complete in box. $15.

Centipede instruction manual (Atari 7800). $2.

Bailey recalled that she never felt intimidated, but that she was treated differently than her male counterparts. "I think that there was a lot of additional pressure just by being the only female," she said. "I think I was watched a lot more than I would have been. I could have blended in a lot better, if not for that one thing."

When asked if things changed once she programmed *Centipede*, Bailey said "yes," but not necessarily for the better. "There was a lot of surly attention after that…people just started, you know…the typical kind of thing that people would say was, either it was a fluke or I didn't really do it, somebody else did it."

According to a 2012 interview published on the Complex Gaming website (complex.com), Bailey got the idea for *Centipede* from a notebook of game concepts collected during an Atari brainstorming session before she got there.

"Most of the other game ideas were based on lasers, wars in space, and shoot down this and that," she said. "Centipede, described as 'a multi-segmented bug crawls out on the screen and gets shot, piece by piece,' sounded the most different from the other game descriptions and the most appealing to me."

Bailey remains proud of her achievement. "I loved it, so I hoped other girls and women would love it, too," she said. "I thought it seemed different, more whimsical and quirky than most games at the time. I still think it is beautiful visually and especially compelling in that way. I think the trackball was a major improvement over other game controls at the time, and I believe that helped make it appealing to girls and women. I didn't expect it to be successful, but I hoped it would be."

Using the precise, whip-smooth trackball Bailey speaks of, players guide a firing implement in all directions around the lower 1/5th section of the playfield, firing upward at a 12-segment centipede that goes back and forth, winding its way downward through the field of mushrooms. The mushrooms can be shot and destroyed incrementally, changing the layout of the mushroom field. Ed Logg has revealed on more than one occasion that the mushrooms could not be destroyed until Dan van Elderen, then VP of engineering with Atari Games, suggested that they should be vulnerable to player shots.

To complete a screen, you must shoot all the centipede segments. As the centipede gets shorter, it gets faster. From time to time, a scorpion will travel across the playfield, poisoning some of the mushrooms. If the centipede comes in contact with a poisonous mushroom, it will plummet straight down.

If the centipede reaches the bottom of the screen, it will start going back up, and more segments will enter the screen, making the game more difficult. Also challenging is the frequently appearing spider, which enters the screen shortly after the game begins, jumping all around. The closer the spider is to your weapon when you kill it, the more points you will score, but firing at such a close range is dangerous because the spider moves quickly. In addition, there are fleas that drop down, adding more mushrooms to the playfield.

Called "relentless and addicting" by Van Burnham, author of *Supercade: A Visual Vistory of the Videogame Age* (2001, MIT Press), *Centipede* was ported to the Atari 2600 in 1981. As with many of the better 2600 adaptations, gameplay mechanics were terrific, but the graphics took a major hit (despite a spiffy title screen). Most notably, the mushrooms were rectangular, as was the firing implement, which the manual called a "magic wand."

The Atari 5200 and ColecoVision *Centipede* ports, which soundly trump the 2600 version, have a lot in common. They're compatible with their respective trackball controllers (the 5200 version is called a "Trak-Ball" while Coleco dubbed theirs a "Roller Controller"), the playfields are widened to fit the TV screen, and, most importantly, they both capture the fun, challenge, and speed of the arcade game (though the arcade version has more robust sound effects). Both games offer three difficulty levels: easy, standard, and hard, but easy is tough enough for all but the best of gamers, especially on the 5200.

The 5200 game, which the late, great Bill Kunkel once called a "high water mark in the home translation of action arcade games," has an edge graphically as the two-tone mushrooms sport outlines like their arcade counterparts; the ColecoVision mushrooms, on the other hand, are mono-colored, as is the wand and the centipede itself. The 5200 spider is smaller and faster, but both spiders can be tough to dodge. As mentioned earlier, both games are trackball-compatible, completing the arcade experience. If you have to play *Centipede* with a joystick, the 5200 version is better. This is one of very few examples in which the non-centering 5200 joysticks have an advantage over a standard digital joystick.

For pure arcade realism and fast shooting action, the Atari 5200 and ColecoVision versions of *Centipede* rank among the best home video games of all time. However, with the introduction of the Atari 7800 version, Atari upped the ante with a pair of ingenious, highly entertaining two-player simultaneous modes: Dual Player Competition, in which scores are separate and players can paralyze one another; and Team Play, in which scores are added together and players can't harm one another. Whether you feel cooperative or competitive, this is a great addition to an already fantastic formula.

Like the Atari 2600 version of *Centipede*, the 7800 port is compatible with the 2600 Trak-Ball. However, it's not as responsive as the 5200 or ColecoVision trackball controllers (at least when it comes to *Centipede*), meaning the joystick is the preferred method of control. Even so, despite this setback, the 7800 game is a must-own and a great reason in and of itself to keep a 7800 system hooked to your television set. Less noteworthy, though still pretty cool, are the 7800 mushrooms, which have a bit of a pseudo-3D look.

Curiously, the 7800 spider only has four legs, and there's an unnecessary white border around the playfield, but these small issues can easily be overlooked.

In 1982, Atari released an arcade sequel to *Centipede* called *Millipede*, which plays a lot like *Centipede*, but adds a number of new insects, including dragonflies, mosquitos, earwigs (same as scorpions), bees (same as fleas), inchworms (slow other enemies when hit), and beetles (turn mushrooms into indestructible flowers). There are also DDT bombs, which are fun to shoot because they destroy all enemies and mushrooms within the explosion radius. For those who had mastered or gotten tired of *Centipede*, *Millipede* was a great new challenge and one of the better sequels of the era.

Unfortunately, *Millipede* never made it to the Atari 5200 (though a prototype was found), 7800, or ColecoVision, but it did show up on the 2600 (1984) and the Nintendo NES (1988). The former was a nice port, despite the requisite rectangular mushrooms and wand, but the latter, though entertaining, was a disappointment because of an unnecessarily small playfield—a large border and scoreboard take up way too much screen space.

Getting back to *Centipede*, which inspired Buckner & Garcia's "Ode to a Centipede" (a song on the *Pac-Man Fever* album), every classic gamer needs at least one excellent version of the arcade classic in his or her game room. If you don't have the actual cabinet, you definitely need one or more of these console ports. If you only get one, grab the 7800 game (also available on the original Atari Flashback console from 2004) as there are few things in this world more entertaining than two-player simultaneous *Centipede*.

FUN FACT:
In addition to appearing on numerous consoles (game.com, Intellivision, Game Boy Color, etc.), Centipede was reimagined in 1999 for the Dreamcast and PlayStation. The game also spawned Centipede: Infestation (2011) for the Nintendo Wii and 3DS.

WHY IT MADE THE LIST:
Centipede is a shooter that even those who don't usually like the genre can enjoy, and the 5200, 7800, and ColecoVision versions are among the best arcade ports of the 1980s.

CHAPTER 20

CHOPLIFTER

SEGA MASTER SYSTEM
GENRE: SIDE-SCROLLING SHOOTER
PUBLISHER: SEGA
DEVELOPER: SEGA
1 OR 2 PLAYERS (ALTERNATING)
1986

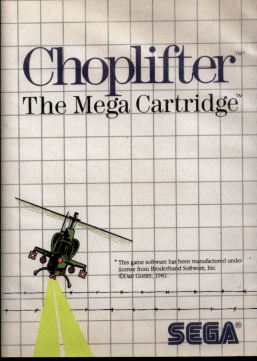

Choplifter for the Sega Master System, complete in box. $12.

"CONSIDERED A BONA FIDE CLASSIC BY MOST SHOOTER FANS."

In 1982, Dan Gorlin, working for Broderbund, programmed *Choplifter!* for the Apple II. The game was ported to various other computers and consoles, including the Commodore 64, Atari 5200, and ColecoVision. In 1985, Sega licensed the game for the arcades (one of the relatively few times a console game has been made into a coin-op title), adding music, voice effects, a fuel gauge, a points system, new environments, and parallax scrolling.

The Sega Master System version of *Choplifter* (note the missing exclamation point) is a straight-up port of the coin-op game, and, despite the missing voice effects and occasional slowdown, it mimics the arcade experience extremely well.

Players, at the helm of a HAWK Z rescue chopper, fly horizontally over the Middle East, over the South Seas, and in underground caverns, landing in strategic spots to rescue hostages who are being held in barracks and caverns.

When you land near the site of hostages escaping, which they will do after you shoot the stronghold where they are being held, the hostages will automatically run toward your helicopter and get onboard. There are 16 hostages per building (compared to eight in the arcade game), and the helicopter's capacity is 16 passengers. Once this number is reached, you should fly the hostages to the home base, land, and let them exit the helicopter to safety.

To complete a level, you must rescue at least 40 of the 64 hostages (only 20 hostages needed rescuing in the arcade game). If too many hostages are killed, the game will end (if too many hostages died in the arcade version, players would simply have to restart the level). Rescuing the hostages is gratifying and fun, but it's not easy—only those who put in a lot of practice will make it as far as the third level, the caverns.

During your mission, you will be besieged by Jaguar tanks, Big Shark battleships, Bat MR11 fighter planes, and Goblin air mines. When you are on the ground to rescue hostages, for example, a tank will roll out and begin firing at you. To prevent this—here's a tip you won't find in the manual—move the helicopter up and down a bit to keep the tank from firing. Even with this helpful hint, this is a challenging game.

The HAWK Z can be maneuvered in eight directions. The control pad guides the chopper, of course, but button 2 changes its forward direction. Button 1 shoots and drops bombs. When the chopper flies forward, it tilts downward, letting you shoot angled shots at enemies on the ground and at sea. When the chopper backs up, it shoots at an upward angle. When the chopper is facing toward the screen, pressing the fire button drops bombs, which are useful for destroying tanks.

One of the better-looking shooters of the era, *Choplifter* oozes with graphical detail, from the mountainous

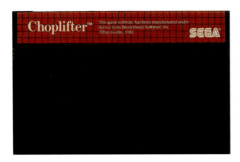

Choplifter game cartridge. $4.

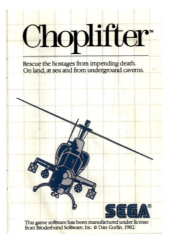

Choplifter instruction manual. $2.

Advertisement for the Sega Master System video game console.

backgrounds to the nicely drawn ships and barracks to the craggy stalagmites and stalactites of the underground caves. The sound effects are pretty bland, but the music is catchy, and the game has the overall look and sound of a quality, next-gen title that is more technologically sophisticated than games for such previous systems as the Atari 5200 and ColecoVision.

Compared to the Atari 7800 version of *Choplifter!*, which was released in 1987, *Choplifter* for the Master System, programmed by "Drunkard Kagi," blows it out of the water. In addition to weaker graphics and sounds, the 7800 game lacks surface-to-air missiles. More importantly, the 7800 game comes to an abrupt ending after 64 hostages have been rescued or killed (the Master System cartridge could theoretically be played forever), which it has in common with the Apple II original.

Speaking of the Apple II game, it was a huge commercial success and is still fondly remembered. In an interview conducted by James Hague and published on www.dadgum.com, Gorlin said: "At Broderbund we had the general feeling that the game would do well since kids would line up to play it at the trade shows, but the way it took off was something no one could anticipate. It was a good product, but we had big-time help from the Iran hostage crisis; believe it or not, the tie-in with current events was something that never really crossed my mind until we published."

Indeed, when creating *Choplifter!*, which took six months to program, Gorlin had far simpler things occupying his mind than geopolitical concerns. "Being fascinated with helicopters, I started out by making one fly around using a joystick," he said. "It was really cool, so I kept adding things to shoot at."

A popular arcade game at the time played a role in the creation process as well. "We had this local kid doing some repairs on my car just outside, and he used to come in and play with it," Gorlin said. "He was a big *Defender* freak, and one day he said, 'You should have some men to pick up.' I walked over to the Laundromat and took a closer look at *Defender* to see what he was talking about—never played it

myself—and damned if I could see any men, but I took his word for it, and it seemed like a cool idea."

Getting back to the console scene, *Choplifter* for the Master System is the best home version of the game and, along with *Fantasy Zone*, *Fantasy Zone II*, *R-Type*, and *Zaxxon 3-D*, one of the better shooters for the system.

As Stan Stepanic of Game Freaks 365 (www.gamefreaks365.com) said, "It's often mentioned in SMS fans' 'Top Ten,' and I think it deserves a position there."

However, Stepanic does find a few imperfections with the game, calling the sound effects "lacking," the hostages "blocky" looking, and one aspect of the controls, which "take some time getting used to," annoying: "The only major problem [with the game] is that if you stop your chopper near the end of the screen on the right or left, you have to first move back in the opposite direction, otherwise you just hang on the edge and pass over everything."

Considered a bona fide classic by most shooter fans, *Choplifter* was the subject of a several remakes and sequels, including: *Choplifter II* (Game Boy), *Choplifter III* (SNES, Game Gear), and *Choplifter HD* (PlayStation Network, Xbox Live Arcade).

FUN FACT:

The reason the original *Choplifter!* for the Apple II lacks a traditional points system is that programmer Dan Gorlin "finds seven-digit scores boring."

WHY IT MADE THE LIST:

A huge upgrade over the Apple II computer program and an excellent port of the arcade game, *Choplifter* for the Master System is a terrific shooter that Defender fans will love.

CHAPTER

CIRCUS ATARI

ATARI 2600
GENRE: BALL-AND-PADDLE
PUBLISHER: ATARI
DEVELOPER: ATARI
1 OR 2 PLAYERS (ALTERNATING)
1980

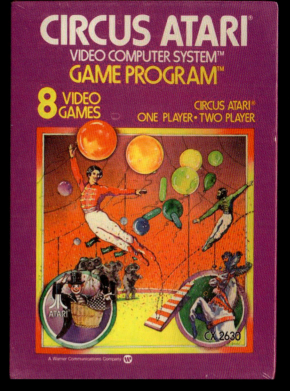

Circus Atari for the Atari 2600, complete in box. $10.

"ONE OF THE BEST GAMES USING PADDLES."

Before I discuss *Circus Atari*, let me apologize up front for endlessly extolling the virtues of the Atari 2600 paddle controllers, which help make such games as *Kaboom!* and *Super Breakout* so much fun.

Scratch that—I make no apologies: Atari's rotary paddles, some of the best controllers ever made for any console, give players smooth, speedy, precision control and do an excellent job of recreating the arcade experience at home.

I agree with Keita Iida (atarihq.com), who called *Circus Atari* and paddle games in general among his favorites. "I absolutely *looooooooove* paddle games," he said. "There's nothing like the feeling of complete and utter control, whether it be playing *Tempest*, *Breakout*, or *Night Driver*. Atari might not have sold many VCS systems because of the paddles alone, but I still applaud them to this day for having the foresight to include the paddle controllers with every system purchase."

In issue #1 (summer, 1983) of the British publication, *TV Gamer*, the writer called *Circus Atari* "One of the best games using paddles." The Video Game Critic (videogamecritic.com) said he enjoys "the frantic nature of the game," which "puts your reflexes to the test," but he posits that "few would consider *Circus Atari* a great game."

Count me among the "few," the proud, who do consider *Circus Atari* to be great.

Programmed by Mike Lorenzen (*Oink*, *Pitfall II: Lost Caverns*), *Circus Atari* is similar to *Breakout*, but with balloons replacing bricks and a pair of clowns hopping on a teeter-totter taking the place of a simple ball and paddle. Players maneuver said teeter-totter back and forth along the bottom of the screen, bouncing a pair of stick figure clowns in the air—in alternating fashion—into three rows of balloons positioned along the top of the playfield.

The further away a clown lands from the fulcrum of the teeter-totter (but without missing the teeter-totter altogether), the higher the clown will bounce. When a balloon gets hit by a clown, it pops. Each time an entire row of balloons is popped, another row takes its place.

If the player pops the entire top row, he or she will earn an extra life. Unlike the items to destroy in most ball-and-paddle games, the balloons in *Circus Atari* actually scroll (horizontally), entering the playfield from the opposite side once they've left the screen.

If you remember playing a similar coin-op game during the late 1970s, you'd be correct. *Circus Atari* is a blatant clone

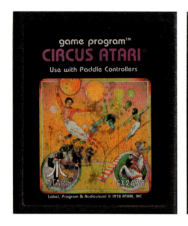
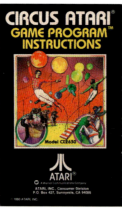
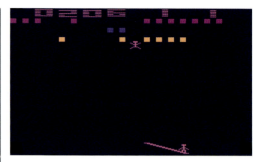

Bouncing clowns in *Circus Atari* for the Atari 2600. Courtesy of AtariAge.com.

Circus Atari game cartridge. $4.

Circus Atari instruction manual. $2.

of *Circus* (programmed by Edward Valeau and Howell Ivey), which Exidy released to the arcades in 1977. In fact, the Sears release of *Circus Atari* is called *Circus*. (Another similar title of the era is Bally/Midway's *Clowns*, which was released to the arcades in 1978.)

The balloons in the *Circus* arcade game are vaguely spherical in appearance, while the balloons in *Circus Atari* are square (the only real weakness of the game). *Circus* has primitive music, including two measures of the funeral march in Frédéric Chopin's "Piano Sonata No. 2" that play upon the death of a clown, while *Circus Atari* has none at all. On the other hand, *Circus Atari* has colorized graphics while *Circus* is rendered in black-and-white (though it does have a color overlay to make the top row of balloons blue, the middle row green, and the bottom row yellow).

Both *Circus* and *Circus Atari* feature amusing death scenes when a clown misses the teeter-totter; in the 2600 version, the clown's arms and legs wildly flail about. This was rather shocking back in the early 1980s, as evidenced by this evaluation of the carttridge in *Ken Uston's Guide to Buying and Beating the Home Video Games* (1982, Signet): "A rather macabre game that some mothers may find unfit for young children. Forgetting the theme, the game is an intriguing hand-eye coordination contest of above-average interest."

As with most early Atari 2600 games, *Circus Atari* has some nifty play options. Depending on the variation selected, the clown will bounce off the balloons he pops or go through the balloons in order to pop more. Also, the game can be played with or without barriers below the balloons. In two-player alternating action, both players share the same wall of balloons, with the computer tracking each player's score individually.

While obviously a *Circus* knockoff, *Circus Atari* inspired a copycat of its own: *P.T. Barnum's Acrobats* (1982) for the Odyssey2. The game benefits from somewhat rounded balloons and compatibility with The Voice speech module ("Oh no!", "Look out!", "Hurry!"), but suffers from the lack of rotary control.

Prior to that, there was the Astrocade cartridge *Clowns/Brickyard* (1978), which includes clones of both *Circus Atari* and *Breakout*. Astrocade controllers come equipped with a rotary knob, helping make *Clowns/Brickyard* a solid two-in-one package.

Unlike *P.T. Barnum's Acrobats* and *Clowns/Brickyard*, however, *Circus Atari* is a game I still play on a semi-regular basis.

If you don't own an Atari 2600, you can play *Circus Atari* on such compilation discs as *Atari Anthology!* (2004, PS2, Xbox) and *Atari Classics: Evolved* (2007, PSP). In 2010, Microsoft made *Circus Atari* available as a downloadable title for the Xbox 360 Game Room service. The game is also built into the Atari Flashback 3 console (2011).

FUN FACT:

In an interview published on the Digital Press website (digitpress.com), Atari alumnus Harry Brown said that *Circus Atari* programmer Mike Lorenzen helped him get the job at Atari by explaining that it was "a fun place to work and they were hiring game testers."

WHY IT MADE THE LIST:

Circus Atari has great rotary controls, and it's a ton of fun to bounce the clowns off the teeter-totter and up into the balloons.

CHAPTER **22**

COMBAT

ATARI 2600
GENRE: NON-SCROLLING SHOOTER
PUBLISHER: ATARI
DEVELOPER: ATARI
2 PLAYERS (SIMULTANEOUS)
1977

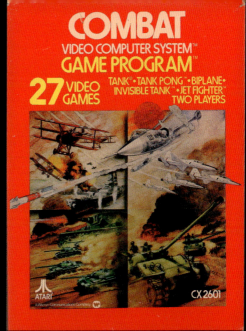

Combat for the Atari 2600, complete in box. $10.

"ANYONE COULD PICK UP AND PLAY COMBAT, THE CONTROLS WERE THAT SIMPLE…"

The original pack-in game with the Atari 2600 console (then called the Atari VCS), *Combat*, along with *Asteroids*, *Pac-Man*, and *Space Invaders*, is one of the most common games in the system's library. Back when Atari titles would regularly show up at flea markets and garage sales and in pawn shops and thrift stores, *Combat* would almost always be among the classic video game offerings, giving it an undeserved reputation as "junk." While it's not worth much to collectors, it's invaluable in terms of fun factor and playability.

Like *Pong* before it, *Combat* is a relic of another time, but it holds up extremely well as an excellent two-player game. During the late 1970s, when I would ride my bike to various friends' homes to play their Atari (I didn't get my own game system until Christmas of 1982), we would invariably play *Combat*, not only because everyone had it, but because it was enormously enjoyable, offering up a fair, competitive challenge each and every time.

As most 2600 fans know, each player commandeers a vehicle in a one-on-one test of wills and skill. Depending on the variation selected (there are 27 in all), gamers guide a tank, an invisible tank, a bi-plane, or a jet-fighter around the playfield (an open area or a maze), with the exquisitely simple task of trying to shoot the other player's vehicle. The tank and jet-fighter games are viewed from overhead while the bi-plane view is from the side.

In addition to different vehicles, *Combat* offers a variety of other choices (again, depending on the variation selected), including straight or guided missiles, easy or complex maze, clouds or no clouds, and direct hits or billiard hits (missiles can bounce off walls and barriers in variations called Tank-Pong). Tanks move at a steady pace while bi-planes and jet-fighters can go slow, medium, and fast.

According to some sources (including *Atari Inc.—Business is Fun*), Joe Decuir and Larry Wagner are credited with programming *Combat*. In an interview conducted by Scott Stilphen and published on www.digitpress.com, Decuir deferred much of said credit, saying: "Ron Milner and Steve Mayer conceived of what became *Combat*; I was an implementer…I worked on it mostly as a test case for the hardware…Larry Wagner, who hired most of the early VCS programmers (including the founders of Activision and Imagic), made the *Combat* display engine a lot more fun."

Speaking of fun, Matt Fox truly "gets" the appeal of *Combat*. In his book, *The Video Games Guide* (2006, Boxtree), he called it "the greatest two-player game of its day." He went on to say, "Anyone could pick up and play *Combat*, the controls were that simple…back in those days there were few finer feelings than shooting your friend's tank and seeing it spin around helplessly in defeat."

In the premiere issue of *Classic Gamer Magazine* (fall, 1999), D.B. Caufield said, "*Combat* is still an outstanding two-player game. What it lacks in graphics is more than made up for in gameplay. There are many tank and fighter plane game variations to keep even the most jaded classic gamer happy."

  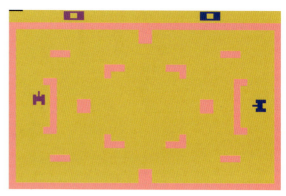

Combat game cartridge. $2.

Combat instruction manual. $2.

Tanks prepare for battle in Combat for the Atari 2600. Courtesy of AtariAge.com.

In the seventh edition of the *Digital Press Collector's Guide* (2002), Joe Santulli had this to say about the game: "Outstanding in its simplicity, it's mano-a-mano in tanks, jets, or bi-planes with changing physics accessible by game options. Break it out and play it again—you may be surprised at how much fun it still is."

On the other hand, The Video Game Critic (videogamecritic.com) admitted that he was "never a huge fan" of *Combat*, but he did have some interesting things to say about the game, especially in terms of the zeitgeist: "This game is an enigma. In the '80s, all of my friends detested *Combat*, often poking fun at its plain graphics and simplistic gameplay. But now, 20 years later, everybody I know swears that it's one of the greatest games ever made…*Combat* is an archaic, simplistic game, but after all these years it's finally getting some respect."

Walter Lowe, Jr., author of *Playboy's Guide to Rating the Video Games* (1982, PBJ Books), failed to see a bright future for the game, giving it a mere star-and-a-half rating and saying, "We've rated *Combat* only because it's the cartridge you get with your VCS."

Ditto author Ken Uston, who, in *Buying and Beating the Home Video Games* (1982, Signet), wrote, "It's not fair to be too critical because, after all, this cartridge is nearly five years old; and in this age of rapid computer technology, that makes it almost an 'antique.'"

In Craig Kubey's *The Winners' Book of Video Games* (1982, Warner Books), the author called *Combat* merely "adequate" and said that the secret of its commercial success "lies only in the fact that it is provided at no additional charge with every Atari console."

In issue #2 (autumn, 1983) of the British publication, *TV Gamer*, reviewer Sonya Bradford surely wouldn't have predicted that *Combat* would gain the reputation as an all-time great when she said, "Initially the controls take some getting used to. But once these are mastered the game becomes a bit monotonous, which is not helped by poor graphics."

"Archaic" or not, "monotonous" or not, "poor graphics" or not, *Combat*, which has clearly aged like a fine wine, inspired a sequel, *Combat Two*, which was originally scheduled to hit stores in 1984, but was a victim of The Great Video Game Crash of 1983. It existed only in prototype form until the 2001 Classic Gaming Expo, where a limited quantity was offered for sale.

Combat Two, which was also made available in 2005 via the Flashback 2 dedicated console (as *Combat 2*), takes place in 2037, during a new kind of war: the Combat Duels. Tanks must be shot three times to be destroyed, and the playfield includes a bridge, a river, woods, and a pair of bases from which players can launch surface-to-surface missiles that home in on the enemy tank. However, the game lacks planes, invisible tanks, and bank shots, probably because it was never completely finished.

Programmed by Steve Mayer, Joe Decuir, Larry Kaplan, and Larry Wagner (project manager), the original *Combat* has been re-released for modern systems on such compilation discs as *Atari Anthology!* (2004, PS2, Xbox) and *Atari Classics: Evolved* (2007, PSP). It's also built into Atari Flashback consoles 2 and 3. In 2010, Microsoft made *Combat* available as a downloadable title for the Xbox 360 Game Room service.

Intellivision owners can play a similar game called *Armor Battle* (ported to the 2600 as *Armor Ambush*), which has better graphics, but slower, less enjoyable gameplay.

FUN FACT:

Combat is essentially an unofficial port of Tank (the Sears version of *Combat* is called *Tank Plus*), which Kee Games, a division of Atari, released to the arcades in 1974.

WHY IT MADE THE LIST:

As video games have gotten longer and more complex, *Combat* is a nice throwback to a simpler time, when all each player needed was a joystick, one fire button, and a few minutes to kill

CHAPTER 23

COMMUNIST MUTANTS FROM SPACE

ATARI 2600
GENRE: SLIDE-AND-SHOOT
PUBLISHER: ARCADIA/STARPATH
DEVELOPER: ARCADIA/STARPATH
1-4 PLAYERS (ALTERNATING)
1982

Communist Mutants from Space for the Atari 2600, complete in box. $15.

> "…IF FAST SCI-FI SHOOT 'EM UPS ARE YOUR THING THEN THIS GAME IS A MUST."

Produced under the working title of "Galactic Egg," *Communist Mutants from Space* was designed for the Starpath Supercharger, a brilliant peripheral for the Atari 2600.

In the May, 1983 issue of *Electronic Games*, Bill Kunkel and Arnie Katz described the Starpath Supercharger clearly and succinctly: "This remarkable new device plugs directly into the VCS cartridge slot. Its wire and male plug are then inserted into the earphone jack on any audio-cassette recorder. The software comes on cassettes—making them far less expensive than cartridges—and have more room for both programming code as well as increased screen RAM."

The brainchild of Steve Landrum, who also programmed *DragonStomper* and *The Official Frogger*, *Communist Mutants from Space* takes nice advantage of the added power with numerous moving objects and crisp, non-blinking graphics.

In an interview published in the instruction manual for *Stella Gets a New Brain* (the Starpath Supercharger collection on CD published by CyberPunks in 1996), Landrum said, "I was trying to push the limits of the 2600 to see what I could get it to do…The fact that I had six digits of score on one side of the screen, and another digit on the other side, or that the flags could show more than six on a row were believed impossible until *Communist Mutants* did them."

The game has players maneuvering an "anti-mutant cannon" along the bottom of the screen, firing upward at waves of enemy warriors. Said warriors were made that way by a "cunning Mother Creature" on the planet "Rooskee." Filled with "irradiated vodka," the Mother Creature "transforms slaves captured on peaceful planets into bloodthirsty Communist Mutants."

In an interview with Landrum published in *Electronic Fun with Computers & Games* #2 (Dec., 1982), he explained the genesis of the game's B-movie title. During a discussion with the advertising agency and executives at Starpath, someone said, "Hey, why don't we just call it *Communist Mutants from Space*? That got a big round of laughs, and nobody took it seriously… but over the next few weeks, we did some surveys with kids… everybody said they liked *Communist Mutants from Space* and so that had to be the name…my parents were really upset…they thought it was inappropriate…they thought I should protest… but the name was an attention-getter and it had a nice ring to it."

In that same interview, Landrum spoke about designing the characters.

"They evolved slowly," he said. "The initial idea for the game—the egg field at the top and the creature laying the eggs—was there from the beginning. But the shapes went

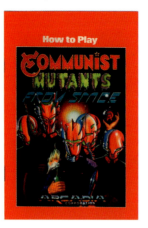

Battling the baddies in *Communist Mutants from Space* for the Atari 2600. *Courtesy of AtariAge.com.*

The back of the *Communist Mutants from Space* box.

Communist Mutants from Space instruction manual. $3.

through quite a few changes. At first, the creatures were a single graphic with essentially no animation. The first characters I drew looked a lot like *Space Invaders*. But I made changes here and there. I started animating them. I made one look like a bird—flapping its wings and flying around."

Landrum also talked about why he made the eggs block-shaped. "The system I was programming for, the Atari VCS, is a fairly limited system in what it will do for you," he said. "With the knowledge that I have now, I would have spent more time and effort to make round eggs. But that was the first time I had written for the system, and while I was writing the game, I was still reverse-engineering the system."

In the *Stella Gets a New Brain* interview, Landrum admitted that his game wasn't particularly original, saying it was "based on coin-op games that I liked at the time: *Space Invaders* [1978], *Galaxian* [1979], *Eagle* [1980], and others."

Despite its derivative nature, *Communist Mutants* is a fast, exciting shooter that is "difficult to dislike" (*Electronic Games*, May, 1983), giving such better known titles as *Demon Attack* and *Phoenix* a run for their proverbial money. The true standout feature of the game is its ridiculous number of options that give players a variety of experiences with the same basic slide-and-shoot setup.

Prior to playing, you'll select the number of players (1-4), the difficulty level (1-9), yes or no shields (similar to the shields in *Phoenix*), yes or no time warp (slows down the mutant attack), yes or no penetrating fire (bullets keep going after they hit a mutant), and yes or no guided fire (lets you steer bullets with the joystick). You can also toggle the difficulty switch to "A" for slow cannon and "B" for fast cannon.

In issue #2 (autumn, 1983) of the British publication, *TV Gamer*, the reviewer gave *Communist Mutants from Space* high marks, saying, "One of the nice things about this game, apart from the graphics and the sound, is the wide selection of gameplay…If fast sci-fi shoot 'em ups are your thing then this game is a must."

In an article about Landrum published on www.thenextlevel.com, Sean Wheatley said that *Communist Mutants from Space* "wasn't much for originality but the gameplay was solid, and it had some of the most fluid animation on the system."

In *Electronic Fun with Computers and Games* #1 (Nov., 1982), reviewer Walter Salm gave the game 3 (out of 4) joysticks, calling it "an action-packed update on the *Space Invaders* theme."

When I was writing this book, narrowing the titles down to 100, I had all but decided to relegate *Communist Mutants from Space* to "The Next 100" section in the back. It's a quality game, but the slide-and-shoot genre was already very well represented by such titles as *Demon Attack*, *Galaga*, *Galaxian*, *Phoenix*, and *Space Invaders*.

However, a few minutes after reacquainting myself with the game, marveling over its strong sound effects, sharp graphics, and intense gameplay, I quickly decided that it had to make the cut. It was simply too challenging, too polished, and too much fun to leave out. Hours later, I managed to break myself away from the game long enough to write about it.

FUN FACT:

Communist Mutants from Space creator Stephen Landrum also programmed *Blue Lightning*, an Atari Lynx launch title.

WHY IT MADE THE LIST:

With its arcade-quality gameplay and downright silly number of options, *Communist Mutants from Space* easily belongs in the top tier of classic shooters.

CHAPTER

DEFENDER

ATARI 5200
GENRE: SIDE-SCROLLING SHOOTER
PUBLISHER: ATARI
DEVELOPER: ATARI
1 OR 2 PLAYERS (ALTERNATING)
1982

COLECOVISION
GENRE: SIDE-SCROLLING SHOOTER
PUBLISHER: ATARISOFT
DEVELOPER: ATARISOFT
1 OR 2 PLAYERS (ALTERNATING)
1983

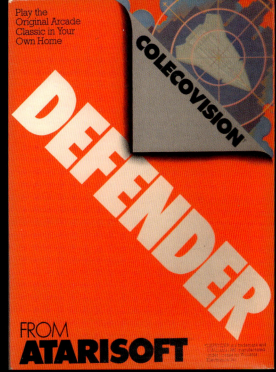

Defender for the ColecoVision, complete in box. $15.

"DEFENDER HAS THE REPUTATION OF A TOUGH, INTENSE, REVOLUTIONARY ARCADE SHOOTER."

Confession time: I stink at *Defender*. More specifically, I'm terrible at the original 1981 Williams arcade version of *Defender*, the world's first side-scrolling shooter—I can only score 25,000 or so on a good day. Not because of the complex control scheme (five buttons and a joystick was considered mind boggling in 1981), but because those darned landers capture my humanoids time and again before I can get to them.

Luckily, the Atari 5200 and ColecoVision ports are slower and easier, making for a longer, more pleasurable gaming experience, at least for me. (I'm good at certain other intense arcade games, such as *Robotron: 2084* and *Asteroids Deluxe*, but I just never could get the hang of *Defender*.)

Purists may argue that the ColecoVision version—with its single skill level—is in fact too easy (unlike Atarisoft *Centipede* for ColecoVision, which is plenty difficult). 5200 owners, on the other hand, can brag that their rendition of the game includes three difficulty levels: easy, normal, and hard. The 5200 game also benefits from a better looking ship, which, like the coin-op classic, has fire shooting from the aft section (the ColecoVision ship is solid white and lacks said flames).

Both versions offer solid controls, long laser fire, fun shooting action (using a smart bomb at just the right time, mowing down tons of enemies with laser fire, barely managing to save a humanoid—these things are a blast), smooth scrolling (not always a given with the ColecoVision), nice explosions (the effect of your ship blowing up offers fireworks-like awesomeness), and a nifty faux vector graphics mountain range along the bottom of the playfield.

In issue #34 (Nov./Dec., 1997) of the *Digital Press* fanzine, video game veteran Jeff Cooper reviewed the Atari 5200 version of *Defender*, calling it "very close to the Williams classic" and saying that it "showed very quickly why the [Atari 5200] SuperSystem was super."

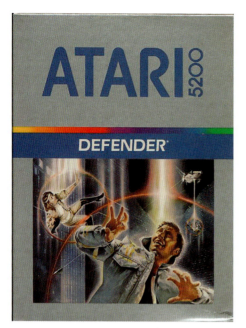

Defender for the Atari 5200, complete in box. Courtesy of AtariAge.com. $15.

The back of the *Defender* box (Atari 5200). Courtesy of AtariAge.com.

In *Electronic Games* magazine #32 (Feb., 1985), Dan Persons, writing about the ColecoVision port, said it is "merciless, action-packed, and well up to its reputation as one of the most exciting games ever created…a real beauty…no library is complete without it."

For the few of you not familiar with *Defender* (if that's possible), the game is a wraparound side-scroller, meaning it scrolls right and left, but you'll come back to where you started if you keep flying in one direction. In the arcade version, the joystick moves the ship up and down while separate thrust buttons are used for flying right and left. In the home renditions, the joystick guides the ship up, down, right, and left. In all three versions, buttons are used for hyperspace and smart bombs.

As you fly over the aforementioned mountain range, quirky aliens and alien ships with names like landers, swarmers, baiters, mutants, pods, and bombers crowd the skies, making your job of staying alive a challenge. The enemies should be shot, of course, but special care should be taken to keep landers from swooping down and stealing humanoids that dot the mountainous landscape.

When a lander does capture a humanoid, you should try to shoot the lander while avoiding the humanoid. After the lander is shot, the humanoid will float down. If the humanoid is close to the ground when the lander is shot, it will be fine, but if it has to fall too great a distance, it will be destroyed upon impact. Fortunately, you can grab a floating humanoid out of the sky and take it safely down to the planet's surface. If a lander makes it to the top of the screen with a humanoid, the humanoid will turn into a mutant and the lander will speed up and home in on your ship.

At the end of each wave, you score bonus points for each humanoid survivor, multiplied by the number of the wave just completed. To help keep track of the enemies, including the positions of the landers abducting the humanoids, a radar scanner is positioned along the top middle section of the screen. There's also an audio cue (a cry for help, one presumes) when a humanoid is being abducted by a lander.

When all the humanoids become mutants, the planet will explode, but you can still play on. If you somehow manage to last a few more waves, the humanoids will reincarnate and the planet will be rebuilt.

The original arcade version of *Defender* was designed by Eugene Jarvis (with assistance from Larry DeMar, Sam Dicker, and Paul Dussault), a pinball programmer who went to Chicago and began working at Williams after the pinball division at Atari shut down.

"I was totally psyched to work with [Williams] Steve Ritchie, perhaps the greatest pinball designer of our time," Jarvis said in an interview published on www.dadgum.com. "At about this time [1978-79], the first microprocessor video games came out. *Space Invaders*, *Space War*, and *Asteroids* were the rage, and I could see the incredible universe now open to video game designers. This led to the *Defender* project at Williams."

Decades earlier, in *JoyStik* magazine #1 (Sept., 1982), Jarvis spoke about the idea that sparked the eventual creation of *Defender*: "Steve Ritchie and myself were sitting in a room toying with concepts and game ideas. Steve said: 'Wouldn't it be neat if you were flying over a planet on a screen.' And we tried to figure out what to do with it. You could be flying over the planet, you could go up and down in any direction

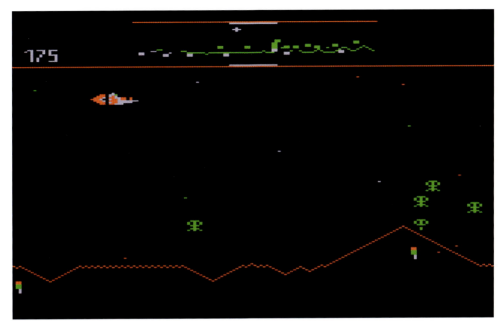

Defender for the Atari 5200 in action.
Courtesy of AtariAge.com.

you want…I eventually said: 'We can't do that yet, but what we can do is fly left and right,' and so on."

Steve Baker ported *Defender* to the Atari 5200. Scott Stilphen interviewed Baker for the *2600 Connection*, the late, lamented fanzine (http://2600connection.atari.org/baker.html). In one point during the interview, Stilphen said, "I must say that your Atari version of *Defender* was simply incredible! Did you have the chance to meet with Eugene Jarvis when doing your version, or did he offer any help/advice?" To which Baker replied: "I had originally done *Defender* for the Apple II as an exercise in programming. Atari wanted it for the 400/800/5200, so that was the first game I did for them. Yes, Eugene and I had an informal meeting at a park near Atari, and I just told him how I programmed it from what I saw and he confirmed it. I did find out the swarmers (little red ones) do not fire behind themselves… LOL! It's a great trick to approach them, get behind them, and then flip around quick and pick them off at your leisure."

Defender has the reputation of a tough, intense, revolutionary arcade shooter, and it made a smooth transition to the next generation consoles of the early eighties. The Atari 2600 port didn't fare so well (the mountains were replaced by buildings, the ship blinks when it fires, the one-button controls are awkward), but the Atari 5200 and ColecoVision versions come highly recommended.

Stargate (1981), the sequel to *Defender*, was ported remarkably well (by Bill Aspromonte) to the Atari 2600 as both *Stargate* (1984), which you'll find in "The Next 100" appendix near the back of this book, and as *Defender II* (1988).

Baker worked on a version of *Stargate* for the 5200, but that port wasn't released back in the day. The game does exist, however, as a homebrew prototype reproduction.

In addition to *Stargate*, *Defender* spawned another sequel/remake in *Defender 2000* (1996) for the Atari Jaguar. Games similar to, but not directly related to *Defender* include such titles as *Chopper Command* (1982) for the Atari 2600 and *Nova Blast* (1983) for the ColecoVision and Intellivision.

FUN FACT:

The original arcade version of *Defender* sold more than 55,000 units; to celebrate the 50,000th machine, a special gold-colored edition was produced.

WHY IT MADE THE LIST:

Both the Atari 5200 and ColecoVision versions of *Defender* are terrific translations of the arcade classic, the first—and still among the best—side-scrolling shooter.

CHAPTER 25

DEMON ATTACK

ATARI 2600
GENRE: SLIDE-AND-SHOOT
PUBLISHER: IMAGIC
DEVELOPER: IMAGIC
1 OR 2 PLAYERS (SIMULTANEOUS)
1982

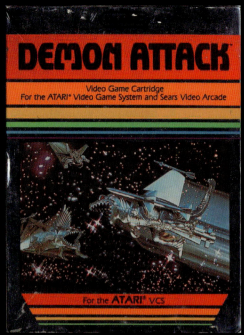

Demon Attack for the Atari 2600, complete in box. Courtesy of AtariAge.com. $8.

"VIBRANTLY COLORFUL, HIGHLY IMAGINATIVE AND CHALLENGING GAME."

A must-own for fans of such coin-op classics as *Moon Cresta* (1980) and *Phoenix* (1980), *Demon Attack* for the Atari 2600 was produced by Imagic, the second most important third-party company for the console.

Like Activision, the first and most important third-party developer for the 2600, Imagic was founded by programmers who left other companies (primarily Atari) because they wanted more money and more credit for the games they were creating. Among these founders was ex-Atari employee Rob Fulop (*Night Driver*, *Missile Command*), who created *Demon Attack*.

In this game, players guide a laser cannon left and right along the bottom of the screen, shooting bullets at colorful, beautifully animated birds that attack from above in waves of three. Beginning with wave five, demons will begin dividing in two when shot. These smaller enemies unleash bullets and fly back-and-forth and diagonally, but they also drop kamikaze-style toward the player's ship. There are seven enemy types with eight different color patterns, for a total of 56 variations.

In addition to standard play, *Demon Attack* offers Tracer Shot mode, in which moving the laser cannon also aims the shots. There's also a Special Co-Op Version of the game where players alternate control of the laser cannon against the same waves of attack (control of the cannon alternates every four seconds). Both of these modes of play add some nice variety to the action.

According to an interview published in *Electronic Games* magazine #11 (Jan., 1983), Fulop originally designed *Demon Attack* to end after the 84th wave, but when a kid beat the game after it was on the market for a mere two days, he reprogrammed it (by changing one line of code) where it could be played indefinitely (but without getting harder past the 84th wave).

Fulop admits he should have made the game more challenging. "I was a little disappointed in *Demon Attack*," he said. "It tops off too quickly. I'm able to consistently get through every level."

Going further behind the scenes, Fulop told *Video Games* magazine (issue #15, Dec., 1983) that the idea for *Demon Attack* "started with two shapes rushing together to create an object." Describing the gameplay and title, he said, "Everything moving on the screen is trying to kill you and you have to shoot everything. I wanted to title the game 'Death from Above' but our marketing department knew better and gave it a more 'marketable' name."

In a 1993 interview with Scott Stilphen (digitpress.com), Fulop got more technical in explaining the creation process: "The trick to the *Demon Attack* graphics was it was the first game to use my Scotch taped/rubber banded dedicated 2600 sprite animation authoring tool that ran on the Atari 800 [computer]," he said. "The first time Michael Becker made a little test animation and we ran Bob Smith's utility that successfully squirted his saved sprite data straight into the *Demon Attack* assembly code and it looked the same on the VCS as it did on the 800 was HUGE! Before that day, all 2600 graphics ever seen were made using a #2 pencil, a sheet of graph paper, a lot of erasing, and a list of hex codes that were then retyped into the source assembly code, typically introducing a minimum of two pixel errors per 8*8 graphic stamp."

Techno jargon aside, *Demon Attack* is a spectacular title that will appeal to a variety of tastes, as evidenced in issue

Demon Attack for the Atari 2600 in action. Courtesy of AtariAge.com.

Demon Attack instruction manual. $2.

Demon Attack magazine ad.

#39 of the *Digital Press* fanzine, where Keita Iida revealed that he's "not much of a fan of the stationary, slide-and-shoot *Space Invaders/Galaxian*-type genre," but that even he enjoys *Demon Attack*'s "brilliant graphics" and that he "can't help but appreciate the care and effort put into the game."

Demon Attack is a fan favorite among those who still play their Atari consoles, but it was especially popular and critically acclaimed during the Golden Age of Video Games.

It won the "1983 Arcade Award" for "Videogame of the Year" in the Jan., 1983 issue of *Electronic Games*, and it was named one of the "50 Best Games" in the March, 1984 issue of *Electronic Fun Magazine*.

In *Electronic Games* #6 (Aug., 1982), Bill Kunkel and Arnie Katz said *Demon Attack* has "fantastic play value, ever-changing, state-of-the-art visuals, and, generally, coin-op quality production values and superior packaging."

In *Electronic Fun with Computers & Games* #2 (Dec., 1982), Randi Hacker called *Demon Attack* a "vibrantly colorful, highly imaginative and challenging game." In *Video Games* #2 (Oct., 1982), the reviewer said "Imagic's first game" was a "terrific debut."

In the aforementioned Stilphen interview, Fulop referenced the arcade classic *Galaxian* (1979) as an inspiration for *Demon Attack*. However, as Stilphen pointed out, the game more resembles *Phoenix* (1980).

The Intellivision version of *Demon Attack*, which Gary Kato programmed later the same year, is even more similar to *Phoenix*, thanks to the addition of a Pandemonium flagship, which serves essentially the same purpose as the mother ship in *Phoenix*. To defeat Pandemonium, which is a visual marvel with slanted eyes, a fiery grin, and devilish horns, players must erode the shield protecting the underbelly of the ship and then shoot through the revolving Window of Vulnerability.

Atari sued Imagic over the similarities between *Demon Attack* and *Phoenix*. Imagic settled out of court and went on to produce *Demon Attack* for a variety of consoles and computers.

Opinions among classic gamers are mixed on the Intellivision version of *Demon Attack*. I'm a big fan of the cartridge, for example, but Classic Gaming Expo organizer Joe Santulli ranked the game the 9th worst in the Intellivision library in issue #4 (March/April) of the *Digital Press* fanzine, citing its "sluggish controls" and "undetailed and predictable" enemies.

The Intellivision version's enemies are definitely blockier and less colorful than their Atari 2600 counterparts, but the game does add such visual flourishes as a cratered moon surface along the bottom of the screen and a portion of planet Earth showing in the background.

In an interview published on the Australian website, www.classic-consoles-center, Kato spoke about the appearance of the Intellivision rendition. "Due to the differences in graphics capabilities, I couldn't make it look exactly like the Atari version," he said. "Intellivision had more moving objects while Atari had more colors."

In that same interview, Kato credited Michael Becker, Imagic's "head art guy," with creating the look of the Pandemonium flagship. "When my eyes saw this, my mouth was hanging open," he said. "As soon as people started coming into work, I rushed back down and said…I HAVE to have this in the game!" Further deferring to Becker, Kato said, "I have to say if it looks good, it was Michael's art. If it looks clunky, it was mine."

In 1983, Dave Johnson ported *Demon Attack* to the Odyssey2 (*Demon Attack* and *Atlantis* were the only U.S.-released third-party games for the system). While the game is one of the O2's better shooters (Adam Smith, in *Creative Computing Video & Arcade Games* #2, called it "quite possibly the best Odyssey2 cartridge on the market today"), it comes up lacking in the graphics department when compared to the Atari 2600 and Intellivision versions. Also, the demons in the Odyssey2 game attack in pairs instead of threes.

Unless you count *Super Demon Attack* (1983) for the Texas Instruments TI-99, *Demon Attack* never got a remake or a sequel, which is a shame—it's a terrific shooter that deserves a modern updating.

FUN FACT:
Demon Attack creator Rob Fulop also programmed *Cosmic Ark*, *Fathom*, and *Cubicolor*, the latter of which Imagic refused to publish; the game was later released by Fulop himself in limited quantities.

WHY IT MADE THE LIST:
A huge hit in its day, *Demon Attack* remains a colorful, dynamic, nicely animated shooter.

CHAPTER 26

DIG DUG

ATARI 7800
GENRE: MAZE
PUBLISHER: ATARI
DEVELOPER: GENERAL COMPUTER CORP.
1 OR 2 PLAYERS (ALTERNATING)
1987

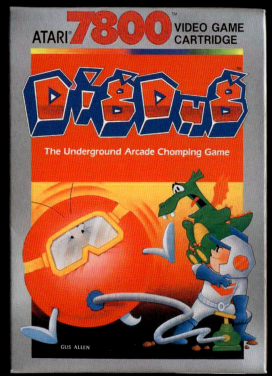

Dig Dug for the Atari 7800, complete in box. *Courtesy of AtariAge.com.* $8.

"GREAT VERSION OF ONE OF THE MORE TIMELESS ARCADE CLASSICS."

For the many of you who dig the original arcade version of *Dig Dug* (developed by Namco in Japan and published in North America by Atari in 1982), you would do well to pick up a copy of the Atari 7800 port. It's an excellent translation of the beloved coin-op classic, though it does move at a slightly faster pace (and certainly faster than the 2600 and 5200 versions).

Also, the final score doesn't stay onscreen after the game is over, frustrating those of us who keep track of such things (yes, I'm nerdy enough to have a notebook filled with my all-time high scores on various classic games).

Minor differences aside, this is a great cartridge.

For those living under the proverbial rock, *Dig Dug* is a legendary classic in which players guide the begoggled (as opposed to bespectacled) title character as he burrows underground, using a shovel to dig tunnels (or gain access to existing ones) and an air gun to stun (a stunned enemy can be walked through with impunity), pump up, and kill two types of enemies: the round, goggle-wearing Pooka; and the green, dragon-like Fygar (who breathe fire).

The Pooka and Fygar cannot dig tunnels, but they can turn into ghosts and maneuver through solid ground to pursue Dig Dug. Pumping up the enemies until they explode is a blast, but it's even more rewarding (in terms of your score) to drop rocks on them. Rocks are initially stagnant, but will plummet downward if Dig Dug walks under them (a rock will fall until it hits dirt).

Strategies in *Dig Dug* are virtually endless, meaning no two games are the same. The deeper you are underground when you kill a monster, the more points you will get for that kill. Other point-boosting maneuvers include eating the vegetables that appear one at a time near the center of the screen and dropping rocks on multiple monsters by skillfully luring them into position.

Although programmed in 1984 (when the Atari 7800 was supposed to come out), *Dig Dug* was published for the Atari 7800 in 1987, the same year as such original, genre-defining titles as Nintendo's *Metroid* and *The Legend of Zelda* for the ubiquitous NES. In the view of many gamers perusing the shelves of Toys "R" Us and KB Toys at the time, the *Dig Dug* cartridge seemed quaint and even stale by comparison. However, that doesn't make it any less of a great game.

Ethan C. Nobles, writing for The Atari Times (ataritimes. com), called *Dig Dug* "perhaps the best arcade port on the system" and said that he "really can't find a flaw" with the game.

The Video Game Critic (videogamecritic.com) only gave the game a "B," but he did call it a "great version of one of the more timeless arcade classics." He also said, "The biggest thrill is to time your boulder drops to take out multiple baddies at a time…the risk reward ratio is perfectly balanced…the memorable 'banjo' music is perfectly

  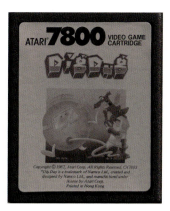

Blowing up a Pooka in *Dig Dug* for the Atari 7800. Courtesy of AtariAge.com.

Dig Dug instruction manual. $1.

Dig Dug game cartridge. $3.

reproduced." (The arcade game's distinctive music was composed by Yuriko Keino.)

For a 7800 title, the coloring is quite good, though it's not quite as rich as in the arcade game. Also, as The Video Game Critic rightly points out, the screen is cropped (square and smaller), making it seem slightly claustrophobic, at least when compared to the rectangular coin-op classic. Luckily, however, gameplay remains largely the same.

When compared to the 5200 version of *Dig Dug* before it, the 7800 rendition has more detailed graphics, such as white teeth and eyes on the Fygar (the 5200 port has solid green Fygar). *Dig Dug* was programmed for the ColecoVision as well, but that version went unreleased until 2001, when CGE Services released it in cartridge form in limited quantities at the 2001 Classic Gaming Expo.

Atari also produced *Dig Dug* for the Atari 2600 and Intellivision. The 2600 game has square rocks, basic lines instead of textured dirt, and flickering, mono-colored enemies, but, as in so many nicely programmed VCS carts, the game captures the essence of the arcade cab.

The Intellivision version has similar graphical shortcomings (including the lack of flower level indicators), but it offers one of the coolest Easter eggs ever seen in a video game. By holding down 4 and 7 on both controllers, you can unlock *Deadly Dogs*, a *Tron Deadly Discs* clone with *BurgerTime* characters. Unfortunately, the Intellivision cartridge is one of the harder to find games for the system.

Arcade *Dig Dug* spawned a sequel in 1985 called *Dig Dug II*, which was ported to the NES in 1989 as *Dig Dug II: Trouble in Paradise*. Here's a portion of the review I wrote for *Trouble in Paradise* in my second book, *Classic Home Video Games, 1985-1988* (2009, McFarland Publishers):

> An obscure sequel to the popular coin-op classic *Dig Dug*, *Dig Dug II: Trouble in Paradise* is a nice port (despite blinking when the screen gets busy) of Namco's 1985 arcade game (which was simply called *Dig Dug II*). Once again, Dig Dug walks around the screen, using a pump (called an "inflator" here) to blow up and destroy round, goggles-wearing Pooka and fire-breathing Fygar. However, unlike the original *Dig Dug*, which found the title character digging maze trails, *Dig Dug II* has players drilling on fault lines to sink sections of an island, killing nearby enemies in the process. Drilling three pieces of an island into the ocean makes a bonus vegetable appear, and flying fish can be caught as well. There are 72 islands in this fun, addictive, strategy-intensive game.

In 1992, Namco released *Dig Dug* for the Game Boy. It includes a straightforward port, plus an adventure mode called *New Dig Dug*. In 2005, the company released *Dig Dug: Digging Strike* for the Nintendo DS. This game has screens similar to those found in both *Dig Dug* and *Dig Dug II*.

Finally, *Dig Dug Arrangement*, which adds such features as giant rocks and power-ups, has appeared in a variety of collections on various modern systems. The game was originally released in 1996 as part of the *Namco Classic Collection Vol. 2* arcade cab.

The various *Dig Dug* offshoots offer varying degrees of entertainment value, but the original *Dig Dug* is the game you'll want to spend the most time with.

FUN FACT:

While I was freelancing for the All Game Guide (allgame.com), I reviewed a PC-only *Dig Dug* sequel called *Dig Dug Deeper*, which Infogrames released in 2001. I called the game "ugly" and "not as fun or as challenging as the original."

WHY IT MADE THE LIST:

Unlike most maze titles, *Dig Dug* lets you dig your own maze pathways, making for a different game each time you play. The Atari 7800 port recreates the arcade action beautifully.

CHAPTER 27

DINER

INTELLIVISION
GENRE: CLIMBING
PUBLISHER: INTV
DEVELOPER: REALTIME ASSOCIATES
1 OR 2 PLAYERS (ALTERNATING)
1987

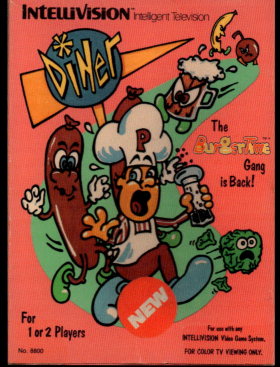

Diner for the Intellivision, complete in box. $85.

"SMOOTH AND FAST-PACED...A WINNER."

The console sequel to *BurgerTime* (arcade sequels to *BurgerTime* include *Peter Pepper's Ice Cream Factory* and *Super BurgerTime*), *Diner* is an Intellivision exclusive and one of the best games for the system. This is an opinion shared by many classic console enthusiasts, including Zach Meston, who gave the game the best score possible in *Video Game Trader* #1 (summer, 2004).

In this great game, players control *BurgerTime* hero Peter Pepper, a short order cook at Ray's Diner, a multi-story building that has a *Congo Bongo*-like, pseudo-3D look. As Peter walks around the floors and climbs the stairs and ladders of the diner, he must kick fresh balls of food (which appear randomly on the floors at the beginning of each stage) onto a plate at the bottom of the screen. Each food ball takes several kicks to reach its destiny (obviously, the food balls on higher floors take more kicks to reach the plate).

As Peter goes about his work, four types of "rotten" food enemies—bananas, hot dogs, cherries, and mugs of root beer—will pester him. Peter should avoid touching these baddies, but he can eliminate them with sprays of pepper and kicked food balls. As in *BurgerTime*, pepper is limited, but players can restock by grabbing "side orders" that randomly appear. These include cups of coffee, hot fudge sundaes, double thick malts, cans of soda pop, and hamburger buns.

Other than *Bounty Bob Strikes Back* for the Atari 5200, *Diner*, weighing in at 15 screens, has more distinct playfields than most any other arcade-style game for a pre-NES system (*Bounty* has a ridiculous 25 levels). I haven't been able to reach all the screens, but the ones I have gotten to are a blast to play, a sentiment shared by the Digital Press staff. In issue #8 (Nov./Dec., 1992) of the *Digital Press* fanzine, the game is called "smooth and fast-paced...a winner."

One of the keys to a good Intellivision game is its ability to make the best of the system's wonky control disc, which doesn't always deliver the most accurate movements. Luckily, as with *Beauty & the Beast* and *Worm Whomper*, the controls work extremely well with *Diner*. Peter moves slowly, but surely, and it's an engaging, non-frustrating challenge to dodge the enemies while trying to save pepper for those times when Peter gets trapped.

Expert players can maneuver in such a way as to manipulate the enemies to line up in a row in order to knock several over at once with the kick of a food ball. This not only racks up big scores, it helps keep the screen uncluttered and Peter alive (which is not always easy).

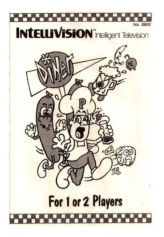  

Diner intro screen.

Diner instruction manual. $15.   The back of the *Diner* box.

Diner was manufactured by INTV Corp., the company that bought the rights to the Intellivision after Mattel, hurting from The Great Video Game Crash of 1983, closed Mattel Electronics in 1984. In addition to marketing the Intellivision II (a small, white version of the Intellivision with detachable controllers), and producing the INTV System III (which is very similar to the original Intellivision, but with an LED on/off light), INTV oversaw production of some of the better, more sophisticated games for the system, such as *Super Pro Football* and *Tower of Doom* (both listed in "The Next 100" appendix near the back of this book).

A game that is relatively hard to find in today's collector's market, *Diner* was designed by Ray Kaestner, who also programmed the excellent Intellivision version of *BurgerTime*. In an interview published in issue #12 (July/Aug.) of the *Digital Press* fanzine, Kaestner gave some insight into the production of *Diner*, which he cited as his favorite game he worked on. "When things went under at Mattel, I was working on a sequel to *Masters of the Universe* with a lot of Escher-looking screens," he said. "After a few mutations and change in characters and storyline, I was able to finish that game as *Diner*, a sequel to *BurgerTime*."

Kaestner, along with graphics artist Connie Goldman, went above and beyond the call of duty with *Diner*. Not only does it offer terrific gameplay, it has many nifty flourishes, such as lighted signs in the restaurant and bonus rounds (after every forth screen) in which Peter catches falling food balls while being careful to avoid deadly blinking ones. It would be nice if the bonus rounds moved a little faster to give it a different feel from the standard action, but this is a small gripe in an otherwise stellar game.

FUN FACT:

Diner programmer Ray Kaestner got his start with Mattel designing handheld electronic games, specifically *Computer Gin* and *World Championship Football*.

WHY IT MADE THE LIST:

Boasting more screens than most arcade-style games of the era, *Diner* is one of the best console sequels ever made.

CHAPTER

DODGE 'EM

ATARI 2600
GENRE: MAZE/RACING
PUBLISHER: ATARI
DEVELOPER: ATARI
1 OR 2 PLAYERS (ALTERNATING, SIMULTA-
NEOUS)
1981

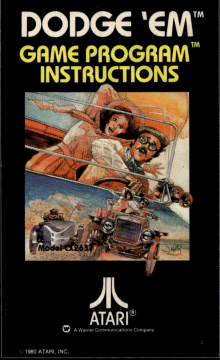

Dodge 'Em instruction manual. $2.

"AS MUCH FUN AS IT IS TO PLAY BY YOURSELF, DODGE 'EM REALLY SHINES IN COMPETITION MODE."

If you were to ask the average gamer what was the first arcade game to have the player maneuver around a maze in order to make dots disappear, the likely answer would be *Pac-Man*. Unfortunately for that hypothetical person's career as a trivia buff, he or she would be wrong. The answer is *Head On*, the Sega/Gremlin arcade game from 1979. (Incidentally, Atari's *Gotcha* from 1973 was the first maze video game of any kind.)

Head On, which was followed later in 1979 by *Head On 2*, was never directly ported to the 2600, but Atari, not wanting to pay licensing fees for the game, cloned it as *Dodge 'Em*, a simple, but engaging maze/racer that was perfectly suited to the confines of the relatively underpowered console.

In both *Head On* and *Dodge 'Em*, players race a car around a top-down maze, driving over (and thus eliminating) dots lining the pathways. The playfield in *Head On* is a grouping of four squares making up a larger concentric square while *Dodge 'Em* is a grouping of four horizontal rectangles making up a larger concentric horizontal rectangle. There are five maze pathways in *Head On*, but only four in *Dodge 'Em*.

The reason the 2600 game is called *Dodge 'Em* is that as players maneuver around the maze, an opposing car drives in the opposite direction. The enemy car doesn't erase dots, but it does tend to change lanes in anticipation of the player's car, causing plenty of head-on collisions (hence the title of the coin-op version). When the player crashes into the oncoming car, the maze starts over, meaning all the erased dots reappear. Once a maze has been completely cleared, the player scores eight bonus points, and the game continues as it started, with a maze full of dots.

Dodge 'Em is simplistic, but super challenging, especially in terms of twitchy, on-the-fly strategy. The car moves at a steady pace automatically, but pressing the action button accelerates it to a higher speed. The racetrack is divided by four intersections (two vertical, two horizontal) in which the player and the opponent vehicle can change lanes. A typical game of *Dodge 'Em* is fast, furious, and fun (if all-too-brief), with players frequently changing lanes and speeding up and slowing down in order to avoid crashing. Once the player crashes three times, the game will end.

Dodge 'Em is indeed a hard game, made more so by a second crash car entering the maze after two mazes have been cleared. Further, when the left difficulty switch on the 2600 console is in the "A" position, the computer car or cars travel at twice their normal speed after the first and third sets of bonus points are awarded. In the "B" position, the car or cars travel at a slower or normal speed. When the right difficulty switch is in the "A" position, the computer car begins the game in different playfield positions. In the "B" position, the computer car always begins next to the player's racecar.

  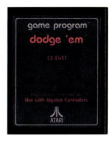

Dodge 'Em for the Atari 2600 in action. *Courtesy of AtariAge.com.*

Atari 2600 video game console. $60.

Dodge 'Em game cartridge. $5.

Unlike certain other early Atari 2600 titles, which offer tons of game modes, *Dodge 'Em* has a mere three, but that's all you really need. Game 1 is for one player while games 2 and 3 let a second gamer in on the action. You can alternate turns against the computer, or, better yet, one player can try to clear the dots while the other drives the crash car. As much fun as it is to play by yourself, *Dodge 'Em* really shines in competition mode. It's one thing to dodge the computer-controlled car, which is robotically predictable (if hard to avoid), but another thing entirely to try and avoid a car driven by a living, breathing, trash-talking human being.

Despite its greatness, *Dodge 'Em* is occasionally underrated, even among classic gaming gurus. In the July/August issue of *2600 Connection* (#94), which contains my listing of "The Ten Best Atari 2600 Games" (*Dodge 'Em* came in at number four), editor and noted collector Al Backiel rebutted with, "I'm not so enthusiastic about *Dodge 'Em*." (To be fair, Backiel didn't infer that he doesn't like the game, just that I ranked it too high.)

Although I'm probably in the minority in proclaiming *Dodge 'Em* a top-10 Atari 2600 title, I'm not alone. In *JoyStik* #4 (Jan., 1983), the game is listed as one of "ten indispensable cartridges" for the system.

Further praise for the game can be found in *Ken Uston's Guide to Buying and Beating The Home Video Games* (1982, Signet), in which the author referred to *Dodge 'Em* as "an exciting, fast-moving maze-type game" that "requires a blend of hand-eye coordination and strategy that will make it of interest to a variety of players."

More recently, the Video Game Critic (videogamecritic.com) called it "a real winner" and a "gem of a game." Keita Iida of Atari Gaming Headquarters (atarihq.com) lavished *Dodge 'Em* with praise—especially the two-player mode—calling it "remarkably fun."

Everyone agrees that *Dodge 'Em* is hardly an audio/visual feast, but it's not an ugly game either. The sounds consist largely of buzzes and beeps, but the graphics, though flat and lacking in detail, are solid enough to get the point across, especially considering the era of release.

Developed by Carla Meninsky, *Dodge 'Em* made its debut in The Atari Video Computer System Catalogue Rev. E (1980), Atari's final game catalogue of that year. The tract hailed the game as "crashing good fun for the whole family," which is a statement that avoids hyperbole since it is true.

In an interview conducted in 2011 by video game historian Will Nicholes (willnicholes.com), Meninsky spoke about her freshman assignment at Atari. "I did *Dodge 'Em* first," she said. "I think it was listed as something like car crash maze game. The name came later from marketing."

Meninsky also spoke about a little-known *Dodge 'Em* variant. "Atari contacted me about turning *Dodge 'Em* into a marketing tool for Mercedes garbage trucks," she said. "They had given it to someone still there to do, but they couldn't figure out the code…I did it in my spare time for free."

Nicholes responded with, "So is there an actual 'Mercedes garbage truck' version of *Dodge 'Em* out there someplace?" To which Meninsky replied, "Yes. I have no idea how that came about…actually, I can guess, now that I think about it…Atari wanted to show how much money they were making…every executive got a brand new Mercedes…I bet someone got a fleet discount and in return they [the car company] got a Mercedes *Dodge 'Em* game."

While working at Atari, Meninsky also programmed *Star Raiders*, *Warlords*, and the unreleased prototype of *Tempest*.

Getting back to *Dodge 'Em*, the next time you fire up your Atari 2600, plug in this exciting maze racer and get ready for fast paced fun. Just be prepared to pull the reset lever again and again as this is one tough, but addicting game.

In 2010, Microsoft made *Dodge 'Em* available as a downloadable title for the Xbox 360 Game Room service. You can also play *Dodge 'Em* on such compilation discs as *Atari Anthology!* (2004, PS2, Xbox) and *Atari Classics: Evolved* (2007, PSP). In addition, it's a built-in title on the Atari Flashback 2 and 3 consoles.

FUN FACT:

Car Wars (1981) for the TI-99 Texas Instruments computer was patterned after *Head On* and *Dodge 'Em*, as was *Power Racer* (1990) for Nintendo's Game Boy.

WHY IT MADE THE LIST:

Although it's brief and simplistic, *Dodge 'Em* is an edge-of-your-seat racer that holds up well to repeated play.

CHAPTER 29

DONKEY KONG

COLECOVISION
GENRE: CLIMBING/NON-SCROLLING PLATFORMER
PUBLISHER: COLECO
DEVELOPER: COLECO
1 OR 2 PLAYERS (ALTERNATING)
1982

NES
GENRE: CLIMBING/NON-SCROLLING PLATFORMER
PUBLISHER: NINTENDO
DEVELOPER: NINTENDO
1 OR 2 PLAYERS (ALTERNATING)
1986

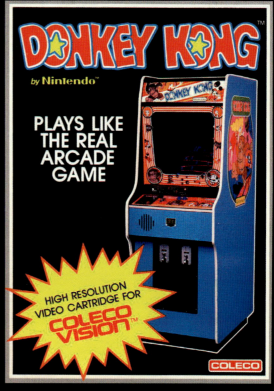

Donkey Kong for the ColecoVision, complete in box. $100.

"DONKEY KONG'S PEDIGREE IS AS RICH AND AS INTERESTING AS ANY VIDEO GAME EVER MADE."

In 1982, when Coleco began hyping their next-gen ColecoVision, I knew I had to get one. The initial television commercial, "The Arcade Experience," was 90 percent hyperbole, showing a guy standing at an arcade cabinet, playing a 3D shooter in which ships actually flew out of the screen.

Even at the tender age of 14, I knew this imagery had little to do with home gaming (I was almost 15, after all). What truly impressed me about the ad was the other 10 percent, which showed the ColecoVision port of Nintendo's arcade classic *Donkey Kong* (1981) in action, looking virtually identical to its coin-op counterpart. Those colorful, detailed, beautifully rendered *Donkey Kong* screenshots were light years above the blocky imagery associated with the Atari 2600, Intellivision, and other previous systems.

Unfortunately, Santa Claus never put gifts under the tree for me totaling more than $100, which was about half the price of a ColecoVision. Stealing one was out of the question, since the systems were kept behind the counter at the various toy and department stores I frequented (and since my conscience wouldn't allow such a thing), so my brain kicked into overdrive, scheming and dreaming of ways to get a ColecoVision.

As fate would have it, summertime was in full swing, which meant there were plenty of lawns to be mowed, and by season's end I had managed to save up more than $130, which was enough to give $100 to Santa Claus (i.e. the folks) and still have enough left over to purchase a copy of *Mouse Trap* (which I gave to my parents to put under the tree).

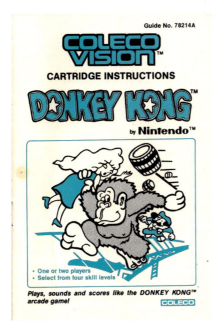
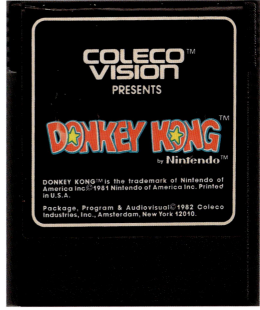

Donkey Kong instruction manual (ColecoVision). $2.

Donkey Kong game cartridge (ColecoVision). $5.

Thus, Christmas of 1982 saw me staying up late into the night with my shiny new console, sitting on my blue bean bag chair in front of the family television set, playing *Donkey Kong* and *Mouse Trap* until my hands and wrists were weary and my eyelids were too heavy to keep open. Over the ensuing months and years, I would add many cartridges to my collection, and to this day, the ColecoVision is my favorite classic console.

In Steven L. Kent's *The Ultimate History of Video Games* (2001, Three Rivers Press), Michael Katz, who was president of marketing at Coleco, recalled Coleco's decision to package *Donkey Kong* with the ColecoVision, a brilliant move that helped sell millions of systems.

"We knew we had to have a hot piece of software to launch the product because software sells hardware," he said. "We got it from a little company called Nintendo—*Donkey Kong*. *Donkey Kong* was exclusive to ColecoVision for the first six months, and we packed it in with the system. If you owned an Atari or Intellivision, you couldn't get *Donkey Kong* for the first six months."

The Ultimate History of Video Games also goes behind the scenes of the licensing arrangement for the game: "On February 1, 1982, Coleco and Nintendo signed an agreement in which Coleco paid Nintendo an undisclosed amount of money and promised royalties of $1.40 for every *Donkey Kong* cartridge and $1 for every tabletop machine sold."

Further, Kent's book details the events surrounding Universal Studios filing suit against Nintendo (on June 29, 1982) for the similarities between *Donkey Kong* and *King Kong*, the rights of which belonged to Universal (thanks to an agreement with RKO Studios, makers of the original 1933 film). Universal lost the case and, in 1985, was ordered "to pay Nintendo $1.8 million for legal fees, photocopying expenses, costs incurred creating graphs and charts, and lost revenues." (Coleco had already cut a deal with Universal, which was essentially "a covenant not to sue.")

As most every human being on the planet knows, *Donkey Kong* has players guiding Mario up and down ladders and across steel girders, jumping over barrels and gaps, pulling up bolts, and smashing fireballs with hammers, all in an effort to rescue Pauline from the titular ape who hangs out at the top of each of the game's three screens.

That's right, as ColecoVision apologists and detractors alike well know, the Conveyor Belt stage from the coin-op classic was left out, leaving just a trio of screens—Girders, Rivets, and Elevators—all of which are fun and nicely emulated. The ColecoVision game is also missing the animated introduction and intermissions. Another difference is that Mario is invincible (as opposed to merely dangerous) when wielding a hammer.

The NES rendition of *Donkey Kong*, which was produced as a single game and as a pairing with *Donkey Kong Jr.* in *Donkey Kong Classics* (1988), is also missing the animations and the Conveyor Belt level, but it has better controls than the ColecoVision version. It also has slightly superior graphics and sounds, and Mario is not invincible when he's got the hammer. Both ports are considerably easier than the arcade game. It's a shame the Conveyor Belt level is missing in both versions because that's a tough level to reach in the arcade, and it would've been nice to be able to play it at home.

Donkey Kong's pedigree is as rich and as interesting as any video game ever made. The world famous arcade version, which was designed by the great Shigeru Miyamoto (*Super Mario Bros.*), featured the first appearances of Mario (then called Jumpman) and Donkey Kong. In addition, it was the first platform game with jumping, it was the second arcade video game with multiple levels (*Gorf* was the first), and it was the subject of *The King of*

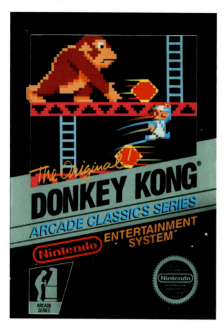

Donkey Kong for the Nintendo NES, complete in box. $300.

for Best Picture and Screenplay…a sophisticated departure from the norm.
—Michael Blanchet (author of *How to Beat the Video Games*), writing in *Electronic Fun with Computers & Games* (Dec, 1982)

…presented in wonderful color and clarity… Virtually everything you like about the arcade original is right here…I commend Coleco for including their best cartridge (to date) in their master unit package.
—Danny Goodman
Writing in *JoyStik* magazine #4 (Jan., 1983)

NES:

In short blasts there is no question this game is still very addictive to this day. You can keep coming back to it time and time again to chip away at your previous high score.
—Darren Calvert
(nintendolife.com)

Prepare for hours of fun and adventure in this home version of monkey madness and mayhem.
—*Pop 'N Play*
Unauthorized Nintendo Instructions (1990)

I've played many home versions of *Donkey Kong*, but this one may be the best.
—The Video Game Critic
(videogamecritic.net)

Kong: A Fistful of Quarters (2007), a documentary chronicling the quest to achieve the world's highest *Donkey Kong* score.

As mentioned earlier, Coleco programmed *Donkey Kong* for the Intellivision and Atari 2600. Unfortunately, the Intellivision version is a two-screen disaster, leading conspiracy theorists to believe that Coleco botched the game on purpose to make their system look even more superior. The Atari 2600 version fares a little better (especially the controls), but Donkey Kong looks like a gingerbread man, and the overall game is a pale shadow of its former self.

Zeroing back in on the specific subject of this chapter—*Donkey Kong* for the ColecoVision and *Donkey Kong* for NES, both of which are hard to find complete in the box—here are accolades for the games from a variety of sources:

ColecoVision:

> We've got to hand it to ColecoVision for the excellent visuals of their *Donkey Kong*. It looks very much like the arcade game in terms of color resolution. The sound effects are also virtually the same.
> —*Playboy's Guide to Rating the Video Games*
> by Walter Lowe, Jr. (1982, PBJ Books)

> A combination of outstanding visuals and variable patterns within the same overall structure are what make *Donkey Kong* so compelling to the solo gamer.
> —Jan., 1983 issue of *Electronic Games Magazine*, in which *DK* won the award for "Best Solitaire Videogame"

If there were Academy Awards for video games, ColecoVision's *Kong* would walk away with Oscars

As a vaunted pack-in title with the ColecoVision (the game was sold separate from the system for only a short time, making the box rare) or as a port of a famous Nintendo arcade game for a famous Nintendo console, *Donkey Kong* holds up extremely well. Some modernists may find it tedious or overly repetitious (walk, climb, jump, repeat), but for us diehard classic gamers, the challenges of *Donkey Kong* never get old.

For those wanting to play the NES version of *Donkey Kong* on something other than an NES console, you can check out the NES Classic Series cartridge (2004) for the Game Boy Advance, or you can download it through the Wii Virtual Console or the 3DS eShop (2006 and 2011 respectively).

FUN FACT:

In the *Guinness World Records: Gamer's Edition 2008*, the arcade version of *Donkey Kong* is credited with having the "First Use of Visual Storytelling in a Video Game."

WHY IT MADE THE LIST:

Donkey Kong is a longtime icon of the video game industry, and it still poses an enjoyable challenge today. The ColecoVision and NES versions, though missing a screen and the intermissions, represent the coin-op classic well.

CHAPTER 30

DONKEY KONG JR.

NINTENDO NES
GENRE: CLIMBING/NON-SCROLLING PLATFORMER
PUBLISHER: NINTENDO
DEVELOPER: NINTENDO
1 OR 2 PLAYERS (ALTERNATING)
1986

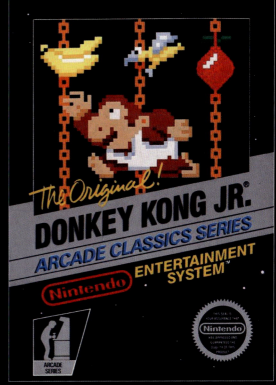

Donkey Kong Jr. for the Nintendo NES, complete in box. $130.

"IT HAS CUTE, COLORFUL GRAPHICS, DELIGHTFUL MUSIC AND SOUND EFFECTS, AND TERRIFIC CONTROLS."

An excellent sequel to the all-time classic *Donkey Kong* (1981), the original arcade version of *Donkey Kong Junior* (1982), like its progenitor, was created by legendary Nintendo designer Shigeru Miyamoto (with assistance from graphics artist Yoshio Sakamoto and music composer Yukio Kaneoka). Also like its progenitor, it is a non-scrolling climbing/platform game that is super challenging and buckets of fun. However, instead of the side-view of a building, the action takes place in a jungle (more accurately, two of the four screens have a jungle setting).

Arcaders guide Donkey Kong's son as he tries to rescue his father from Nintendo mascot Mario (in his only villainous role), who holds Donkey Kong in a cage at the top of the screen in each of the four levels of play. When Junior reaches the top, it's on to the next screen. This continues until players lose all their lives. Junior dies if he touches an enemy (including the stagnant Mario), falls from too great a height or into water, or lets the bonus timer reach zero.

In an interview published in *Nintendo Online Magazine* #18 (2000), Miyamoto, who created the character Donkey Kong Junior because "Donkey Kong is just too darn big," talked a little bit about the son of Kong. "We did a complete one-eighty from the first title and made Mario the villain," he said. "It's the story about Donkey Kong being taken by humans, and his son going to rescue him. In this game, we put in some demo screens that indicated Donkey Kong had been taken from some island in the South, and it seems that those images continue to have an influence on the world of Donkey Kong even now."

Unlike the NES *Donkey Kong* port, which is missing a screen, *Donkey Kong Jr.* for the NES retains all four layouts. They appear in a different order than in the coin-op classic, but they're recreated extremely well.

Depending on the level, Junior: climbs up vines while avoiding Snapjaws (which climb vines and move across platforms); jumps on platforms and climbs across chains while avoiding Nitpicker Birds and the eggs they drop; walks across platforms, climbs poles, and jumps over or otherwise avoids sparks; or pushes keys up chains to reach locks near the top of the screen while avoiding Nitpicker Birds and Snapjaws. To kill enemies and garner extra points, Junior can touch fruit (to make it drop) hanging in certain spots near platforms and on vines and chains.

 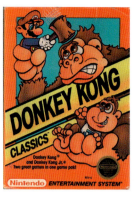 

Donkey Kong Junior for the Atari 7800 is a solid port, but the NES version is better. 7800 cartridge pictured. $6.

Donkey Kong Jr. was re-released with *Donkey Kong* in 1988 as one half of the *Donkey Kong Classics* cartridge. Pictured complete in box. $35.

Donkey Kong Jr. was re-released on the Game Boy Advance e-Reader in 2002 as *Donkey Kong Jr.-e*. The cards you swipe in the e-Reader device are pictured. $4.

Donkey Kong Jr. is a great game for a variety of reasons. It has cute, colorful graphics, delightful music and sound effects, and terrific controls. When Junior climbs up a single vine or chain, he moves slowly, but if he grabs two at once, he scurries upward quickly. Holding two vines or chains, however, makes him a bigger target, so there's some nice strategic potential here. (If Junior goes down holding two vines or chains, he moves slowly, but sliding down a single vine or chain makes him move quickly.) Furthermore, dropping fruit on enemies is tremendously satisfying in terms of both gameplay and audio/visual effects.

As mentioned earlier, the NES game is a faithfully recreated port in terms of graphics and gameplay (only purists will complain that the coin-op version is more difficult and has slightly sharper visuals), but, regrettably, the animated intermissions from the arcade game are absent (a common occurrence with home adaptions, though certain cartridges do retain intermissions, such as *Pac-Man* for the Intellivision). Players can select from game "A," which is for "beginners," and game "B," which is for "experts."

An excellent port of the game was also released for the ColecoVision (Noel Steere with *Electronic Fun with Computers & Games* called it a "must-buy" and said it was "as good as the arcade game"), but that version, despite its high quality, is missing the Hideout screen, giving the NES cart a distinct advantage. The game was also released for the Atari 2600 and Intellivision, but those renditions are hindered by poor controls and ugly character graphics. The Atari 7800 version, produced in 1988, has all four screens, but the music and sound effects are terribly off key.

To give you a little perspective on the release of *Donkey Kong Jr.* for the NES, the console had just launched the previous year during a test-marketing campaign in New York City. During the first year of the system's nationwide release (i.e. 1986), Nintendo mined their early arcade hits, resulting in the "Arcade Classics Series" of games, which consisted of *Donkey Kong*, *Donkey Kong Jr.*, *Donkey Kong 3*, *Mario Bros.*, and *Popeye*. Another related NES title was *Donkey Kong Jr. Math* (1985), which incorporated climbing action with lessons in addition, subtraction, multiplication, and division.

In 1988, Nintendo re-released *Donkey Kong* and *Donkey Kong Jr.* on one cartridge, calling it *Donkey Kong Classics*. NES *Donkey Kong Jr.* was also released for the cumbersome e-Reader device, which was a failed peripheral that plugged into the Game Boy Advance. To play an e-Reader game, the user had to swipe data cards, which most gamers found to be a hassle.

Other systems to receive the NES version of *Donkey Kong Jr.* include the Nintendo Wii (2006, via the Virtual Console) and the Nintendo 3DS (2011, via the Virtual Console).

FUN FACT:

The arcade version of *Donkey Kong Junior* spawned a cereal: fruit-flavored and shaped berries and bananas, produced by Ralston. It was also featured as one of five arcade cabs used in the first broadcast video game championship, airing on ABC TV's *That's Incredible!* on February 21, 1983.

WHY IT MADE THE LIST:

Published before such revolutionary titles as *The Legend of Zelda* and *Metroid* changed the landscape of the NES in 1987, *Donkey Kong Jr.* is a great port and a worthy follow-up to *Donkey Kong*.

CHAPTER **31**

DONKEY KONG 3

NES
GENRE: NON-SCROLLING SHOOTER
PUBLISHER: NINTENDO
DEVELOPER: NINTENDO
1 OR 2 PLAYERS (ALTERNATING)
1986

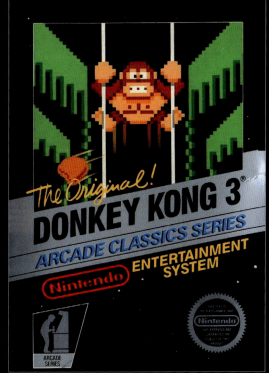

Donkey Kong 3 for the Nintendo NES, complete in box. $125.

"THE SHOOTING ACTION IN DONKEY KONG 3 IS FAST AND FRANTIC."

Donkey Kong 3 isn't quite the black sheep of the *Donkey Kong* family of games (that honor should probably go to *Donkey Kong Jr. Math*), but it is a widely misunderstood, highly underrated game that turned the franchise on its ear—at least temporarily—by switching genres from climbing game to *Galaga*-style shooter.

Originally released in the arcades in 1983, *Donkey Kong 3* is the sequel to the much more popular, much more well-received *Donkey Kong Junior* (1982), which was the follow-up to the legendary coin-op classic, *Donkey Kong* (1981). Instead of climbing a building (*DK*) or vines (*DKJ*), *Donkey Kong 3* has players running around the lower portion of the screen, firing upward at an assortment of enemies. The NES port is a near note-for-note translation of its coin-op cousin.

Centipede and *Gorf* are somewhat similar to *Donkey Kong 3*, but instead of guiding a shooting implement, players maneuver a gardener named Stanley the Bugman as he jumps on and runs across several horizontal platforms. There are three different screens, as opposed to four in the previous *Donkey Kong* games. Stanley shoots bug spray at various creatures, including Beesyps (small bees), Buzzbees (larger bees), Creepy snakes, butterflies, and other pests.

While shooting and trying to avoid getting hit, Stanley should try to keep the flying enemies from swooping down and stealing flowers that are positioned in a row of five along the bottom of the screen. In addition, Stanley must keep Donkey Kong, who throws coconuts, punches beehives (to get the bees to swarm onto the playfield), and climbs down from a pair of vines that is suspended from the top of the playfield from jumping down and killing him. This is done by spraying DK periodically to keep him higher up on the vines. Exterminating all the creatures or shooting Donkey Kong all the way up to the top of the screen completes the level.

The shooting action in *Donkey Kong 3* is fast and frantic, especially given the theme—most shooters this intense are set in outer space. After completing a few screens, the player will be in a near-constant state of panic, shooting bugs, making sure Donkey Kong doesn't jump down, and running and jumping to try and avoid getting touched (narrow misses are frequent).

Stanley is one busy little guy, and he's fun to control. He only has one power-up—a can of power spray dropped once per screen by Donkey Kong—but it's super strong, as it can eliminate snakes (which are otherwise indestructible) and send Donkey Kong faster up the vines.

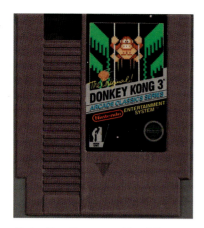

Donkey Kong 3 game cartridge. $10.

Donkey Kong 3 was re-released on the Game Boy Advance e-Reader in 2003 as *Donkey Kong 3-e*. Pictured complete in package. $6.

Nintendo NES video game console. $50.

Apparently, I'm something of a minority in terms of my affection for *Donkey Kong 3*. Darren Calvert, writing for Nintendo Life (nintendolife.com), had this to say when reviewing the game as downloaded for the Nintendo Wii: "For 500 Wii points it is hard to recommend *Donkey Kong 3*. There are far better NES games already on the Virtual Console that offer much more depth and longevity."

Worse, the Video Game Critic (videogamecritic.com) gave the cartridge a confounding "D-", saying the game "stinks" and that it is "an ill-advised game even Nintendo would like to forget." Adding insult to injury, Joe Santulli, the head honcho at Digital Press (digitpress.com), bemoaned the absence of Mario and called the game "about as much fun as being beat over the head with a sack of onions."

Alas, *Donkey Kong 3* may be that third child its parents didn't really want, and it may be that kid on the playground that no one wanted to play with, but I'll happily welcome it into my game room any time, any day. *DK3*, consider yourself adopted (I own a boxed copy of the relatively hard-to-find NES cart, but not, unfortunately, the arcade cabinet).

After *Donkey Kong 3* hit the NES in 1986, the property had a long dry spell that was broken in 1994 by *Donkey Kong* for the Game Boy, a brilliant expansion of the original concept that added puzzle elements and featured 101 stages. Later that same year, the gorgeous platformer *Donkey Kong Country* breathed new life into the Super Nintendo, helping keep that system relevant for a couple of more years.

The *Donkey Kong* franchise continued with *Donkey Kong Land* (1995, GB), *Donkey Kong Country 2: Diddy's Kong Quest* (1995, SNES), *Donkey Kong Land 2* (1996, GB), *Donkey Kong Country 3: Dixie Kong's Double Trouble!* (1996, SNES), *Donkey Kong Land III* (1997, GB), *Donkey Kong 64* (1999, N64), *Donkey Kong Jungle Beat* (2004, GC), *DK King of Swing* (2005, GBA), *DK Jungle Climber* (2007, DS), *Donkey Kong Country Returns* (2010, Wii), *Donkey Kong Country Returns 3D* (2013, 3DS), and *Donkey Kong Country: Tropical Freeze* (2014, Wii U).

In 2003, Nintendo re-released *Donkey Kong 3* on the Game Boy Advance e-Reader as *Donkey Kong 3-e*.

FUN FACT:

Stanley the Bugman first appeared in *Greenhouse*, a Nintendo Game & Watch handheld title from 1982. He also appeared as a trophy in *Super Smash Bros. Melee* (2001) for the GameCube.

WHY IT MADE THE LIST:

A fast, frenetic shooter, *Donkey Kong 3* is one of the most underrated games ever created for the arcades or the home. Forget the *Donkey Kong* theme and treat the game as a hardcore shooter, and you may just find that you enjoy it.

CHAPTER 32

DRAGONSTOMPER

ATARI 2600
GENRE: ROLE-PLAYING GAME
PUBLISHER: STARPATH
DEVELOPER: STARPATH
1 PLAYER
1982

DragonStomper for the Atari 2600, complete in box. Courtesy of AtariAge.com. $20.

"ONE OF THE BEST ADVENTURE GAMES EVER RELEASED FOR THE ATARI 2600."

I'll admit up front that I'm not much of a role-playing game fan. In most cases, I would rather jump straight into the action than wander around for half an hour looking for a sword. However, in going through the painful process of deciding what games to include and not include in this book, I felt I couldn't ignore *DragonStomper* (originally titled "Excalibur," but never produced under that name), an ambitious RPG that disciples of the genre should definitely check out.

Produced in cassette format for the beloved Starpath Supercharger peripheral, *DragonStomper* puts you in the title role of a hero armed with courage, strength, wits, intuition, and resourcefulness. Your mission, as the title implies, is to slay a dragon.

The dragon in question is by no means an innocent or mindless beast. Thanks to powers absorbed by an amulet, the creature is intelligent and wields magical powers. As the dragon got more and more powerful, he became obsessed with evil and attacked a formerly peaceful kingdom, spurring you—the DragonStomper—into action.

The game tasks you with journeying through three levels, each of which loads separately from a cassette recorder into the memory of the Supercharger: The Enchanted Countryside (load one), The Oppressed Village (load two), and The Dragon's Cave (load three).

In The Enchanted Countryside, you, as a small white dot, must traverse the land, keeping your strength up while avoiding traps, gathering gold, weapons, and other useful items (rings, keys, potions, shields, and the like), and battling such enemies as beetles, monkeys, snakes, slimes, spiders, and warriors. As in *Stellar Track*, the battles are text-based (via user-friendly text menus—"move" [i.e. run], "fight," "use" [item]), with the computer giving you play-by-play info on hits connected, who won, what treasure you gained, and how much strength you lost.

If you manage to earn enough money to bribe the guard in order to cross the bridge (or, you can show the guard your scroll), you will enter The Oppressed Village, where you must buy and barter for items (food, magic, medicine) at the Magic Shop, the Trade Shop, and the Hospital. By making the right offer, you can also recruit warriors from the village to help you in your quest. Once you are convinced that you have everything you need to take on the dragon, you should step up to the gate of the Dragon's Cave to enter the third and final level.

The Dragon's Cave scrolls vertically, sending you up a long pathway through a cave riddled with traps, obstacles (watch out for strength-draining darts), guardians, and the

Gaining a handaxe in *DragonStomper* for the Atari 2600. Courtesy of AtariAge.com.

DragonStomper game tape. Courtesy of AtariAge.com. $8.

DragonStomper instruction manual. Courtesy of AtariAge.com. $4.

bones of other would-be DragonStompers. If you get to the end of the cave, you'll reach the Dragon's Lair, where you must use the weapons you've gained to slay the dragon (or at least take back the amulet).

If you manage to beat the game, you'll be treated to a surprisingly good "bleep and bloop" version of the British patriotic song, "Rule, Britannia!" Other tunes in the game include "Taps," which plays when you are killed, and "I'm in the Money," which plays when you take an item from a defeated enemy.

In an interview published in the instruction manual for *Stella Gets a New Brain* (the Starpath Supercharger collection on CD published by CyberPunks in 1996), *DragonStomper* programmer Stephen Landrum (*Communist Mutants from Space*, *The Official Frogger*) said the game took several months to complete and that he chose to do it because "nobody had done a real fantasy role-playing game on the 2600 up to that point. There was *Adventure* (by Atari), but at the time I didn't consider it a real FRP."

The accolades for *DragonStomper* among the classic gaming community are plentiful. In *Digital Press* #12 (July/Aug., 1993), Joe Santulli called it "one of the greatest games ever for the 2600." In the same issue, Liz Santulli said it "really shows off the Atari 2600 potential" while the late Kevin Oleniacz claimed it's "definitely one of the top 10 for this system."

The Video Game Critic, via videogamecritic.com, said, "*DragonStomper*'s graphics are high resolution and meticulously drawn. This is a respectable RPG, and that's no small feat for the Atari 2600." Writing for The Atari Times (ataritimes.com), Darryl Brundage claimed *DragonStomper* was better than any similar game from its era while Lee and Lori Krueger called it nothing less than "the second best 2600 game of all time," citing its "playability, good graphics, and fantastic replay value."

Regarding vintage publications, *The Electronic Games Software Encyclopedia* (1983) gave it an overall rating of 9 out of 10, referring to its "excellent" graphics and sounds, its "outstanding play-action" capabilities, and its greatness as a solitaire experience.

In *Electronic Fun with Computers & Games* #5 (March, 1983), Michael Blanchet called it "a thinking man's game, and a good one at that." He also said it "challenges the mind instead of the wrist, which makes the game closer to a total entertainment experience than almost any other game currently on the market."

In *Video Games* Vol. 2 #2 (Nov., 1983), Dan Persons called *DragonStomper* "one of the best adventure games ever released for the Atari 2600." He said the graphics and sounds were merely "ordinary," but praised the game's interfacing and controls. Moreover, he claimed that the "booby traps in the dragon's cave spring with such a suddenness that I literally jumped from my seat."

If you own a Starpath Supercharger for your Atari 2600, and you enjoy role-playing games, picking up a copy of *DragonStomper* is a no-brainer—though playing it through to the end could strain your brain more than just a bit.

FUN FACT:

In an article entitled "Xbox 360 Has Nothing on Atari 2600" published in the November, 2005 issue of *Forbes* magazine (http://www.forbes.com/2005/11/23/microsoft-xbox-videogames-cx_el_1123oldgames.html), Ed Lin called *DragonStomper* "the best title ever made in the history of U.S. video gaming."

WHY IT MADE THE LIST:

A sophisticated RPG for its time, *DragonStomper* remains a challenging adventure with good interfacing, a variety of ways to solve problems, and randomized monsters and items.

CHAPTER

ESCAPE FROM THE MINDMASTER

ATARI 2600
GENRE: MAZE
PUBLISHER: STARPATH
DEVELOPER: STARPATH
1 PLAYER
1982

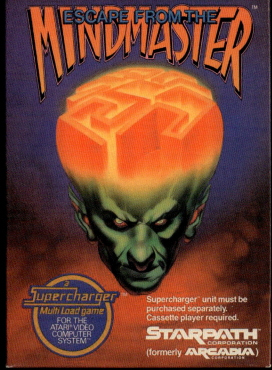

Escape from the Mindmaster for the Atari 2600, complete in box. Courtesy of AtariAge.com. $20.

"THE PSEUDO-3D GRAPHICS ARE VERY IMPRESSIVE LOOKING FOR A 2600 GAME."

Escape from the MindMaster is a multi-load game designed for use with the Starpath Supercharger, which is a cassette-based peripheral sold separately that attaches to the 2600. It requires four loads from the cassette to complete.

One night while sleeping, you were kidnapped from your own bed by the MindMaster, only to awaken in a maze of corridors demarcated by large blue walls. You are trapped in a strange prison and must solve a series of puzzles in order to escape the maze, not to mention preserve the honor of the human race.

The action in *Escape from the MindMaster* is viewed from a first-person perspective—an unusual point of view for the era—and the pseudo-3D graphics are very impressive looking for a 2600 game.

As Mark Brownstein stated in *Electronic Fun with Computers & Games* #5 (March, 1983), "Mattel attempted to corner the market on three-dimensional graphics with *Star Strike*, but they will have to go further to match this game… the limited 3D graphics are excellent…there is something for just about everyone in this game."

As you walk down the maze hallways, turning and reversing direction as needed (certain doors are one-way only), you must locate a number of colored pegs (one at a time) and place them in their corresponding holes (for example, a wing-shaped hole needs a wing-shaped peg).

Each maze has a doorway to the next maze, but these stay locked until you place all the pegs within that maze into the correct holes. To help you keep track of your location, an overhead-view map is positioned near the bottom/center of the screen. To help keep things challenging, the map does *not* show the location of the pegs, doors, or other items, but there is a direction finder arrow that tells you which way you are facing.

While navigating a maze, you must avoid running into sliding force fields, which are basically large square panels that move. If you see one, let it pass before continuing on your way. You must also avoid bumping into the Alien Stalker, which is a creature that is also trying to escape from the maze. When the Alien Stalker gets near, an audio clue will sound.

The reason you are trapped to begin with is that you are the subject of an experiment. The MindMaster watches your every move, testing your intelligence, memory, coordination, and reflexes. To that end, there's a test hidden in each of the game's first five mazes.

These mini-games—another rarity for the era—are as follows (reprinted from the manual):

Starpath Supercharger trade publication ad. Courtesy of Digital Press (digitpress.com).

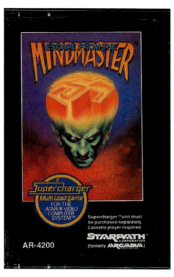
Escape from the Mindmaster game tape. Courtesy of AtariAge.com. $8.

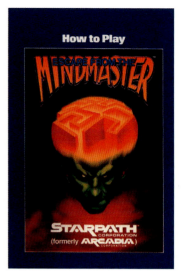
Escape from the Mindmaster instruction manual. Courtesy of AtariAge.com. $4.

Test 1: *Agility*—Dance from side to side to avoid the falling bricks. The fourth collision is a knockout.

Test 2: *Reflexes*—Watch for the flashing arrow. Follow its movement as quickly as you can with your joystick.

Test 3: *Recall*—Memorize the sequence of arrows on the screen. Then recreate the pattern with your joystick.

Test 4: *Dexterity*—Scamper through the stream of bricks without touching any.

Test 5: *Coordination*—Here's a test especially for time-traveling species. Make a nice soft landing on the platform without using too much fuel. You get five attempts.

In an interview published on www.mayhem64.co.uk, *Escape from the MindMaster* creator Dennis Caswell said he doesn't quite remember where the idea for the game came from, but he does "recall being motivated by a desire to create a fun game that had no shooting in it."

Caswell also spoke about the challenge of programming for the 2600. "In *Mindmaster*, the playfield was used for the walls of the maze, with a couple of the other objects overlayed along the tops of the walls to smooth their edges, which otherwise would have been extremely blocky," he said. "One of the players was used for both the alien and the sliding panels (you'll notice they never appear together). The benefit of the first-person format is that I didn't need to use up a graphic object to display the human player. Unfortunately, there wasn't enough computing horsepower available to re-render the entire display in a single video frame, so I rendered half on one frame and half on the next, which is why the display breaks up a bit when you run down the halls."

In addition to being a technically impressive and innovative accomplishment for the Atari 2600, *Escape from the MindMaster* is simply a fun and challenging game, an opinion shared by Digital Press co-founder Kevin Oleniacz (may he rest in peace). In issue #8 (Nov./Dec., 1992) of the *Digital Press* fanzine, he called it "one of the most creative [games] Starpath offered…an addictive mix of memory games and reflex tests…a winner."

In *JoyStik* magazine #6 (July, 1983), Jim Gorzelany gave the game just three out of five stars, calling it "a bit slow" for the "hardcore video action addict." However, he conceded that "if you like mental challenges, this game is for you."

In issue #2 (autumn, 1983) of the British publication, *TV Gamer*, the writer said, "This game is a first-class piece of software for the VCS and one very strongly recommended."

In *Video Games* #11 (Aug., 1983), Perry Greenberg warned action fans that they may be a little disappointed with *Escape from the MindMaster*, saying it is "really a puzzle/memory game." However, he also said it is "more than a little addictive" and that it has "well-conceived visuals and gameplay."

In short, for most gamers, *Escape from the MindMaster* is a good, brain-engaging reason to own a Starpath Supercharger.

FUN FACT:

An Atari 2600 exclusive, *Escape from the MindMaster* should have been released for the ColecoVision in 1983, but was a victim of The Great Video Game Crash. Famed collector and dealer Jerry Greiner discovered an apparently complete prototype of the ColecoVision version a few years ago.

WHY IT MADE THE LIST:

Clearly ahead of its time, *Escape from the MindMaster* was highly sophisticated upon release and is still entertaining today.

CHAPTER 34

FANTASY ZONE, FANTASY ZONE II

FANTASY ZONE
SEGA MASTER SYSTEM
GENRE: SIDE-SCROLLING SHOOTER
PUBLISHER: SEGA
DEVELOPER: SEGA
1 OR 2 PLAYERS (ALTERNATING)
1986

FANTASY ZONE II
SEGA MASTER SYSTEM
GENRE: SIDE-SCROLLING SHOOTER
PUBLISHER: SEGA
DEVELOPER: SEGA
1 OR 2 PLAYERS (ALTERNATING)
1987

Fantasy Zone for the Sega Master System, complete in box. $20.

"THESE ARE GREAT GAMES WITH CONSTANT SHOOTING, CROWDED LEVELS, AND CHALLENGES GALORE."

Released by Sega in 1985, the original arcade version of *Fantasy Zone*, along with Konami's *TwinBee* released earlier the same year, helped pioneer the so-called "cute-'em-up" subgenre, which, as those who hang out on video game message boards know, is short for "cute shoot-'em-up."

Fantasy Zone was heavily influenced by *Defender* (1980), but instead of no-nonsense aliens, a starry outer-space backdrop, and a simple outline of a mountain range, the game has bright pastel coloring, surrealistic flora and fauna, and oddball enemies with names like Moocolon, Quili-Quili, Shatboo, Sourtham (looks like scissors), Onyamma (inflates and deflates), and Poyon (has eyeballs revolving around its body).

Instead of a standard starship, like in *Defender*, players pilot an Opa-Opa, which is a spaceship that is shaped like an egg and can walk along the ground. A merry musical soundtrack and punchy sound effects match the onscreen action, which involves flying around a wraparound world (scrolling is non-forced), firing at airborne enemies while avoiding them and their bullets. To progress to the boss of the level you are in, you must destroy a certain number of enemy-generating bases, which is a gratifying and fun-to-execute objective.

Once you have destroyed the boss, a sprinkling of coins will appear that you should snatch up (coins fall from

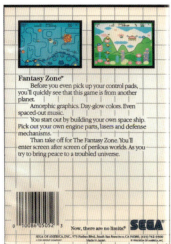
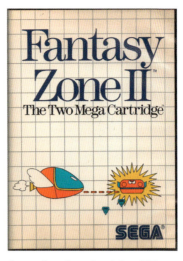
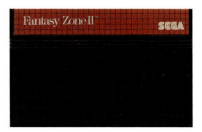

Fantasy Zone II game cartridge. $7.

The back of the Fantasy Zone box.   Fantasy Zone II complete in box. $20.

standard fallen foes as well), and you will then progress to the next planet. Levels include: Plalfeaf (Planet of Greenery), Tabas (Planet of Fire), La Dune (Planet of Sand), Dolimicca (Super Planet), Polaria (Planet of Ice), Mockstar (Planet of Clouds), Pocarius (Planet of Water), and Salfar (Planet of Evil Spirits).

The money earned for beating baddies is used for shopping in a store that carries such power-ups as extra speed, wide beam, laser beam, 7-way shot, twin bombs, smart bombs, fire bombs, heavy bombs, and extra ships (in addition to bases, bosses, and a whimsical theme, power-ups also help separate *Fantasy Zone* from *Defender*). Opa-Opa shoots horizontally (a la *Defender*), but it also drops arcing bombs (a la *Cosmic Avenger*, *Scramble*, and *Super Cobra*).

When I was frequenting the arcades during the mid-1980s, none of the ones I went to had a *Fantasy Zone* machine, and I didn't own the NES or Sega Master System version of the game until years later. Thus, my first experience with this challenging, rapid-fire shooter was via the near-perfect TurboGrafx-16 port, which came out in 1989. I've also spent a fair amount of time playing *Fantasy Zone* via the *Sega Classics Collection* (2005) for the PlayStation 2.

The Master System rendition of *Fantasy Zone* isn't as spot-on as the TurboGrafx-16 game (backgrounds disappear during boss battles and the enemy radar screen is missing, among other niggling points), but it is a terrific port and a great game in general. Despite the cutesy graphics and sounds, *Fantasy Zone* is a hardcore shooter that fans of the side-scrolling genre will love.

Included among these fans is Sean with Game Freaks 365 (gamefreaks365.com), who said that *Fantasy Zone* "bursts right out at you with incredible graphics" and that the soundtrack is one of the most memorable he's ever heard. He also said it's "one of the best Master System games out there and one of the greatest shooters of all time," citing its creativity, presentation, abstract design, and large, nicely detailed bosses.

Tony Takoushi, reviewing the game for issue # 79 of the UK magazine, *Computer and Video Games* (May, 1988), gave *Fantasy Zone* for the Master System a 9 out of 10 rating in all four categories (graphics, sound, playability, and overall), calling it a "beaut of a game" with "very unusual colourful backdrops and aliens."

Anyone who enjoys *Fantasy Zone* will surely appreciate *Fantasy Zone II* (a port of the 1987 Sega arcade game), which sticks to the formula established by the original, but adds some new features and longer, more difficult challenges. Subtitled "The Tears of Opa-Opa" on the title screen (but not on the box nor in the manual), the game takes place 10 years in the future, when Opa-Opa has returned to his homeland. He finds that a group of Blackhearts has taken over and must be destroyed.

Once again, there are eight pastel-colored levels: Pastaria, Sarcand, Hiyarika, Bow Bow, Chaprun, Fuwareak, Sbardian, and Wolfin. In addition to different names, the levels have new graphics and designs, but what really sets them apart is that they are bigger than the levels in *Fantasy Zone*.

Unlike *Fantasy Zone*, certain enemy bases in *Fantasy Zone II* turn into blue warp gates (the manual says they're green, but they're not) that transport you to different scenes within the level (the first two levels have three scenes while the rest have five). Once you have destroyed every base in every scene of a level, a red warp gate will appear. Passing through a red warp gate takes you to that level's boss.

You can still gather money to use in shops (bills in addition to coins), but the shops are set in place this time and don't float around. In addition, there are hidden shops in levels three, five, and six (you must fire bullets in seemingly random areas to locate them). New items to purchase include fireball, 3-way shot, big shot, big bomb, twin big bombs, auto beam, shield, red bottle (increases and prolongs power meter), and blue bottle (replenishes power meter).

There are lots of new enemies as well, including Bigmouth, Barrelface, Kucklejaw, Birdman, Snakebite,

Nuclear Cactus, Beehive, Amoeba, Bulldog, Trash Can Man, Rocketron, Elephant Man, Twister, Slug, and the turtle-like Shell Back.

As with several other titles in this book, *Fantasy Zone II* for the SMS is available on the Nintendo Wii Shop Channel for the Virtual Console. After downloading the game, Corbie Dillard of Nintendo Life (nintendolife.com) heaped praise on it, saying, "*Fantasy Zone II* takes everything that was great about the original and adds in larger levels, a few new gameplay twists, and an increased difficulty to form one of the best cute-'em-ups to come out of the 8-bit era."

Further, Dillard said that the game's "vibrant and contrasting colors really jump off the screen and give the game its unique charm and personality…each level is very distinct in look and feel, and even the various areas within each level show a lot of variety…the bosses are also a bit more imaginative this time around and some are downright enormous in size."

Lucas M. Thomas, also commenting on the Wii download version, is especially fond of the game's graphics. In a review published on ign.com, he said, "The first *Fantasy Zone* was attractive and colorful, but this one took things up a notch with exceptional use of the hardware's palette and engaging, dynamic, and detailed environments…not fixing what wasn't broken and putting extra effort into the visuals was just the right strategy for Sega with this sequel."

Other *Fantasy Zone* sequels include: *Fantasy Zone: The Maze* (1988), a maze shooter for the Master System; *Fantasy Zone Gear* (1991, Game Gear), which added a homing shot and other new weapons; and *Super Fantasy Zone* (1992, Mega Drive), a Japanese and European release that I downloaded from the Wii Shop Channel and have thoroughly enjoyed.

Fantasy Zone also inspired a hard-to-find Sega Mark III (the Japanese Master System) spinoff called *Galactic Protector*, which uses an analog paddle controller to guide Opa-Opa in circles around a planet positioned in the center of the screen, firing outward at a barrage of enemies. *Space Fantasy Zone* for the PC Engine CD-ROM² (the Japanese TurboGrafx-CD), which would have melded the *Fantasy Zone* and *Space Harrier* franchises, was never released and only exists in prototype form.

If you like hardcore side-scrolling shooters and have never given *Fantasy Zone* or *Fantasy Zone II* a try because of their pastel graphics and goofy creatures, you should reconsider. These are great games with constant shooting, crowded levels, and challenges galore.

FUN FACT:

In *Sonic's Ultimate Genesis Collection* (2009) for the Playstation 3 and Xbox 360, you can unlock the arcade version of *Fantasy Zone* by scoring 80,000 in *Flicky*.

WHY IT MADE THE LIST:

Fantasy Zone and *Fantasy Zone II* suck you in (or turn you away) with cute, pastel-colored graphics, but keep you coming back for more with hardcore side-scrolling shooter action.

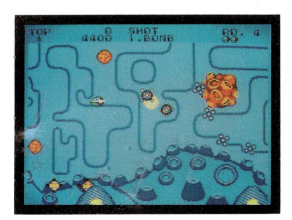

CHAPTER

35

FOOD FIGHT

ATARI 7800
GENRE: ACTION/NON-SCROLLING SHOOTER
PUBLISHER: ATARI
DEVELOPER: ATARI
1 OR 2 PLAYERS (ALTERNATING)
1987

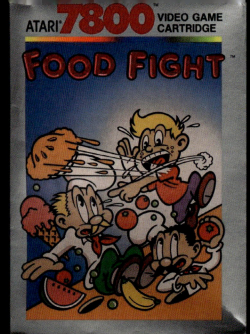

Food Fight for the Atari 7800, complete in box. *Courtesy of AtariAge.com.* $12.

> " THE FOOD IS FUN TO THROW, THE CHEFS AND FOOD PROJECTILES ARE FUN TO DODGE, AND THE ACTION IS NON-STOP."

The video game industry of the late 1970s and early '80s was a hotbed of creativity. Sure, there were plenty of *Pac-Man*, *Pong*, and *Space Invaders* clones, but video games were still in their infancy, and even the larger companies, unrestrained by today's massive budgets and large design teams, were freer to come up with crazy concepts.

One of these crazy concepts was the food-themed game, which included such titles as *BurgerTime*, *Fast Food*, *Jawbreaker*, *Tapper* (beer is a food, right?), and, of course, the 1983 Atari arcade game *Food Fight* (called *Charley Chuck's Food Fight* on the marquee and manual), which has "nice animation" and "interesting play-action" (*Electronic Games* magazine #19, Nov., 1983).

Developed by General Computer Corp., the same company that designed *Ms. Pac-Man*, *Food Fight* has one of the simplest (in a good way) premises ever seen in a cute, character-based arcade game. Players, guiding a blond-haired fellow named Charley Chuck, must walk across the screen to gobble up a large ice cream cone. Upon approach, Charley's mouth opens super wide (creating a mildly amusing visual effect), and he quickly gulps down the ice cream (the kid must be immune to brain freeze). Then, he must perform the same task again and again (and again).

Lucky for those of us who enjoy some degree of challenge, there are obstacles in Charley's way, including manholes, chefs (Angelo, Zorba, Oscar, and Jacques), and flying food (thrown by the chefs). Naturally, falling into a manhole, making contact with a chef, or getting hit by a piece of food will cook Charley's goose. Another obstacle is the 32-second time limit, which kicks in immediately because the ice cream begins melting as soon as each round gets underway. As you work your way through each stage, the action gets progressively faster.

To combat the aforementioned chefs (two to four of them at a time, depending on the level), Charley can walk in all directions, grab food (bananas, pies, tomatoes, and the like) from piles that are scattered about the floor, and throw said food at the chefs in rapid-fire fashion. Throwing the food is essentially a shooting maneuver, making the game feel a little bit like *Berzerk* or *Frenzy*. Charley "shoots" in the direction the joystick is pointing. He can also force the chefs into manholes, which is where they appear from to begin with.

In *Atari Inc.—Business is Fun* (2012, Syzygy Company Press), authors Mary Goldberg and Curt Vendel compared the game to a trio of coin-op classics: "*Food Fight* offers a really enjoyable and less violent alternative to *Robotron* (watermelon, tomatoes, and pies being thrown at others is generally not a leading cause of death…), all in a uniquely colorful experience similar to *Centipede* and *Crystal Castles*. The game becomes a good draw for younger players and

Food Fight game cartridge. $6.

Food Fight instruction manual. Courtesy of AtariAge.com. $3.

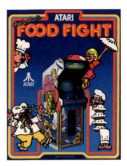
Food Fight arcade flyer.

Charley Chuck gulping down ice cream in Food Fight for the Atari 7800. Courtesy of AtariAge.com.

female players, and proves again that GCC can design unique games."

In an interview published on the American Classic Arcade website (www.classicarcademuseum.org), *Food Fight* creator Jonathan Hurd spoke about how he got the idea for the coin-op classic after playing some of the more violent games of the time. "I wanted to come up with something different—something that was less violent, possibly funny, and that would appeal to both male and female players," he said. "Most games had a 'Fire' button, and so I thought, 'What else could a button do?' I'm a baseball fan, so I thought, 'Throw.' But throw what? I thought, 'Food!' Once I had the idea for *Food Fight*, I immediately realized it was a great name and idea, so I was inspired to create the game quickly before someone else did."

Hurd also discussed the collaborative process of game design: "When I first put up the high score table on *Food Fight*, its title was something generic like 'Food Fight High Scorers.' Mike Feinstein said, 'Why don't you call it something more interesting, like 'Fabulous Food Flingers'?' A few minutes later I changed the title, and that's what stuck."

According to Hurd, Tom Westberg and Larry Dennison designed the hardware, Patty Goodson wrote some of the music (including the instant replay theme), and "Roy Groth designed the sound hardware and developed many of the sounds, such as the food 'splatting' sound."

The Atari 7800 version of *Food Fight*, a game adored by most fans of the system, is very faithful to the arcade original in terms of gameplay and level design, despite a few differences. Unlike the coin-op game, the level select menu in the 7800 version doesn't have ice cream flavors to cycle through. Also, the arcade game has richer, more colorful graphics and more elaborate intro screens. This is nitpicking, though, as the port, which offers four skill levels (beginner, intermediate, advanced, and expert), is a blast to play. As in the coin-op semi-classic, the layout of the manholes and food is different in each of the 16 selectable levels.

As Tom Zjaba of Tomorrow's Heroes (tomheroes.com) wrote, *Food Fight* is "a great port of a great game and one of the reasons to own an Atari 7800." The *Food Fight* review in issue #5 (May/June, 1992) of the *Digital Press* fanzine,

written by Kevin Oleniacz, ends with the following: "With plenty of food to toss, and with comical antagonists present, you can't go wrong with this cart. This is arguably the best arcade translation ever for a classic system."

While I'm not quite ready to crown *Food Fight* the king of all classic arcade ports, it is a game I go back to from time to time, trying to boost my high score. The food is fun to throw, the chefs and food projectiles are fun to dodge, and the action is non-stop, giving owners of the oft-criticized 7800 some much-needed bragging rights.

In 2010, Microsoft made the 7800 version of *Food Fight* available as a downloadable title for the Xbox 360 Game Room service. The game is also built into the original Atari Flashback console (2004).

FUN FACT:

According to atariprotos.com: "Back in 1981 a small company known as General Computer Corporation (GCC) began to sell enhancement kits for Atari's latest smash hit coin-op *Missile Command*. While the public applauded their efforts of breathing new life into the game, Atari was less than amused. As a result, Atari sued GCC for hacking their game, but in a strange twist of fate the two companies actually became partners! GCC agreed to develop three arcade games for Atari (*Food Fight*, *Quantum*, and *Nightmare*)…of these three games, *Food Fight* is most well-known with *Quantum* being released in only limited quantities and *Nightmare* not being released at all."

WHY IT MADE THE LIST:

A charming and challenging action title, *Food Fight* is a great reason to fire up the Atari 7800. It's also a nice change of pace from the many violent shooters produced over the years.

CHAPTER 36

FORTRESS OF NARZOD

VECTREX
GENRE: NON-SCROLLING SHOOTER
PUBLISHER: GCE
DEVELOPER: GCE
1 OR 2 PLAYERS (ALTERNATING)
1982

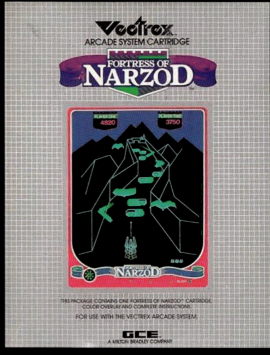

Fortress of Narzod for the Vectrex, complete in box. $70.

"…FAST-PACED, WITH ABOVE AVERAGE GRAPHICS AND UNUSUAL PLAY MECHANICS."

During The Golden Age of Video Games, countless arcade and console titles mimicked *Space Invaders* (1978) and *Galaxian* (1979), with players firing at waves of aliens (or other objects) appearing near the top of the screen and advancing or swooping downward. Many of these games were great, such as *Galaga*, *Phoenix*, and *Demon Attack*, but few of them veered very far from the tried and true formula.

Enter *Fortress of Narzod* (programmed by John Hall), an ingenious old-school shooter that is both great and highly original.

After firing up the game and viewing the title screen, which features a truncated rendition of Wagner's "Ride of the Valkyries" (also heard in *Satan's Hollow*, another brilliant and original take on the genre), gamers will select number of players (1 or 2 alternating) and skill level: 1, 2, or 3 (stick with 1, especially if you are a beginner—it's plenty challenging).

Fortress of Narzod is a non-scrolling game, but it has a nice sense of progression, thanks to its unique structure. The playfield is a series of three mountainous roadways leading to the titular fortress at the top of the screen, which is home to a Mystic Hurler, who is essentially a boss character in an era when bosses were extremely rare (*Zaxxon* has a boss, but not many other games did).

Once all three roadways are complete, gamers go one-on-one against the Mystic Hurler, who moves back and forth, firing Spikers downward at the player's ship. To destroy Mystic, which gives you a much-needed extra hovercraft, you must shoot him six times.

The boss scene is fun, but I'm getting ahead of myself. In the first level of the game, players guide a hovercraft around the base of the Lower Roadway, firing upward at DoomGrabbers (little spaceships that look like pincers) which, like all guardians of the fortress, release spinning, zigzagging Spikers. After all the DoomGrabbers have been destroyed, players must face the Tarantulas and then the Ghouls.

The second level, called the Middle Roadway, adds Warbirds to the mix. Warbirds are deadly, of course, but when you shoot them while they are directly over the roadway, they freeze (temporarily before they disappear) and act as shields against the Spikers. In addition, the Middle Roadway adds the element of Spikers that split in two when shot, doubling the danger.

The Upper Roadway, level three, is similar to the Middle Roadway, but with greater numbers of enemies. Also, the Warbirds are now more hostile, firing bullets when they get within range of your ship.

So, what exactly makes *Fortress of Narzod* so unusual? Isn't it just more shooting and dodging like we've seen in so many other games? I say thee nay!

The zigzagging, mountainous roadway layout is unique, giving the game a distinctive look, but it is more than just an aesthetic flourish. Bullets and enemies bounce off the walls,

Back of the *Fortress of Narzod* box.

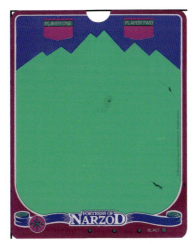
Fortress of Narzod screen overlay. $15.

Vectrex magazine ad.

keeping players on their toes when it comes to maneuvering the ship and firing bullets. Players can also ricochet bullets off walls and into enemies, which is a useful and rewarding strategy. Holding down button 4 allows continuous fire, but this should be used judiciously, since it's all too easy to ricochet a bullet up off a wall at the top of the screen and down into your own ship.

Of course, there are other shooters with ricocheting bullets (*Combat*, *Frenzy*, and *Omega Race* come to mind), but *Fortress of Narzod* uses this gameplay mechanic in a highly original way. I also like that the game lets you move up and down as well as horizontally (a la *Centipede* and *Gorf*), a maneuver that frequently comes in handy in dodging enemy ships and projectiles.

To illustrate level progression, players enter the doorway at the top of the screen. This is a freebie—no challenge involved—but it does give the player a sense of advancement, and it's kind of a fun little breather in between the intense shooting and dodging action required to play the game well.

Among the classic gaming community, I'm far from alone in my appreciation of *Fortress of Narzod*. Here are some accolades from around the web:

> Immensely fun and relentlessly challenging…a must have…entirely original…a shooter I can play over and over again.
> —The Video Game Critic
> (www.videogamecritic.com)

> One of the best games available for the venerable Vectrex…addictive, unique, frantic, and fun.
> —Krooze L-Roy
> (www.krooze.wordpress.com)

> Excellent 3D graphics…challenging gameplay with a frenzied attack of enemies…if you only ever play one Vectrex game, *Narzod* is worthy of your consideration.
> —Vinvectrex
> (www.retroist.com)

In terms of print publications, the Digital Press staff, in issue #6 (July/Aug., 1992) of the *Digital Press* fanzine, called the Vectrex classic "one of the best for the system…fast-paced, with above average graphics and unusual play mechanics."

In a review published in *Electronic Fun with Computers & Games* Vol. 2 #1 (Nov., 1983), Marc Berman said the game has an "original concept" and that, "It comes very close to being a great game, except for one thing: It's so darn hard to win." He also praised the game's visuals, saying, "Vectrex graphics have never looked better."

If you are tired of *Space Invaders*, *Centipede*, *Gorf*, *Demon Attack*, and the like, but you love classic shooters, give the highly original *Fortress of Narzod* a spin—you'll be glad you did.

FUN FACT:
Fortress of Narzod was a Vectrex exclusive upon release, but, in 2009, it was ported to the Commodore 64 by a German company called Tristar & Red Sector Incorporated.

WHY IT MADE THE LIST:
In addition to being a formidable challenge and tons of fun, *Fortress of Narzod* is one of the most original shooters of the era.

CHAPTER 37

FREEWAY

ATARI 2600
GENRE: ACTION
PUBLISHER: ACTIVISION
DEVELOPER: ACTIVISION
1 OR 2 PLAYERS (SIMULTANEOUS)
1981

Freeway for the Atari 2600 game cartridge. $5.

"THE GRAPHICS AND THE SOUND MAKE THIS GAME HIGHLY ENTERTAINING AND GOOD FUN FOR EVERYONE, NOT JUST KIDS."

With the possible exception of *Dodge 'Em*, *Freeway* is the most simplistic form of interactive entertainment listed in this book. The game has each player pushing up on the joystick to get a chicken across a horizontal, 10-lane, top-down street. Pulling down on the joystick makes the chicken back up. Once the chicken reaches the top of the screen, the player will get a point and the chicken will start again at the bottom.

Player one guides the chicken on the left side of the screen, while player two controls the one on the right. After two minutes and 16 seconds have passed, the game will end, and the player with the most points wins. When playing by yourself, which is nowhere near as fun, the other chicken just sits there while you go for a high score.

Freeway plays something like *Frogger*, but is more rudimentary as there's no left or right movement, no bays to jump into, no mates to jump on (in fact, no jumping at all), no way to drown, and no enemies other than vehicles. Getting run over by a car or truck moves the chicken down a lane (difficulty "B") or all the way to the bottom of the screen (difficulty "A").

Designed by David Crane (*Dragster*, *Fishing Derby*), *Freeway* answers that age-old question of "Why did the chicken cross the road?" It's apparently because gamers, wanting points, pushed the joystick. *Freeway* is fun *because* it's simple. When two players of similar skill go at it head-to-head, it's a pure, thoroughly engaging challenge, as the gamer with the best concentration and timing and the fastest reflexes has the distinct advantage—a trademark of classic gaming at its finest.

When Crane was designing *Freeway*, Activision president Jim Levy suggested incorporating traffic patterns from real United States thoroughfares. As such, by toggling the select switch, players can choose from eight game variations: Lake Shore Drive, Chicago, 3 A.M.; Interstate 5, Seattle, 6 A.M.; Santa Monica Freeway, Los Angeles, 10 A.M.; Bayshore Freeway, San Francisco, Midnight; John Lodge Expressway, Detroit, 9 P.M.; The Beltway, Washington, D.C., 6 P.M.; LBJ Freeway, Dallas, 5 P.M.; and Long Island Expressway, New York City, 3 A.M.

Regardless of the city, each roadway is gray and flat. My wife (who calls *Freeway* "the chicken game") and I chuckled over the inclusion of LBJ Freeway, which is pretty close to where we live in Fort Worth, Texas. Trust me when I say the video game version of the highway looks nothing like the real thing, though the traffic patterns from that time may have been similar—who can say?

Seriously, though, the variations are a big plus when it comes to challenge and replay value as each game varies according to the amount and speed of the traffic. In games five through eight, the speeds of the vehicles are increased and decreased at random, making for an especially fun time for veteran players.

The streets may be a boring gray color (you were expecting rainbows?), but *Freeway* nevertheless has nice audio/visuals (it was the first Atari 2600 game to animate 24 sprites simultaneously). The chicken is only vaguely recognizable as such, but the cars and trucks are nicely drawn and, despite moving fast and crowding the screen at times, are entirely lacking in flicker. The car horns sound surprisingly

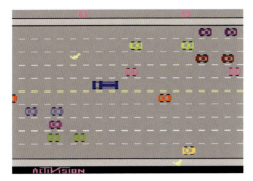
Getting the chicken across the road in *Freeway* for the Atari 2600. *Courtesy of AtariAge.com.*

Freeway magazine ad. *Courtesy of Digital Press (digitpress.com).*

Freeway instruction manual. $2.

realistic, and when a chicken gets run over, it emits a sadly amusing "cheep cheep" sound.

In issue #1 (summer, 1983) of the British publication, *TV Gamer*, the writer praised *Freeway* as an all-ages game, saying, "The graphics and the sound make this game highly entertaining and good fun for everyone, not just kids."

Jim Leonard, writing in *Video Game Collector* #8 (spring, 2007), discussed how *Freeway* pushed the Atari 2600 to its technological limits: "Just sit back and try to figure out how David Crane achieved not 4, not 8, but 24 moving sprites onscreen simultaneously, with two vertically moving sprites, with no flicker whatsoever. You can look at a disassembly of the game cartridge and you'll still have trouble trying to figure some of it out."

In *Ken Uston's Guide to Buying and Beating the Home Video Games* (1982, Signet), the author said, "This is a colorful, fast-moving game…[for those] who are into working out patterns and spatial relationships, this game could provide hours of challenge, and even perplexity."

Many people who play *Freeway* assume that it was inspired by the arcade classic, *Frogger*, which came out the same year. However, the "Inside Gaming" feature in the debut issue of *Electronic Games*, which hit the stands during the winter of 1981, tells a different tale:

> The story of Freeway begins at a trade show and convention in Chicago. Dave and some friends accidentally left the convention center from the wrong exit. The only way to get where they wanted to go was to brave crossing the Windy City's busiest thoroughfare at the height of the mid-afternoon crush.
>
> As they bobbed and weaved across the mighty multi-lane road, carefully picking their path lane by lane, someone commented brightly, "Gee, this would make a great video game!"
>
> Crane and his buddies got safely across the highway, but the idea might well have died there. You know, just another passing joke that's soon forgotten.
>
> And so it might have been if fellow Activision designer Larry Kaplan had not experienced a strikingly similar revelation. "Later that day," explains David Crane, "Larry was riding a bus, also along Lake Shore Drive. He saw some poor guy trying to cross it against the traffic, too. The man was going crazy, dodging and darting between cars and trucks, first going forward a little and then backing up."
>
> The sight impressed Kaplan enough that he mentioned it to Dave, who suddenly began to realize that this might, indeed, be the basis for a video game after all.

Crane initially considered having a human character cross the road, but that seemed a little morbid so Activision considered a tie-in with the San Diego Chicken, the mascot for Major League Baseball's San Diego Padres. The deal never materialized, but the chicken idea took hold.

Like *Combat* and *Air-Sea Battle*, *Freeway* is an excellent two-player experience for the venerable 2600. Opinions on the game are mixed, but I agree with the editors of *The Electronic Games Software Encyclopedia* (1983), who called it "excellent" and "outstanding" in every respect.

Freeway has been re-released on a number of compilation discs for various modern systems, including *Activision Classics* (1998) for the PlayStation, *Activision Anthology* for the PlayStation 2 (2002), and Game Boy Advance (2003). In 2012, *Activision Anthology* hit the iPad, iPhone, Android Phone, and Android Tablet.

FUN FACT:

In an interview with Good Deal Games (www.gooddealgames.com) owner Michael Thomasson, *Freeway* designer David Crane said his creation probably owes "some allegiance" to Atari's arcade classic *Space Race* (1973), in which two players race up the screen, avoiding asteroids that fly in from the left.

WHY IT MADE THE LIST:

In two-player *Freeway*, you can't help but laugh and have a good time while you frantically guide your chicken across the road, dodging traffic, trying to get to the other side as quickly as possible.

CHAPTER

38

FRENZY

COLECOVISION
GENRE: MAZE SHOOTER
PUBLISHER: COLECO
DEVELOPER: COLECO
1 OR 2 PLAYERS (ALTERNATING)
1983

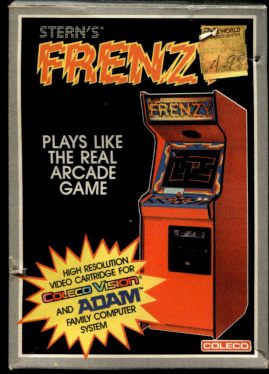

Frenzy for the ColecoVision, complete in box. *Courtesy of Bryan C. Smith.* $40.

"FRENZY IS AN EVEN BETTER GAME THAN BERZERK."

During the console wars of the early 1980s, Atari 5200 owners could boast that their system had a stellar port of *Berzerk*, the 1980 coin-op classic from Stern. While the ColecoVision never went berserk (unless you count playing the Atari 2600 version of *Berzerk* on Expansion Module #1), Coleco fans were in a frenzy over *Frenzy* (based on the 1982 Stern arcade game), an excellent port of the excellent sequel to *Berzerk*.

The game has players guiding a nicely animated Commando through contiguous, non-scrolling maze rooms of a "bizarre, alien high tech structure," shooting skeletons and robotic tanks that shoot back (the enemies shoot each other as well). The Commando can only shoot in the direction he is moving, and the enemies, who roam the mazes and frequently surround you, are fairly intelligent, giving *Frenzy* much of its challenge.

Unlike *Berzerk*, the walls in *Frenzy* aren't electrified, meaning they are not deadly to the touch. Rather, there are solid walls that ricochet bullets (a bullet will stay onscreen through multiple bounces) and there are walls comprised of dots that can be shot and destroyed, which adds an exciting element of play when you need to blast your way through a wall to escape a maze.

The objective in each maze room is to destroy all the skeletons and tanks and escape to a conjoining room. If you stay in a room too long, a bouncing face called Evil Otto, who can go straight through walls, will enter the scene and head toward you.

In *Berzerk*, Evil Otto was indestructible. However, he can be killed in *Frenzy*. One shot removes his smile, a second shot makes him frown, and a third shot is deadly (in skill level 4, it takes four shots to destroy him). Killing Evil Otto, one of the coolest enemies in classic gaming, scores bonus points and is fun, but it brings about a faster Evil Otto.

Certain maze rooms contain a "feature cell" at their center. By shooting this centrally located target, players earn bonus points. Three of the four feature cells affect the onscreen action when shot: the Power Plant freezes robots, the Computer makes robots move and shoot erratically, and the Robot Factory stops the endless generation of robots in that room (in the arcade version, shooting the Robot Factory had no affect on gameplay).

Shooting Big Otto, who smiles when you die, doesn't alter the robots' actions, but killing Evil Otto during the Big Otto feature screen is ill-advised, since four super fast Evil Ottos will take his place and almost surely kill your Commando.

The back of the *Frenzy* box. *Courtesy of Bryan C. Smith.*

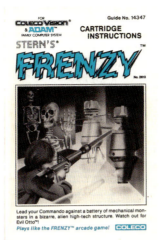

Frenzy instruction manual. $8.

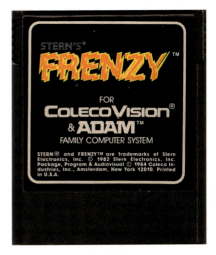

Frenzy game cartridge. $12.

The arcade version of *Frenzy*, which was designed by Alan McNeil, is less talkative than *Berzerk* (also designed by McNeil), and the ColecoVision version is entirely lacking in voice effects (as with the Coleco versions of *Gorf* and *Space Fury*), depriving home gamers of such phrases as "Robot attack!" and "The humanoid must not destroy the robot." This is regrettable considering the fact that such third-party titles as *Sewer Sam* and *Squish'em featuring Sam* had a character who could talk. ColecoVision *Frenzy* does add music, which is nice, and, unlike such early titles as *Donkey Kong* and *Venture*, there is a pause button.

Thanks to more colorful graphics and more strategically inclined gameplay (brought about by the aforementioned ricocheting bullets and walls that can be shot through), *Frenzy* is an even better game than *Berzerk*. Shooting diagonally isn't as easy a maneuver as it should be (something *Venture* fans will sympathize with), but the game is otherwise above reproach, offering shooter fans a formidable challenge and hours and hours of fun.

Jeff Cooper, writing in issue #29 (March/April, 1996) of the *Digital Press* fanzine, agrees with my assessment of *Frenzy*, calling it, "A highly polished and beautifully crafted piece of programming." He also praised the game's audio/visuals. "The graphics are colorful and smoothly animated," he said. "The music and sound effects—right down to the eerie pause music—rate a 10: they are simply fantastic and succeed in creating an atmosphere unlike any other classic game I can think of."

Summing up the game for www.thelogbook.com, Earl Green said, "The ColecoVision plays a damn near perfect game of *Frenzy*, except the bloody thing plays faster than the arcade game." For precision control, Green recommends using Coleco's Super Action Controllers.

In *Video Magic* #139 (June/July, 1998), Chris Federico and Adam Trionfo called the game superior, involved, smooth and varied (referring to the animation), superbly crafted, and consistently exciting.

When *Frenzy* was new in stores, Noel Steere, writing in *ComputerFun* #1 (April, 1984), said the game is "what every good shoot-'em-up fan is looking for—lots of action, a bit of strategy, and lots of surprises…the graphics are just like the arcade…the action is unbelievable."

Frenzy isn't as well known as *Berzerk*, which is fitting considering the plethora of excellent ports of under-appreciated arcade games for the ColecoVision. The game was never produced for another console (which is one of many reasons every retro gamer should own a ColecoVision), but it was ported to the Sinclair ZX Spectrum home computer.

FUN FACT:

The obscure 1982 LP, *Get Victimized*, recorded by R. Cade and the Video Victims, contains a song called "Frenzy," which includes sound effects from the coin-op classic.

WHY IT MADE THE LIST:

Frenzy, ported masterfully to the ColecoVision, is a sequel that is even better than the original game (*Berzerk*, which is also great).

CHAPTER

FROGGER, THE OFFICIAL FROGGER

FROGGER
COLECOVISION
GENRE: ACTION
PUBLISHER: PARKER BROTHERS
DEVELOPER: PARKER BROTHERS
1 OR 2 PLAYERS (ALTERNATING)
1983

THE OFFICIAL FROGGER
ATARI 2600
GENRE: ACTION
PUBLISHER: STARPATH
DEVELOPER: STARPATH
1 OR 2 PLAYERS (ALTERNATING)
1983

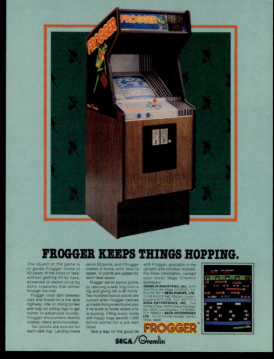

Frogger arcade flyer.

"A HIGHLY ORIGINAL CREATION AND ONE OF THE MOST FONDLY REMEMBERED GAMES OF THE GOLDEN AGE OF THE ARCADES."

Developed by Konami and licensed by Sega/Gremlin, the original coin-op version of *Frogger* hit the arcades in 1981. The game's cute graphics and simple four-way control were inspired by *Pac-Man* (1980), but *Frogger* could hardly be considered a *Pac-Man* clone—in fact, it's a highly original creation and one of the most fondly remembered games of the Golden Age of the arcades.

Viewing the single screen, non-scrolling action from a top-down perspective, players guide a frog up an obstacle-ridden screen, hopping right, left, up, and down, trying to make it into one of five bays positioned along the top of the playfield. In some bays, a deadly alligator will appear while in certain other bays a fly can be eaten for bonus points. Once the frog is safely inside a bay, it's time to do it again until all five bays contain a frog. Once this occurs, the action repeats itself, but is more difficult.

The bottom half of the screen is a busy highway filled with opposing lanes of horizontally moving cars, trucks, buses, bicyclists, bulldozers, dune buggies, motorcycles, taxis,

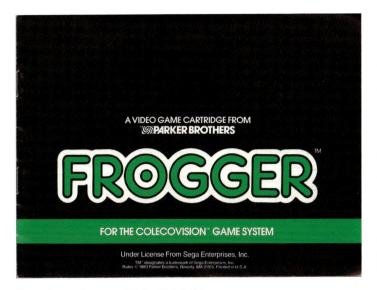
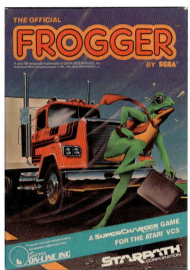

Frogger instruction manual (ColecoVision). $3.

The Official *Frogger* for the Atari 2600, complete in box. *Courtesy of AtariAge.com.* $90.

and/or vans. The vehicles move at varying speeds, so they can be tricky to dodge as you maneuver the frog across the street.

A horizontal stripe in the center of the screen is a median—a safety zone of sorts—but a slithering snake can crawl along this stripe and kill the frog dead.

The top half of the screen is a horizontally flowing river containing floating logs of varying sizes and rows of swimming turtles. To make it across the river, the frog can hop on logs and on the backs of turtles, but some turtles will dive underwater, killing the frog if the frog doesn't hop off before it submerges completely. The frog can also ride on the backs of alligators, but you should be sure to avoid their gaping mouths.

Jumping into the river water is deadly, and players must also be careful to avoid crocodiles, snakes, and otters, the latter creature appearing in later screens. Sometimes a lady frog will appear on a floating object in the river, and the frog can hop on her and escort her across the river and into a bay for extra points (insert "the frog scored" joke here).

When I would go with my older brother to The Land of Oz arcade at the Northeast Mall in Hurst, Texas (near Fort Worth) during the early 1980s, I played *Frogger* fairly often, but I could never beat my brother, who could weave in and out of traffic and hop across the point with lightning speed and pinpoint accuracy. No matter when we would go or how busy the arcade was, he would always play *Frogger*, and he would always far surpass whatever high score was currently on the machine.

Frogger is timed, but in the film *Chasing Ghosts: Beyond the Arcade* (2007), *Frogger* champion Mark Robichek, who scorekeeper extraordinaire Walter Day said has "a cool hand, almost like a Clint Eastwood movie," stressed patience as a key to playing the game well. "With *Frogger*, my style was not to go as fast as I can to get to the home," Robichek said. "My style was, take my time; if the traffic gets a little too busy, backup and start over again. There was enough time for me to be patient, make sure I do it right, and to not worry about going as fast as possible."

Whether you employ the speedy version my brother used or the methodical method preferred by Robichek, there's no doubting that *Frogger* is an all-time classic. When Parker Brothers ported the game to the ColecoVision back in 1983, I eagerly purchased it, knowing that the system had a great track record for arcade conversions. Coleco is obviously the king of ports when it comes to the ColecoVision, but Parker Brothers is no slouch, producing great versions of such classics as *Popeye*, *Q*bert*, and *Tutankham*.

Frogger is, in fact, the best, most accurately translated Parker Brothers game for the ColecoVision, recreating the arcade experience almost note for note (though nitpickers will notice that the colors aren't quite as rich). It has excellent graphics and sound effects and includes lively renditions of the classic folk tunes "Camptown Races" and "Yankee Doodle," which were so memorable in the arcade game.

In the 2006 issue of *Retro Gaming Times Monthly* (retrogamingtimes.com), Alan Hewston, in his "The Many Faces of *Frogger*" article, pointed out that the ColecoVision version of *Frogger* looks almost identical to the TI/99 computer port, speculating that it "was probably programmed by the same person, or ported over from the TI code."

In the original coin-op *Frogger*, the arcade operator could set the game to give players three, five, or seven lives. In the ColecoVision version, players begin with five lives and can set the game to play at a slow or fast speed. In the latter mode, the floating objects start off slow, but increase in velocity after a short period of time. Despite the fact that the music is pleasurable to listen to, it can be turned off.

Programmed by Stephen Landrum, *The Official Frogger* for the Atari 2600 also came out in 1983. To play that game, which was produced as a cassette and published by Starpath, you needed a Starpath Supercharger, which plugged into the 2600 to give it more processing power, and a tape recorder.

When I was a teenager, I had a tape recorder (or at least my sister did), but we didn't own a Supercharger, so I didn't

The back of *The Official Frogger* box. Courtesy of AtariAge.com.

Frogger magazine ad.

get to play *The Official Frogger* until years later. Turns out I was missing a great game that, like the ColecoVision version, was extremely faithful to the arcade original.

In *The Official Frogger*, which is the hardest Supercharger game to find, you begin the game with seven lives. When the difficulty switch on the 2600 console is in the "A" position, you lose a life when you float beyond the edge of the river, as in the original *Frogger*. However, when it's in the "B" position, you'll simply appear on the other side of the screen, making the game much easier. Like all Supercharger games, *The Official Frogger* was republished as part of the *Stella Gets a New Brain* CD (1996).

In 1982, Parker Brothers released *Frogger* for the Atari 2600 in standard cartridge form (as opposed to Starpath's *The Official Frogger* cassette). The game has the expected graphical shortcomings (flickering, ovals instead of turtles), and the otters are missing, but the gameplay is spot-on, and it includes some features not seen in the arcade game, such as the difficulty switch options found in *The Official Frogger*, along with a special Speedy Frogger mode.

The Atari 5200 version, released in 1983, looks nice, and it has two game speeds. However, to use the infamous non-centering Atari 5200 joystick, you also have to press the lower button on the side of the controller to get the frog to hop, which makes quick, precise movements tough to pull off. Luckily, you can use the keypad to control the frog (2 hops forward, 8 back, 4 left, 6 right), and this works quite a bit better, though it's hardly what you'd call arcade-like. As with the Atari 2600 version, the 5200 game's music only plays between levels.

Frogger was also released for the Intellivision (decent gameplay, large, blocky graphics, off-key music, otters included), Game Boy Color (a nice port for a handheld), Sega Genesis (a near-perfect port and the last official release for the system), Super Nintendo (a lazily produced, oddly quiet port), and numerous other systems, plus it had a little-known arcade sequel, 1991's *Ribbit*, which offered two-player cooperative action.

Various remakes, re-imaginings, and sequels have been released for various modern consoles, such as *Frogger Beyond* (2002) for the GameCube and Xbox, *Frogger: Ancient Shadow* (2005) for the GameCube, Xbox, and PlayStation 2, and *Frogger 3D* (2011) for the Nintendo DS.

Personally, I've had a blast playing *Frogger Returns* (2009), a downloadable title for the Nintendo Wii. The controls aren't perfect, but it's a fun, old-school challenge.

The most notable console sequel for retro gamers is *Frogger II: Threeedeep!* (1984), produced for the Atari 2600, Atari 5200, and ColecoVision. You can find this game listed in "The Next 100" section at the back of this book.

The *Frogger* formula is simple, but timeless. If you dig the '80s like I do, you'd do well to pick up the ColecoVision port. Or, if you have a Starpath Supercharger, *The Official Frogger* will certainly suffice.

FUN FACT:

Frogger wasn't released for the Odyssey2 in the U.S., but it was produced for the Videopac, which is the European equivalent of the console; in this version, the highway and the river are on two separate screens.

WHY IT MADE THE LIST:

Sporting simple controls, cute graphics, charming music, and fun gameplay, *Frogger* for the ColecoVision and *The Official Frogger* for the Atari 2600 are terrific ports of an all-time great arcade classic.

CHAPTER 40

GALAGA

ATARI 7800
GENRE: SLIDE-AND-SHOOT
PUBLISHER: ATARI
DEVELOPER: GENERAL COMPUTER CORP.
1 OR 2 PLAYERS (ALTERNATING)
1987

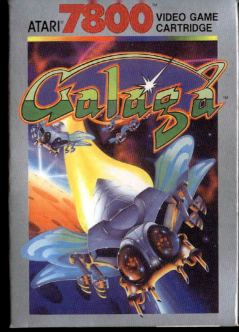

Galaga for the Atari 7800, complete in box.
Courtesy of AtariAge.com. $12.

"GALAGA IS ONE OF THE MOST SUCCESSFUL, MOST VISIBLE (NOT TO MENTION MOST VENERABLE) ARCADE GAMES OF ALL TIME."

Before you play the Atari 7800 version of *Galaga*, rip out the standard joystick for the system and throw it in the trash (your left thumb will thank you). Actually, you'll need to keep it for games that require both fire buttons (and it works fine for certain one-button titles), but set it aside for *Galaga* and plug in your favorite Atari 2600 controller. Or, better yet, hook up a Sega Genesis control pad, prepare to have a blast, and start firing away.

If you're a *Galaga* veteran, you'll want to select the export mode of play, which is faster and more arcade-like than the other two choices: advanced and novice. Speaking of arcade-like, this port doesn't perfectly mimic Namco's 1981 coin-op classic (the colors are a little washed out, the player's ship is smaller, stage indicator badges are now numerals, and the timing is a little off), but it plays enough like that great game to make it a highly enjoyable cartridge.

Along with *Ms. Pac-Man*, *Galaga* is one of the most successful, most visible (not to mention most venerable) arcade games of all time. Many restaurants, bars, and, yes, even arcades still have a *Galaga* machine, and it's frequently cited by joystick jockeys as one of the greatest shooters in the history of the industry, regardless of the era. However, it never made it to the Atari 2600, Atari 5200, ColecoVision, or other pre-NES console, so the Atari 7800 cartridge was a welcome sight when it was finally released in 1987 (it was

programmed in 1984, when the Atari 7800 console was supposed to come out).

The NES has a better, more accurate port of *Galaga* in *Galaga: Demons of Death* (the subtitle is purely superfluous), but *Demons of Death* was released in 1988, meaning it doesn't qualify for inclusion in this book. The 7800 port doesn't exactly earn its place by default (it's a great game), but it helps that the NES game wasn't a part of the equation when I was going through the painstaking process of boiling an entire decade's worth of games down to a measly 100 titles.

Brian C. Rittmeyer, in a review published on the Atari Times website (www.ataritimes.com), is a big fan of the 7800 version, saying he was "once a *Space Invaders* loyalist," but that he's "come to appreciate *Galaga*, especially in its incarnation on the Atari 7800." He said he finds himself "playing again and again" and that "it's among the 7800's arcade translations that can still be enjoyed today."

On a less positive note, Earl Green, via www.thelogbook.com, said the Atari 7800 conversion of *Galaga* is "pretty decent" and that "everything is there," but notes that a home version of *Galaga* should have been released years earlier. "It must've looked pretty silly going up against the NES games that were on the market at the time," he said, "including that system's version of the very same game."

Galaga game cartridge. $5.

Galaga instruction manual. $2.

The player's ship getting captured in *Galaga* for the Atari 7800. Courtesy of AtariAge.com.

Acting on behalf of the Intergalactic Warrior Fleet (the 7800 manual adds the typical-for-Atari sci-fi storyline), *Galaga* has players guiding a "command ship" horizontally along the bottom of the screen, firing upward at waves of ships and bug-like aliens called "Galagans." These airborne enemies fly in various zigzagging patterns out onto the playfield, gather into formation near the top, and then dive-bomb and shoot toward the bottom of the screen, oftentimes directly at the command ship.

Galaga owes its existence to *Space Invaders* (the first game of the slide-and-shoot subgenre) and *Galaxian* (the first *Space Invaders*-type game in which the invaders broke away from the pack to attack the player), but it adds a couple of features to the formula that make it truly spectacular. By letting an enemy capture the command ship, players can then shoot that enemy and regain the ship, giving the player a double ship and, more importantly, dual firepower. Also, the challenge stages, in which the enemies move in creative patterns but can't attack, are a blast to play, especially when your ship is equipped with double missiles.

Regarding my comments earlier that *Galaga* for the 7800 isn't arcade-perfect, I can see The Video Game Critic's (videogamecritic.net) point when he said, "In a way, I like that this version is unique, because I've already played the original one to death…the gameplay is still fast and furious."

This doesn't necessarily excuse the game's shortcomings, but it does present an altered challenge and something of a fresh gaming experience for grizzled *Galaga* fans. Of course, you could say that about a lot of classic console games, but it is a good point and a great reason to keep the old systems.

The original *Galaga*, which was a sequel to *Galaxian*, was followed in the arcades by *Gaplus* in 1984 (also called *Galaga 3* in the U.S.), *Galaga '88* in 1987, and *Attack Of The Zolgear* in 1994. *Galaga '88* was ported to the TurboGrafx-16 in 1989 as *Galaga '90*, one of my all-time favorite console video games.

In addition to the 7800 and NES, *Galaga* has been ported to a number of other home systems, including the Game Boy (bundled with *Galaxian*), Nintendo 64 (via *Namco Museum 64*), and Xbox 360 (via *Namco Museum Virtual Arcade*), among others. The game has also been remade for the Game Boy Color and PlayStation, the latter as *Galaga: Destination Earth*.

Lately, I've been playing a lot of *Galaga Legions*, a modernized version of the game for the Xbox 360. Developed by the same team that created *Pac-Man Championship Edition*, *Galaga Legions*, included on the *Namco Museum: Virtual Arcade* collection (2008), doesn't play a whole lot like the original, but it is great fun.

Despite all these ports and remakes, I still plug *Galaga* into the 7800 from time to time, making sure I have a Genesis controller handy. And, whenever I see the arcade game somewhere, I usually pop in a quarter or two.

FUN FACT:

In *Game Informer* #100 (Aug, 2001), the arcade version of *Galaga* was listed as the 19th greatest game of all time. The writer said, "The fear of getting trapped in a corner by shots, the agony of accidentally shooting your own ship and receiving a measly 1,000 points as compensation, and the thrill of scoring perfectly on a Challenge Stage have not been tempered by time, and the pull of a *Galaga* upright is still an undeniable force for any quarters in your pocket."

WHY IT MADE THE LIST:

Simply put, *Galaga* for the 7800 is a very nice port of one of the greatest arcade games of all time.

CHAPTER 41

GALAXIAN

COLECOVISION
GENRE: SLIDE-AND-SHOOT
PUBLISHER: ATARISOFT
DEVELOPER: ATARISOFT
1 OR 2 PLAYERS (ALTERNATING)
1983

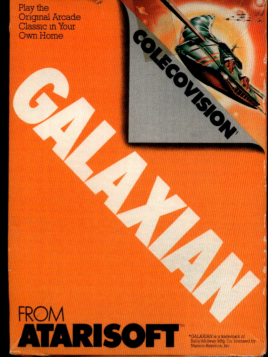

Galaxian for the ColecoVision, complete in box. $140.

"ONE OF THE MOST INGENIOUS, YET SIMPLISTIC STRATEGY ELEMENTS EVER DEVISED IN A VIDEO GAME."

When I was in the planning stages of writing this book, narrowing hundreds of games down to the 100 best, around 50 or 60 titles were no-brainers. Such transcendent games as *Pitfall!* for the Atari 2600, *Lady Bug* for the ColecoVision, and *Super Mario Bros.* for the NES were obvious choices.

Once I got deep into the book, however, I had to make some painful decisions about what to include, what to leave out, and what to relegate to the honorable mentions section (called "The Next 100") at the back of the book. I had all but decided to dismiss *Galaxian*, a game I had grown somewhat tired of, when fate intervened in the form of an online competition.

I was perusing the Retroboards on retrocademagazine.net, where high scores are tracked, and noticed that someone named Jeff Adkins had scored 43,220 on *Galaxian* for the ColecoVision. I knew that was a pretty good score, but not astronomical, so I figured I could beat it. It took the next three or four hours of playing and replaying the game, but I finally beat the score, but only by 400 points. Nevertheless, a win is a win, so I posted my score to the site.

During that gaming session, which I thoroughly enjoyed, it occurred to me how well *Galaxian* has held up over the years, even in the wake of hundreds of similar games that came after it. *Galaxian* isn't my favorite console slide-and-shoot game of the era (2600 *Space Invaders* holds that honor), but it is a great game with one of the most ingenious, yet simplistic strategy elements ever devised in a video game.

Before I get to that strategic element, however, a little history is in order. Namco produced the original arcade version of *Galaxian* in Japan in October of 1979. Midway brought the game to the United States in December that same year, introducing a number of "firsts" to American gamers.

According to *Supercade: A Visual History of the Videogame Age 1971-1984* (2001, The MIT Press), *Galaxian* was the "first video game to display graphics in three-channel RGB color." The logical extension of the slide-and-shoot concept pioneered by *Space Invaders*, *Galaxian* was also the "first to introduce attack formations—enemies that would break off from the marching rows of invaders to swoop down toward the ship—a popular gameplay device that was later used in such classic games as *Phoenix* [1980], *Radarscope* [1980], *Galaga* [1981], and *Gyruss* [1983]."

 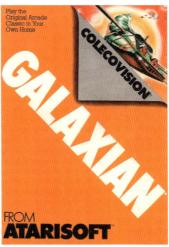 

Galaxian game cartridge. $45.   *Galaxian* instruction manual. $20.   *Galactic Invasion* for the Astrocade, complete in box. $10.

Further, in an article entitled "The Evolution of Space Games: How We Got from *Space Invaders to Zaxxon*," published in *JoyStik* magazine #1 (Sept., 1982), the writer said that *Galaxian* introduced a "strong evolutionary concept" in the form of "enemies with individual personalities."

While the word "personalities" may be a bit of a stretch, the enemies in *Galaxian* do have varying behaviors, which gets us back to the strategic element I mentioned earlier. As you guide your ship left and right along the bottom of the screen, firing upward at rows of invaders, some of which break off kamikaze-like toward your "intergalactic command ship" (as it's referred to in the ColecoVision port's manual—the arcade version is called a "Galaxip"), you'll notice a couple of yellow enemies at the top of the formation.

When one of these yellow ships attacks, it is often accompanied by a pair of red ships. If you shoot both red ships prior to shooting the yellow ship as the trio descends, the yellow ship will be worth 800 points, which is a lot in this relatively low-scoring game. This is a fun strategy to employ, but it is also risky; part of the expertise of the great *Galaxian* player is to know when to try and shoot down the trio and when to stay out of the way.

In addition, ships that are in attack mode are worth more points when destroyed than ships in formation, and a patient player with good aim will take advantage of this when shooting for a high score.

The ColecoVision version of *Galaxian*, which Tracie Forman of *Electronic Games* magazine called "solid gold" (Oct., 1984 issue), is one of the most faithful arcade ports of the 8-bit era, emulating the graphics and sounds almost note for note, even improving upon the original in some areas, as The Video Game Critic (videogamecritic.com) notes: "This adaptation of the classic space shooter is absolutely superb in every way. Your ship's explosion is impressive—far better than the arcade. What really makes the game special is the speed. Your shots move much faster than the arcade game, but this is offset by the aliens, who are faster and more aggressive."

In the audio department, Forman pointed out that the "alien's high-pitched attack squeals have been modified to suit the ColecoVision sound capabilities," but that this "minor change has no bearing on the game's play-action or its overall enjoyability."

When I play ColecoVision *Galaxian*, which was programmed by James Eisenstein, I replace the standard Coleco joystick with a controller for the Personal Arcade, which is a console manufactured by Telegames that plays most ColecoVision cartridges (Telegames bought the rights to the ColecoVision console following The Great Video Game Crash of 1983). This NES-like D-pad works very well with slide-and-shoot titles and is less tiring on the hands.

One thing to be careful of when playing *Galaxian* on the ColecoVision is the keypad controls. The # key will pause the game, which is nice, but the * key will reset the game, even during the middle of play. This is a convenient feature, but be sure not to reset the game when you are just trying to pause it. The keypad also lets you select from three skill levels: novice, intermediate, and advanced.

Galaxian was also produced for the Atari 2600 and Atari 5200. The 2600 version, which lets you turn continuous fire on and off, is pretty decent, despite the lack of a starry playfield and the inclusion of a superfluous and distracting orange border. The 5200 port, on the other hand, "looks, plays, and sounds more like an unauthorized knockoff than an official port," as I wrote in my first book, *Classic Home Video Games, 1972-1984* (2007, McFarland Publishers). If you do play the 5200 version, be sure and use the Trak-Ball for precise, accurate control (the standard non-centering joystick is a nightmare in this game as the ship frequently moves of its own accord).

Considering the next-gen console wars of the early 1980s, it's fairly amusing that Atari did a far superior job in porting *Galaxian* to the ColecoVision than they did their own 5200 console.

Galaxian was also ported to the Bally Astrocade. That version, which was later called *Galactic Invasion* because of copyright issues, definitely has the three "F"s: fast, furious, and fun. It has excellent sound effects as well. However, the game only has 16 invaders per wave (as opposed to 48), and the phalanx of invaders is closer to the player's ship, giving the action something of a claustrophobic feel.

The original coin-op *Galaxian*, which was created by Kazunori Sawano (designer), Kōichi Tashiro (programmer), and Shigekazu Ishimura (hardware designer), begat a number of sequels, including the great *Galaga* (1981), the very good, but obscure *Gaplus* (1984, a.k.a. *Galaga 3*), the incredible *Galaga '88* (1987), and *Galaxian 3* (1990). It was also released for numerous modern consoles through the various *Namco Museum* collections.

As I mentioned earlier, ColecoVision *Galaxian*, which is a hard game to find nowadays, was a close call in making it into this book, but, like *Pac-Man* for the NES, it's a largely accurate port that has, surprisingly, stood the test of time. Just be sure and steer clear of the 5200 version, especially if you don't own a Trak-Ball.

FUN FACT:

In 1995, a nice port of *Galaxian* was released for the original Game Boy as part of the *Arcade Classic No. 3: Galaga/Galaxian* cartridge.

WHY IT MADE THE LIST:

A pick-up-and-play title that requires good aiming and a bit of strategy for scoring big, *Galaxian* has a simple formula that still works, especially when played on the ColecoVision.

CHAPTER 42

GHOSTS 'N GOBLINS

NES
GENRE: SIDE-SCROLLING PLATFORMER
PUBLISHER: CAPCOM
DEVELOPER: MICRONICS (UNCREDITED)
1 OR 2 PLAYERS (ALTERNATING)
1986

Ghosts 'n Goblins for the Nintendo NES, complete in box. $50.

> "EMBELLISHED WITH A TERRIFIC MUSICAL SCORE, GHOSTS 'N GOBLINS IS AN ATMOSPHERIC GAME WITH FIERCE ACTION."

Like *Castlevania*, *Metroid*, and *The Legend of Zelda*, *Ghosts 'n Goblins* is an NES institution, helping define the console as a hardcore system for hardcore gamers. Famous for its extreme—one might say ridiculous—level of difficulty, the game humiliates many of the most nimble-thumbed among us, yet is fondly remembered and still widely played today.

Ghosts 'n Goblins begins with a dramatic introductory scene in which a winged demon called the Red Devil swoops down and kidnaps the beautiful Princess from her lover, the brave Knight, who dons his armor and is ready to get her back at all costs.

Armed with an unlimited supply of javelins, which fire straight to the right or left (depending on which way you are facing), you as the Knight can run, climb ladders, duck, jump, and throw said javelins in rapid-fire succession.

Throughout each of the game's seven brief, but brutal, levels (graveyard and forest, town, caves, bridge, castle lower level, castle upper level, final boss), there are jars hiding five different weapon types: javelins, torches (which form an arc when thrown), swords (which are similar to javelins, but faster), axes (which form an arc when thrown), and crosses (which fly straight). When the Knight picks up a weapon, he forfeits the one he was holding, and he keeps the new weapon even after he dies (which can be good or bad depending on which weapon you prefer).

Embellished with a terrific musical score, *Ghosts 'n Goblins* is an atmospheric game with fierce action. Zombies come out of the ground and attack. Ravens stand on tombstones and fly toward you. Green monsters open their mouths to fire projectiles. Forest ghosts fly and throw spears. Flying knights move up and down and are protected by shields. Big Man fires hard-to-dodge projectiles horizontally and downward. Tower Monster shoots out of both of his faces. Finally, Satan must be shot eight times, and The Devil must be shot 10 times.

And there are other enemies and bosses that make staying alive tough, including the requisite bats, dragons, and skeletons. Moving platforms add to the fun and frustration.

Part of what makes *Ghosts 'n Goblins* so hard, other than the quick, frequently appearing enemies, is the fact that the Knight, who is somewhat clumsy, can only fire horizontally. Diagonal shots would be helpful in certain situations, as

The back of the *Ghosts 'n Goblins* box.

Ghosts 'n Goblins game cartridge: $10

Ghosts 'n Goblins instruction manual. $6.

would straight up or down. As the Video Game Critic (www.videogamecritic.com) states, "It's a shame you can't fire upward, because many stages feature multi-tiered platforms with enemies above and below…part of the problem is the controls, which are rigid and unforgiving. It's very easy to get stuck in a crouch position or become caught up on the edge of a gravestone. Taking a hit knocks you back, sometimes sending you into a pit!"

Ironically, this extreme difficulty is part of the game's charm. Most games that are this hard I don't have patience for, but *Ghosts 'n Goblins* somehow gets a pass. After you die, the game shows you a layout of how much longer you have to trek, daring you to stick with it. Unlimited continues with checkpoints that stay intact after a game is over inspire you to keep playing the game "just one more time." Other helpful aspects include "hidden characters" (as the manual calls them) in the form of replacement armor and extra lives.

Perhaps it's the game's comedy that makes the frustration easier to forgive. When the Knight is wearing standard armor and gets hit, he's reduced down to his boxers (another hit will kill him unless he finds replacement armor first). When the Magician casts his spell on the Knight, he becomes a frog. In short, *Ghosts 'n Goblins* may not kill with kindness, but at least it does so with a sense of humor.

Ranked #129 on *Nintendo Power*'s list of "Top 200 Games" on a Nintendo console (2005), *Ghosts 'n Goblins* is a faithful, but imperfect port of the less famous arcade game of the same name, which Capcom released in 1985. The coin-op semi-classic, which was programmed by Nobuyuki Matsushima, has better controls, richer coloring, and less (i.e., nonexistent) flickering, but the games are otherwise very similar.

Ghosts 'n Goblins was also ported to the Game Boy Color, complete with passwords for saving progress. When the "Classic NES" cartridges came out for the Game Boy Advance, I assumed *Ghosts 'n Goblins* would make the cut, but it didn't, at least not in America (in Japan, it was included as part of the series). Luckily, NES *Ghosts 'n Goblins* has made it to the Nintendo Wii, 3DS, and Wii U as part of Nintendo's Virtual Console program.

Ghosts 'n Goblins sequels include *Ghouls 'n Ghosts* (arcade, Master System, Genesis), *Super Ghouls 'n Ghosts* (SNES, Game Boy Advance), and *Ultimate Ghosts 'n Goblins* (PSP). Spinoffs include *Gargoyle's Quest* for the Game Boy, *Gargoyle's Quest II* for the NES, *Demon's Crest* for the Super Nintendo, and *Maximo: Ghosts to Glory* (one of my favorite modern games) and *Maximo vs. Army of Zin* for the PlayStation 2.

As I've mentioned on more than one occasion, I received my original Nintendo NES as a birthday present from my brother in August of 1986 and kept busy for months playing *Super Mario Bros.*, *Duck Hunt*, and *Hogan's Alley*. For Christmas that same year, my parents got me *Ghosts 'n Goblins*, a game I have never beaten, but have had lots of fun trying.

During the late 1990s, when the Internet became ubiquitous, I found out that if you defeat the final boss in *Ghosts 'n Goblins* for the NES, you have to beat the game all over again to battle the true boss. As much as I enjoy the game, I get the distinct feeling that I'll never achieve that goal.

FUN FACT:

In the manual for *Ghosts 'n Goblins* for the NES, and in the original arcade manual, the protagonist is generically called the "Knight" and his girlfriend the "Princess"; later games, such as *Super Ghouls 'n Ghosts*, refer to them as "Arthur" and "Guinevere" respectively.

WHY IT MADE THE LIST:

Although it can be terribly frustrating, *Ghosts 'n Goblins* has enough horror, humor, and hardcore gameplay to make it a legendary NES classic.

CHAPTER 43

GRADIUS

NINTENDO NES
GENRE: SIDE-SCROLLING SHOOTER
PUBLISHER: KONAMI
DEVELOPER: KONAMI
1 OR 2 PLAYERS (ALTERNATING)
1986

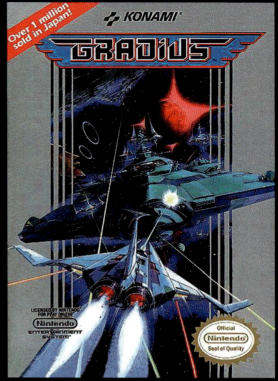

Gradius for the Nintendo NES, complete in box. $25.

"GRADIUS FOR THE NES IS EASILY ONE OF THE BEST SHOOTERS OF THE ERA."

Gradius for the NES is a nicely programmed port of the coin-op classic of the same name, which Konami released to the arcades in 1985. Influenced by such forced-scrolling shooters as *Cosmic Avenger* and Konami's own *Super Cobra* and *Scramble*, each of which came out in 1981, *Gradius* advanced the genre forward with its constant barrage of firing, detailed graphics, lively musical score, and ingenious power-up system.

According to Machiguchi Hiroyasu, who at age 23 was the team leader for the arcade game's development group, *Gradius* was a direct outgrowth of *Scramble* and was inspired by Namco's *Xevious*. "I started off by asking everyone what kind of game they wanted to make," Hiroyasu told shmups.system11.org. "To my surprise, everyone responded 'STG!' [shooting game], and with that we began planning. It was the golden age of *Xevious*, and everyone was driven by the enthusiastic sentiment that, 'If we're going to make a STG, let's surpass *Xevious*.' As for our choice to make a horizontal scroller, it was because we had materials for *Scramble* and decided to reuse those as much as possible. In fact, *Gradius* originally started as *Scramble 2*."

Gradius was a huge influence on Hideki Kamiya, the brains behind *Devil May Cry*, *Resident Evil 2*, and *Viewtiful Joe*. In an interview with www.1up.com, he said:

When you saw *Gradius*, and you'd hear the music, and the sounds, even though they were old-school synthesizer sounds, it was still just amazing—the world, the options. You'd have tons of lasers flying all at once. During summer, whenever I'd find the 50 yen I needed to play a game, I'd hop on my bike and race down to the arcade to play *Gradius*. It so filled my consciousness that even in class I'd daydream about *Gradius* and draw the ships, shooting everything.

Regarding the NES port, *Gradius* was one of the five initial Konami releases for the console, along with *Castlevania*, *Double Dribble*, *Rush 'N Attack*, and *Track & Field*. The game puts players in the role of the sleek and versatile Warp Rattler, trying to save the planet Gradius from the amoeboid Bacterions, a race of beings from the sub-space star cluster of Bacterion. The ultimate goal is to destroy Xaerous, the Bacterion super fortress.

The Warp Rattler flies from left to right, firing at a variety of targets, most notably alien ships that fly in an assortment of patterns and attack from all directions. Other enemies include: Fan (neutral zone patrol craft), Dakker (ambulatory anti-aircraft robot cannon), Jumper (mobile robot), Dai #01

Gradius game cartridge. $8.

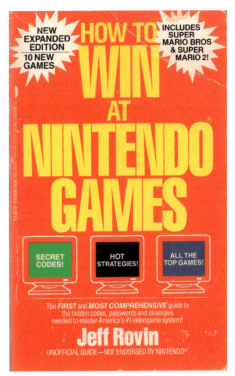

How to Win at Nintendo Games: Updated and Expanded Edition (1989, St. Martin's Press) contains tips and tricks for *Gradius* and various other NES carts.

(anti-aircraft plasma cannon), Tild (midget ring flier), Venus (commando reconnaissance craft), and more.

Levels to battle your way through include: The Volcanic Stage, The Stonehenge Stage (an asteroid belt), The Inverted Space Volcano Stage, The Moai Stage (Moai are huge heads that resemble the Easter Island statues), The Antennoid Stage, The Amoeboid Stage, and The Xaerous Superfortress Stage. Certain areas contain pre-drawn pathways to navigate and/or obstacles that must be blasted through in order to create new pathways.

By shooting certain enemies and eliminating certain enemy formations, players uncover power capsules, which should be grabbed in order to power-up the Warp Rattler. When you get a power capsule, it advances the power boost selection indicator strip along the bottom of the screen. When a desired indicator lights up, players should press the boost button (B) to activate that power boost.

Power-ups include speed up, missile (air-to-surface missiles), double (a double-beam cannon, with one beam firing diagonally upward), laser (a high-penetration laser-beam cannon), option (up to two doppelganger ships), and ?, which is a much-needed force field barrier. By being able to select which power-up to equip, players are given strategic control of their ship. If the player's ship is destroyed, all power-ups are lost, helping make the game extremely challenging.

Thanks to its many attributes and influential gameplay, *Gradius* for the NES is easily one of the best shooters of the era, an opinion shared by many. The Video Game Critic (www.videogamecritic.com) agrees, calling it an "innovative"

and "insanely addictive" game that is "well-designed" and has "superb graphics and audio." Other accolades include:

Nothing short of sensational.
—www.allgame.com

A very deep shooter…one of the best for the console.
—www.nes-bit.com

Wonderful graphics and perfect control.
—Joe Santulli
via the seventh edition of the *Digital Press Collector's Guide* (2002)

Clean and crisp, this NES port worked with the technical limitations of the 8-bit hardware and produced a faithful representation of the original arcade game.
—www.ign.com

Gradius controls just as you would expect from a classic Konami shooter. It's flawless.
—psatoshimatrix.wordpress.com.

Gradius instruction manual. $5.

It'll be a warm day on Pluto before you've completely mastered the intricacies of *Gradius*.
—Jeff Rovin
via *How to Win at Nintendo Games: Updated and Expanded Edition* (1989, St. Martin's Press)

The depth and variety of the game's power-ups was an immediate draw for players back in the '80s, and still holds up today.
—Damien McFarren
Reviewing the Wii Virtual Console release (2007) for www.nintendolife.com

Numerous like-minded shooters followed in the wake of *Gradius*, including *R-Type* (1987), *ThunderForce II* (1989), and *Gaiares* (1990). A plethora of sequels, spinoffs, remakes, and re-releases also followed, most of which kept the basic gameplay intact, but added such elements as humor (*Parodius*), the weapon edit method of selecting weapons (*Gradius III*), portability (the Game Boy version of *Nemesis*, the eShop download of *Gradius* for the 3DS), and home exclusivity (*Gradius Gaiden*, the Japanese game brought to America via *Gradius Collection* for the PSP). PlayStation 2 owners can enjoy *Gradius III and IV*, a disc collecting two arcade games, and *Gradius V*, which features graphics rendered in 3D.

In addition to revolutionizing the shooter genre, the NES version of *Gradius* introduced the famous "Konami Code" (which *Contra* popularized). When the title screen stops scrolling, press up, up, down, down, left, right, left, right, B, A, and Start to begin the game with a full weapons complement.

FUN FACT:

Life Force for the NES is a *Gradius* spinoff, adding vertical scrolling levels and a two-player simultaneous mode.

WHY IT MADE THE LIST:

Ported masterfully to the NES, *Gradius* took the side-scrolling action of *Scramble* and added weapons upgrades and more detailed graphics.

CHAPTER 44

GREMLINS

ATARI 5200
GENRE: ACTION
PUBLISHER: ATARI
DEVELOPER: ATARI
1 OR 2 PLAYERS (ALTERNATING)
1986

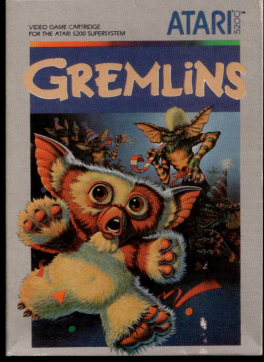

Gremlins for the Atari 5200, complete in box. $35.

"GREAT LOOKING, NICELY ANIMATED GAME."

Faithful to its source material and a heck of a lot of fun, *Gremlins* for the Atari 5200 is nothing less than one of the best movie-based video games ever developed.

Prior to covering the cartridge itself, however, a little history is in order regarding the film (since the game captures the essence of it so well).

Directed by Joe Dante (*The Howling*) and produced by Steven Spielberg (*E.T. the Extra Terrestrial*), *Gremlins* is a "wonderfully demented" (*Terror on Tape*, Billboard Books) movie about creatures run amuck. Inventor Randall Peltzer, played by Hoyt Axton, goes Christmas shopping for his teenage son, Billy (Zach Galligan). Instead of going to K-Mart and buying an Atari console, the man goes to an antique store in Chinatown and purchases a small, furry creature called a Mogwai.

More high maintenance than a dog or a cat, the Mogwai comes with three rules, each of which has reached iconic status as the film's legend has grown: never get it wet (which will cause it to multiply), never expose it to direct sunlight (which is fatal), and never, ever—under any circumstance—feed it after midnight.

After purchasing the Mogwai, Randall nicknames it "Gizmo" and takes it home to his family in the picture postcard-like town of Kingston Falls, New York. If the above rules were obeyed, you wouldn't have a movie, so, of course Gizmo gets wet (from a spilled glass of water) and reproduces. His spawn trick Billy into feeding them after midnight and, after a cocooning process, they hatch into the titular monsters, who ravage the small town in an orgy of cartoonish (if decidedly violent) mayhem—a gremlin explodes in a microwave, among other horrors.

The violent nature of *Gremlins*, which some parents mistook as a children's movie (the cuddly cute Gizmo gave it that appearance), helped lead the Motion Picture Association of America to adopt the PG-13 rating, which was put into use just two months after the release of *Gremlins* (*Red Heat* was the first PG-13 film).

Gremlins opened to mixed reviews and is still divisive in some circles, though it has gotten better in many viewers' minds with age. Some see the film as needlessly violent while others champion its frenzied, frantic nature and its "deft, satiric edge" (*VideoHound's Golden Movie Retriever*, Invisible Ink Press). One of the film's biggest detractors is dark fantasy author Harlan Ellison, who called it "a corrupt thing, vicious at its core, mean-spirited, and likely to cause harm to your moral sense" (*Harlan Ellison's Watching*, Underwood, Miller).

I enjoy *Gremlins* for what it is—a fun horror comedy loaded with references to other films, including *Invasion of*

Gremlins game cartridge. $18.

Gremlins for the Atari 5200 in action. *Courtesy of AtariAge.com.*

the *Body Snatchers* (1956), *The Howling* (1981), *Forbidden Planet* (1956), and *The Wizard of Oz* (1939). In fact, the movie's climax takes place during a Christmas Eve screening of *Snow White and the Seven Dwarfs* (1937). Dante is an avowed film buff, and it shows. An inferior sequel followed, 1990's *Gremlins 2: The New Batch*.

Now, on to the game.

A major departure from the more prosaic Atari 2600 version of *Gremlins*, which featured slide-and-shoot and slide-and-catch gameplay (a la *Space Invaders* and *Kaboom!* respectively), *Gremlins* for the Atari 5200, which was designed by John Seghers, Courtney Granner, and Robert Vieira, is a closed-room (Billy's living room, to be precise) action title containing strategies derived straight from the film.

Players guide Billy as he maneuvers around the room, grabbing Mogwai and taking them to a pen located at the upper/right section of the screen. You can only carry one Mogwai at a time (in addition to Gizmo, who rides in Billy's backpack) and, if you don't watch it, Gremlins will release Mogwai from their cage, making Billy's task harder and more time-consuming. Billy must return all Mogwai to their pen, eliminate all Gremlins, and survive until six a.m.

To destroy Gremlins, which have a tendency to clutter up the screen, Billy can kill them with his sword. This is one aspect of the game that deviates widely from the film, but it's a welcome addition. The combat is challenging and fun, and it predicted the sword-swinging action found in *The Legend of Zelda* for the NES.

In addition to a sword, Billy is equipped with three flash cubes and will gain a new one with each new life (you win a bonus life with every 10,000 points scored). Flash cubes are used for temporarily stunning Mogwai and Gremlins. Also distracting the creatures is a TV set located in the upper/left portion of the screen. The TV turns on when Billy, a Mogwai, or a Gremlin touches it, prompting the creatures within range to stand still and watch it.

Three other mechanical objects affect gameplay. In the lower/right section of the screen, there's a Peltzer Popcorn Popper that spews popcorn that the Mogwai will eat, turning them into pupas and then Gremlins. Walking over pupas makes them disappear, but it's dangerous since they hatch so quickly. A refrigerator also flings out food, and its icemaker spits ice cubes randomly onto the living room floor, melting shortly thereafter. Obviously, the Gremlins and Mogwai multiply if they touch the melted ice.

In my first book, *Classic Home Video Games, 1972-1984* (McFarland Publishers, 2007), I called *Gremlins* a "great looking, nicely animated game" and "an essential part of the Atari 5200 library."

Unfortunately, the game had limited distribution since it was released after the fall of the Atari 5200, meaning many owners of the system have never played it.

According to the seventh edition of the *Digital Press Collectors Guide* (2002), "*Gremlins* was actually completed in June, 1984 but not released until 1986. The reason: the game was released to manufacturing the day before the Tramiels took over Atari and halted all game manufacturing. Rumor has it that Steven Spielberg was pissed and his company, Amblin Entertainment, tried to buy the product, but Atari wouldn't sell. *Gremlins* was supposed to be released in conjunction with the movie along with a promotional campaign for Like Cola."

Most people who have actually played *Gremlins*, including me, like it a lot.

Giving the game a rating of 9 out of 10, Karlis Povisils of Atari Gaming Headquarters (atarihq.com) called it "incredibly addictive" with "good graphics, sound, and music." Gregory D. George of The Atari Times (ataritimes.com) said it's one of the few movie-to-game translations he enjoys, citing its adherence in spirit to the film and its superb animation and sound.

The Video Game Critic (videogamecritic.com) gave *Gremlins* an "A" for its "ominous musical theme," "well-animated characters," and fun, frantic, intense gameplay. In issue #15 (Nov./Dec., 1993) of the *Digital Press* fanzine, Edward Villalpando said it is "one of the best games made for the Atari 5200" and that the "graphics seem to exceed the capabilities of the system, putting more than 30 moving objects on the screen at once, without flickering."

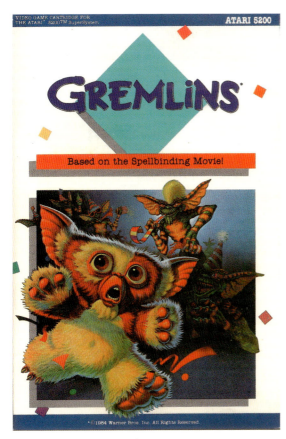

Gremlins instruction manual. $8.

Going back a couple of decades, Tracie Forman, writing in *Electronic Games* magazine # 29 (Nov., 1984), said *Gremlins* "has all the thrills, chills, and offbeat sense of humor that kept the lines so long at the box office." She also called it a "rare find for action lovers, requiring split-second decision making and skillful swordplay to survive…one of the best games ever made for the 5200." (Since the *Digital Press* guide claims *Gremlins* didn't hit stores until 1986, Forman apparently had access to an advance review copy.)

When one thinks of Atari and movie adaptations, visions of the infamously bad *E.T. The Extra-Terrestrial* for the 2600 typically come to mind. It's a shame more gamers don't know about *Gremlins*, one of the few original, console-exclusive titles for the Atari 5200.

FUN FACT:

Gremlins Gizmo, a collection of mini-games based on the original *Gremlins* film, was released for the Nintendo DS and Nintendo Wii in 2011.

WHY IT MADE THE LIST:

Not only is *Gremlins* a gem in the crown of the Atari 5200, it's one of the best movie-based video games ever made.

CHAPTER 45

H.E.R.O.

ATARI 2600
GENRE: ACTION/ADVENTURE
PUBLISHER: ACTIVISION
DEVELOPER: ACTIVISION
1 PLAYER
1984

COLECOVISION
GENRE: ACTION/ADVENTURE
PUBLISHER: ACTIVISION
DEVELOPER: THE SOFTWORKS
1 PLAYER
1984

H.E.R.O. for the ColecoVision, complete in box. $35.

"TEXTURED TUNNELS, DETAILED PLANT LIFE AND LAVA, NICELY ANIMATED CREATURES, AND CRAGGY ROCKS."

A game that calls to mind such properties as *Raiders of the Lost Ark* (1981), the Rocketeer (a comic strip character created by Dave Stevens), and *King of the Rocketmen* (a Republic serial from 1949), H.E.R.O. does indeed put you in the role of a hero—named, appropriately enough, Rod Hero—rescuing miners trapped "miles under the surface of the earth."

To hover and fly through the underground tunnels and caves, you are equipped with a helicopter backpack, which the manual calls a "prop-pack." In addition, you tote a limited number of dynamite sticks, which are used for blowing up cave walls that act as barriers. To shoot the various creatures inhabiting the caves, your helmet fires "microlaser" beams.

Lava rivers and molten magma deposits should be avoided, and if you touch or shoot a lantern, that section of the mine goes dark, making your task more difficult. Rescuing a miner completes the level and refills your fuel tank, and you earn extra points for each dynamite stick that you don't use.

If you run out of dynamite, but still need to blast your way through barrier walls, you can do so with laser beams, but this is a slower method. It's all too easy to accidentally push the dynamite button instead of the laser button, so focused concentration is a crucial component of the game. The action gets tough beginning with level seven, and only the best of players will make it to the 10th level and beyond, where hazards, dark areas, and blocked passages increase in number.

John Van Ryzin programmed the original Atari 2600 version of H.E.R.O. In the instruction manual for the game, he provides the following tips:

- The dynamite R. Hero carries is potent. He doesn't need to be right next to a wall in order to blow it up.
- If R. Hero runs out of dynamite, he can burn through walls with the microlaser beam. The closer he stands to a wall, the faster he'll break through.
- If a lantern goes out, find mineshafts by looking at rough edges along the bottom of the screen.
- When flying above the river, ride the ceiling by pushing up as well as to the left or right.

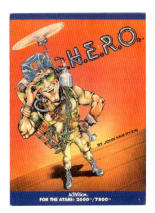

H.E.R.O. for the Atari 2600, complete in box. *Courtesy of AtariAge.com.* $45

H.E.R.O. game cartridge (ColecoVision). $18.

H.E.R.O. in action (Atari 2600). *Courtesy of AtariAge.com.*

- Ride rafts whenever possible, since it is easier than trying to go under a lava ceiling.
- A word about tentacles: they don't move fast, so try to outrun them.

In issue #21 (Sept/Oct, 1994) of the *Digital Press* fanzine, Van Ryzin spoke with Tim Duarte about his method for creating games for the Atari 2600. "I would write the program on the PDP-11 [a 16-bit minicomputer] and then compile the program," he said. "It was then transferred, or downloaded to a development system—a box that emulates an Atari 2600. The box had a joystick coming out of it, so I could sit there and play it. I didn't have to burn a ROM. I could make changes to the program on the PDP-11, and transfer it to the box again for testing. Inside the box was a 2600, but a number of 'tools' were connected to it. I could stop the game, and examine what was going on. I could de-bug my program."

For the ColecoVision version of *H.E.R.O.*, Activision handed adaptation duties over to The Softworks, and the company did a great job. Unlike most other Activision-published games, which look virtually identical on the ColecoVision, *H.E.R.O.* takes advantage of the system's extra processing power. As I wrote when I was freelancing for the All Game Guide (allgame.com), the game has "textured tunnels, detailed plant life and lava, nicely animated creatures, and craggy rocks."

That's not to say the 2600 game is ugly—far from it. Consider the words of Dave Giarusso, writing in issue #45 (Jan./Feb., 2001) of the *Digital Press* fanzine: "*H.E.R.O.* has long been my favorite Atari 2600 game, and for good reason...it has incredible graphics and colors that were rarely seen on the 2600 up to that point, no onscreen flicker, and there are lots of levels to explore...an excellent game for players of all skill levels...it was the one game that my friends couldn't believe they were playing on the 2600."

In issue #5 (April, 1984) of the British publication, *TV Gamer*, the writer spoke to the well-roundedness of the 2600 cartridge, giving it 4 out of 5 stars in all four categories—value, graphics, sound, and gameplay—and calling it: "All and all an excellent game."

In *Electronic Games* magazine #27 (Sept., 1984), the late, great Bill Kunkel called *H.E.R.O.* "graphically appealing," "surprisingly endearing," and "a plus on any gaming system."

Of the three console versions produced, the Atari 2600 rendition has the best controls. The ColecoVision game also handles pretty well, but the 5200 game (programmed by Van Ryzin) has controls that are *too* responsive, meaning it's far too easy to run into obstacles when precise movements are called for (thus the exclusion of the 5200 game from this book).

Short for "Helicopter Emergency Rescue Operation," *H.E.R.O.* makes you feel like a true adventure hero (or as close as you can get to that feeling while staring at a TV screen), a rare feat in the pre-NES era of gaming. It's not as famous or as common as such Activision titles as *Kaboom!*, *Pitfall!*, and *MegaMania*, but, like those titles, it belongs in any worthwhile classic video game library.

The Atari 2600 version of *H.E.R.O.* has been re-released on a number of compilation discs for various modern systems, including *Activision Classics* (1998) for the PlayStation and *Activision Anthology* for the PlayStation 2 (2002) and Game Boy Advance (2003). In 2012, *Activision Anthology* hit the iPad, iPhone, Android Phone, and Android Tablet. In 2010, Microsoft made *H.E.R.O.* available as a downloadable title for the Xbox 360 Game Room service.

FUN FACT:

John Van Ryzin, who designed *H.E.R.O.* for the Atari 2600, also programmed *Cosmic Commuter* for the 2600 and *F-18 Hornet* for the 7800.

WHY IT MADE THE LIST:

A good looking and sounding game, *H.E.R.O.* casts the player in the role of an adventure hero and does so convincingly.

CHAPTER 46

THE INCREDIBLE WIZARD

ASTROCADE
GENRE: MAZE SHOOTER
PUBLISHER: ASTROCADE
DEVELOPER: ASTROCADE
1 OR 2 PLAYERS (SIMULTANEOUS)
1982

The Incredible Wizard instruction manual. $3.

"BEST WHEN PLAYED WITH ANOTHER PLAYER."

When *The Incredible Wizard* for the Astrocade hit store shelves in 1982, the Atari 2600 was by far the most popular console on the planet, with the Intellivision and Odyssey2 a distant second and third respectively (the ColecoVision and Atari 5200 would arrive on the scene a short time later). The Astrocade, on the other hand, was an obscurity that the average man (or woman) on the street hadn't even heard of. Unfortunately, this meant that most gamers didn't get a chance to play *The Incredible Wizard*, one of the best cartridges ever produced for any system.

An exciting and dynamic port of Midway's *Wizard of Wor* (1981), *The Incredible Wizard* puts arcaders in the role of a humanoid "Worrior" armed with a "Concentrated Unified-Field Disturbance Rifle," which can only maintain one bullet in the air at a time. The Worrior walks around a series of non-scrolling, single-screen maze dungeons, firing away at three types of standard enemies: Burwors, Garwors, and Thorwors.

Burwors are slow and always visible. Thorwors are fast, and both Thorwors and Garwors are invisible until they are in the same corridor as the player. To help gamers keep track of the invisible enemies, there's a *Defender*-like radar at the bottom of each maze.

After players shoot all the monsters in a maze, a flying creature called Worluck will enter the scene. The Worluck is fast, but always visible and will try to escape. If you manage to shoot the Worluck, you'll get double score for the next maze.

After the Worluck is shot or escapes, the Wizard may appear, firing lightning bolts and disappearing and reappearing. The Wizard doesn't show up on radar and he cannot be avoided—you have to kill him or be killed. Shooting the Wizard shakes the screen for a nice, dramatic effect.

As Digital Press head honcho Joe Santulli pointed out in his review of the game, which was published in *Digital Press* #28 (Jan/Feb, 1996), *The Incredible Wizard*, which is a cross of sorts between *Berzerk* and *Pac-Man*, was released the same year as the "laughably bad" Atari 2600 version of *Pac-Man*, making the cart's excellent graphics, sounds, and gameplay even more impressive in comparison.

The Incredible Wizard is a fine solo title, but it's best when played with another player. Calling the cartridge one of his "top 10 classic games of all time," Santulli did a good job describing the appeal of the two-player mode:

> The two-player strategy in this game can really get intense! Because you can only have one bullet on the screen at a time, you have to plan carefully where and when you want to execute the other player. Once done, you can lurk outside of his little cubbyhole where he will pop out for his next "life." He can wait there for ten seconds, leaving at any time, but is then forced into play by the computer. It's often that two or three more lives will be lost to the lurking player, but eventually one of those damn Worluks will happen by and catch

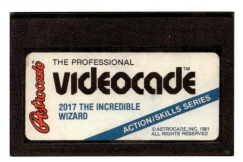

The Incredible Wizard *for the Bally Astrocade game cartridge: $5*

Art for an article on *The Incredible Wizard*, featured in *Videogaming Illustrated* magazine.

Bally Astrocade magazine ad. *Courtesy of Digital Press (digitpress.com).*

him off-guard, then it's out of the hole and back to the hunt. What a game. What a damn good game.

In the Jan., 1983 issue of *Electronic Games* magazine, *The Incredible Wizard* won the "Arcade Award for Best Multi-Player Videogame." The editors called it "the best multi-player game of all time and the best single title ever released for use with the Astrocade…a breathtaking experience."

In *Video Games* #5 (Feb., 1983), Roger Dionne said the cartridge is as fascinating as the arcade version of *Pac-Man* and that it's "at the very top of my TV-game list." In *Playboy's Guide to Rating the Video Games* (1982, PBJ Books) by Walter Lowe Jr., the author gave the game five (out of five) stars, calling it a "very attractive game" with "excellent long-term player interest" and "plenty of intellectual stimulation."

In *Electronic Fun with Computers & Games* #4 (Feb., 1983), Michael Blanchet said *The Incredible Wizard* is "the closest thing to arcade action I've come across in a long time…a must-have for Astrocade owners…a home cartridge has finally done justice to an arcade game!"

Regarding the original arcade classic, Bob Ogden, who designed *Wizard of Wor*, spoke about the genesis of the game to *Electronic Games* magazine co-founder Arnie Katz for the May, 1982 issue, saying, "We wanted to get away from simply moving the gun left and right and shooting upward, and we wanted a game that two people could play together or against each other."

Regarding the memorable voice effects, which *The Incredible Wizard* lacks, he said: "When we put a voice into the machine, that got us into the mythology of who, exactly, was doing the talking. So we invented the Wizard. We used the Wizard to disrupt the flow of the game."

Ogden made the Wizard a "mystery" so that "players would have to work to get at him."

The interview with Ogden also mentioned that the *Wizard of Wor* characters were originally intended to be small, but when he saw *Pac-Man*, a new arcade game at the time, he decided to make the characters larger.

According to the *Digital Press Collector's Guide* #7 (2002), Ogden also designed *The Incredible Wizard*. This would appear to be verified by a 1982 Astrocade, Inc. press release for the game, which says it "comes to you from the same team that designed the famous *Wizard of Wor* coin-op arcade game." However, the instruction manual for *The Incredible Wizard* cartridge says the game was created by Tom McHugh, Scot Norris, and Julie Malan.

Regardless of who created what, *The Incredible Wizard* is a great game and, obviously, a must-own for the console.

Wizard of Wor was also ported to the Atari 2600 and 5200, but under the actual *Wizard of Wor* title. The 2600 version suffers from excessive flickering, odd looking enemies, and the lack of a computer-controlled Worrior in one-player mode (something the *The Incredible Wizard* also lacks), but it still manages to be a lot of fun.

Unfortunately, considering the extra power of the system, the 5200 version looks (and plays) a lot like the 2600 game (sans flickering). Like the 2600 version and *The Incredible Wizard*, it is missing the arcade game's voice effects, which is inexcusable since the 5200 version of *Berzerk* has very nicely replicated speech.

For a near-perfect home version of the *Wizard of Wor* arcade game, complete with voice effects, check out the *Midway Arcade Treasures 2* (2004) collection for the PlayStation 2, GameCube, and Xbox.

However, if you want to go strictly old-school on an obscure console, you'll want to fire up a Bally Astrocade and plug in a copy of *The Incredible Wizard*.

FUN FACT:

As noted on Wikipedia, *Wizard of Wor* (and *The Incredible Wizard*) "begins with a five-note opening from 'Danger Ahead'—the theme to the radio and television series *Dragnet*—with the fifth note only playing on the 'double score dungeon' screen."

WHY IT MADE THE LIST:

The Incredible Wizard may have a different name, but it's a spectacular port of *Wizard of Wor*, one of the most ruthless two-player simultaneous games ever created.

CHAPTER 47

INDY 500

ATARI 2600
GENRE: FORMULA-1/INDY RACING
PUBLISHER: ATARI
DEVELOPER: ATARI
1 OR 2 PLAYERS (SIMULTANEOUS)
1977

Indy 500 for the Atari 2600, complete in box. $25.

"SIMPLICITY IS WHAT GIVES INDY 500 MUCH OF ITS CHARM, AND IT PLAYS WAY BETTER THAN IT LOOKS."

A launch title with the Atari 2600 system (then called the Atari VCS), *Indy 500* was the first console driving game to require the use of a special controller.

When *Indy 500* was new in stores, it came packaged in a large box with two driving controllers, which are similar to the standard paddle controllers, but with two differences: the paddles have stops, while the driving controllers can rotate continuously, and the paddles are paired to a single plug on the 2600 console, while each driving controller connects to a separate plug.

The racing action is viewed from a top-down perspective, with players maneuvering a boxy, mono-colored car around one of several tracks.

As with many early 2600 titles, *Indy 500* has numerous variations. Some are quite different than the others, but all 14 variations maintain the basic gameplay of the first option, which is the Grand Prix Track. In this mode, gamers race around a vertical oval track, trying to be the first player to complete 25 laps. Game 2, Grand Prix Race Track (Time Trial), is for one player, racing around the track as many times as possible in 60 seconds.

Game 3 is the Devil's Elbow Track, which is similar to Grand Prix, but with sharper twists and turns. Devil's Elbow Track also has a Time Trial option, bringing us to Game 5, Crash 'n Score I Track. In Crash 'n Score, players drive around the screen, running into a small square. When the square is hit, it warps to another spot on the screen. The first player to crash into the square 50 times is the winner. A Time Trial mode is available as well.

Game 7, Crash 'n Score II Track, ups the ante with six square barriers on the track (as opposed to two rectangular barriers in Crash 'n Score I Track), making running into the hit square a little more challenging for both players. A Time Trial mode is also available.

Game 9 is Tag-Barrier Chase Track, which, as the title suggests, is a game of tag like you might have played as a kid. However, instead of running, you are driving a car. When your vehicle is blinking, you should avoid getting hit by the opposing player's car as you score a point for every second you are not "it." If you get tagged, your car will stop blinking and you must chase and tag the blinking car. The first player to 99 is the winner. Game 10, Tag-Motor Hunt Track, is similar to Game 9, but with six square barriers on the track (as opposed to two rectangular barriers in Tag-Barrier Chase Track).

Game 11, Ice Spring Track Race, evokes Grand Prix Race Track, but with slippery roads that make steering more difficult. A Time Trial mode is available as well. Game 13, Ice Rally Track, is similar to Ice Spring Track Race, but has more twists and turns. It also includes a Time Trial mode.

While the Time Trial options give *Indy 500* some value as a one-player title, the cartridge truly shines in two-player mode. The driving controller works extremely well in turning the car with pinpoint precision (in *Ken Uston's Buying and Beating the Home Video Games*, the author said the controllers are "excellent for steering games of this type"), and the fire button is perfectly serviceable as an accelerator.

In these days of such feature-rich, photorealistic racing titles as *Forza Motorsport 4* (2011) for the Xbox 360 and *Gran Turismo 6* (2013) for the PlayStation 3, *Indy 500* for the

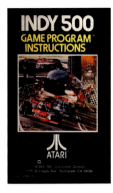
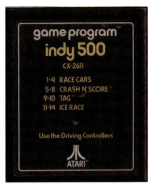
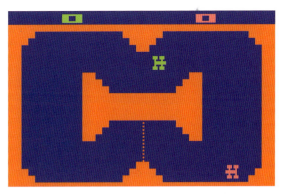

Indy 500 instruction manual. $2.

Indy 500 game cartridge. $3.

Indy 500 for the Atari 2600 in action. *Courtesy of AtariAge.com.*

Atari 2600 can only look primitive to the modern gamer, like comparing a 2013 Lamborghini Aventador to an 18th century steam wagon. However, simplicity is what gives *Indy 500* much of its charm, and it plays way better than it looks.

The Video Game Critic agrees. On his website (videogamecritic.com), he wrote:

> *Indy 500*'s beauty lies in its simplicity, and like wine, this classic racer seems to improve with age. Compared to most modern racers with their complicated control schemes and unpredictable handling, this game is like a breath of fresh air… the action is wild and competitive…After all these years, *Indy 500* is one of the best racing games around, so grab a friend and give it a go.

Darryl Brundage with Atari Times (www.ataritimes.com) said he only paid $10 for *Indy 500* during The Great Video Game Crash of 1983, but from the sound of his review, he would have gladly paid more. "I really like this game, it's a lot of fun, and I'm really pleased that I own it," he said. "Even though the sounds and graphics are nothing spectacular—they're adequate and do their job, and that's pretty much it—but the controls are great."

In *Electronic Games* magazine #5 (July, 1982), in a feature called "Player's Guide to Summer Sports Videogames," the uncredited writer called *Indy 500* "pure action from start to finish," referencing the ice modes as the "most exciting" variations.

Released as *Race* under the Sears Telegames label, *Indy 500* was inspired by such arcade games as Kee Games' (a division of Atari) eight-player *Indy 800* (1975) and Atari's four-player *Indy 4* (1976). Both cabinets were massive and featured steering wheels, pedals, and buttons, the latter used for honking a horn. Other arcade games from the series include *Sprint 2* (1976, Kee Games), *Sprint 4* (1977, Atari), *Sprint 8* (1977, Atari), and *Sprint One* (1978, Kee Games).

In 1986, Atari released the two-player *Championship Sprint* and the three-player *Super Sprint*, full-color arcade games that added such features to the formula as pop-up posts, automatic doors, prize money, and vehicle upgrades.

In 1988, Atari released *Sprintmaster*, an Atari 2600 game with nine tracks, three road surfaces (pavement, dirt, ice), lap number selection (1-50), and the option to have cars bounce off of or crash against the walls. Unfortunately, *Sprintmaster*, which is based on *Super Sprint*, is not compatible with the driving controllers (in fact, *Indy 500* was the only game to make use of the driving controllers), making it far inferior to *Indy 500*.

Indy 500 was designed by Ed Riddle. In the May 11, 2013 episode of Robert Ferguson's *2600 Game by Game Podcast*, the host discusses a conversation he had with Riddle about creating the game. Here's a transcribed portion of that episode:

> When Mr. Riddle arrived at Atari in 1977, The Stella chip for the 2600 was being breadboarded or prototyped. He designed the software development systems that were used to program the first 2600 games. He was asked to program a game despite not having programmed a game before. He was given a program called "drive start" by Larry Wagoner, which was the architectural skeleton of the game. He learned how to program, and he came up with the game variations. Mr. Riddle says he enjoyed learning how to make the cars skid in the ice race variations. He also mentioned that *Indy 500* is largely table-driven, and the playfield, cars, motion vectors, and skid parameters all come from tables.

Although it was released more than three decades ago, *Indy 500* holds up remarkably well and is a must-own for old-school racing fans.

FUN FACT:

In 1982, Atari released *Racing Pak*, a boxed set that includes *Indy 500*, *Slot Racers*, and a pair of driving controllers.

WHY IT MADE THE LIST:

Indy 500 is a nice change of pace from all the complex modern racers. Using the driving controller to guide your car around the twisting, turning, top-down tracks is super fun, especially when you are challenging a friend.

CHAPTER 48

JAWBREAKER

ATARI 2600
GENRE: MAZE
PUBLISHER: TIGERVISION
DEVELOPER: TIGERVISION
1 OR 2 PLAYERS (ALTERNATING)
1982

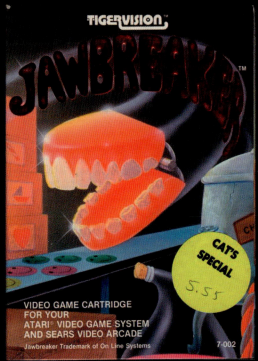

Jawbreaker for the Atari 2600, complete in box. Courtesy of AtariAge.com. $45.

"EXCITING GAMEPLAY, NON-STOP ACTION, AND DEAD-ON CONTROLS."

The original *Jawbreaker* for the Atari 400/800 (1980) and the Apple II (1981) published by On-Line Systems was a *Pac-Man* clone, with players guiding a pair of hungry choppers around a traditional maze (called a "candy store"), eating dots ("sweets") while avoiding, and, when energized, turning the tables on, four round faces ("jawbreakers").

John Harris developed the game, and when he brought it to the Atari 2600 for Tigervision, he changed the formula to make it very different from *Pac-Man*. Some have speculated that Harris altered gameplay to avoid a lawsuit from the litigious Atari, which had sued Magnavox for the similarities of the Odyssey2's *K.C. Munchkin!* to *Pac-Man*, but this isn't necessarily the case (or it only tells half the story).

In an interview published on www.dadgum.com, Harris said, "The 2600 version of *Jawbreaker* had to be written considerably differently from the original computer version, due to the 2600's limitation of only two player objects per line. The game was redefined into a format where I could maintain only one adversary per line and still keep the game enjoyable."

They say that necessity is the mother of invention. With 2600 *Jawbreaker*, Harris didn't reinvent the wheel (so to speak), but the Atari 2600's limitations did force him to be creative in coming up with a decidedly new twist on a well-worn genre.

The set of chomping teeth ("jaws") players control in 2600 *Jawbreaker* eats rectangular dots ("candy bars"), but instead of maneuvering in a *Pac-Man*-like maze, gamers travel around a playfield consisting of nine horizontal rows. In order to move up and down from row to row, each line delineating the pathways has an open doorway that constantly moves left and right at differing speeds (players can also move up and down on the far left and right sides of the screen).

With its horizontal rows, *Jawbreaker* looks more simplistic than *Pac-Man*, but this is deceptive as the movement of the gaps creates a constantly changing maze. This, along with enemies that appear in your path virtually every time you start down a row, creates an unusual challenge. The enemies in question are round twirling faces that are difficult to avoid, but utilizing the gaps can help you evade them. To turn the tables on the enemies, you can eat a vitamin pill positioned at the center of the maze (three will appear during each level).

If you expect to do well in this game, you should work to clear rows while you are energized and eat whatever enemies that happen to get in your way, as opposed to strictly going after as many enemies as possible.

Jawbreaker moves at a hectic pace, so players have to be on their toes and make quick strategic decisions in order to clear a maze. Once all the candy bars are gone (there are 135 per maze), a toothbrush comes out to brush the set of chomping teeth (a cute touch), and it's on to the next

Jawbreaker magazine ad.

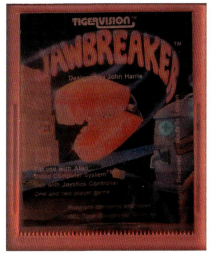

Jawbreaker game cartridge. $18.

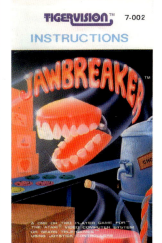

Jawbreaker instruction manual. $8.

level. After clearing two screens, players earn an extra set of choppers (up to three extras total).

As stated earlier, *Jawbreaker* is different enough from *Pac-Man* to stand on its own, but it also provided a nice alternative to the anemic Atari 2600 release of *Pac-Man*, which, though fairly entertaining on some level, disappointed gamers with its blocky title character, puke-yellow mazes, and pale, blinking enemies.

As Perry Greenberg, commenting in *Video Games* #5 (Feb., 1983), said: "Tigervision's *Jawbreaker* is heaven-sent, especially for anyone who's still smarting from the turkey of 1982—Atari's *Pac-Man*." Perry also said the game has "some charm" and that the action is "fast and furious."

With its red cartridge casing and great gameplay, *Jawbreaker* is regarded among collectors and critics alike as a highly desirable title. The Video Game Critic (videogamecritic. com) said it's the "cream of the crop" of *Pac-Man* clones, citing its exciting gameplay, non-stop action, and dead-on controls.

Writing for IGN (www.ign.com), Levi Buchanan called *Jawbreaker* "one of the better *Pac-Man* clones for the Atari 2600…you'll want it to play, not just to stick on a shelf and use as a museum piece." Darryl Brundage of Atari Times (www.ataritimes.com) called it "addicting and fast-paced."

When *Jawbreaker* was new in stores, Arnie Katz and Bill Kunkel reviewed it in *Electronic Games* magazine #13 (March, 1983). The duo loved the cartridge, calling it "definitely recommended" and "the most innovative variant on the maze chase/gobble game ever developed." Further, they enjoyed the game's "state-of-the-art" graphics and sounds, and they said that it was even better than the original computer version.

In *Electronic Fun with Computers & Games* #2 (Dec., 1982), Raymond Dimetrosky said the game is "similar to *Pac-Man*, but not a ripoff…very interesting…colorful…[filled with] personality."

On the other hand, in the second (and final) issue of *Creative Computing Video & Arcade Games* (Fall, 1983), Martha Koppin clearly didn't get the appeal of *Jawbreaker*, saying it is just "another in the apparently unending series of maze games" and that "you only need so many of this variety of game." (No wonder *Creative Computing* only lasted two issues.)

Jawbreaker II followed in 1983 on the Atari 400/800, Apple II, and Texas Instruments TI99/4A. *Jawbreaker II* is similar to, but nowhere near as good as the Atari 2600 version of *Jawbreaker*. In the interview referenced earlier, Harris explained why. "*Jawbreaker II* came later, written by someone else," he said. "The programmer had never seen the 2600 version of *Jawbreaker*, and so [Sierra On-Line founder] Ken Williams drew a quick sketch to show him what to do, but didn't explain it very well. This rough sketch had only five horizontal pathways on it, and so that is all that were programmed into the game…the open passageways at the edges of each line weren't drawn in Ken's sketch, and so they didn't get included in the game."

Though not exactly rare, *Jawbreaker* for the Atari 2600 is one of the harder-to-find games referenced in this book. If you do stumble across a copy, especially boxed with the manual, you should definitely pick it up.

FUN FACT:

Jawbreaker was released for the Commodore 64 in 1983; it's basically the same disappointing game as *Jawbreaker II*.

WHY IT MADE THE LIST:

Although it doesn't veer too terribly far from the *Pac-Man* formula, the expertly programmed *Jawbreaker* adds enough twists to make it a special challenge.

CHAPTER 49

JOUST

ATARI 7800
GENRE: NON-SCROLLING PLATFORMER
PUBLISHER: ATARI
DEVELOPER: GENERAL COMPUTER CORP.
1 OR 2 PLAYERS (SIMULTANEOUS)
1986

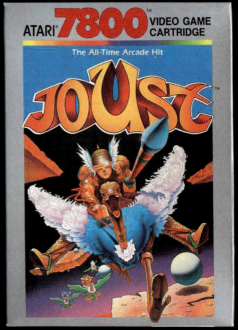

Joust for the Atari 7800, complete in box. $10.

"JOUST IS A TIMELESS CLASSIC THAT IS A BLAST TO PLAY AGAIN AND AGAIN."

A fantastic port of Williams' 1982 coin-op favorite, *Joust* for the Atari 7800 puts players in the role of a bird-borne, lance-wielding Knight, riding an ostrich into battle against wave after wave of Buzzard Riders. To win a joust, you must have your lance higher than your enemy's at the moment of contact. If both mounts are at the same level when contact is made, the joust is a draw.

When you win a joust, the defeated, suddenly rider-less bird will lay an egg, which will float through the air until it lands on a platform or falls into the lava pit below and is destroyed. You should grab the egg for extra points. If you leave an egg on a ledge for too long, it will hatch into another enemy. If you hover too close to the lava pit, the Troll of the Lava Pits can rise up and grab you.

There are three types of Buzzard Riders: the Bounder (weakest of the three types) wears red; the Hunter wears gray; and the Shadow Lord (the most powerful) wears blue. The Buzzard Riders attack in waves, meaning the screen gets crowded at times, making for a tough game. Adding to the challenge is the frequent appearance of a pterodactyl that moves fast and is hard to kill—precise contact is a must, so avoidance is usually a better strategy for the novice.

The *Joust* playfield is non-scrolling and viewed from the side, featuring eight ledges that act as platforms. Guiding the ostrich around the screen is achieved with the joystick, but players must keep pressing the fire button to keep the bird in the sky (the ostrich can stand on and walk across the ledges without the aid of the fire button). The side buttons on the 7800 joysticks make staying airborne a tiring chore, so players should use a 2600 joystick instead.

When compared head-to-head with the arcade version, 7800 *Joust* isn't quite as detailed graphically, but it looks and plays like a champ nevertheless. It has four difficulty levels, and it's an upgrade over the 5200 port (and, of course, the 2600 cartridge). As I mention in *Classic Home Video Games, 1985-1988* (McFarland Publishers, 2009), "the 7800 game features several details that the 5200 version left out, including the engine-like roar of enemies at the beginning of each level and the buzzards that fly in to pick up the riders that hatch from the eggs (in the 5200 game, eggs simply hatch into riders that are already mounted atop buzzards)."

Joust was originally programmed for the 7800 in 1984 by Pete "Kid" Gaston, but it didn't hit store shelves until 1986 (since the 7800 console was delayed until then). It may have seemed dated to many gamers at the time—especially to younger NES owners—but *Joust* is a timeless classic that is a blast to play again and again, especially in two-player simultaneous mode.

Speaking of the NES, it has an excellent port of *Joust* as well, but that version wasn't released until 1988, making it ineligible for inclusion in this book. (Fans of the game should also check out the 1992 Atari Lynx version, which adds a two-player Gladiator mode without enemies.)

As a testament to the greatness of *Joust*, which is one of the finest finesse games ever created, here are accolades for the 7800 version, culled from various sources:

Joust game cartridge. $5.

Joust for the Atari 7800 in action. *Courtesy of AtariAge.com.*

Joust instruction manual. $2.

…a fantastic port, retaining almost everything that made the game a fun experience in the arcade…fast and furious with virtually no instances of slowdown or lag…includes all the little touches of the arcade game—the survival waves, the little quotes [PREPARE TO JOUST BUZZARD BAIT], the bird flying off when you kill its rider…
—DTM Review Archive
(dtmreviewarchive.blogspot.com)

I'm happy to say this version is nearly identical to the arcade.
—The Video Game Critic
(videogamecritic.com)

It looks, sounds, and, most importantly, plays pretty much like its arcade cousin.
—Darryl Brundage of The Atari Times
(www.ataritimes.com)

A great translation of an arcade classic. Another great two-player game, which is one of the strong points of the 7800 system.
—Tom Zjaba of Tomorrow's Heroes
(www.tomheroes.com)

The original arcade version of *Joust* was programmed by John Newcomer (aided by Bill Pfutzenrueter, Jan Hendricks, Python Anghelo, Tim Murphy, and John Kotlarik), who was interviewed about the game as a special feature in *Williams Arcade's Greatest Hits* (1996) for the PlayStation. "Compared to now, we were working with bubblegum and rubber bands and hot glue," he said. "The memory in the game I believe was 96K, which was just nothing. We waste that on title screens nowadays. The real challenge in creating games back then was how do you do something interesting with some nice animation…how do you do it in such a small package, because that doesn't allow us a lot of variety."

Despite that lack of processing power, *Joust* is a masterpiece of classic coin-op programming and was a financial success at the time, selling 26,000 units. A cocktail version was produced, but only 500 were manufactured, making it a collector's item today.

In 1986, Williams released a sequel, *Joust 2: Survival of the Fittest*, which was nowhere near as good. Here's the review I wrote about the game for the All Game Guide (allgame.com):

The sequel to the far more popular, far more common *Joust*, *Joust 2: Survival of the Fittest* is an arcade oddity that plays somewhat similar to the original game. However, it has a number of alterations, most prominently thunderous sound effects and more robust, more detailed graphics. In the sequel, players can transform their mount into a Pegasus, which is stronger but harder to control than the ostrich. Other differences include a vertical (as opposed to horizontal) screen, varied level environments (natural as well as industrial), additional enemies (such as bats and cyber-pterodactyls), and much more. Despite the game's bolder, brasher look, feel and sound, *Joust 2* is more convoluted and less enjoyable than its progenitor. Manufactured during an era of decline at the arcades, *Joust 2* was produced in limited quantities. An estimated 500-1,000 units were released.

In addition to the sequel, *Joust* inspired a number of similar games, including *Balloon Fight* (1986) for the NES and *Sir Lancelot* (1983) for the Atari 2600 and ColecoVision. Speaking of the ColecoVision, Atarisoft created a ColecoVision port of *Joust* back in the day, but it only existed as a prototype until 2001, where it was released in limited quantities at the Classic Gaming Expo in Las Vegas. Unfortunately, it has no sound as the game was never completed to begin with.

FUN FACT:

Like *Space Invaders*, *Joust* had a pinball spinoff; it was called, appropriately enough, *Joust Pinball* (1983).

WHY IT MADE THE LIST:

Adapted in near perfect form for the Atari 7800, *Joust* is a wonderful finesse game that is great fun, whether you play it solo or with a friend.

CHAPTER 50

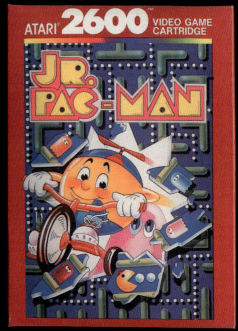

JR. PAC-MAN

ATARI 2600
GENRE: MAZE
PUBLISHER: ATARI
DEVELOPER: GENERAL COMPUTER CORP.
1 OR 2 PLAYERS (ALTERNATING)
1987

Jr. Pac-Man for the Atari 2600, complete in box. Courtesy of AtariAge.com. $10.

"ONE OF THE BEST ARCADE-TO-HOME TRANSLATIONS OF THE CLASSIC ERA."

Most everyone with any sense of video game history knows that the 1981 release of *Pac-Man* for the Atari 2600 was a disaster. Based on Midway's famous arcade classic (1980), which revolutionized the coin-op industry with its cute characters, charming gameplay, and simple, four-way controls, 2600 *Pac-Man* failed its progenitor in almost every imaginable way.

Designed by Tod Frye, who was working under severe time constraints to complete the project, the port was playable (Pac-Man could eat dots and avoid ghosts in reasonably efficient fashion, and fans burned out on the arcade version had a new challenge), but it was plagued by washed-out graphics, a blocky maze that bore little resemblance to the original, and flickering ghosts that were barely discernible in color from one another. Most notoriously, Pac-Man faced sideways while traveling up and down.

Regardless of its flaws, at seven million copies sold, *Pac-Man* was the best-selling Atari 2600 cartridge of all time (*Pitfall!* was second at more than four million). However, 12 million cartridges were produced, making it as disappointing commercially as it was critically (numerous *Pac-Man* cartridges, as well as copies of the also-disastrous *E.T. The Extra-Terrestrial*, were buried in a New Mexico landfill, the famously dubious pinnacle of The Great Video Game Crash of 1983).

Atari rectified the *Pac-Man* situation to some extent with the 1982 release of *Ms. Pac-Man*, which was a far more faithfully adapted port of its respective coin-op counterpart (Midway, 1981) and a superior game overall. Buoyed by crisp controls, colorful graphics, and delightful sounds (purists bemoaned the lack of intermissions, but most could overlook such a minor setback), *Ms. Pac-Man* is one of the greatest Atari 2600 games of all time.

Amazingly, *Jr. Pac-Man* is even better than *Ms. Pac-Man*. A stunning port of Bally/Midway's 1983 arcade game, which was produced without Namco's authorization (Namco developed *Pac-Man*), and which never got its due in terms of widespread acclaim, *Jr. Pac-Man* trumps *Ms. Pac-Man* with faster gameplay, smarter enemy A.I., seven scrolling mazes (as opposed to four non-scrolling mazes), and a sartorial accessory that sets the protagonist apart from his Pac parents: a beanie cap with a spinning propeller.

As Junior Pac-Man travels around each maze, eating dots, he is chased by one, two, three, or four ghosts—Inky, Blinky, Pinky, and Tim (taking the place of Clyde)—depending on the difficulty level selected by the player. When Junior eats one of several power pills scattered about the maze, he can temporarily turn the tables on the pursuant ghosts. However, after a couple of mazes have been completed, the power becomes very short lived, making it tough to gobble more than one ghost.

Instead of edible fruit like in *Pac-Man* and *Ms. Pac-Man*, *Jr. Pac-Man* features toy-shaped candy, including a tricycle, a kite, a drum, a balloon, a train, a kitty, and root beer. The candies roam the mazes and can be snacked on for bonus points. Interestingly, when a toy touches a dot, that dot gets bigger and is worth more points (50 as opposed to 10) when eaten. Players should beware, though, because Junior slows down

Jr. Pac-Man for the Atari 2600 in action. Courtesy of AtariAge.com.

Jr. Pac-Man game cartridge (Atari 2600). $5.

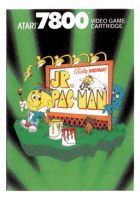

Jr. Pac-Man homebrew for the Atari 7800, complete in box. $50.

while eating big dots, making him more likely to get caught by a ghost. In addition, toys can destroy power pills by simply making contact with them (creating a cool explosion effect).

While *Jr. Pac-Man* is indeed a fantastic take on the coin-op classic, there's no such thing as an arcade-perfect port for the Atari 2600. Niggling differences include: mazes that scroll up and down instead of left and right, the lack of an animated intro scene, maze walls that lack pinstripe outlines, a beanie that is yellow instead of red, and the missing whites of the ghosts' eyes.

Regardless, *Jr. Pac-Man* is a terrific game that critics love.

Writing for The Atari Times, Dan Loosen, praising the cart's quality gameplay and "great graphics," called it "hands-down my favorite *Pac-Man* on the 2600." Dave Mrozek, better known as The Video Game Critic, favors the cartridge over *Pac-Man* (poor graphics) and *Ms. Pac-Man* (too easy), saying, "this time Atari got everything right." Earl Green, who hosts the website Phosphor Dot Fossils (www.thelogbook.com/phosphor/), is also a big fan of the game, calling the graphics, music, and sound effects "absolutely spot-on."

In issue #24 (March/April, 1995) of the *Digital Press* fanzine, various contributors weighed in on *Jr. Pac-Man*, calling it "addictive" and "my favorite *Pac-Man*-style game." In the seventh edition of the *Digital Press Collector's Guide* (2002), the cart is called "one of the most graphically impressive games on the VCS in regards to matching its arcade counterpart."

The Atari 2600 is home to lots of interesting maze titles, most of which were influenced by *Pac-Man*. These include *Alien*, *Dodge 'Em*, *Jawbreaker*, *Lock 'N' Chase*, *Mouse Trap*, *Shark Attack*, and the recently released *Lady Bug*, which is a surprisingly good homebrew of Universal's 1981 coin-op game. However, *Jr. Pac-Man* beats them all in terms of shear arcade quality and entertainment value.

In my article, "The 10 Best Atari 2600 Games," which was published in issue #94 of the late, great *2600 Connection* fanzine, I ranked *Jr. Pac-Man* number one, ahead of such classic carts as *Space Invaders*, *Kaboom!*, and *River Raid*.

In my first book, *Classic Home Video Games, 1972-1984* (McFarland Publishers, 2007), I called *Jr. Pac-Man* "one of the best arcade-to-home translations of the classic era." More telling, I still play the game on a regular basis, trying again and again to boost my high score.

Although programmed in 1984 (by Ava Robin-Cohen of General Computer Corp.), *Jr. Pac-Man* was shelved until 1987, during a resurgence of sorts for the 2600. The previous year, Atari, bolstered by Nintendo's success in the marketplace with the NES, re-released the Atari 2600 in a smaller format.

Euphemistically called the "2600 Jr.," the little system that tried couldn't compete with the NES and such cutting edge titles as *Super Mario Bros.*, *The Legend of Zelda*, and *Metroid*.

Thus, *Jr. Pac-Man* was relegated to relative obscurity. Very little in the way of promotion was spent on the game, though it did appear in three catalogs: Atari (CO25618-001 Rev. A) from 1984; Atari 1987 (CO34003 Rev. A); and Atari Advantage-2600 (C300592-001W.F. 03-1989). Luckily, despite its lack of fame, it is fairly easy to find. On a related note, *Jr. Pac-Man* should have been released for the Atari 5200, but it was cancelled when Jack Tramiel bought the computer and console divisions of Atari, Inc.

Today, *Jr. Pac-Man* may be a small, beanie-wearing player in a virtual world filled with first-person shooters, 3D graphics, and complex controls, but it is absolutely required playing for anyone even remotely interesting in classic gaming. If you've only played *Jr. Pac-Man*'s parents, *Pac-Man* and *Ms. Pac-Man*, you owe it to yourself to spend a little time with their oft-neglected offspring. You'll eat him up.

FUN FACT:

In 2009, programmer Bob "PacManPlus" DeCrescenzo created a homebrew version of *Jr. Pac-Man* for the Atari 7800. It includes the intermissions and is a more accurate port in general than the already excellent 2600 game (which is only fitting given the superior processing power of the 7800).

WHY IT MADE THE LIST:

Jr. Pac-Man is the most arcade-like of the various Atari 2600 ports, so it was an obvious choice for inclusion in this book.

CHAPTER  51

K.C. MUNCHKIN!, K.C.'S CRAZY CHASE!

K.C. MUNCHKIN!
ODYSSEY2
GENRE: MAZE
PUBLISHER: NAP
DEVELOPER: NAP
1 PLAYER
1981

K.C.'S CRAZY CHASE!
ODYSSEY2
GENRE: MAZE
PUBLISHER: NAP
DEVELOPER: NAP
1 PLAYER
1982

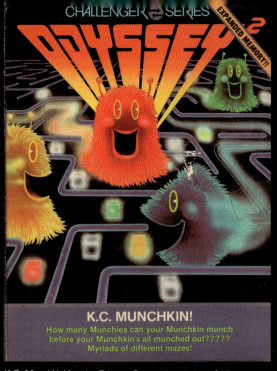

K.C. Munchkin! for the Odyssey2, complete in box. $12.

"BOTH ARE DIFFERENT ENOUGH FROM PAC-MAN (AND OTHER MAZE TITLES) TO OFFER THEIR OWN BRAND OF ENTERTAINMENT."

I'll admit up front that I'm cheating a bit with this chapter by including two games. I did this for two reasons: one, *K.C. Munchkin!* and *K.C.'s Crazy Chase!* are forever intertwined in the annals of video game history; and two, it gave me the ability to add another game to this book, the confines of which left many quality titles by the wayside.

Now that I've gotten that out of the way, let's consider the greatness and contextual importance of *K.C. Munchkin!* and *K.C.'s Crazy Chase!*

Shortly after the coin-op classic *Pac-Man* was released in 1980, scores of imitators followed, including such dot-munching games as *Lady Bug*, *Mouse Trap*, and *Lock 'N Chase*, each of which was released to the arcades in 1981. Also released in 1981 was *K.C. Munchkin!* for the Odyssey2, a cartridge that obviously borrowed from *Pac-Man*, but is a great game in its own right.

K.C. Munchkin! is indeed similar to *Pac-Man*, but with a number of key differences. The dots to be eaten are called

 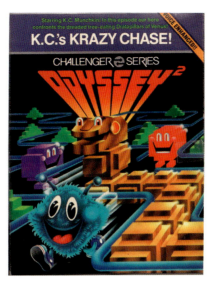 

K.C. Munchkin! game cartridge. $5.   *K.C.'s Krazy Chase!* complete in box. $15.   *K.C.'s Krazy Chase!* game cartridge. $6.

"munchies," and they move around the maze independently, making for more on-the-fly decisions for the gamer. There are only 12 munchies per screen, including four that blink with color and can be eaten to turn the tables on the enemies. Instead of four ghost enemies roaming the mazes, *K.C. Munchkin!* has three "munchers," which can be eaten when the player is energized with a blinking munchie.

Pac-Man has a single maze design, but, like *Ms. Pac-Man*, *K.C. Munchkin!* has four different mazes. And, like the Atari 2600 version of *Mouse Trap*, players can elect to play the game with disappearing mazes. Even better, gamers can create (but not save) their own mazes, making for a virtually limitless number of game screens. The character K.C. Munckin! looks a lot like Pac-Man, but is adorned with antennae. The munchers have antennae as well.

Unfortunately, *K.C. Munckin!* was the subject of a lawsuit.

According to *Atari Inc.—Business is Fun* (2012, Syzygy Company Press): "On March 18, 1982, Federal Judge George N. Leighton ruled in favor of Atari versus Magnavox when Atari accused Magnavox of creating a game too similar to its licensed *Pac-Man*, *K.C. Munchkin!* Atari had purchased the exclusive rights to *Pac-Man* prior to the *K.C. Munchkin!* release. The earlier ruling in the Federal Court had ruled that the game by Magnavox was not in violation of any copyright laws because the source codes of the two games were different. That while there were similarities, there were also differences in the gameplay of the two games. However, Atari appealed the decision and the new ruling went in Atari's favor. Magnavox was ordered to stop selling *K.C. Munchkin!* and to pull the game off store shelves immediately, making it a collector's item for fans of the Magnavox's Odyssey2 system."

Luckily, despite the purported "collector's item" status, the game stayed on store shelves long enough to satisfy thousands of eager Odyssey2 owners. It was the best-selling title for the system, and it helped reinvigorate the market for the O2, meaning the game is easy to find today.

In an interview published on www.dadgum.com, *K.C.* programmer Ed Averett spoke about the influence behind the creation of the game. "*Pac-Man* was the hit of the day, and I was asked to design a game that would compete with the game concept of *Pac-Man* without violating copyright laws," he said. "But there were no copyright laws at that time concerning video games. A three-way design effort was begun by marketing, who wanted to come as close to *Pac-Man* as legally possible; the Magnavox legal department, who wanted something they could easily defend in court; and me, who wanted to design a game that would eat *Pac-Man*'s lunch from an interactive play point of view. Everyone was pleased with the results."

Averett also talked about how the lawsuit was "one of the landmark legal rulings in video games, and it was fun to be in the middle of it."

Undaunted by their defeat in court, North American Philips released *K.C.'s Krazy Chase!* the next year, but changed the formula enough to avoid further lawsuits.

"*K.C.'s Krazy Chase!* was designed soon after the *K.C. Munchkin!* court exercise and did a good job of capturing the moment at Magnavox," Averett said. "There was something about the adversary biting the behind of little *K.C.* that appealed to everyone at the moment."

In *K.C.'s Krazy Chase!*, gamers once again guide K.C. Munchkin! as he maneuvers his way around a series of mazes. However, instead of eating munchies, he chases a "Dratapillar" comprised of a deadly head and multiple body segments. Some say the centipede-like Dratapillar, which should only be approached from the rear, is a potshot at Atari, which produced the *Centipede* arcade game.

By consuming a Dratapillar body segment, K.C. becomes energized and can temporarily turn the tables on two skull-like "Drats" that roam the mazes and follow K.C. Also on the screen are regenerating, randomly placed trees, which both the player and the Dratapillar can eat. The trees are worth extra points, but slow the player down. The trees also slow down the Dratapillar, which can be strategically useful to the player.

Like *K.C. Munchkin!*, as the game progresses, the action gets faster. Also like *K.C. Munchkin!*, *K.C.'s Krazy Chase!* lets players program their own mazes. One new addition is support of The Voice speech module, which adds laughter and such exclamations as "Go!", "Run!", "Watch out!", and "Incredible!"

Best of all, the two new enemy types combined with the trees helps make for a distinctive, hugely entertaining sequel.

In the Jan., 1983 issue of *JoyStik*, the reviewer called *K.C.'s Krazy Chase!* "lots of fun" and a "pleasant sequel." In *Electronic Games* magazine #12 (Feb., 1983), Arnie Katz and Bill Kunkel called the game a "welcome addition to the Odyssey2" and "absolutely top drawer." In *Electronic Fun with Computers & Games* #2 (Dec., 1982), Art Levis said, "*K.C.'s Krazy Chase!* is more complex, faster, and more interesting than its predecessor and K.C.'s new nemesis—the dreaded Dratapillar and her Drats—are far more menacing than the original Munchkin monsters."

On The Odyssey2 Home Page! (www.the-nextlevel.com/odyssey2), William Cassidy said the game "succeeds at retaining the basic fun of a maze munch title while moving well beyond the essential sameness of *Pac-Man*." He also called it "a more-than-worthy follow-up to Odyssey2's most successful game."

According to the seventh edition of the *Digital Press Collector's Guide* (2002), which refers to the game as "excellent" and "phenomenal," *K.C. Munchkin!* is Ed Averett's favorite cartridge that he designed, which is saying a lot since he programmed a whopping 24 games for the Odyssey2.

Both *K.C. Munchkin!* and *K.C.'s Krazy Chase!* are great games with sharp graphics, nice animation (especially considering the limitations of the system), excellent controls, and fast, fun, challenging gameplay, and both are different enough from *Pac-Man* (and other maze titles) to offer their own brand of entertainment. When compared to the anemic Atari 2600 version of *Pac-Man*, which was hampered by flickering graphics, dull sound effects, and an ugly title character, the "K.C." games look and play like arcade games.

FUN FACT:

K.C. Munchkin! was named after Kenneth C. Menkin, who was president of Philips Consumer Electronics at the time. Overseas, the game was simply called Munchkin.

WHY IT MADE THE LIST:

K.C. Munchkin! and K.C.'s Crazy Chase! are two of the best maze games ever created for any system, offering sharp graphics and fantastic gameplay.

CHAPTER 52

KABOOM!

ATARI 2600
GENRE: ACTION
PUBLISHER: ACTIVISION
DEVELOPER: ACTIVISION
1 OR 2 PLAYERS (ALTERNATING)
1981

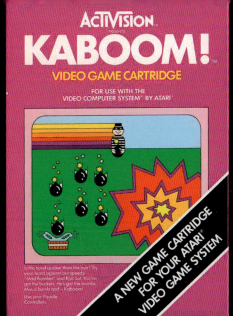

Kaboom! for the Atari 2600, complete in box. Courtesy of AtariAge.com. $12.

"EXTREME CONCENTRATION AND TOP-NOTCH REFLEXES ARE REQUIRED, CREATING A TENSE, THOROUGHLY GRATIFYING EXPERIENCE."

In *Kaboom!*, the player uses an Atari paddle controller to guide a trio of horizontally stacked, water-filled buckets left and right along the bottom of the screen, catching bombs that are raining down from the fiendish Mad Bomber, who zips back and forth across the top of the playfield. If the player lets a bomb get by, a bucket will disappear. When all the buckets are gone, the game is over.

The action starts off slowly, letting the player get accustomed to things, but with each successive round, the Mad Bomber begins moving and dropping bombs more quickly, forcing the player to operate the buckets faster and with laser precision and focus. When the game gets especially intense, extreme concentration and top-notch reflexes are required, creating a tense, thoroughly gratifying experience.

Kaboom! is a simple title, borrowing its gameplay mechanic from Atari's *Avalanche* (arcade, 1978), but with bombs instead of falling rocks. In an interview published on the Digital Press website (www.digitpress.com), designer Larry Kaplan said [laughing], "I just ripped off *Avalanche*, but I had to fit it into 2048 bytes and [I was] limited to VCS graphics. So, unable to display a bunch of rocks on top, I changed it to a single figure dropping bombs. David Crane came up with the Mad Bomber and the buckets, both of which he designed for me."

The Mad Bomber, with his pin-striped prison uniform, looks great—he even smiles when a bomb gets past—and the little bombs have flickering fuses and sound good when exploding. However, the emphasis is clearly on the action—keeping the buckets in front of the bombs—and in this regard the game delivers in spades. The game has one basic screen, and players do the same thing over and over again, which in this case is not a negative—you'll be too involved in the immersive gameplay to care.

The Video Game Critic (videogamecritic.com) is a huge fan of *Kaboom!*, calling it "mesmerizing" and "arguably the most fun Atari 2600 game ever." He and I are hardly alone in our appreciation of *Kaboom!* as it's regarded in most gaming circles as one of the better games of the era.

Here's a sampling of accolades:

Taxing, insane, and narcotic!
—*The Complete Guide to Conquering Video Games*
by Jeff Rovin
(1982, Collier Books)

An "interesting" and "addictive" game that "excels in imagery, graphics, and sound effects."
—*Ken Uston's Guide to Buying and Beating the Home Video Games*
(1982, Signet)

"A stimulating and challenging game of skill" with "fine graphics" and "smooth animation."
—*The Book of Atari Software*
(1983, The Book Company)

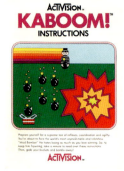

Kaboom! for the Atari 2600 in action. Courtesy of AtariAge.com.

Kaboom! game cartridge. $5.

Kaboom! instruction manual. $2.

Kaboom! is without a doubt one of my favorite games and deserves mention as one of the greatest games of all time.

—Game Freaks 365
(www.gamefreaks365.com)

"Original" and "clever" with "great" graphics, sounds, and controls.

—Darryl Brundage of The Atari Times
(www.ataritimes.com)

A blast…a hard game to put down…a good reason to dust off the Atari 2600.

—Scott Alan Marriott of the All Game Guide
(www.allgame.com)

In the reviews section of the first issue of *Electronic Games* magazine (winter, 1981), Bill Kunkel and Frank Laney, Jr. gave *Kaboom!* high marks, saying that the cartridge "shows off the approach to game design that has vaulted Activision into the video game big time almost overnight" and that it is "infinitely more enjoyable than the commercial arcade game upon which it is loosely based, *Avalanche*" because of Kaplan's "delightful electronic artwork."

In his review, The Video Game Critic pointed out a key *Kaboom!* strategy that I try to use whenever possible: "When you have all three buckets, it's a good idea to mess up intentionally just before obtaining your bonus bucket at 1000 points. This will slow down the bombs temporarily, and you'll get your third bucket right back."

In the instruction manual for *Kaboom!*, Kaplan described this bucket-sacrificing strategy, as well as making the following observations about the game: "To do well in the *Kaboom!*, you'll need all the reflexes, endurance, and concentration you can muster. Don't be frustrated if things don't go well at first. It takes a fair amount of practice, especially to catch the bombs at higher speeds."

As you get better at the game, Kaplan noted, "You'll notice that you'll be improving in stages. The first plateau is the 1,000 point mark. Mastery at Bomb Groups 5 and 6 is necessary to do well here. Conquering Bomb Group 7 will place you at the 2,000 point level. As you develop the stamina and concentration needed to progress, you'll conquer Bomb Group 8. From then on, it's a matter of fine-tuning your skills and extending your endurance to improve your score. If you hit the 10,000 point level, that really impresses the Mad Bomber, and he'll show you his appreciation. Watch for it."

In 1983, Paul Willson adapted *Kaboom!* for the Atari 5200. Since that system lacks paddle controllers, the 2600 version is by far the superior cartridge. However, the 5200 game adds a fairly enjoyable Pitch & Catch mode in which players take turns controlling the Mad Bomber. In terms of audio/visual improvements, the 5200 version depicts buildings in the background, and every time the player catches a bomb, a note of "The Toreador Song" plays.

Atari 2600 *Kaboom!* has been re-released on a number of compilation titles for various modern systems, including *Activision Classics* (1998) for the PlayStation and *Activision Anthology* for the PlayStation 2 (2002) and Game Boy Advance (2003). In 2012, *Activision Anthology* hit the iPad, iPhone, Android Phone, and Android Tablet. In 2010, Microsoft made *Kaboom!* available as a downloadable title for the Xbox 360 Game Room service.

Despite its greatness, *Kaboom!* never received a sequel. *Kaboom: The Mad Bomber Returns*, also known as *Kaboom! 2*, was in development in 1993/1994 (by High Voltage Software) for the Super Nintendo, but was never released. According to an article in volume 5 # 11 of *VideoGames* magazine (Nov., 1993), Activision displayed *Kaboom: The Mad Bomber Returns* at the Summer CES in Chicago in 1991, side-by-side with the also-cancelled *River Raid: The Mission of No Return*.

FUN FACT:

Kaboom! and *Bridge* programmer Larry Kaplan also designed two Atari 2600 launch titles: *Air-Sea Battle* and *Street Racer*.

WHY IT MADE THE LIST:

More than most any game ever programmed for any console, *Kaboom!* requires laser focus and steady controller movement.

CHAPTER 53

KILLER BEES!

ODYSSEY2
GENRE: ACTION
PUBLISHER: NAP
DEVELOPER: NAP
1 PLAYER
1983

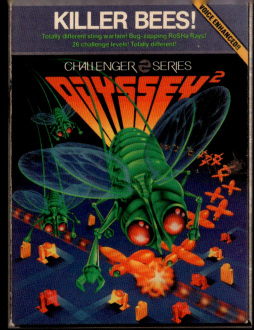

Killer Bees! for the Odyssey2, complete in box. $35.

> "SMOOTH DIFFICULTY PROGRESSION, GOOD CONTROLS, SHARP SOUND EFFECTS, AND THAT CERTAIN SOMETHING THAT MAKES THE RETRO GAMER IN ALL OF US KEEP SAYING "JUST ONE MORE TIME.""

A hidden gem in the Odyssey2 library, *Killer Bees!* is nothing short of one of the most original games of the Golden Age. Players guide a swarm of 12 tiny white bees around the playfield, stinging several enemy Beebots that slow down with each sting. Hover over a Beebot long enough (or enough times) and it will die, leaving a grave marker in its place. Left alone, a Beebot will speed up, making it harder to kill.

Guarding the Beebots, which look like armless alien humanoids, are colorful swarms of bees, which should be avoided. Letting an enemy swarm touch the player's swarm reduces the number of the player's bees, making them less powerful in stinging the Beebots. The player's swarm can be reduced all the way down to one (a nice touch), but players start with a new swarm of 12 with each of the game's 26 levels defeated (killing all the Beebots finishes a level).

In addition to wearing down and killing Beebots, players can fire "RoSHa Rays" at swarms of bees. RoSHa Rays are beams that stretch horizontally across the playfield, destroying any swarm in its path. Players are only armed with one ray at a time, but killing a Beebot recharges the weapon (RoSHa Rays are ineffective against Beebots). As play progresses, the action gets considerably faster, making for a challenging, enjoyable contest.

When I began researching and writing my first book, *Classic Home Video Games, 1972-1984* (2007, McFarland Publishers), *Killer Bees!* was one of the few Odyssey2 titles that I had never played before, so I had to get a copy of the game off eBay in order to review it. Twenty-something dollars and a few days later, a complete copy arrived in the mail, much to my delight (I still get excited when the mailman brings something other than bills or junk mail).

After spending a couple of hours with *Killer Bees!*, it became one of my favorite Odyssey2 titles. Not only is it stunningly original, it has nifty graphical flourishes (such as a rainbow title screen and the aforementioned gravestones), smooth difficulty progression, good controls, sharp sound effects, and that certain something that makes the retro gamer in all of us keep saying "just one more time."

The Voice, which is the Odyssey2's speech synthesis module, gives *Killer Bees!* its aural kick, emitting some pretty spiffy buzzing sounds. Without the module, however, the buzzing, beeping sound effects, though strong, can become grating after extended play (if you don't own The Voice, you may want to play the game with the audio turned low, but not off).

Killer Bees! is a relatively hard-to-find title that deserves a bigger fan base. Back when the game was new in stores, a review, written by Art Lewis, appeared in the July, 1983 issue of *Electronic Fun with Computers and Games*. In addition to complimenting the game's "great play value," "vivid" visuals, and "great sound effects," Lewis bemoaned its obscurity, saying "only an eccentric handful of game players will ever know its joysticks."

William Cassidy, writing for the All Game Guide (allgame.com), enjoys the fun, but little known game as well, calling it a "winner" and saying that, "There may be no other game quite like the addictive and fast-paced *Killer Bees!*"

In *Classic Gamer Magazine* #5 (fall, 2000), Odyssey2 enthusiast Earl Green called *Killer Bees!* "fast," "strangely

The back of the *Killer Bees!* box.   *Killer Bees!* game cartridge. $15.   *Killer Bees!* magazine ad.

addictive," and "possibly the most original and unusual game ever released under the quasi-prestigious 'Challenger Series' banner." In the seventh edition of the *Digital Press Collector's Guide* (2002), the game is called "one of the 'must-haves' for any semi-serious Odyssey2 player."

Not everyone "gets" it, though. In issue #11 (May/June, 1993) of the *Digital Press* fanzine, the staff severely underrated *Killer Bees!*, giving it mixed reviews. Kevin Oleniacz called it "far from the perfect game," but admitted that it is "very addictive." Joe Santulli referred to it as being "one of the strangest [games] of all time," but only gave it a 6 out of 10 in terms of gameplay. Liz Santulli appeared to miss the appeal of the game altogether, saying it "gets boring really fast."

In an interview published on the Classic Consoles Center (classic-consoles-center.at) website, Bob Harris, who programmed *Killer Bees!*, shared his feelings about the cartridge.

"I think what made the game is that it is faster-paced than the other Odyssey games, and had some features the others didn't have," he said. "Many of the other games locked the characters into a maze, and I let the character move around at will. Other objects in the game had gradual acceleration, rather than only one or two speeds. Death (of opponents) was a gradual thing, as opposed to an event. Even your own death is gradual."

Harris is also quoted in the Museum section of classicgaming.gamespy.com, where he said: "I was experimenting with a lot of different techniques with *Killer Bees!*, most of which stayed in the released version. The death concept was a little unusual. It may not be obvious, but you actually lose bees (in your swarm) gradually. The longer you are in contact with the bad swarm, the more bees you lose. I don't know if anyone ever figured this out—the reviewer at *Games Magazine* (Burt Hochberg) asked why I didn't allow multiple lives like every other game did."

As Odyssey2 fans well know, the system had a fixed set of characters, meaning the men, planets, trees, and other objects were identical in many of the games. In *Classic Gamer Magazine* #5, Harris discussed how he used a bug in the programming to circumvent this limitation. "There was a flaw in the video chip that allowed you to use any bottom segment of any character," he said. "Thus, the *Killer Bees!* robots used the legs from the walking figures, and half-8's for the helmets."

The inspiration for *Killer Bees!* was derived from a couple of unlikely sources. "The idea for *Killer Bees!* came from one of the sounds of the Voice module," Harris said. "It was supposed to sound like a 'boing,' but actually sounded like buzzing bees."

Killer Bees! plays nothing like *Centipede*, but that classic title played a role in the creation of the cartridge as well. "Everything was trying to duplicate the feel of the arcade game *Centipede*," Harris said. "I definitely wanted something fast paced...One of the things I liked in *Centipede* was that a smart player could make use of the patterned behavior of the centipede to force it into a channel of mushrooms and pick it off easily. The corresponding concept in *Killer Bees!* was the predictable behavior of the robots...You could take advantage of this by killing a robot or two in the right place, which forced another robot into a tight loop, making it easier to kill."

Anyone looking for something a little (make that a lot) different and a whole lot of fun should definitely pick up *Killer Bees!*, a truly unique game in an industry filled with copycats and imitators.

FUN FACT:

Killer Bees! programmer Bob Harris also designed *Nimble Numbers Ned!* and *Type & Tell!* for the Odyssey2, along with *War Room* for the ColecoVision.

WHY IT MADE THE LIST:

There's no other video game quite like the quirkily cool *Killer Bees!*

CHAPTER 54
LADY BUG

COLECOVISION
GENRE: MAZE
PUBLISHER: COLECO
DEVELOPER: COLECO
1 OR 2 PLAYERS (ALTERNATING)
1982

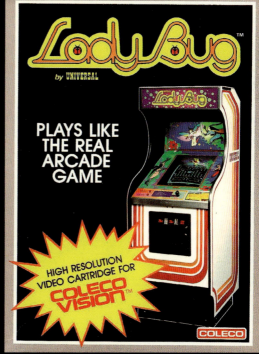

Lady Bug for the ColecoVision, complete in box. $15.

"THE PATIENT, STRATEGY-MINDED GAMER WILL BE REWARDED TREMENDOUSLY BY PLAYING THE GAME TO ITS FULLEST POTENTIAL."

In issue #93 of *Game Informer* (Jan., 2001), a review of *Lady Bug* for the ColecoVision appeared in the "Classic GI" section near the back of the magazine. The unnamed author ended the review with: "It is true that *Lady Bug* isn't very original in concept, but it still provides an addicting and entertaining experience."

Although a fair assessment of the game, the writer of the piece didn't go far enough in extolling the virtues of this great cartridge, which is nothing short of one of the best maze games of all time.

John Sellers, author of *Arcade Fever* (2001, Running Press), agrees with me, calling *Lady Bug* "arguably the strongest of all *Pac-Man* clones." (Sellers was discussing the arcade original, but the ColecoVision game is such a strong port that the same critique applies.)

Universal released the original arcade version of *Lady Bug* in 1981 to little fanfare, though it was featured in an episode of the early '80s TV game show, *Starcade*, in which the hapless contestants had to score as many points as possible on the game in only 50 seconds. Most arcade denizens saw *Lady Bug* as nothing more than an effeminate *Pac-Man* wannabe and failed to appreciate (or even attempt) its varied, nuanced strategies.

As in *Pac-Man*, players guide a cute character around a maze, gobbling up dots and avoiding a foursome of creatures (flies, beetles, and other insects in this case). However, there's much more to it than that, and the patient, strategy-minded gamer will be rewarded tremendously by playing the game to its fullest potential.

As in *Lock 'N' Chase* (1981) and *Mouse Trap* (1981), the maze in *Lady Bug* has walls that can be manipulated. By using the title character to rotate the walls, changing the layout of the maze in the process, players can create barriers against attack (though it's impossible to isolate a portion of the playfield entirely) and divert the course of enemies, preferably into one of several deadly skulls lying about the playfield.

In the Aug., 1982 issue of *Videogaming Illustrated*, designer Tom Helmer of Coleco explained that the location of the doors differs in the ColecoVision port because "the arcade game is longer than it is wide, unlike most televisions—and we can't very well ask people to put their TVs sideways to play the game."

Unlike most maze games, *Lady Bug* does not allow players to kill, eat, shoot, chase, or otherwise attack the enemies. However, eating a vegetable will temporarily freeze the insects. A vegetable will appear when all four enemies

Lady Bug catalog ad.

Lady Bug instruction manual. $2.

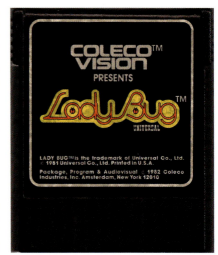
Lady Bug game cartridge. $5.

have left their centrally located base and entered the maze pathways. Enemies enter the maze one at a time, adhering to a schedule set in place by a timer that is backed by some fairly intimidating sound effects. Entering the insects' starting base to eat the veggie for extra points gets difficult in later rounds when the enemies are moving at ridiculously high speeds.

In addition to movable walls and freezable enemies, *Lady Bug* offers tantalizing treats in the way of letters spelling out EXTRA (a feature also found in Universal's *Mr. Do!*) and SPECIAL. At the beginning of each level, a trio of letters appears within the maze. The letters change in color cyclically, from blue to red to yellow and back again. Eating a letter when it is blue simply grants the player a minimum number of points, but eating a letter while it is yellow or red scores extra points and a letter needed to spell out EXTRA or SPECIAL (respectively).

In the arcade game and in the ColecoVision port, spelling out EXTRA grants players a bonus life. However, SPECIAL is a different story. In the coin-op classic, players earn an extra credit (!) and a wedding ceremony (!) for spelling out SPECIAL. In the ColecoVision version, since gamers can play the game over and over again without inserting quarters, earning an extra game would be redundant, so the programmers added an ingenious feature: a maze garden challenge stage. Here players guide the Lady Bug through an enemy-less maze, gobbling up as many vegetables as possible prior to time running out.

This delightful and rewarding vegetable garden feature sends scores skyrocketing and adds tremendously to the enjoyment of the game, but spelling out SPECIAL is a daunting challenge, even for the pros. In the Jan., 1983, issue of *Electronic Games*, a "devoted fan of the fantastic new ColecoVision system" wrote in asking what happens when you light up all the letters in SPECIAL. Bill Kunkel, a.k.a. The Game Doctor, replied, saying he "sat up for three hours" to accomplish this formidable task. (From time to time, I can spell out SPECIAL twice during a game, but that's a rare feat.)

Another fun feature in *Lady bug* is a trio of hearts scattered about the maze. If the player eats a heart when it is blue, it will advance a pinball-like bonus multiplier (2x, 3x, 5x), adding another layer to the game's plethora of strategic scoring opportunities.

Lady Bug is one of my favorite all-time games, so I've gotten pretty good at it (though there are certainly better players). During the early '80s, the highest score I achieved in the ColecoVision version (skill level 1) was 401,430, which just missed the mark of 407,470 set by Dean Odice of Bridgeport, CT, whose score was posted in the Aug., 1983 issue of *Electronic Games*.

In the past few years, several players have scored in the millions, as reported on the Twin Galaxies Official Electronic Score Board.

Although *Lady Bug* never caught on in the arcades, the ColecoVision game was one of the better sellers for the system. It ranked #3 in the "Most Popular Videogame Cartridges" section of the Jan., 1983 issue of *Electronic Games*, and today is a common (and therefore inexpensive) cartridge in the collector's market.

Back in the day, *Lady Bug*, which is just as challenging as the arcade original, was rightfully hailed by critics as a great game. In the *Electronic Games 1983 Software Encyclopedia*, the cartridge was given an overall rating of a perfect 10. In the "Programmable Parade" section of *Electronic Games* magazine #10 (Dec., 1982), the reviewer called it an "addictive" game with "superb" graphics, a "virtually perfect recreation of the Universal coin-op."

In his book, *Ken Uston's Home Video '83—The 20 Best New Games and How to Beat Them…Plus 5 Great Classics*, Uston said, "*Lady Bug* could possibly be regarded as the top maze-type TV-game in existence." In issue #1 of the short-lived (two issues) *Creative Computing Video & Arcade Games* (spring, 1983), Owen Linzmayer said the game is "just as much fun as the original."

More recently, Scott Stone, writing for Digital Press (www.digitpress.com), said: "I strongly suggest you find this game for your own collection or play it on an emulator."

During an interview published in 2008 on 8-Bit Rocket (www.8bitrocket.com), Bill Kunkel cited *Lady Bug* as one of his favorite games of all time, telling interviewer Steve Fulton, "I was an absolute sucker for *Lady Bug* on the ColecoVision."

In issue # 2 (Nov./Dec., 1991) of the *Digital Press* fanzine, edtior Joe Santulli placed *Ladybug* #1 on his list of "Top 10 ColecoVision Carts." In issue # 24 (March/April, 1995), Kevin Oleniacz said, "There is more than enough intense action, strategy, and variables to make this more than just another dot-gobbling maze chase."

Lady Bug was also produced for the Intellivision (1983), but the letters spelling out SPECIAL are absent, as is the vegetable garden (though the game is still fun). *Lady Bug* was featured on the cover of Coleco's Atari 2600 catalogue, but the game never was released to stores, and a prototype of the cartridge was never found.

Luckily, John W. Champeau took it upon himself to create a homebrew version of *Lady Bug* for the 2600, and he did a great job, going so far as to include SPECIAL and the bonus vegetable garden. This homebrew masterpiece was released in 2006 and was made available through the AtariAge Store (atariage.com).

Despite its status among video game philistines as a *Pac-Man* poseur, *Lady Bug* for the ColecoVision is easily one of the 100 greatest console games of all time, regardless of the era. Its inclusion in this book was one of the easiest decisions I've ever had to make.

FUN FACT:
The original arcade version of *Lady Bug* was designed by Kazutoshi Ueda, who also created *Mr. Do!*

WHY IT MADE THE LIST:
Thanks to its many strategies and scoring opportunities, *Lady Bug* is at or near the top of the pack when it comes to the heavily populated maze genre.

CHAPTER 55
THE LEGEND OF ZELDA

NINTENDO NES
GENRE: ACTION ROLE-PLAYING GAME
PUBLISHER: NINTENDO
DEVELOPER: NINTENDO
1 PLAYER
1987

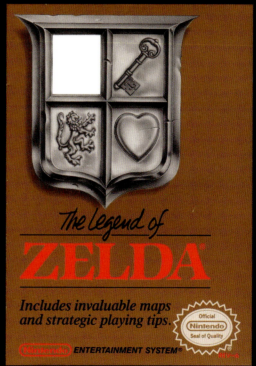

The Legend of Zelda for the Nintendo NES, complete in box. $150.

"WHATEVER SYSTEM YOU PLAY THE LEGEND OF ZELDA ON, YOU'LL LIKELY HAVE A BLAST."

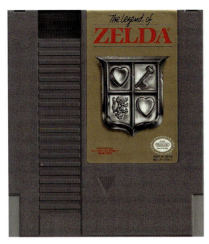
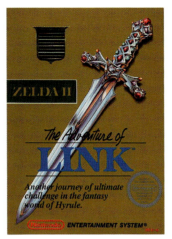

Gray *The Legend of Zelda* game cartridge. $20.

The Legend of Zelda spawned numerous sequels, including Zelda II: The Adventure of Link. Pictured here complete in box. $80.

The Legend of Zelda was re-released on the Game Boy Advance in 2004. Pictured complete in box. $40.

Created by Shigeru Miyamoto (with assistance from Takashi Tezuka and Eiji Aonuma), the man responsible for such classics as *Donkey Kong* and *Super Mario Bros.*, *The Legend of Zelda* was, for many Americans, their first role-playing game. In fact, worried that the game might confuse players, Nintendo included a toll-free number in the manual so players could call the company for help. This was the genesis of Nintendo's game counselor hotline, which, during its peak, maintained a staff of 200 operators.

An action-oriented RPG, *Zelda*, which is viewed from a top-down perspective, borrowed some of the exploration elements of *Adventure* for the Atari 2600, but advanced the genre considerably (to put it mildly) with larger worlds to explore, vastly superior graphics, ingeniously conceived puzzles, a sweeping musical score, and a much greater emphasis on hack-and-slash swordplay.

As with virtually any RPG, gameplay, which takes place long ago when the world was in chaos, is story-driven. Players control a young, elfin hero named Link as he journeys through Hyrule, hoping to defeat the evil Ganon, rescue Princess Zelda (who Ganon is holding captive), and restore the fabled land to its former glory. To perform this considerable task, Link must find the eight fragments of the Triforce of Power (also called the Triforce of Wisdom).

The Legend of Zelda plays out in two areas: the Overworld, which is brightly lit and filled with forests, lakes, and mountains; and the Underworld, which is an underground maze of dangerous labyrinths. The Triforce segments are hidden within the Underworld. The action starts in the Overworld, but there are many entrances to the Underworld, including some hidden deep in the forests and mountains. The intricate world Miyamoto created for the game was inspired by the programmer's childhood, in which he explored the caves, lakes, forests, and villages of his native Sonobe, Japan.

Link relies heavily on his sword and shield to fight the assortment of creatures he will encounter in the land of Hyrule. He can upgrade his standard weaponry, and he can use (and store in inventory accessible via a sub-screen) such items as a compass, a map, keys, a ladder (for crossing holes and rivers), a raft (for crossing seas and lakes), boomerangs (wooden and magical), bows, arrows (wooden and silver), rings (which reduce damage inflicted by enemies), a magical clock (for freezing enemies), a power bracelet (for lifting rocks), candles (to light the way), a magic wand and book (for casting fiery spells), and bombs (for destroying enemies and opening holes in walls).

Rubies, which act as currency for purchasing items from merchants, are scattered throughout the kingdom, and the items can be used in a variety of ways to solve puzzles, including tantalizing moments when you can see items and areas, yet not access them directly. The combat is better than in most RPGs, with Link battling a nice assortment of creatures that pounce, fly, fire spears, shoot fireballs, walk in varying patterns and at different speeds, and more. Enemy types include Tektite (spidery things), Octorok (octopi that spit rocks), Peahat (flower ghosts), Molblin (bulldog-like goblins), and Armos (stone soldiers), among others.

In *High Score! The Illustrated History of Electronic Games* (2002, McGraw-Hill/Osbourne), Miyamoto spoke about designing the game: "The first *Legend of Zelda* was created based upon the original concept of a 'miniature garden that you can put inside your drawer,' inside of which the player can freely explore…I tried to make a game where the next move the player is supposed to make is not already determined. Each player has to decide the route he or she thinks is best and take the best possible action. Another big element is that players themselves can grow…you see and feel that Link actually grows."

Only those gamers who are turned off by its non-linear play and epic scale can help but love *The Legend of Zelda*, which has countless admirers. In *High Score!*, the authors said that *Zelda* "may be the most perfect game ever made."

In *Game Informer* #100 (Aug., 2001), *Zelda* was referred to as "perfect in every conceivable way," earning the number one spot in the issue's list of "Top 100 Games of All Time." In *Electronic Gaming Monthly* #200, *Zelda* came in at number five in their list of "The Greatest 200 Videogames of Their Time," which ranked the titles in terms of influence on their generation of games.

Matt Fox, in *The Video Games Guide* (2006, Boxtree), said that many things about *The Legend of Zelda* were special, "but most special of all was the feeling of deep immersion you got while on Link's quest. The forests, seas, towns, and dungeons of Hyrule are seen from a top-down view and together make up a hugely expansive and convincing game-world. All it took was a couple of hours spent exploring this world, to make discovering every last location and hidden secret a burning obsession."

The Legend of Zelda does indeed offer much to explore, but visuals aren't its strong point (at least compared to certain other NES titles from the same year), as Steven Schwartz pointed out in *Compute!'s Guide to Nintendo Games* (1989, Compute! Books): "The graphics are *The Legend of Zelda*'s greatest weakness. Particularly in the outerworld, Link and the creatures he meets are a bit too much like Munchkins and Muppets to evoke any real feelings of fear. Everything—including Link—seems a few sizes too small."

Like most everyone else, however, Schwartz is a big fan of the game, calling it "an adventure in every sense of the word…the game offers days (or weeks) of exciting play."

Schwartz has mixed feelings about the sound, saying, "The music is good, especially the haunting tune played in the dungeon and the one used for the opening screens. The outerworld music is more cartoonish and wears thin quickly. The sound effects are handled well."

Encased in a shiny gold cartridge (and later in traditional gray), *The Legend of Zelda* was the first NES game to feature battery backup for saving progress (there are three save slots), it's the fourth-best selling NES title of all time (though it's now hard to find complete in box), and it's one of the most influential games in the history of the industry, paving the way for numerous like-minded action RPGs to follow, including such brilliant sequels as *The Legend of Zelda: A Link to the Past* (1992, Super Nintendo), *The Legend of Zelda: Ocarina of Time* (1998, Nintendo 64), *The Legend of Zelda: Twilight Princess* (2006, GameCube, Wii), *The Legend of Zelda: Skyward Sword* (2011, Wii), and *The Legend of Zelda: A Link Between Worlds* (2013, 3DS).

The first *Zelda* sequel was *Zelda II: The Adventure of Link*, which was released for the NES in 1988 (and the Game Boy Advance in 2004). It's a quality title that would've made this book if released a year earlier, but it did disappoint certain fans of the original with its altered gameplay, steep difficulty level, and side-scrolling viewpoint.

Getting back to the original *The Legend of Zelda*, it was also released for the Game Boy Advance (2004, via the "Classic NES Series"), the Nintendo Wii (2006, via the Virtual Console), and the Nintendo 3DS (2011, via the Virtual Console).

Whatever system you play *The Legend of Zelda* on, you'll likely have a blast. Just stay away from those awful Philips CD-i sequels: *Link: The Faces of Evil* (1993), *Zelda: The Wand of Gamelon* (1993), and *Zelda's Adventure* (1995). (Trust me on this.)

FUN FACT:

Citing the name's "pleasant and significant" sound, Miyamoto named Princess Zelda after the wife of F. Scott Fitzgerald, the American novelist.

WHY IT MADE THE LIST:

Considered by retro gamers and modernists alike to be one of the greatest games of all time, *The Legend of Zelda* will forever hold a significant place in the annals of video game history.

CHAPTER 56

MARIO BROS.

NINTENDO NES
GENRE: NON-SCROLLING PLATFORMER
PUBLISHER: NINTENDO
DEVELOPER: NINTENDO
1 OR 2 PLAYERS (SIMULTANEOUS)
1986

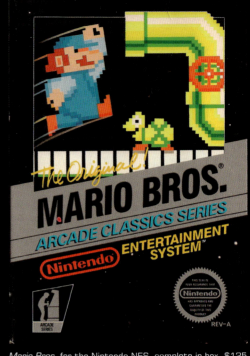

Mario Bros. for the Nintendo NES, complete in box. $125.

"MARIO BROS. WAS NINTENDO'S FIRST SIMULTANEOUS TWO-PLAYER TITLE."

Released in June of 1983, the same year as the vastly underappreciated *Donkey Kong 3*, the original coin-op version of *Mario Bros.* is an excellent successor to *Donkey Kong* and *Donkey Kong Junior*. It is also a nice prelude to the side-scrolling classic, *Super Mario Bros.*, the game that would change the industry forever.

Mario Bros. was designed by Shigeru Miyamoto and Gunpei Yokoi, two of the lead programmers on *Donkey Kong*. When it was new and arcades were still going strong, it came to the Land of Oz at the Northeast Mall in Hurst, Texas, a place I liked to frequent as a teenager.

Mario Bros. quickly became one of my favorite games. I was 16 at the time, and my best friend Johnnie and I would play the game for hours on end. The two-player mode was great, and Johnnie and I would laugh hysterically as we tried to bump, kick, trick, and otherwise get each other killed—we NEVER cooperated—it was much more fun to fight!

In *High Score: The Illustrated History of Video Games* (2002, McGraw-Hill/Osborne), Rusel Demaria and Johnny L. Wilson agree that *Mario Bros.* is better when played with a pal. "The game was at its best as a two-player game," they wrote. "You could play cooperatively, but more often than not, one person would flip something over and the other player would go grab the points. Not fair, you say? But that was *Mario Bros.* And you could get revenge with a well-timed bump on your buddy, sending him to an oncoming enemy. So there!"

Matt Fox understands the appeal of *Mario Bros.* as well. In his book, *The Video Games Guide* (2006, Boxtree), he wondered "why there weren't more twin-player platform games" and said that "*Mario Bros.* is an absolute riot."

In 1986, which was the year I got my NES, Nintendo brought *Mario Bros.* into the living rooms of gamers everywhere. Like other early NES titles, it came in a black box. I immediately picked up a copy. During this time, video game magazines had yet to resurface after The Great Video Game Crash of 1983, so I was pretty much buying blind—there were no reviews to consider, or at least none that I knew of.

I didn't care about the lack of information because I knew I wanted the game, and I was confident that Nintendo would do a bang-up job with the home release. Fortunately, my confidence was not misplaced.

It wasn't a perfect port (character animations and designs were slightly different, the falling icicles were missing, and the colorful title screen and demonstration mode was replaced by the standard NES Game A and Game B title screen), but gameplay remained a blast.

It was refreshing playing *Mario Bros.* without having to pump in quarter after quarter, and I discovered that the one-player version is awesome as well. Since the two-player mode was always competitive, at least when it came to me

  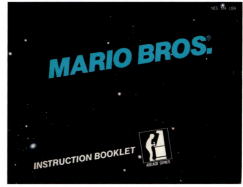

The back of the *Mario Bros.* box.   *Mario Bros.* game cartridge. $20.   *Mario Bros.* instruction manual. $15.

and my friends, games never lasted very long. However, when playing by myself, I managed to get deep into the game, when the screen would get crowded and the action would demand the utmost in control finesse and the direction and timing of jumps.

For those of you who have only played *Super Mario Bros.* and beyond, the original *Mario Bros.* is a non-scrolling, side-view platformer in which the titular plumber (player one) and his brother Luigi (player two) run and jump on seven fixed platforms (picture a *Joust*-like playfield, but set in a sewer) plus a brick floor, grabbing coins while trying to get rid of crabs, fighter flies, and turtles, which come out of pipes. There are four pipes, one in each corner of the screen. Fireballs come out of the pipes as well. They can be destroyed, but it's usually easier to avoid them. After you defeat all the creatures, the screen starts over at a harder, more enemy-filled pace.

To stun a creature and knock it over, you must maneuver your character under said creature and jump, bumping (and creating a ripple on) the platform it is walking on. While the stunned creature lies motionless, you must jump up to the creature and run into it to knock it off the screen before it has time to recover. If it does manage to get up, it becomes faster and, as a result, harder to defeat than it was before it fell.

By bumping a "POW" button near the bottom of the screen, you can stun or revive all the creatures simultaneously (depending on the current status of said creatures). Knocking several creatures off the screen in quick succession results in more points.

In the vaunted two-player mode, you can assist your gaming partner by stunning creatures for him or her to kick off the screen. Or, better yet, you can foil your fellow gamer's plans with trickery and conniving by reviving a creature just as your opponent is preparing to kick it. It's also good fun to bump the other player into creatures and fireballs

In later levels, you must deal with freezies, which are ice creatures that, if not destroyed, will spread out across a platform and harden, making that platform slippery. It takes longer to come to a stop on a slippery platform, adding another level of challenge and urgency to the game.

In addition to being fun, *Mario Bros.*, at least the original arcade version, is historically important. Technically, Mario's first appearance was in *Donkey Kong* (1981), but he was called Jumpman in that game. The first time he was called Mario was in *Mario Bros.*—he was named after Nintendo's landlord at the time, Mario Segali. The coin-op classic, which introduced Mario's penchant for coin collecting, also featured the debut of Mario's stalwart sibling, Luigi. Further, *Mario Bros.* was Nintendo's first simultaneous two-player title.

Mario Bros. is one of the most adapted games of all time. As Lucas M. Thomas wrote in a review of the Virtual Console version of the NES game, *Mario Bros.* was "recast as a two-player challenge contained within the later generation NES masterpiece, *Super Mario Bros. 3*. Then it came back again in *Super Mario All-Stars.* Then, again, reimagined as *Mario Clash* as a launch title for Nintendo's ill-fated Virtual Boy system."

Thomas continued: "After that, *Mario Bros.* began seeing further reissue through the *Super Mario Advance* series of Game Boy Advance cartridges—all four of those titles, as well as *Mario & Luigi: Superstar Saga*, contain a GBA rendition of the game. It came back again in *Animal Crossing*. And in e-Card form, for the GBA's e-Reader device."

Prior to those versions, *Mario Bros.* was ported to the Atari 2600, 5200, and 7800, all of which are nicely programmed, but inferior to the NES game.

FUN FACT:

Programmed by Jimmy Huey of Designer Software, the Apple II version of *Mario Bros.* had something the NES and Atari ports lacked: falling icicles.

WHY IT MADE THE LIST:

Mario Bros. offers stellar two-player action—bumping each other into enemies can be hilariously entertaining—but the one-player mode is terrific as well.

CHAPTER 57

MEGA MAN

NINTENDO NES
GENRE: PLATFORM SHOOTER
PUBLISHER: CAPCOM
DEVELOPER: CAPCOM
1 PLAYER
1987

Mega Man for the Nintendo NES, complete in box. $250.

"CRISP GRAPHICS, EXCELLENT CONTROLS, CHALLENGING GAMEPLAY, AND EXPANSIVE, GENRE-DEFINING ACTION."

Mega Man is a key game in the NES library, characterized by crisp graphics, excellent controls, challenging gameplay, and expansive, genre-defining action.

Released at the tail end of 1987, it is a platform shooter that's as hard and (almost) as fun as 1988's *Contra* (the greatest platform shooter for the NES), but with anime-style characters instead of muscle-bound commandoes. Unlike Lance and Bill, the heroes of *Contra*, Mega Man—the human-like experimental robot that players control—can't shoot diagonally or up or down.

Clad in a round helmet and blue costume, Mega Man must run, jump, shoot, and climb his way through six levels, each of which scrolls horizontally and vertically, and each of which ends in a humanoid robot boss: Cutman, Gutsman, Iceman, Bombman, Fireman, or Elecman. After beating all six levels, Mega Man must face Dr. Wily, the mad scientist responsible for programming the bosses to be evil.

The benevolent Dr. Wright, who is Dr. Wily's boss, had originally created the boss robots to perform such industrial functions as transporting boulders (Gutsman), cutting down trees (Cutman), and supervising nuclear power plants (Elecman). However, Wily had other plans. He wanted to control the world and its resources. Luckily, Mega Man, who was also created by Dr. Wright, resisted Dr. Wily's programming and is here to save the day.

As Mega Man, players can select the order in which to play the first six levels, each of which has a theme that reflects its boss's weapons and intended function. After Mega Man defeats a boss, he will acquire that boss's weaponry (such as fireballs or boomerangs), which can be used to exploit other bosses' weaknesses, meaning there is some strategy involved for the experienced player in deciding which order to play the levels in.

In addition to end-level bosses, the game is riddled with other obstacles, including such oddball enemies as Screw Bomber, Octopus Battery, Killer Bullet, Flying Shell, Bombomb, Sniper Joe, Tackle Fire, Crazy Razy, Picket Man, and Blader (a flying pair of eyes with teeth). There are also helpful items to grab that increase the player's life energy, weapon energy, and point total. In addition, there are 1ups and magnet beams, the latter of which create steps for climbing up.

Thanks in part to platforms that disappear in sequence and hard-to-dodge projectiles, *Mega Man* is a difficult game. However, it does have a generous health meter and unlimited continues, making it beatable for those who chose to stick with it and don't mind repeating earlier parts of levels again and again until you can manage to get past them (a common occurrence in '80s gaming).

In 2004, Capcom released *Mega Man Anniversary Collection* for the GameCube and PlayStation 2 (the Xbox version hit store shelves in 2005). The disc features 10 complete games in the series (including the original *Mega Man*), plus unlockable bonus features. The GameCube version includes an interview with *Mega Man* producer and illustrator Keiji Inafune (working with Akira Kitamura and Tokuro Fujiwara), who co-designed the lead character.

Shortly after graduating (art school? high school? college?—the interview doesn't say), Inafune went to work for Capcom. "The very first project I ever did was an arcade game called *Street Fighter* [1987]," he said. "Then after that, when we were done

The back of the *Mega Man* box.

Mega Man Anniversary Collection for the GameCube includes an interview with Mega Man producer and illustrator Keiji Inafune.

Mega Man spawned numerous sequels, including Mega Man 2. Pictured complete in box. $100.

with the project, they said 'we are working on a new title for the home consumer division, and we'd like you to participate.' So it was at that time that I joined the *Mega Man* project."

With its cutesy, rounded, big-eyed characters, *Mega Man* was obviously inspired by anime. "A lot of the character design for *Mega Man* is based on the Japanese cartoons I saw when I was a child," Inafune said. "And when I was making the game, I felt like I was going back to my roots, back to my childhood. It was very fun to design that character."

In Japan, where the game was developed, *Mega Man* is known as *Rockman*, but that title came about after a few other names were considered. "It was originally going to be 'Mighty Kid' or 'Knuckle Kid,'" Inafune said. "And that's how we were doing the package until we decided on *Rockman*. And in the end, it did become *Mega Man* in the states."

Inafune continued: "It's not a rock like a stone or a pebble. That's not where the name 'Rockman' comes from. It comes from rock 'n' roll. When I first designed the character, I had rock 'n' roll in mind. That was the back image I was going off of when I designed the artwork. For me, *Rockman*—or *Mega Man*, has always been a game that's been designed with music in mind. Music's always been an important part of the series."

Looking back at his original sketches for the game, Inafune shook his head, smiling. "Man, I really wasn't that good, was I?," he said. "If one of my character designers that work under me now were to bring something like this to me, I'd probably take one look and say 'no way, this sucks, try again.'"

Commenting on *Mega Man*'s gameplay mechanics, Inafune said: "When you think about it, there's not something in the world that is stronger than everything else. Almost everything has something that it's stronger than and something that it's weaker than. Sort of like in rock/paper/scissors. Scissors will beat paper, but it loses to the rock. Paper will beat the rock, but it loses to the scissors. That's how the *Mega Man* weapons work."

Upon completing *Mega Man*, Inafune, Akira Kitamura (who applied the rock/paper/scissors theory to the weapons), and producer Tokuro Fujiwara were convinced that they had a commercial failure on their hands. "After we got the game done,"

Inafune said, "we took it over to sales, and they said there's no way this is going to sell. So I was really disappointed, of course."

Capcom proceeded to release the cartridge as *Rockman* in limited quantities (at least at first) in Japan. Luckily, the game became a big hit, thanks in large part to that unpredictable arbiter of the marketplace: word of mouth. Capcom brought *Mega Man* to the U.S. shortly thereafter, and it enjoyed brisk sales as well, despite crummy box art that in no way reflected the actual game.

The follow-up cartridge, *Mega Man 2* for the NES, is generally considered to be even better than the original *Mega Man* (thanks to more detailed graphics, larger enemies, more intricate level designs, and the inclusion of passwords), but that title was released in 1989, meaning it doesn't fall within the parameters of this book. Luckily, *Mega Man* is no slouch.

The success of *Mega Man*, which has been re-released through the Wii, Wii U, and 3DS Virtual Consoles, led to numerous other sequels, including titles for the NES, Game Boy, Game Boy Color, Game Boy Advance, Game Gear, Super NES, Sega Saturn, Game Gear, GameCube, Nintendo DS, Nintendo 64, PlayStation, PlayStation 2, PlayStation 3, Wii, and Xbox 360.

Mega Man also spawned a syndicated cartoon series, which aired from 1994-1995.

FUN FACT:

In *Rockman*, which is the Japanese version of *Mega Man*, the title character has a female counterpart named "Roll."

WHY IT MADE THE LIST:

Anyone who likes anime-style characters, crisp graphics, and hardcore platform shooting action will love *Mega Man*.

CHAPTER 58

METROID

NES
GENRE: ADVENTURE/PLATFORM SHOOTER
PUBLISHER: NINTENDO
DEVELOPER: NINTENDO
1 PLAYER
1987

Metroid for the Nintendo NES, complete in box. $80.

"METROID IS OLD-SCHOOL DIFFICULT, SEPARATING THE HARDCORE GAMER FROM THE CASUAL FAN."

In the year 20X5, space pirates have stolen a mysterious new life-form called Metroid, a being so powerful that it probably wiped out the entire civilization of Planet SR388. If the space pirates were to multiply the life-form and use it as a weapon, the entire galaxy could be destroyed. To prevent this unimaginable disaster, the Federation Police have sent a cyborg space hunter named Samus Aran to penetrate the enemy fortress on Planet Zebes and destroy big boss Mother Brain, which would put a stop to the entire operation.

The player controls Samus Aran, an agile, now-iconic character who can run, jump, and fire short-range beams. However, by finding rooms that contain power items, Samus can add the following strategic, fun-to-use weapons to his arsenal: bombs, long beam, ice beam, wave beam, screw attack, high jump, missile rockets, varia (which makes Samus lose less power when hit), and maru mari (which lets Samus roll into a ball to access narrow passages). Samus can also find tanks for storing energy.

A game that is now hard to find complete in box, *Metroid* is anything but a garden-variety platform shooter. Rather, it's an epic adventure taking place in a vast, non-linear underworld of connecting rooms, confounding dead ends (or are they?), and exotic enemies—some that crawl, some that fly, some that swoop down at you. The player could use a map or some kind of guidance system, but none exist—those features would come later in such sequels as *Super Metroid* (1994, Super Nintendo) and *Metroid Prime* (2002, GameCube).

Metroid is old-school difficult, separating the hardcore gamer from the casual fan.

Luckily, *Metroid* is equipped with a then-cutting edge password system for saving progress. *Kid Icarus*, which was released at the same time as *Metroid*, shares the honors for being the first video game cartridge to use passwords. Also like *Kid Icarus*, *Metroid* scrolls vertically as well as horizontally. Both games are super tough to beat.

While *Metroid*'s solid black backgrounds seem dated today, the game was a thing of beauty at the time of its release. Samus is nicely animated, the creatures look cool, and the platforms in the underground caverns Samus explores are a nice variety of colors, designs, and textures. The game sounds great as well, with catchy, memorable, upbeat music (by Hip Tanaka) to complement the daunting nature of Samus's lonely task. Players truly get the sense that Samus is alone and lost in a hostile alien environment—the unadorned backgrounds actually add to the game's creepy atmosphere.

When I got my NES, *Metroid* was one of the first cartridges I bought with my own money. I typically prefer straightforward action games to adventure titles (I tend to get lost, bored, and/or frustrated with games in which the emphasis is on exploration), but, as with *The Legend of Zelda*, I somehow managed to stick with the game long enough to get to the end. Speaking of which, the game has a major, now-famous surprise at the end, in which—SPOILER WARNING—Samus is revealed to be a woman!

The back of the *Metroid* box.

Metroid spawned numerous sequels, including *Metroid II: Return of Samus*. Pictured complete in box. $70.

Metroid was re-released on the Game Boy Advance in 2004. Pictured complete in box. $20.

Created by Makoto Kano (scenario writer), Hiroji Kiyotake (character designer), Yoshio Sakamoto (director and character designer), and Gunpei Yokoi (producer), *Metroid* may test the patience and resolve of the modern gamer, but it will forever hold its place as one of the greatest cartridges of the 8-bit era.

Here are a few of the countless accolades for *Metroid*:

Intelligent mix of platform exploration and shoot-'em-up action.

—*Videogames: The Ultimate Guide* (2001, Carlton)

Metroid is pure gaming genius at its finest, because you don't play it, you experience it.

— *Game Informer* #100 (Aug., 2001) in which *Metroid* is ranked sixth on the list of "Top 100 Games of All Time"

Listed as one of the "99 Favorite Classics" by Digital Press in 1997

One of the greatest games of all time.

—gamestyle.com

Metroid's not just a classic because of its astounding graphics, cinematic sound effects, accurate control, and fresh gameplay, but also because of its staying power.

—Benjamin F. Norris IV (allgame.com)

In issue #200 of *Electronic Gaming Monthly* (Feb., 2006), *Metroid* ranked number 11 on the list of "The Greatest 200 Videogames of Their Time." In that issue, the director of *Metroid*, Yoshio Sakamoto, gave a little insight into the origins of the groundbreaking nature of the game. "When we were working on the original *Metroid*, we didn't have much development experience," he said. "We were trying to establish a brand-new type of game: the sci-fi adventure.

Even though we [had to feel] our way to completion, we never lost our ambition. Now, looking back at how we were at that time, our attitude was like that of Samus Aran, who had to rush headlong into the vast and dangerous planet Zebes without hesitation."

Metroid inspired a variety of sequels, including: *Metroid II: Return of Samus* (1991, Game Boy), which added spring ball and spider ball weapons, along with battery backup; *Super Metroid* (1994, Super Nintendo), which added a moon walk maneuver, an inventory screen, and weapon combining; *Metroid Fusion* (2002, Game Boy Advance), which added wall climbing, ledge grabbing, and aliens that release power-ups; the *Metroid Prime* series (GameCube, Wii), which changed the genre to first-person shooter; and *Metroid: Other M* (2010, Wii), a third-person 3D action title taking place right after *Super Metroid*.

In 2004, Nintendo released an enhanced remake of *Metroid* for the Game Boy Advance called *Metroid: Zero Mission*. That same year saw the original *Metroid* re-released on the Game Boy Advance as part of the "Classic NES Series."

In 2005, the franchise took a curious turn with *Metroid Prime Pinball* for the Nintendo DS.

In 2007, the original *Metroid* became a downloadable title via the Virtual Console for the Nintendo Wii, and in 2011 for the 3DS.

FUN FACT:
Entering JUSTIN BAILEY as the password lets players start *Metroid* with most of the power-ups already acquired, and with Samus wearing a pink, one-piece swimsuit.

WHY IT MADE THE LIST:
Dark, mysterious, adventurous, and weapons-filled, *Metroid* is one of the cornerstone titles of that beloved gray box we call the NES.

CHAPTER 59

MINER 2049ER

COLECOVISION
GENRE: CLIMBING/NON-SCROLLING PLATFORMER
PUBLISHER: MICRO FUN
DEVELOPER: MICRO FUN
1 OR 2 PLAYERS (ALTERNATING)
1983

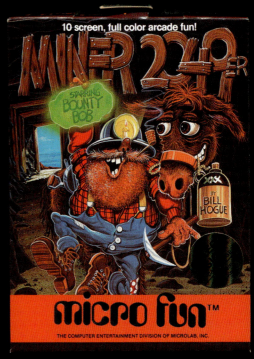

Miner 2049er for the ColecoVision, complete in box. Courtesy of Bryan C. Smith. $30.

"IT'S FUN TO TRY AND FIGURE OUT THE BEST PATHWAY THROUGH EACH LEVEL."

The first third-party release for the ColecoVision, *Miner 2049er* brings 11 levels of action to the family television set (or, these days, more likely your game room, since the family TV is probably a high-def flat screen with an Xbox One, PS4, or Wii U hooked up to it). Instead of digging for coal, diamonds, gold, or some other valuable substance (like a normal miner might do), you, as Bounty Bob, must walk on the complete surface of all the platforms in each level, effectively "masking" in the mineshaft framework.

Along with scurrying over platforms, players will jump, climb up and down ladders, ride on moving platforms, be hoisted by a hydraulic pump, go down slides (ladders and slides connect girders in each level), use elevators (pressing 5 on the keypad retrieves the elevator while 1-4 takes Bob to the desired floor), ride a small crane, and even get shot out of a cannon. Once Bob has masked all of the framework within a set time period (the faster you finish a level, the more points you get), it's on to the next screen.

While working his way through each level, Bob must jump over or otherwise avoid roaming mutants. If Bob grabs one of the floating mining tools available at different areas throughout the game, the mutants change color and smile, becoming vulnerable for a few seconds. During this time, Bob can destroy them with a mere touch. This is similar to the power pellets in a certain dot-eating maze game. In short, *Miner 2049er* is a cross of sorts between *Pac-Man* and *Donkey Kong* (with a number of unique elements mixed in), a pleasurable concoction indeed.

The platforms and other items in each level are laid out in deviously clever fashion, forcing the player to work quickly, smartly, and strategically, especially in later levels. Bounty Bob moves with great speed relative to most non-scrolling platformers, and it's fun to try and figure out the best pathway through each level. Sometimes it's wise to walk on certain platforms prior to working on other areas of the screen, and expertly timed jumps are often necessary. It's a particularly fun strategy to destroy a mutant while sliding down a slide, having recently grabbed a mining tool.

When *Miner 2049er* first hit stores, it retailed for approximately $50, which was almost twice as much as the average ColecoVision cartridge (*Zaxxon* also debuted for around $50). A friend of mine named Brian bought the game and got tired of it (I'm not sure how—I still love playing it), and he sold it to me for $30 (he also sold me his copy of *Zaxxon*, but I digress…). I was happy for the discount, but I would've gladly paid the full price, even though my funds were limited at the time—it's that great of a game.

Admittedly, *Miner 2049er* doesn't look like much. The colors are sharp, and the graphics are flicker-free, but the mutants are simplistic in design, and Bob appears as though he were drawn by a four-year-old. The play's the thing, though, and in this regard *Miner 2049er* has few peers. Fans

The back of the *Miner 2049er* box. Courtesy of Bryan C. Smith.

Miner 2049er game cartridge. $12.

Miner 2049er instruction manual. $5.

of such titles as *Space Panic*, *Mr. Do!'s Castle*, and *Lode Runner* will love it.

In a 2007 interview with Syd Bolton published on The Armchair Empire website (www.armchairempire.com), Bill Hogue, who created the original computer version of *Miner 2049er*, summed up the appeal of the cartridge thusly: "It's a simple game and it's clear at first glance what needs to be done to finish a level. But as you're playing along you discover it wasn't quite as easy as you thought. I wonder, though, if kids of today think of *Miner* like we do. *Miner* returns us to a simpler time and perhaps that's why people like to play it again."

In *JoyStik* Vol. 2 #2 (Nov., 1983), the reviewer gave *Miner 2049er* for the ColecoVision five out of five stars, saying it "has the potential to be the best game of the year" and that it "makes *Donkey Kong* look like a warm up." He also said, "This is a game that will have you thinking and planning strategy hour after hour and wanting to come back for more."

The ColecoVision version of *Miner 2049er* is the best because it has 11 screens (in an era when most games of its type had just 1-4 screens). The original computer version has 10 screens, as does the Atari 5200 version (which benefits from intro animations in which Bob walks around displaying the title and credits). For the Atari 2600, the action was divided among two cartridges (*Miner 2049er* and *Miner 2049er II*) containing just three screens apiece.

Mike Livesay adapted *Miner 2049er* for the ColecoVision. In a gamespy.com interview conducted in 2001, Livesay said, "One of my most enjoyable times during the *Miner 2049er* experience was when the ColecoVision came on the market. I immediately ran out and bought one…after playing a few games I decided to crack open the unit and see what was inside. To my delight, I found that it was made from many off-the-shelf parts—no custom chips, really. It was based on a Z80 and used a GI sound chip and a TI graphics chip. I was able to get the data sheets for all the chips."

Livesay approached Micro Fun about adapting *Miner 2049er* for the ColecoVision, but Coleco turned them down, saying they didn't want any third-party games. Undeterred, Livesay "went ahead and reversed engineered the Coleco and put together my own development kit, based on the Apple II CP/M system. I was able to rewire one of their game carts to use a zip socket so I could insert EPROMs in them. Thus I was able to develop games by coding them on the Apple II system, burning the code into an EPROM which could be run as a game cart on an actual retail system."

A short time later, Livesay "got the okay from Micro Fun to do Coleco *Miner*, and four months or so later we released it… We even had room to throw in an extra level, the impossible-to-get-to 11th level…the game flew off the shelves and outsold the Apple version by over two to one. Six months later I was making $15,000 per month in royalties, which was a huge amount of money for a single, 24-year-old kid in the early '80s."

Despite the critical and commercial success of *Miner 2049er*, the sequel, *Bounty Bob Strikes Back* (featured in this book), was only released for the Atari 5200 and Commodore 64, leaving ColecoVision fans out in the cold.

Luckily, said fans can return to *Miner 2049er* again and again.

FUN FACT:

A sequel to *Miner 2049er* called *Scraper Caper* was tantalizingly advertised in various magazines of the era, but was never released. According to the Armchair Empire interview referenced earlier, Hogue admits that he threw away the disks and tapes containing the game many years ago.

WHY IT MADE THE LIST:

An ingenious mixture of *Donkey Kong* and *Pac-Man*, *Miner 2049er* is one of the greatest climbing games ever made. The later screens are tricky puzzles, requiring brains and dexterity to solve.

CHAPTER 60

MINESTORM/ MINESTORM II

VECTREX
GENRE: NON-SCROLLING SHOOTER
PUBLISHER: GCE
DEVELOPER: GCE
1 OR 2 PLAYERS (ALTERNATING)
1982

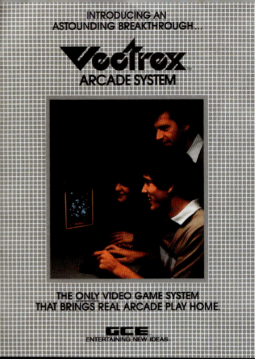

Vectrex press kit, showing *MineStorm* in action. $100.

"MINESTORM IS WIDELY REGARDED AS ONE OF THE BEST GAMES OF THE GOLDEN AGE."

Some of the games in this book, such as *Adventure* and *Pitfall!*, are highly original creations, while others, such as *Demon Attack* and *K.C.'s Krazy Chase!*, borrow heavily from earlier games. *MineStorm*, which is built into the Vectrex console, clearly falls into the latter category, mimicking the classic, vector-based arcade shooter *Asteroids* (1979) in fine fashion.

Like the ship you control in *Asteroids*, the space craft you pilot in *MineStorm* can rotate, thrust, shoot, and warp into hyperspace. The ship maneuvers in all directions and will appear on the opposite side of the star-studded playfield when you fly off-screen.

Hitting hyperspace, which makes the ship disappear and reappear in another part of the playfield (called a "galaxy" in the manual), is a desperate maneuver—it can save your life when you are surrounded by enemies, or it can place you immediately in harm's way.

In *Asteroids*, players shoot at space rocks, which break into smaller shapes when hit. In *MineStorm*, the rocks are replaced by—you guessed it—mines, which come in four varieties: floating mines resemble three-pointed stars and simply drift through space; fireball mines, which are four-pointed, semi-square stars with a dot in the middle, hurl a fireball your direction when they are shot; magnetic mines are four-pointed stars that follow your ship around the playfield; and magnetic-fireball mines possess properties of both magnetic and fireball mines, making them especially dangerous.

By having fireballs hurled at you when you shoot fireball mines, the programmers infused *MineStorm* with a challenging, on-the-fly strategic consideration as players must quickly decide the safest, most efficient way to shoot those types of mines. The preferred method is to put some distance between your ship and the fireball mine and open fire, being careful to shoot the fireball as soon as it's released. It's also a good idea to clear out some of the floating and magnetic mines prior to taking on the fireball mines in order to give your ship room to operate.

Each mine appears in three sizes: small, medium, and large. When a large mine is destroyed, two medium-sized mines take its place. When a medium-sized mine is destroyed, two small mines take its place. Shooting small mines removes them entirely from the playfield. Flying saucers periodically appear, and players can shoot them right away or let them lay even more mines (for the potential to score extra points). After the playfield has been completely cleared out, it's on to the next minefield.

In the instruction manual for *MineStorm*, it says that you will "enter a new type of universe after you complete 13 mine fields" and that "space dust and alien forces make this new world a difficult challenge." The truth is that the game has a bug that skips the action ahead to mine field 15 and reduces many of the mines to mere floating dots. Gameplay and scoring continue, but it's an annoying bug, not an intentional feature to make the game more challenging.

Page three of Vectrex press kit.

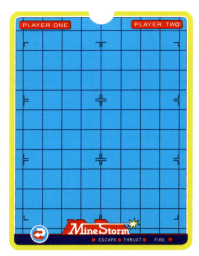
MineStorm screen overlay. $35.

Vectrex magazine ad; *MineStorm* was built into the Vectrex console.

In many *MineStorm* cartridges, the game crashes altogether after level 13. Some of these cartridges included an extra slip of paper in the instruction manual advising the player to press reset if the game screen goes blank after level 13.

MineStorm gets pretty hard after the sixth or seventh screen, and most players never make it to the 13th screen and beyond. However, during the short-lived heyday of the Vectrex, if you wrote GCE to report the bug that appears after minefield 13, the company would send you a bug-free version of the game called *MineStorm II*. Very few people did this, so *MineStorm II* is extremely rare.

Even though their system eventually failed on a retail level, GCE opting to feature *MineStorm* as the built-in game was a genius move. It does an excellent job showing off the standalone console's sharp, vector-based graphics, it seems ideally suited to the system's control panel, and it's the type of pick-up-and-play game that anyone can jump right into. Like many of the great classics, it's simple to play, but very tough to master.

In the premiere issue of *Passport Magazine* (1984), *MineStorm* programmer John Hall spoke briefly about the difficulties in developing the game, saying it took more than four months to complete. "The first third of that project went very smoothly," he said. "But like most of the games I've worked on, it's the final two-thirds that take all the time. All the detail work can make you crazy! During the game programming process I have to include input from the game designers, the marketing department, and the many people who actually play-test the games—all of whom have changes they want made to the game."

MineStorm is widely regarded as one of the best games of the Golden Age, regardless of the system. George Roush, writing for IGN (ign.com), said that *MineStorm* is a classic that he still enjoys playing and that it has excellent controls and sound effects. The Video Game Critic (videogamecritic.com) called the game "a brilliant *Asteroids* adaptation" and "reason enough to purchase the Vectrex."

Also comparing the cart to *Asteroids*, Joe Santulli, writing in *Digital Press Collectors Guide #7* (2002), inferred that *MineStorm* is more fun and more challenging than the game that inspired it.

"*MineStorm* not only contains the point busting, rock blasting, run 'n' shoot offense that made *Asteroids* a hit, but it also has levels," he said. "Levels! New tougher enemies appear each stage until you just can't match their speed."

In a feature called "Farewell to the Vectrex," published in the Sept., 1984 issue of *Electronic Games* magazine, *EG* cofounder Joyce Worley wrote that *MineStorm* is a "high energy one- or two-player contest that's so good most gamers would want to buy it separately if it didn't come with the system."

In issue #1 (summer, 1983) of the British publication, *TV Gamer*, the writer called *MineStorm* "both challenging and impressive to look at" and "a game that should have long lasting appeal." He also said, "This is to date the probably the best game to come with a console," which is high praise considering the fact that *Donkey Kong* was packaged with the ColecoVision.

Of all the titles in the Vectrex library, I've spent more hours playing *MineStorm* than any other game. I like the rapid fire and quick ship, the non-stop action, the starburst explosions when you destroy a mine, the impending doom sound of the musical intro, the spaceship that brings out the mines as play begins, and that compulsive feeling I have to play "just one more game" every time I lose all my ships.

FUN FACT:

A 3D version of *MineStorm* called, appropriately enough, *3D MineStorm* was also released for the Vectrex; it was the pack-in title with the 3D Imager glasses.

WHY IT MADE THE LIST:

Of the countless console games obviously inspired by an arcade classic (*Asteroids* in this case), *MineStorm* ranks right up there with the best of the best.

CHAPTER 61

MISSILE COMMAND

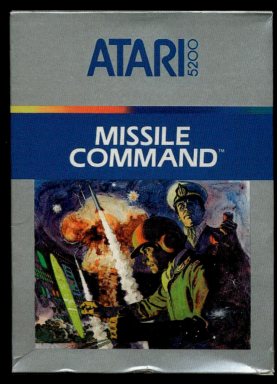

ATARI 2600
GENRE: NON-SCROLLING SHOOTER
PUBLISHER: ATARI
DEVELOPER: ATARI
1 OR 2 PLAYERS (ALTERNATING)
1981

ATARI 5200
GENRE: NON-SCROLLING SHOOTER
PUBLISHER: ATARI
DEVELOPER: ATARI
1 OR 2 PLAYERS (ALTERNATING)
1982

Missile Command for the Atari 5200, complete in box. Courtesy of AtariAge.com. $15.

> "THE FIRING SYSTEM IN MISSILE COMMAND WAS UNIQUE WITH THE RELEASE OF THE ARCADE ORIGINAL AND IS STILL UNUSUAL TODAY."

Like the Atari 2600 port, *Missile Command* for the Atari 5200 eschews any Cold War era implications of Atari's 1980 coin-op classic by incorporating a science fiction plotline into the manual. The resource-rich Zardon, an Earth outpost colony, is under attack by Krytolia, a planet plagued by poverty, crime, and civil unrest.

The accompanying gameplay is similar, however, as players must defend six cities along the surface of a planet from IPBMs (interplanetary ballistic missiles), MIRVs (multiple independent reentry vehicles), smart missiles, killer satellites, and bombs. This is done by guiding a targeting site around the screen, firing ABMs (anti-ballistic missiles) at the various enemies and enemy projectiles dropping from the sky.

The firing system in *Missile Command* was unique with the release of the arcade original and is still unusual today. When players push the fire button, a missile from a base at the bottom/center of the screen shoots toward the current position of the targeting site, exploding upon arrival and destroying anything in the immediate vicinity. By moving and shooting quickly, players can create up to eight ABM explosions onscreen at once. Missiles should be used judiciously, though, since they are limited—one key strategy is to aim for enemy missile intersections.

Regrettably, like the Atari 2600 version, the 5200 game, which was designed by Rob Zdybel, only has the single missile base. In the arcade version, that base was flanked by

Missile Command for the Atari 2600, complete in box. *Courtesy of AtariAge.com.* $8.

Missile Command instruction manual (Atari 2600). $1.

two more bases: one in the bottom left corner and one in the bottom right corner. However, the 5200 rendition retains the bombers and the flashing, famously ominous two-word ending, THE END, elements missing from the 2600 cart.

With only one of three bases intact, and with blockier graphics, you might think *Missile Command* for the home is drastically downgraded from the arcade game. While the shortcomings in the 2600 and 5200 versions are unfortunate, the games remain a blast to play, thanks in part to the basic gameplay mechanics remaining firmly intact, and to excellent trackball control, which gives you firm command of the targeting site, whether you are moving it slowly or zipping it around the screen with reckless abandon.

The appeal of *Missile Command*, whether you are playing it on the Atari 2600, 5200, or in the arcades, lies in its ever-maddening fast pace, which has you in a near-constant state of "putting out fires." As enemy missiles rain down from above, you must quickly move the targeting sight all over the screen, timing your barrage of shots with rough precision (I say "rough" because near-misses count since explosions expand).

As the protector of six cities, you feel a sense of responsibility and increasing doom as you inevitably lose one city after another. For each 10,000 points scored, you gain an extra city, which always comes as a relief. On the sixth wave, the alien invaders launch smart missiles that home in on your cities and missile base, making an already challenging game even more difficult. For those who want a stiff challenge from the get-go, you can go to Skip Wave Mode and bypass up to nine waves.

The original arcade version of *Missile Command* was a huge hit and something of a cultural icon, appearing in an episode of the *Barney Miller* television program (a detective was hooked on the game) and in the films *Fast Times at Ridgemont High* (1982) and *Terminator 2: Judgment Day* (1991).

The game was designed by Dave Theurer, who, in *High Score: The Illustrated History of Electronic Games*, described the genesis of the coin-op classic thusly: "Gene Lipkin told Steve Calfee that we should do a game where the country was being invaded by missiles. They showed me a picture of a radar screen and said to take it from there. I hated the radar screens because of the vanishing info, so I got rid of it. I had used the Trak-Ball in my previous *Soccer* game and decided it was the best controller for the task."

Getting back to *Missile Command* for the home, Walter Lowe, Jr. praised the 2600 version in his book, *Playboy's Guide to Rating the Video Games* (1982, PBJ Books), calling it "extremely intense" with "very good long-term player interest." In *Ken Uston's Guide to Buying and Beating the Home Video Games* (1982, Signet), the author wrote, "If you like the arcade *Missile Command* game, the chances are high you'll like this game too. While it's of necessity simpler than the arcade game due to computer capacity and graphics limitations, it's almost as much fun to play."

In Craig Kubey's *The Winners' Book of Video Games* (1982, Warner Books), the author said the 2600 game "admirably reproduces most of the characteristics of the popular, unique, and ultra-challenging parent of the same name."

Rob Fulop designed 2600 *Missile Command*, but he was unhappy with the compensation he received. In *Atari Inc.—Business is Fun* (2012, Syzygy Company Press), authors Marty Goldberg and Curt Vendel wrote that Fulop was expecting a bonus of "perhaps $10,000-$15,000 or who knows, perhaps even more" since Atari "had just made millions" from the game. However, all he got beyond his normal salary was a certificate for a free turkey. This insult helped Fulop decide to leave Atari and, along with Dennis Koble and a few others, form Imagic.

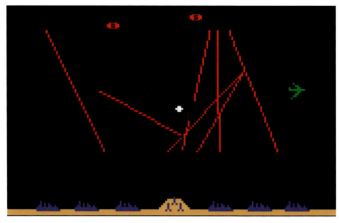

Missile Command for the Atari 5200 in action. Courtesy of AtariAge.com.

Despite its greatness on the 2600, the 5200, and in the arcades, *Missile Command* never received a proper sequel—in 1992, Atari Games developed *Arcade Classics* containing *Missile Command II* and *Super Centipede*, but that arcade cab only exists as a prototype. However, the game was reimagined for the Atari Jaguar in 1995 with *Missile Command 3D*, which included three games: *Missile Command*, *3D Missile Command*, and *Virtual Missile Command*.

The previous year, Atari released *Super Asteroids and Missile Command* for the handheld Lynx, containing *Super Asteroids* and *Super Missile Command*. Both games add power-ups and updated graphics to the original formula, and *Super Missile Command* features different types of terrain to protect.

In 1999, *Missile Command* was remade for the PlayStation, with fancy graphics and an elaborate musical score, and for the Game Boy Color, with animations, different city backgrounds, and rumble effects. In 1992, *Missile Command* was ported to the original Game Boy as part of *Arcade Classic No. 1: Asteroids/Missile Command*, which also added different city backgrounds.

In 2007, Atari brought the original *Missile Command* arcade game to the Xbox 360 (via XBLA). It includes the standard game, plus versions with updated graphics and different modes of play, such as Throttle Monkey Mode, which increases the speed and challenge of the game. In 2010, Microsoft made *Missile Command* for the arcade and the 2600 available for the Xbox 360 Game Room service.

Finally, *Missile Command* ports have been included in various compilation titles over the years, including *Arcade Classics* (1996) for the Game Gear and Genesis and *Arcade's Greatest Hits: The Atari Collection 1* for the PlayStation (1996), Sega Saturn (1997), and Super Nintendo (1997).

But if you want to get back to basics and have smooth trackball control, stick with the Atari 2600 or the Atari 5200 version, the next best thing to playing the arcade original.

FUN FACT:

Rob Fulop encoded his initials into the 2600 port; in level 13, if you use all your missiles without scoring any points, the city on the right will become "RF." This Easter egg was documented in volume 1 issue 2 of *Atari Age* via a letter to the editor from Joseph Nickischer.

WHY IT MADE THE LIST:

As *Missile Command* champion Roy Schildt said in *The King of Kong: A Fistful of Quarters* (2007), "The prestige of *Missile Command*" is great "because it's a macho game...it has a lot of paramilitary association." Schildt was referring to the arcade game, but the 2600 and 5200 versions are just as macho.

CHAPTER 62

MOON PATROL

ATARI 5200
GENRE: SIDE-SCROLLING SHOOTER
PUBLISHER: ATARI
DEVELOPER: ATARI
1 OR 2 PLAYERS (ALTERNATING)
1983

Moon Patrol for the Atari 5200, complete in box. $12.

"OFFERS ENOUGH ON-THE-FLY STRATEGIES AND HARDCORE ACTION TO PLEASE THE MOST DISCERNING OF JOYSTICK JOCKEYS."

A science fiction game that puts players in a moon buggy, rolling along the ground (as opposed to the far more common ship flying through space), *Moon Patrol* is a creatively designed horizontal shooter that moves in a strictly linear, auto-scrolling fashion, but it offers enough on-the-fly strategies and hardcore action to please the most discerning of joystick jockeys.

As the moon buggy drives to the right, UFOs appear overhead, and these, along with their missiles, can be shot out of the sky with a gun fixed atop the car that shoots straight upward. There's also a short-range gun on the front of the car, which is useful for removing rocks from the pathway. Certain rocks roll, adding to the challenge.

A versatile vehicle, the moon buggy can jump over craters, some of which automatically appear in the roadway, some of which are created by missiles dropped by the UFOs. Rocks and landmines can also be jumped over. By pressing left and right on the joystick, the buggy can be slowed down and sped up (respectively).

The key to success in this super fun, super challenging game is timing jumps just right in conjunction with the obstacles and working the speed controls in a way to get through the course safely and quickly. The timing of shots plays a role as well.

Williams released the original coin-op version of *Moon Patrol* in 1982. It was likely influenced by Rockola's *Jump Bug*, a vehicle-based side-scroller that appeared in the arcades the previous year. *Moon Patrol* was designed by the legendary Takashi Nishiyama, who would go on to conceive the original *Street Fighter* at Capcom. A pioneer of the fighting genre, Nishiyama also developed such titles as *Fatal Fury*, *King of Fighters*, and *Samurai Shodown*.

According to *High Score: The Illustrated History of Video Games* (2002, McGraw-Hill/Osborne), *Moon Patrol* was "the only imported game licensed by Williams (from Irem in Japan)." It was also "the first game to feature parallax scrolling, in which the background moved at a different rate than the foreground," giving the graphics "a slightly more realistic distance effect." (Oddly, the book also says *Moon Patrol* does "not qualify as one of the all-time greats," which is an opinion I strongly disagree with.)

The Atari 5200 version of *Moon Patrol* mimics the parallax scrolling nicely, and the game is an excellent port overall. As with virtually all ports of the era, however, there are a couple of shortcomings, in this case a moon buggy that looks like a mechanical aardvark and blocky UFOs that lack the classic sci-fi appearance of their coin-op counterparts. The mountainous backgrounds look fantastic, however, as do the buildings, which are wonderfully futuristic in a surreal kind of way.

Another positive with the 5200 game is that it includes the checkpoints found in the original, along with players getting bonus points for moving quickly. These attributes give gamers a real sense of progression as they go from point A to point Z (with E, J, O, and T checkpoints in between). In the arcades, *Moon Patrol* was one of the first games to let you

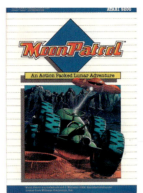
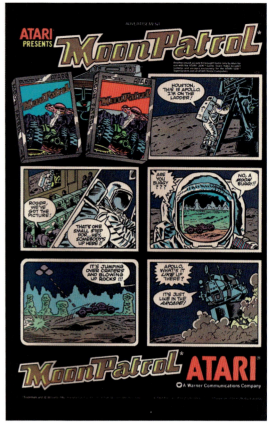

The back of the *Moon Patrol* box.

Moon Patrol instruction manual. $2.

Moon Patrol comic book ad.

continue the action (by inserting more quarters), and it's nice that you can do this at home free of charge.

Unlike certain 5200 titles, the controls for *Moon Patrol* work great. Not surprisingly, the game as a whole is a nice upgrade over the 2600 version, which is playable, but suffers visually and, of course, doesn't have a separate button for jumping (players must press up on the joystick). Both versions include the background music from the arcade game, but the 5200 music is more on key.

Atari produced *Moon Patrol* for the ColecoVision in 1984, but, sadly, that version only exists in prototype form. I've never played the *Moon Patrol* prototype, but the YouTube videos I've seen of the game in action look very impressive.

James Bond 007, released for the Atari 2600 in 1983 and the 5200 and ColecoVision in 1984, mimics the action of *Moon Patrol* to some degree, but it's a vastly inferior title.

In 2007, Left Turn Only produced *Space Patrol*, a spectacular *Moon Patrol* clone for the Intellivision. Programmed by Joe Zbiciak, the game offers the same type of side-scrolling shooter action, but adds Mercury, Mars, and Pluto as selectable stages.

If you want to play a near-perfect port of *Moon Patrol*, pick up *Arcade's Greatest Hits: The Midway Collection 2* (1997) for the PlayStation.

Getting back to the Atari 5200, the system's biggest strength is its stellar line of cartridges based on famous arcade games, including *Moon Patrol*, a very nicely programmed port of a true classic.

FUN FACT:

According to an interview with Takashi Nishiyama published on www.1up.com, arcade *Moon Patrol* was the second game he developed for Irem. "The first game design I worked on was *UniWar S*," he said. "I doubt you're familiar with it, but it was a ROM-based game that used Namco's *Galaxian* hardware."

WHY IT MADE THE LIST:

Moon Patrol is a side-scrolling shooter with a twist. Instead of piloting a ship through space, you drive a buggy along the moon, jumping and shooting—a great combination.

CHAPTER 63

MOUSE TRAP

COLECOVISION
GENRE: MAZE
PUBLISHER: COLECO
DEVELOPER: COLECO
1 OR 2 PLAYERS (ALTERNATING)
1982

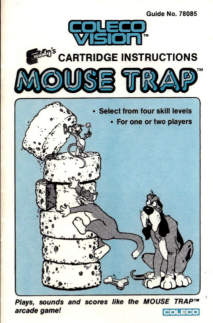

Mouse Trap instruction manual. $2.

> "THE GRAPHICS, SOUND EFFECTS, AND MUSIC ARE ABOUT AS GOOD AS YOU COULD ASK FOR FROM A COIN-OP CONVERSION OF THE ERA."

Flash back to the summer of 1982. Virtually all of my friends and cousins had game consoles, whether it was an Atari 2600, an Intellivision, an Odyssey2, or one of the other, more obscure systems of the time (oddly enough, my two best friends each had a Fairchild Channel F). During this era, I didn't know a single person who had two or more systems—it simply wasn't the norm as it seems to be now.

Alas, despite my love for all things video game, I had yet to acquire a game system of my very own. Sure, I had several of the old Mattel (and other company) handhelds, my brother and I were frequent fixtures at the Land of Oz and Malibu Grand Prix arcades, and I was always going over to other people's houses to play their games (I wasn't above inviting myself over), but an actual game console with cartridges was financially out of my reach.

However, when Coleco began showing ads on television for the new state-of-the-art ColecoVision, with its drop-dead perfect (or so it seemed) port of *Donkey Kong*, I knew I had to have one, regardless of the cost. Santa's gifts always topped out at around $100, so I had to pitch in $100 or so of my lawn mowing money to get a ColecoVision (which retailed for $189.99 plus tax) for Christmas of that year.

Donkey Kong came packaged with the ColecoVision, of course, but I also found *Mouse Trap* under the tree (actually, truth be told, I bought *Mouse Trap* myself and gave it to "Santa" to put under the tree). I had played the arcade version of *Mouse Trap* (1981, Exidy) before at the Land of Oz, and I enjoyed the game as a more complex take on *Pac-Man*. However, it wasn't until I brought the game home that I truly began to appreciate its cat-and-mouse charms.

Like many of the better ColecoVision titles, *Mouse Trap* is an excellent, highly faithful port of a relatively obscure arcade game. The graphics, sound effects, and music are about as good as you could ask for from a coin-op conversion of the era. The maze and items are colorful, the mouse, dog, and cats are cartoonish, and the audio does a nice job mixing cheerful (when you grab a bonus item) and cautionary (when a vulture appears) sounds.

Mouse Trap has player guiding a mouse (actually, a mouse head) around a *Pac-Man*-like maze, eating dots of cheese lining the pathways while avoiding making contact with cats that roam said maze. Instead of gobbling one of four power pellets to turn the tables on the enemies like in *Pac-Man*, players can push button 5 on the controller keypad to temporarily turn into a barking dog. Players can only turn into the dog if they have at least one dog bone in stock. Each time the player begins a maze, there are four bones to be eaten, and they can be stocked up to use at any time.

The controller keypad is also used to open and close 13 color-coded doors within the maze (1 operates red doors, 2 yellow, and 3 blue). Newbies may find themselves looking down to push the buttons, but veterans of the *Mouse Trap* wars will get to know the controller and the positioning of the buttons by feel and memory, enabling them to keep their eyes on the screen at all times. The action gets fast and intense after a few rounds, so this is important. Regarding maze games with operable doors, *Mouse Trap* isn't quite as good as *Lady Bug*, but it's better than *Lock 'N' Chase*.

Mouse Trap doesn't control as smoothly as *Pac-Man*, but I like the strategic maneuvering of the doors (blocking cats is especially fun), and it's extremely rewarding to turn into a dog and gobble up as many cats as possible before the timer runs out. There's definitely strategy involved in using the bones. Saving them for later is recommended, as long as you can stay safe while doing so. If you need to make an emergency escape, you can enter the IN box at the center of the screen, which will warp you to one of the four corners.

Like most early ColecoVision titles, *Mouse Trap* has four skill levels. In numbers 2, 3, and 4, a vulture will periodically appear in the maze, zigzagging across the screen and in general getting in the way. The vulture is invulnerable to dogs, so beware. One of the coolest aspects of *Mouse Trap* is the bonus prize system. When players eat a bonus prize, such as a key or a pair of glasses, another appears somewhere in the maze. There are six possible prizes in the first maze, seven in the second, and on up until a maximum of 15 prizes. This sense of progression in a single-screen game was rare in 1982.

In short, *Mouse Trap* is an excellent port and is easily one of the best console maze games of all time, making it a shoe-in for inclusion in this book. If my recommendations aren't enough, consider this from *Electronic Games* magazine #14 (April, 1983): "*Mouse Trap* is a fast, fun maze contest, enlivened by perky graphics and an entertaining concept. Chalk up another winner for Coleco."

Further, in issue #1 (summer, 1983) of the British publication, *TV Gamer*, the reviewer said *Mouse Trap* was of a "much higher caliber" than *Pac-Man* and that it "runs rings around" the more famous maze chase. In *Video Games* #7 (April, 1983), Phil Wiswell said, "If you like maze games at all, you'll probably love *Mouse Trap*. And if you liked the arcade game, suffice it to say there are no disappointments in the cartridge."

Coleco also brought *Mouse Trap* to the Atari 2600 and Intellivision. Both are playable (despite blocky graphics), but the 2600 version lacks hawks, color-coded doors (the fire button opens and closes all the doors at once), prizes to grab, and the IN box. The Intellivision cart, which also lacks hawks, is a more accurate conversion (complete with keypad overlays), but the disc controllers are hardly ideal for this type of game.

Mouse Trap was never given the sequel treatment, but the arcade game was commemorated in song on Buckner & Garcia's *Pac-Man Fever* novelty album from 1982. The ditty is called "Mousetrap," a slight misspelling of the name of the game.

Mouse Trap game cartridge. $5.

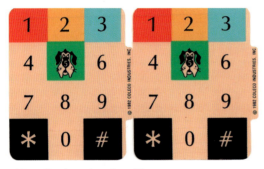

Mouse Trap keypad overlays. $2.

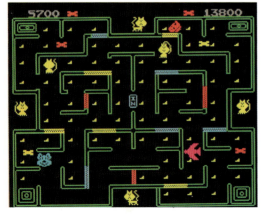

Mouse Trap for the ColecoVision in action.

FUN FACT:
In the Atari 2600 version of *Mouse Trap*, flipping the color switch on the 2600 console to B/W makes the mazes, cheese, and bones invisible (pressing pause causes this effect when the game is played on the 7800).

WHY IT MADE THE LIST:
Mouse Trap for the ColecoVision is a near-perfect port of a terrific arcade game. Turning into a dog and gobbling cats is a blast, as is blocking cats with doorways.

CHAPTER 64

MR. DO!

COLECOVISION
GENRE: MAZE
PUBLISHER: COLECO
DEVELOPER: COLECO
1 OR 2 PLAYERS (ALTERNATING)
1983

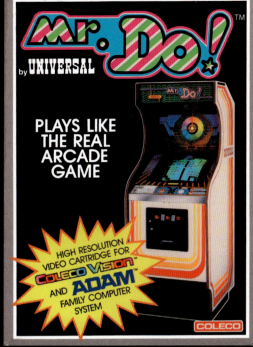

Mr. Do! for the ColecoVision, complete in box. $12.

"IT'S CLOSE ENOUGH TO THE HUGELY ENTERTAINING ORIGINAL TO MAKE IT A MUST-OWN CARTRIDGE."

Based on Universal's 1982 coin-op classic, which is nothing less than one of the greatest games of all time, *Mr. Do!* is hardly the most accurately ported arcade conversion for the ColecoVision (*Lady Bug* and *Mouse Trap*, for example, are far more faithful), but it's close enough to the hugely entertaining original to make it a must-own cartridge.

Players control a goofy looking little clown as he digs tunnels, gobbles rows of cherries (eating a grouping of eight cherries in succession grants extra points), and throws a power ball at big-headed Badguys that prowl a maze in hot pursuit of our hero. As Mr. Do! digs tunnels, he alters the maze (if he digs enough real estate, he can make the entire playfield disappear, but that's not a good strategy, just an observation), meaning the game is different each time you play it.

After Mr. Do! throws the ball and kills an enemy, the ball will reappear in his hands a few seconds later. However, if the ball gets stuck in limbo, bouncing around the orchard somewhere, he must retrieve the ball himself. A more lucrative, more strategic way to kill enemies is to have Mr. Do! walk under apples to make them drop on top of them—killing multiple monsters with a single apple is a good way to score tons of points. Mr. Do! can also push the apples.

Near the center of each maze lies a food item, which when eaten brings forth an Alphamonster and his henchmen. Killing Alphamonsters, each of which contains a letter, can spell out EXTRA, giving players an additional life. Occasionally, a sparkling diamond will appear. Grabbing this goodie is worth 10,000 points and advances the action to the next maze. (In the arcade game, the diamond grants 8,000 points and an extra credit.) Level progression otherwise requires eating all the cherries, spelling out EXTRA, or killing all the enemies, which also include Diggers and Blue Chompers.

Each of the enemies in this game serves a different purpose, but they are all out to get Mr. Do! Alphamonsters release Blue Chompers, which are very fast and can eat the apples. Badguys are pretty basic (one could compare them to the ghosts in *Pac-Man*), but they can turn into Diggers, which create their own pathways.

Mr. Do! is sometimes dismissed as a poor man's *Dig Dug* by philistines of the gaming world. While it was indeed inspired by that great game, it's an excellent title in its own right. Throwing a ball at enemies may not be as satisfying as blowing them up with a pump, but watching helplessly as the ball bounces around the tunnels, missing the enemies when you desperately need the ball back, is excruciating—in an exhilarating kind of way. More importantly, spelling out EXTRA adds a strategic

The back of the *Mr. Do!* box.

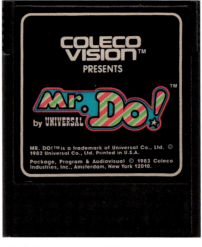

Mr. Do! game cartridge. $5.

Mr. Do! instruction manual. $2.

dimension to the action, and the "pushable" apples in *Mr. Do!* are far more versatile than the "unpushable" rocks in *Dig Dug*.

Indeed, *Mr. Do!* is strategically diverse and endlessly entertaining, and it has smooth difficulty progression, meaning anyone can play. In later levels, it takes tremendous skill to survive, but the game never gets frustrating. Upping one's high score to the nth degree can be a fun, rewarding, years-long objective and a great way to blow off steam after a long day at work.

Getting back to the arcade original, *Mr. Do!* is more than just entertaining—it's historically important. Check out this article excerpt taken from Examiner.com, celebrating the 30th anniversary of the little clown that could:

[*Mr. Do!*] instantly gained the label of being a *Dig Dug* clone, a game that appears very similar at a glance. This label combined with the name of a lesser known arcade company caused initial sales of *Mr. Do!* to be rather soft. Universal then opted to try a different approach by releasing *Mr. Do!* as a conversion kit.

Conversion kits are retrofit kits designed to transform an older arcade title into a new one. During this time in the industry, most games were released as "dedicated" cabinets with the design and artwork meant to be just that one game title. As 1983 came around, arcade game operators were flooded with dedicated cabinets of titles that had stopped earning money and had little to no resale value in a crowded market.

While previous companies had tried to sell conversion kit games, the titles were typically of poor quality and failed to earn well. Some companies such as Sega and Data East had tried to introduce entire lines of games designed around the concept of conversion kits, but failed to support these systems with top titles. *Mr. Do!* broke this mold, becoming the first commercially successful conversion kit in arcade history.

For the price of under $500, operators began to convert older titles into *Mr. Do!* machines, quickly paying off the price of the kit in a short period of time. By the end of its run, Universal sold around 30,000 *Mr. Do!* kits, which actually means the title was in almost twice as many locations across the United States than *Dig Dug*.

The article goes on to say that *Mr. Do!*, which was designed by Kazutoshi Ueda (*Lady Bug*), was the seventh best-earning arcade game on average for 1983, beating out *Q*bert*, *Ms. Pac-Man*, *Galaga*, *Super Pac-Man*, *Moon Patrol*, *Donkey Kong Junior* and *BurgerTime*. (The first six were *Pole Position*, *Star Trek*, *Gyruss*, *Time Pilot*, *Popeye*, and *Joust*.)

So, what about those differences between the ColecoVision version of *Mr. Do!* and the arcade game? The music and sound effects are similar, but the home game is missing the animation sequence that follows the spelling of EXTRA. Also, the character sprites are a single color, and the scrolling isn't quite as smooth. Luckily, the basic gameplay elements are largely the same (though, as with many home games, the arcade version is more difficult).

In *Video Games* #17 (Feb., 1984), Mike Sittnick wrote that the Coleco game was "very entertaining," but he did acknowledge the differences between it and the original. "It isn't a perfect clone of the arcade version," he said. "The Mr. Do! character is only a white figure in the home cart while he looks like a fully detailed, multi-colored clown in the arcade version. The intermissions are gone, and the monsters are not as aggressive. Sometimes it is difficult to move Mr. Do! properly when he is next to an apple."

In a review published in *Electronic Fun with Computers & Games* Vol. 2 #1 (Nov., 1983), Gary Miller also mentioned the game's shortcomings, but called the action "fast and furious" the graphics "well done" and the sounds "virtually identical to the arcade game."

In *JoyStik* Vol. 2 #3 (Dec., 1983), the reviewer said, "The game has the bright colors, great graphics, and cheerful music that have become Coleco trademarks." He also called *Mr. Do!* "a versatile game that is fun for the casual player and an endless challenge to the strategist."

Mr. Do! inspired several sequels, including *Mr. Do!'s Castle* (arcade, various), *Mr. Do's Wild Ride* (arcade), *Do! Run Run* (arcade), and *Neo Mr. Do!* (Neo Geo), and it was ported to the Atari 2600 (sans diamonds, mid-maze items, and in-game music), Game Boy (with scrolling mazes), and Super Nintendo (with a two-player battle mode, which is as quirky and as fun as it sounds).

A similar, but inferior game, *Quest: Fantasy Challenge*, was released for the Game Boy Color in 1999.

As the author of the *Classic Home Video Games* book series (McFarland Publishers), I'm often asked to name my favorite video game of all time. My answer is always the same: *Mr. Do!*

FUN FACT:

My review of the Super Nintendo version of *Mr. Do!* appeared in *Game Informer* #113 (Sept., 2002) as an installment of the late, lamented "Greatest Game of All Time" feature.

WHY IT MADE THE LIST:

Mr. Do! for the ColecoVision isn't quite as accurate an arcade conversion as it could be, but it mimics the greatness of the original enough to keep you entertained indefinitely.

CHAPTER 65

MR. DO!'S CASTLE

ATARI 5200/COLECOVISION
GENRE: CLIMBING
PUBLISHER: PARKER BROTHERS
DEVELOPER: PARKER BROTHERS
1 OR 2 PLAYERS (ALTERNATING)
1984

Mr. Do!'s Castle arcade flyer.

"EASY TO LEARN, BUT DIFFICULT TO MASTER, AND NO TWO GAMES ARE THE SAME."

The first and best sequel to *Mr. Do!*, which is my favorite video game of all time, Universal's *Mr. Do!'s Castle* was released to the arcades in 1983.

According to Wikipedia, *Mr. Do!'s Castle* "began life as a game called 'Knights vs. Unicorns,' but the U.S. division of Universal persuaded the Japanese arm to modify the graphics into a *Mr. Do!* game, taking into account the first game's popularity." According to The Arcade Museum (www.arcade-museum.com), the Japanese version is called *Mr. Do! Vs. Unicorns*.

Taking a different path (so to speak) than its *Dig Dug*-inspired predecessor, *Castle* is a climbing game that borrows from such classic titles as *Donkey Kong* and, more prominently, *Space Panic*.

Players once again control Mr. Do!, a semi-cute little clown with an affinity for cherries. However, instead of digging in an orchard, our hero must clear his castle home of red, blue, and green unicorns that roam the hallways. As with so many other cutesy, non-scrolling games in which several enemies pursue the protagonist, one bite from a unicorn kills Mr. Do!, so those pestiferous perpetrators should be avoided at all costs.

Unless, of course, the unicorns have been turned into bonus letter unicorns. But I'm getting ahead of myself.

Mr. Do!'s Castle is comprised of eight different screens, each of which consists of seven side-view floors. Each floor is connected by ladders, some of which are diagonal and can be pushed a little to reach a neighboring platform. The middle five floors largely consist of blocks. *Mr. Do!* is armed with a hammer and can knock out blocks to kill unicorns as they pass by underneath. If you knock out a block and a unicorn falls into the hole you made, it will temporarily trap the unicorn.

Ordinary blocks contain cherries, but three of the blocks contain keys. After knocking out all three key blocks, you should go up to the door at the top of the castle and touch the blinking plus sign. This will briefly enable Mr. Do! to turn the tables on his enemies (a la *Pac-Man*). Hitting a bonus letter unicorn with the hammer earns the player that letter, and if you can spell out EXTRA at any point in the game, you'll get an extra life (a la *Mr. Do!*).

Another type of floor block is the skull block. If a skull block is at either end of a section of flooring, and there are unicorns on that section, knocking out both skull blocks drops that entire section, meaning you can eliminate several unicorns at once.

As I mentioned earlier, there are three colors of unicorns. Red are standard, green are a bit trickier than red,

 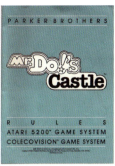  

Mr. Do!'s Castle for the ColecoVision, complete in box. $85.

Mr. Do!'s Castle instruction manual. $12.

Mr. Do!'s Castle game cartridge (ColecoVision). $30.

Mr. Do!'s Castle game cartridge (Atari 5200). $30.

and blue are the toughest of all to defeat because they can split themselves into two separate unicorns, and because you can't pull the *Space Panic*-like maneuver of knocking them down through to the lower floor when they have fallen into a hole.

Like many of the best classic video games, *Mr. Do!'s Castle* is easy to learn, but difficult to master, and no two games are the same. There are several different strategies for killing unicorns, and, similar to *Mr. Do!*, there are two ways to beat a level: knock out all the cherry blocks or eliminate all the unicorns. And, of course, the challenge to spell out EXTRA adds a nice dimension to the action.

I'm a huge *Mr. Do!'s Castle* fan, as is Earl Green, who runs the popular gaming site, Phosphor Dot Fossils (www.thelogbook.com/phosphor). There he wrote: "Another of my favorite obscure games, *Mr. Do!'s Castle* is truly cool, fun, and addictive—all the requisite qualities of a good video game. In my mind, it easily outshines the original *Mr. Do!* by miles, and is one of the most unique and original entries in the ladders-and-levels genre since *Donkey Kong*."

In bringing *Mr. Do!'s Castle* to the ColecoVision and Atari 5200, Parker Brothers kept the basic gameplay elements intact, making for a terrific port. The game's myriad strategies are perfect for a home setting since players can stick with the game for as long as they like without inserting more quarters.

I got *Mr. Do!'s Castle* for ColecoVision when it first came out (the 5200 version was a later acquisition). I played it for hours and hours and still play it on occasion to this day. My all-time high score is 324,960, which is pretty darned high, if I do say so myself. I say that not to brag, but to illustrate how much time I spent honing my skills at the game. (I would've gotten tired of it long before reaching that score if it were a less enjoyable cartridge.)

Graphically, both the ColecoVision and Atari 5200 ports have nice looking castles, and the cherries and Mr. Do! himself are recognizable as such. However, the unicorns, which are mono-colored, appear sickly and deformed, as though E.T. and Mr. Kool-Aid had a litter of mongoloid love children.

One variance the ColecoVision version has from the 5200 game is that the red unicorns in the ColecoVision cart will turn green if you hit them too many times with your hammer. If you hit a green unicorn with the hammer, it will turn blue. Predictably, the ColecoVision version has better, more precise controls.

Despite its greatness, not everyone "gets" *Mr. Do!'s Castle*. Writing for HonestGamers (honestgamers.com), "LowerStreeBlues," complaining about the game's high level of difficulty, said it's "an arcade game that isn't much fun, with console ports all the more fleeting and pointless."

More egregiously, Dave "The Video Game Critic" Mrozek (videogamecritic.com) gave the 5200 version a surprisingly low "D-", complaining that it's "too complicated for its own good" and that it "seems intriguing at first but eventually you may want to just throw it out the window." Mrozek offers sound opinions in most cases, but I think he should have stuck with this game a while longer to better figure it out.

Mr. Do!'s Castle was also produced for the Atari 2600. Like so many 2600 ports, that rendition has blocky, but discernible graphics and is highly playable.

Mr. Do!'s Castle was followed in the arcades by two largely unsuccessful sequels—*Mr. Do's Wild Ride* and *Do! Run Run*—both of which were released in 1984, and both of which never made it to a classic console in the United States.

FUN FACT:
While the arcade, Atari 5200, and ColecoVision versions of *Mr. Do!'s Castle* have eight screens, the Atari 2600 rendition has just six.

WHY IT MADE THE LIST:
Like *Miner 2049er* and *Space Panic*, *Mr. Do!'s Castle* is an intricate climbing game that devoted fans of the genre will love, especially those gamers who stick with it long enough to learn to play it well.

CHAPTER 66

MS. PAC-MAN

ATARI 7800
GENRE: MAZE
PUBLISHER: ATARI
DEVELOPER: GENERAL COMPUTER CORP.
1 OR 2 PLAYERS (ALTERNATING)
1986

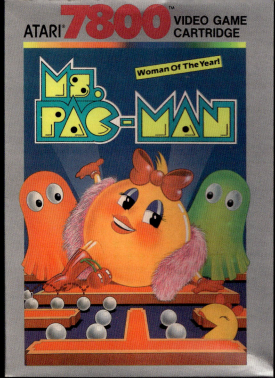

Ms. Pac-Man for the Atari 7800, complete in box. $10.

"SIMPLE FOUR-WAY CONTROLS, FAST GAMEPLAY, CUTE VISUALS, AND CHARMING MUSIC."

When *Ms. Pac-Man* was released for the Atari 2600 in 1982, fans of the always-famished female, grateful that the game was a much better port than the anemic looking *Pac-Man* for the 2600, breathed a collective sigh of relief. The Atari 5200 version released the next year was also a solid arcade-to-home translation (despite iffy controls), improving upon the 2600 rendition with better graphics and sounds and the inclusion of the animated intermissions.

Programmed by Alan Wells, the Atari 7800 cartridge is even better (not to mention faster), giving gamers a near-perfect arcade experience (though nitpickers will point out that the title character's lipstick is missing), along with a special bonus feature: the ability for players to level-select. This means anyone can begin the game from any screen, including the vaunted banana level. The 7800 game also lets players start on an easy teddy bear stage.

In issue #24 (March/April, 1995) of the *Digital Press* fanzine, Jeff Cooper, a *Pac-Man* collector since the 1980s, said: "7800 *Ms.* was encoded by the same individual who encoded the [1982] Bally/Midway coin-op. While it's not *exactly* arcade quality, it's pretty damn close…a superb version of a great game…as fun to play today as it was many years ago…it alone is worth the price of a 7800."

Classic gamer Earl Green put the 7800 cartridge in historical perspective, pointing out that the late release of the game hurt it in the marketplace, and in the eyes of gamers spoiled by the expansive, graphically advanced *Super Mario Bros.* "The Tramiels did their new company—and gamers everywhere—a grievous disservice by putting the 7800 on ice until the NES was on top of the world," he said, referring to Atari's Jack Tramiel shelving the 7800 console, which was completed in 1984, until 1986. "This game is *Namco Museum* good, with the music, graphics and even the intermissions brought home in one excellent, perfectly balanced package."

Unlike the Atari 7800 versions of *Asteroids* and *Centipede*, 7800 *Ms. Pac-Man* does not offer a two-player simultaneous mode. For that, you'd have to play the unlicensed Tengen version of the NES game, which came out in 1990, making it ineligible for this book. (Or, you could go the 16-bit route and play the Genesis or SNES version.)

For those of you living under the proverbial *Pong* machine for the last 35 years, *Ms. Pac-Man* is based on Midway's 1981 coin-op classic of the same name, in which gamers guide the yellow, pie-shaped femme around a series of four different non-scrolling mazes (as opposed to one maze design in the original *Pac-Man*), gobbling up pellets

Ms. Pac-Man instruction manual. $2.

Ms. Pac-Man game cartridge. $5.

Ms. Pac-Man for the Atari 7800 in action. *Courtesy of AtariAge.com.*

while avoiding four roaming ghosts. Blinky, Pinky, Inky, and Sue in *Ms. Pac-Man* are less predictable than Blinky, Pinky, Inky, and Clyde in *Pac-Man*, preventing the use of pattern-memorization to beat the levels.

Eating items that bounce—one at a time—around the maze pathways, including teddy bears, cherries, strawberries, oranges, pretzels, apples, pears, and bananas, gives players bonus points. Gobbling one of the four energy pills (often called power pellets) positioned in each corner of the maze temporarily turns the ghosts blue and lets players eat them for extra points. Eating two or more ghosts in succession ups your score even higher. After a ghost is gobbled, it will return to the center of the screen and begin the chase anew.

Although it's basically a faster, more diverse *Pac-Man*, *Ms. Pac-Man* was historically important in the arcades as it featured the first female lead character in a video game. Further, it has held up extremely well over the years and can still be found in arcades, bars, movie theaters, and other locations across America (sometimes as *Ms. Pac-Man/Galaga: Class of 1981*, a 20th anniversary release). The game's continued success can be attributed to its simple four-way controls, fast gameplay, cute visuals, and charming music (composed by Naoki Higashio), elements that combine to make it a favorite among gamers of both genders and all ages.

Most "civilians" know that *Ms. Pac-Man* was the sequel to *Pac-Man*, but only joystick junkies know of the arcade game's somewhat convoluted production history. In *High Score! The Illustrated History of Electronic Games* (2002, McGraw Hill), Rusel Demaria and Johnny L. Wilson revealed the following:

*Ms. Pac-Ma*n came into being not in some Japanese pizza parlor (a la *Pac-Man*), but around the MIT campus in Boston, and was the result of work done on enhancement boards for existing arcade machines.

The original intent was to create add-on boards that improved on game play for existing arcade games, thereby extending their viable life span in the arcade. However, after a lawsuit by Atari [over the *Missile Command* conversion kit, *Super Missile Attack*] and subsequent out-of-court settlement, the designers [working for General Computer Corporation] approached Midway with an add-on board for *Pac-Man*. Midway, instead, suggested putting out a whole new game.

The original add-on had a Pac-Man-like character with legs [Crazy Otto], but that was not an acceptable option. Ultimately, however, the concept of a female Pac-Man came up. She was first Miss Pac-man, then Mrs. Pac-Man, and ultimately she became the ultraliberated Ms. Pac-Man, the protagonist of the best-selling arcade game in U.S. History.

In addition to the 7800 release, *Ms. Pac-Man* was ported to the Atari Lynx (1990), Game Boy (1993), Game Gear (1995), Game Boy Color (1999), PlayStation (1996, via *Namco Museum Vol. 3*), Xbox 360 (2007, via XBLA), iPhone (2008), and various other platforms.

In 2000, *Ms. Pac-Man* spawned *Ms. Pac-Man: Maze Madness*, a popular console sequel for the PlayStation, Dreamcast, and Nintendo 64. In 2004, *Ms. Pac-Man: Maze Madness* hit the Game Boy Advance.

The arcade classic *Ms. Pac-Man* is one of the greatest video games of all time, so it only stands to reason that the highly accurate 7800 port is one of *The 100 Greatest Console Video Games: 1977-1987.*

FUN FACT:

Ms. Pac-Man is the most successful U.S.-produced coin-op game of all time, selling more than 115,000 units.

WHY IT MADE THE LIST:

Fast, fun, and festive, *Ms. Pac-Man*, adapted brilliantly for the 7800, is a timeless classic that people will still be playing—in one form or another—30 years from now.

CHAPTER **67**

PAC-MAN

NES
GENRE: MAZE
PUBLISHER: TENGEN
DEVELOPER: NAMCO
1 OR 2 PLAYERS (ALTERNATING)
1987

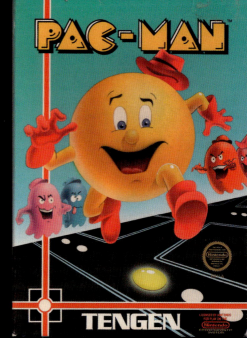

Pac-Man for the Nintendo NES, complete in box. $30.

"THE NES GAME IS A LARGELY FAITHFUL PORT OF THE ARCADE CLASSIC."

While doing research for this book, part of which involved replaying most of the better games of the era, I hadn't planned on including *Pac-Man* as a main selection—I figured it would be relegated to "The Next 100" appendix. After all, subsequent maze titles, including *Ms. Pac-Man*, *Lady Bug*, and *Mouse Trap*, all of which easily made the cut, added various features to make the action more dynamic and more versatile than this crusty old favorite.

However, after playing a few rounds of the NES version of the game using the NES Advantage joystick (a very common peripheral, not like those tough-to-find alternative joysticks for the Atari 5200), I quickly changed my mind. If you've only played NES *Pac-Man* with the standard control pad, which isn't as sure or as tight in telling the yellow fella which direction to go, you haven't gotten the most out of the game. And, if you haven't played *Pac-Man* for any console in a few years (as I hadn't), you may be surprised that the game holds up extremely well.

As everyone reading this likely knows, *Pac-Man* is the prototypical maze game, with players guiding the pie-shaped title character up, down, right, and left around a single maze, gobbling up dots along the way while avoiding the ghostly quartet of Shadow (nicknamed Blinky), Speedy (Pinky), Bashful (Inky), and Pokey (Clyde). The NES game is a largely faithful port of the arcade classic, but it doesn't include the ghost nicknames on the introductory screen (a small oversight to be sure).

In each of the four corners of the maze lies an energizer (sometimes called a power pill or a power pellet), which when eaten turns the ghosts blue and lets Pac-Man chase after his enemies for a short time. Gobbling the ghosts in succession scores extra points: 200, 400, 800, 1600. Another way to boost your score is to eat a piece of fruit that will appear periodically near the lower center of the maze (the exact center is the square where the ghosts enter the maze).

The fruit, along with a pair of charm-like items, also acts as a level marker as players work their way up the food chain (so to speak): cherry (level 1), strawberry (level 2), peach (levels 3 and 4), apple (levels 5 and 6), kiwi (levels 7 and 8), orange (levels 9 and 10), bell (levels 11 and 12), and key (levels 13 and up). The fruit in the NES game looks a little flat and washed out in comparison to the arcade, but this is a small complaint. After you clear the screen of dots, the maze flashes, just like in the coin-op game, and then it's on to the next level.

Likely programmed by Hiroki Aoyagi (his name is credited in the ROM text), NES *Pac-Man* starts off slowly—slower, in fact, than the arcade version—but it does pick up steam after a couple of screens. In fact, the difficulty level amps up nicely as the action gets faster and the period of time Pac-Man can gobble the ghosts grows shorter.

In *Compute!'s Guide to Nintendo Games* (1989, Compute! Books), Steven Schwartz said that "in many respects, *Pac-Man* is faithful enough to the original arcade version—in features,

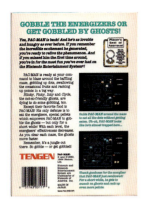  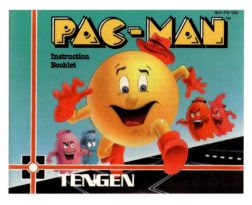

The back of the *Pac-Man* box.   *Pac-Man* game cartridge. $10.   *Pac-Man* instruction manual. $4.

design, and sound—to bring a nostalgic tear to any older game player's eye."

However, Schwartz did lodge two complaints against the game, both of which have some merit, but both of which are arguable. He said, "responsiveness to the control pad isn't what it might be," which is true, but he apparently didn't have access to an NES Advantage joystick controller, even though it came out in 1987. He also lamented that the arcade patterns are missing, but to me that's a strength rather than a weakness since the action presents a new challenge to those who mastered the coin-op game.

Pac-Man was ported to the NES three different times, first as a licensed game from Tengen (traditional gray cartridge) and then as an unlicensed game from Tengen (black cartridge). In 1993, it was Namco's turn. All three versions look and play exactly the same.

Speaking of Namco, the company developed the original coin-op version of *Pac-Man*, which Midway licensed for distribution in the United States in 1980. The game was originally called *Puck Man* (*Pakkuman* in Japan), but the name was changed out of fear that vandals would alter the "P" to create the "F" word.

Designed by Tōru Iwatani and a nine-man team (including programmer Shigeo Funak and musical composer Toshio Kai), *Pac-Man* impacted the industry in ways that few games have before or since. It wasn't the first dot-eliminating maze title (that would be Sega/Gremlin's *Head On* from 1979, which inspired *Dodge 'Em* for the Atari 2600), but it was the first video game to incorporate cute character graphics, creating the hobby's first unofficial mascot and gaming's first marketing frenzy.

According to *Pac-Man Collectibles: An Unauthorized Guide* (2002, Schiffer), more than 500 *Pac-Man* and *Pac-Man*-related items were manufactured between 1981 and 2001 (many more items have been produced since). The addictive nature of *Pac-Man*, along with the ubiquitous merchandising that accompanied the game, spawned "Pac-Man Fever," a condition popularized in the 1982 album and song of the same name by Buckner & Garcia.

In Steven L. Kent's indispensable *The Ultimate History of Video Games* (2001, Three Rivers Press), Iwatani shed some light on the creation process of the famous arcade game. "At the time, as you will recall, there were many games associated with killing creatures from outer space," he said. "I was interested in developing a game for the female game enthusiast. Rather than developing the character first, I started out with the concept of eating and focused on the Japanese word 'taberu,' which means 'to eat.'"

The Pac-Man character design occurred to Iwatani during a meal. "The figure of Pac-Man came about as I was having pizza for lunch," he said. "I took one wedge and there it was, the figure of Pac-Man."

According to Kent, Iwatani wanted to make sure Pac-Man's enemies were cute in order to appeal to the female audience he was trying to court, so he came up with "colorful 'ghosts' that looked like mop heads with big eyes."

It took Iwatani and company "just over a year to produce a working prototype of the game."

Pac-Man's simple, yet timeless maze formula spawned countless copycats and arcade sequels, the latter of which includes the great *Ms. Pac-Man* (1981), the underrated *Super Pac-Man* (1982), *Pac-Man Plus* (1982), the brilliant pinball/video game hybrid *Baby Pac-Man* (1982), *Professor Pac-Man* (1983), *Pac & Pal* (1983), the super challenging *Jr. Pac-Man* (1983), *Pac-Land* (1984), *Pac-Mania* (1987), *Pac-Man VR* (1996), and *Pac-Man Battle Royale* (2011).

Numerous console exclusive sequels to *Pac-Man* were released as well, including such stellar titles as *Pac-Man World 20th Anniversary* (1999) for the PlayStation and *Pac-Man Championship Edition DX* (2010) for the Xbox 360. Pac-Man even got his own *Super Mario Kart*-style racer with *Pac-Man World Rally* (2006) for the PlayStation 2 and GameCube.

The most infamous version of *Pac-Man* is the Atari 2600 port. Although not a total disaster (I still play and enjoy it on occasion), the widely ridiculed game was a pale shadow of its coin-op counterpart, thanks to washed-out graphics, horribly blinking ghosts, an inaccurate maze, an odd color scheme, and a lead character who continues looking to the right or left when going up or down (strangely, 2600 Pac-Man has eyes).

Getting back to the NES port, the 1987 release stood in the shadow of such cutting edge titles as *Castlevania*, *The Legend of Zelda*, *Mega Man*, and *Metroid*. As such, it was ignored by many gamers at the time of its release. Also, since *Pac-Man* has been ported to so many systems since, including pitch-perfect emulations for modern consoles, the NES version is still frequently overlooked.

The only real disappointment with the game is playing it in the wake of the Tengen version of *Ms. Pac-Man* (1990) for the NES, which not only featured a straight port of *Ms. Pac-Man*, but also added a number of (sometimes wild) features, including: four difficulty levels (normal, easy, hard, and crazy), four types of mazes (arcade, mini, big, and strange), and the super speedy Pac-Booster option.

FUN FACT:
In 2004, Nintendo ported the NES version of *Pac-Man* to the Game Boy Advance as part of its "Classic NES Series."

WHY IT MADE THE LIST:
Most longtime gamers have enjoyed *Pac-Man* in various forms many, many times, but the NES port, when played using an NES Advantage joystick, is still great fun.

CHAPTER 68

PBA BOWLING

INTELLIVISION
GENRE: BOWLING
PUBLISHER: MATTEL ELECTRONICS
DEVELOPER: MATTEL ELECTRONICS
1-4 PLAYERS (ALTERNATING)
1981

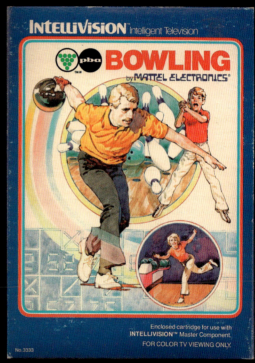

PBA Bowling for the Intellivision, complete in box. $5.

"AHEAD OF ITS TIME IN TERMS OF AUTHENTIC FEATURES AND TV-STYLE PRESENTATION."

The Intellivision, which is short for "intelligent television," is known for a variety of things, including its quirky disc controllers, its relative degree of stodginess, and the fact that it has more graphical processing power than the Atari 2600.

It's also known for its many realistic sports simulations, none of which is more impressive than *PBA Bowling*, a cartridge that was clearly ahead of its time in terms of authentic features and TV-style presentation. Designed for up to four players and licensed by The Professional Bowlers Association, the game lets you select handedness, ball weight (7-16 pounds), and lane slickness. According to the manual, 0 is the slowest alley with maximum curve, while 10 is the fastest alley and the most difficult.

Gamers can maneuver their bowler at the starting line, set the curve on the ball with the directional disc, and employ an optional "loft" maneuver that makes the ball break sharply at the far end of the alley (this is useful for picking up difficult

The back of the *PBA Bowling* box.

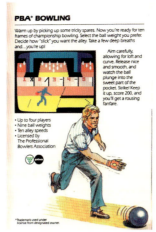
PBA Bowling catalog advertisement.

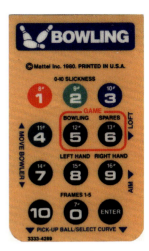
PBA Bowling keypad overlay. $1.

spares). To help you aim the ball, there's a white "spotter ball" that sweeps repeatedly across the lane.

The bowler, who looks like a skinny Rock 'Em Sock 'Em Robot, is very nicely animated, going through a full range of motions as he rolls the ball. He's viewed from the side, with a window above showing the pins. After the ball is released, the view switches to behind the ball as it rolls toward the pins. Once struck, the pins bounce around in lively fashion and can knock over other pins.

Two games are included in the program: Regulation Bowling and Pick-up Spare, the latter of which lets you practice knocking down difficult pin arrangements—"10 frames of spare setups randomly presented from 32 possibilities."

According to www.intellivisiongames.com, a site ran by former Intellivision programmers, "*PBA Bowling* was the first Intellivision game actually programmed by Mattel employees: Mike Minkoff and Rick Levine from the handheld-games department. Since Mattel didn't have development equipment yet (1980), Mike and Rick commuted from Mattel in Hawthorne to APh in Pasadena three days a week. Mike gives Rick, an avid bowler, credit for the many realistic details in the game."

When *PBA Bowling* hit stores in 1981, it was preceded by several primitive bowling games for other systems: *Bowling* for the Atari 2600 (overhead view of square pins, bowler appears to be on his side); *Bowling!/Basketball!* for the Odyssey2 (overhead view, no bowler is visible—just the ball, lane, and square pins); and *Bowling* for the handheld Microvision (simple squares represent the ball and pins).

PBA Bowling was also preceded by *3D Bowling* for the Arcadia 2001, a fine simulation that fans of the sport should consider checking out. It's not as good as the Intellivision game (the pins don't appear to bump into each other, for example), but it does let you line up the bowler, hook the ball right or left, and continually press a "duration" key to keep putting spin on the ball as it rolls (an unusual feature). In addition, you get penalized in *3D Bowling* if you step over the foul line (also unusual).

When *PBA Bowling* was new, Bill Kunkel and Frank Lane Jr. said, "there's no bowling cartridge quite as enjoyable as this one" in issue #2 of *Electronic Games* (March, 1982). In issue #11 of *EG* (Jan., 1983), the game won a Certificate of Merit for "Best Multi-Player Videogame" (*The Incredible Wizard* was the winner).

In *Playboy's Guide to Rating the Video Games* (1982, PBG Books), author Walter Lowe, Jr. gave *PBA Bowling* an overall 3.5 rating out of 5 stars, praising the sim for its realism, "intellectual challenge" (relative to other bowling titles), and "surprisingly good visual effects."

In *Ken Uston's Guide to Buying and Beating the Home Video Games* (1982, Signet) the author called *PBA Bowling* an "intriguing" game that is "realistic" and has the "best graphics of all the video bowling games." Uston cited the game's strategic possibilities as well, saying, "If you happen to like developing *Pac-Man* patterns, or blackjack or backgammon solutions, you might well become addicting to this game, as I have."

Issue #1 (summer, 1983) of *TV Gamer* gave readers a British perspective of the simulation: "Bowling, although a popular sport in the States, hasn't much of a following over here. Nevertheless this is a commendable effort. The graphics as well as the sound effects are good. If you like bowling then you'll enjoy this cartridge."

PBA Bowling has withstood the test of time, despite significant advances in sports video games. The bowling titles I spend the most time with these days are *Championship Bowling* (1993) for the Sega Genesis, which also has lots of options, and the bowling game on *Wii Sports* (2006), which has you physically going through the motions of rolling a ball. However, I still manage to get in a game of *PBA Bowling* when the mood strikes (so to speak).

Jonathan Sutyak, writing for the All Game Guide (allgame.com), agrees that the game has held up, saying, "*PBA Bowling* is a lot of fun if you enjoy the actual sport." He also likes the accurate sound effects and the fact that when you score over 200 points you get to hear special music.

The Video Game Critic (videogamecritic.com) gave the game an "A", saying it's "incredibly deep and expertly designed" and "by far the best classic bowling game I've come across."

As a genre, older sports video games have, in some respects, aged very poorly. There are still plenty of fun vintage sports games (*Baseball Stars*, *Double Dribble*, and *Tecmo Bowl* for the NES come to mind), and there's a lot to be said for the simplistic joys of a game like *Bowling* or *Boxing* for the Atari 2600, but photorealistic graphics, updated rosters, the ability to manage teams, and other modern features make current sports titles awfully appealing.

Regardless, *PBA Bowling* is just as fun to play now as it was 30+ years ago.

FUN FACT:
The Sears release of this game, which was not licensed by The Professional Bowlers Association, is simply called *Bowling*.

WHY IT MADE THE LIST:
Loaded with realistic features, *PBA Bowling* represents its sport better than just about any video game of the 1980s.

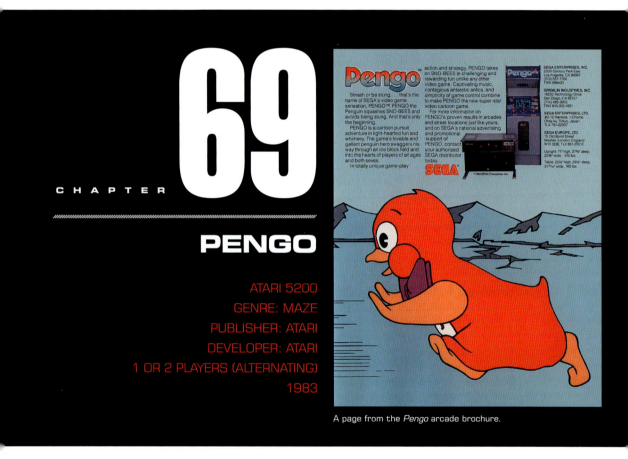

CHAPTER 69

PENGO

ATARI 5200
GENRE: MAZE
PUBLISHER: ATARI
DEVELOPER: ATARI
1 OR 2 PLAYERS (ALTERNATING)
1983

A page from the *Pengo* arcade brochure.

"FUN-TO-DEFEAT ENEMIES, CHARMING VISUALS, AND CHALLENGING, BUT NON-FRUSTRATING GAMEPLAY."

When I was in junior high school, I would draw mazes to pass the time after I had finished my work (and sometimes when I was supposed to be doing my work). I would hand out the mazes to my friends, and they had fun doing them. I've always loved mazes, and I remember getting a boxed set of monster maze books one year for Christmas.

I don't do pencil-and-paper mazes anymore, but I still love maze video games, especially the many excellent arcade-to-home ports of the early 1980s (which should be obvious as you read this book). I also tend to enjoy action titles with puzzle elements, so it should come as no surprise that *Pengo* is one of my favorite games.

Pengo for the Atari 5200 in action. Courtesy of AtariAge.com.

Pengo game cartridge. $8.

Pengo for the Atari 5200, complete in box. Courtesy of AtariAge.com. $20.

Pengo instruction manual. $3.

Sega released the original arcade version of *Pengo* in 1982, the year after Midway's *Ms. Pac-Man* was produced. According to Steve Sanders, writing in *JoyStik* #5 (April, 1983), character games were on the decline around this time. "Cute games are in trouble," he wrote. "*Pac-Man* isn't the reliable quarter-sucker it once was, and recent character games have had trouble even making a name for themselves (witness *Kangaroo*)."

Created by Tsutomu Iwane, Nobuo Kodera (director), Akira Nakakuma (programmer), and Shinji Egi (designer), *Pengo* may not have been a blockbuster in the arcades—it fell far short of the heights reached by Sega's *Turbo* (1981), which revitalized the racing genre, and *Zaxxon* (1982), which reenergized the space shooter genre—but it's a terrific game that works better as a home cartridge where players can learn its many strategies without having to spend zillions of quarters. In this respect, it's a lot like such ColecoVision titles as *Pepper II* and *Lady Bug*, which found their true footing at home.

In *Pengo*, players guide Pengo the Penguin as he walks around the screen, kicking blue blocks of ice, rearranging the playfield in the process. When an ice block is kicked, it will move in that direction until it touches another block of ice or a wall. If a block of ice is kicked while it is up against another block of ice or a wall, it will be destroyed. There are 16 different block formations; beginning with round 17, the playfields begin repeating themselves.

The objective in this game is to destroy the pursuing Sno-Bees, which can be crushed between blocks of ice, or between a block of ice and a wall. Also, if an ice block containing a Sno-Bee is destroyed, the Sno-Bee will die. Finally, if a Sno-Bee is walking next to a wall, Pengo can kick the wall to stun the enemy and then touch the enemy to make it go away—a good strategic maneuver when you are not in position to destroy the enemy with a block of ice.

Pengo as I've described it so far is a great game, with its constantly changing playfields (no two games are the same), fun-to-defeat enemies, charming visuals, and challenging, but non-frustrating gameplay. What makes the cartridge even better is a trio of diamond blocks that, when lined up, grants the player big bonus points (lining them up in the middle of the playfield—a difficult task—is worth twice as much as lining them up along a wall). This adds a key strategy element and is a worthy goal for more experienced players to achieve.

Even though it's a maze game, *Pengo* works fairly well with the Atari 5200's much criticized controllers, which are problematic in terms of quick, precise moves with such titles as *Pac-Man* and *Ms. Pac-Man*. Earl Green (thelogbook.com) disagrees with me in this regard, calling *Pengo* "very frustrating due to the non-self-centering joysticks" of the 5200.

Phil Wiswell, writing in *Electronic Fun with Computers & Games* #11 (Sept., 1983), also disparages the game, saying it is "very slow because the joystick is less responsive than most, and you end up overrunning lots of blocks because the joystick is not self-centering."

True, the 5200 controllers are less than ideal for any maze title (getting *Pengo* to turn the opposite direction quickly and with exact precision can be problematic), but I don't find the game as a whole to be frustrating at all.

Perceived control issues aside, 5200 *Pengo*, which was programmed by Sean W. Hennessey, is a very nice translation of the original arcade cab. The port, though it has charming (if repetitious) music, is missing the animated intermissions from the coin-op classic, but this was pretty common for the time, as anyone who has played the many *Donkey Kong* home ports of the era will tell you.

There aren't a whole lot of reviews of the Atari 5200 version of *Pengo* online or elsewhere (leading me to believe it's a severely underappreciated game), but Matt Fox, writing in *The Video Games Guide* (2006, Boxtree), did call the arcade rendition "addictive" and "good, clean fun."

The same could apply for the 5200 port, which Tom Zjaba (via www.tomheroes.com) called "a fun little game." In *Electronic Games* magazine #25 (May, 1984), Bill Kunkel said that *Pengo*'s "animation is wonderful, with appropriately lighthearted theme music churning happily throughout the game." He also said the home version was "an excellent addition to the already imposing 5200 collection" and that it gave players time—without spending tokens—to get "more deeply involved with this game's strategic possibilities and its challenging eye-hand coordination."

A predictably blocky version of *Pengo* was released for the Atari 2600. It's one of the harder to find first-party titles for the system, but don't go out of your way to look for it unless you are a completist—it's not that good, as Kevin Oleniacz, in issue #6 of the *Digital Press* fanzine (July/Aug., 1992), said: "This is a very lackluster arcade translation [with] mediocre graphics, limited sounds, and simple gameplay."

In 1992, *Pengo* was ported to the Sega Game Gear, but only overseas. Luckily, that version, if you can find it, will work on your U.S.-released system.

FUN FACT:

In 2010, Sega released an eight-player version of *Pengo* for its Ringwide arcade board.

WHY IT MADE THE LIST:

Thanks to its ever-changing playfields, numerous strategies, and cute graphics, playing *Pengo* never gets old.

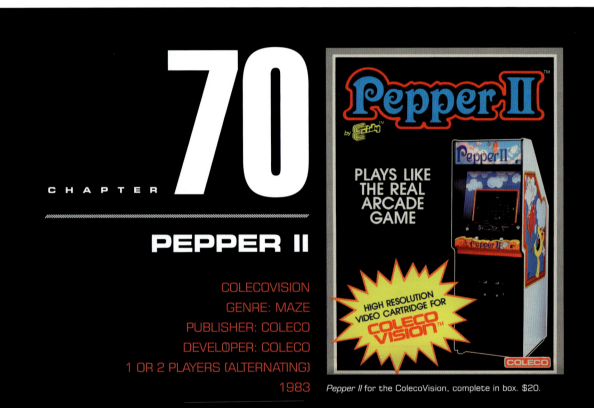

CHAPTER 70
PEPPER II

COLECOVISION
GENRE: MAZE
PUBLISHER: COLECO
DEVELOPER: COLECO
1 OR 2 PLAYERS (ALTERNATING)
1983

Pepper II for the ColecoVision, complete in box. $20.

"A STELLAR ENTRY IN THE LANDSLIDE OF MAZE GAMES."

A triumph of classic gaming, *Pepper II* for the ColecoVision is one of the best console video games of all time. It's a stellar entry in the landslide of maze games unleashed on the public in the aftermath of *Pac-Man* (1980), but instead of munching dots as in *Pac-Man* (and *Lady Bug* and *K.C. Munchkin*, etc.), players enclose preconfigured areas. This made the game similar to (but better than) the coin-op semi-classic *Amidar*, which was released in 1982, the same year as Exidy's original arcade version of *Pepper II*.

The character players control is an angel named Pepper, who busily zips along tracks in four different mazes. After those mazes have been completed, another four appear, but this time with tracks that turn invisible. Each maze has its own screen, but by going through exits along each of the four walls of the maze, players can enter and exit mazes at will and complete them in any order.

While Pepper works hard to zip up each area in each maze, Roaming Eyes (similar in execution to the ghosts in *Pac-Man*) will wander the mazes, making life difficult for our hero. In addition, a fiendish looking Zipper Ripper will frequently appear on the scene, unzipping tracks that haven't completely enclosed an area.

To help even the odds against his foes, Pepper temporarily turns into a devil when he encloses an area

The back of the *Pepper II* box.

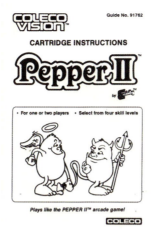
Pepper II instruction manual. $2.

Pepper II game cartridge. $6.

containing a pitchfork or a magic box (other items that appear onscreen offer multiplying bonus points). Once in devilish form, Pepper can turn the tables on the Roaming Eyes and touch them to remove them from the screen—shades of Pac-Man chasing after the ghosts. Yes, *Pepper II* borrows from *Pac-Man*. It was also inspired by *Qix* (1981), but with tracks of demarcation instead of an open playfield. Indeed, *Pepper II* isn't terribly original, but it's a great game.

In addition to frantic maze action, quick, crisp maneuvering, and an uncanny resemblance to its coin-op counterpart (coloring is a little different, but this is no big deal), *Pepper II* for the ColecoVision has terrific music, especially Charles Gounod's "Funeral March of a Marionette" (popularly known as the theme from *Alfred Hitchcock Presents*), which helps get things underway, and "Zip-a-Dee-Doo-Dah" (from Disney's *Song of the South*), which plays after a maze has been completed.

One admirer of *Pepper II* is Bruce Consolazio, who, in a review posted on the Digital Press website (digitpress.com), praised the game's arcade-like qualities, its "incredibly colorful graphics," and its excellent controls, which he prefers over those of *Lady Bug* and *Mouse Trap*. In the "Closet Classics" section of issue #4 (March/April, 1992) of the *Digital Press* fanzine, the staff cited the game's "excellent challenge, fast-moving gameplay, and frenzied music."

In *Video Game Collector* #9 (2008), video game historian Michael Thomasson lauded *Pepper II* for its frantic pace, sprawling maze layouts, and intelligent enemies. "*Pepper II* is a challenging delight to play and never leaves the player feeling restricted," he wrote.

In the August, 1983 issue of *Electronic Fun with Computers & Games*, reviewer George Kopp praised the cartridge thusly: "In gameplay, graphics, and sound, *Pepper II* is an outstanding game and an outstanding arcade translation."

Kopp also copped to being addicted to the game. "Filling in those boxes satisfies some deep-seating craving—and, like most habits, it's a hard one to break," he said.

In *Video Games* #11 (Aug., 1983), Perry Greenberg called *Pepper II* an excellent port with responsive controls, excellent graphics, and terrific sound effects—a game that "complements Coleco's other hits of this genre such as *Mouse Trap* and *Lady Bug*."

In a review published in *Video Game Player* Vol. 2 #2 (Oct./Nov., 1983), Raymond Dimetrosky said, "The designers of *Pepper II* have taken all the characteristics that make up good maze games and added extra touches to produce a contest that is exceptional…*Pepper II* is excellent."

Another highly positive vintage review can be found in *JoyStik* Vol. 2 #1 (Sept., 1983), where the writer said, "*Pepper II* is a maze game *par excellence* in the best traditions of *Amidar* and *Pac-Man*…the game action is very intriguing and very well executed graphically…the easy controller action will allow more than just the hardcore player to perform well."

There are certainly worse things in life than being addicted to a great game like *Pepper II*, a cartridge I still plug into my ColecoVision on a regular basis. In fact, as of this writing, I hold the number two spot on the *Retrocade Magazine* (www.retrocademagazine.net) score submission leader boards with a score of 875,270 points.

FUN FACT:

Despite the sequel-sounding name of *Pepper II*, there's no such thing as "Pepper I."

WHY IT MADE THE LIST:

A wonderful maze game, *Pepper II* is the prototypical ColecoVision cartridge: an obscure coin-op title that achieved mainstream success in the home.

CHAPTER 71

PHOENIX

ATARI 2600
GENRE: SLIDE-AND-SHOOT
PUBLISHER: ATARI
DEVELOPER: ATARI
1 PLAYER
1982

Phoenix arcade flyer.

"DOES AN ADMIRABLE JOB IN CAPTURING THE ORIGINAL ARCADE CLASSIC'S BASIC GAMEPLAY ELEMENTS AND ESSENTIAL FUN FACTOR."

Released by Centuri in 1980, the original arcade version of *Phoenix* wasn't exactly a novel concept, but it did expand upon the slide-and-shoot genre pioneered by *Space Invaders* (1978) and fleshed out by *Galaxian* (1979).

Among numerous other groundbreaking elements (such as destructible barriers, a savable high score, and multiple lives), *Space Invaders* invented the concept of a downward-advancing alien invasion, with players guiding a ship along the bottom of the screen, firing upward at said aliens. The aliens in *Space Invaders* appeared in rows, marched horizontally back and forth, and descended gradually (each time the grouping would reach the edge of the screen, it would move downward one level), making for a daunting and incredibly entertaining, but highly ordered attack.

Galaxian featured rows of alien invaders, but instead of advancing as a unit, they would break off individually (and as two- and three-ship tandems), move in swirling patterns, and attack the player's ship, advancing the genre in terms of varied challenges and unpredictability of enemy movement. *Galaxian* wasn't necessarily a better game than *Space Invaders*, but it did shake things up quite a bit. *Phoenix* ran with this formula, changing the aliens to birds and altering enough features to give it a personality and inventiveness all its own.

When I was in junior high, I rode my bike to school each morning. Near the school was a convenience store called Quickway, which had three arcade cabs in the back corner: *Asteroids*, *Pac-Man*, and *Phoenix*. Oftentimes I would stop by the store after school to play a few rounds, and sometimes I would even try to squeeze in a game or two before school (unfortunately, this had a tendency to make me tardy).

Of the three games, I mastered *Asteroids* and was only mediocre at *Pac-Man* (I never did try to memorize the patterns), but *Phoenix* held the distinction of being my favorite.

Both the arcade and Atari 2600 versions of *Phoenix* consist of five different screens: two waves of smaller, quicker birds; two waves of larger, slower birds; and a massive alien mother ship (at a time when bosses were rare in games). As is the case with many of the better Atari 2600 ports, while the game loses something in translation when it comes to audio/visual effects, it does an admirable job in capturing the original arcade classic's basic gameplay elements and essential fun factor. In short, it maintains the spirit of its progenitor.

Atari 2600 *Phoenix* is missing the following elements from the coin-op classic: music ("Für Elise" by Beethoven and "Romance de Amor" a.k.a. "Spanish Romance" by an unknown composer), the ability to save the player's high score, the title screen with the smaller birds spelling out "Phoenix," the starry background (which scrolls downward to give the illusion of movement), numerals appearing onscreen (indicating points earned) whenever the larger birds get shot, and smaller birds appearing on the mother ship screen. To

Phoenix for the Atari 2600, complete in box. *Courtesy of AtariAge.com.* $12.

Phoenix instruction manual. $2

Phoenix magazine ad.

Firing at the mother ship in *Phoenix. Courtesy of AtariAge.com.*

account for the latter absence, the port simply increases the number of bullets firing downward from the mother ship.

Fortunately, the essential elements are intact:

- Pulling back on the joystick (pushing a button in the arcade game) activates the ship's protective force field (called shield in the arcade game), which prevents the ship from moving (briefly), but protects it from enemy fire and contact.
- Using the force field to kill a large, swooping bird is a total blast.
- The second screen has rapid fire, giving it a different feel than the first screen.
- The larger birds have regenerating wings that can be shot off for extra points (only a center shot to a larger bird kills it).
- To defeat the mother ship, players must fire away at its thick underbelly, which is destroyed incrementally with each shot (similar to the barriers in *Space Invaders*). Once a hole has been shot through the underbelly, a rotating strip must be shot through. Once this has been done, a single shot will kill the animated alien pilot within the ship, ending the screen.

Like many Atari 2600 cartridges, *Phoenix* is embellished with a story told via the manual. According to myth, a great Arabian bird once lived for more than 500 years. Upon his deathbed, the legendary bird built itself a funeral pyre/nest comprised of frankincense, myrrh, and other aromatic spices. The bird proceeded to set the nest on fire and engulf itself in the flames, only to have a young, revitalized Phoenix take its place.

The above story will be familiar to anyone even remotely familiar with Greek mythology, but the 2600 version adds a unique twist. The nest has been contaminated by radioactive fallout, mutating the Phoenix into a bird of prey. In addition, a number of other birds have risen from the ashes. Unlike the friendly bird from the popular legend, these birds are decidedly mean, attacking the player's ship with reckless abandon.

A colorful game with rich graphics, crisp sound effects, and excellent gameplay, *Phoenix* is widely regarded as a standout in the Atari 2600 library. In the June, 1983 issue of *Electronic Games*, Arnie Katz and Bill Kunkel referred to *Phoenix* as "perhaps the finest invasion title ever produced for the 2600," citing the cartridge's "fantastic graphics and unexcelled gameplay."

In the April, 1983 issue of *Electronic Fun with Computers & Games*, Noel Steere overstated matters a bit when he called the game "a perfect arcade adaptation" and said that "the birds look exactly like they do in the arcades," but he was right on the money when he called the cartridge great and said that the game "made up for the sin of *Pac-Man*."

Conversely, Jim Gorzelany with *JoyStik* magazine (July, 1983) gave the game a mere two stars (out of five), saying "much of the challenge of the arcade original has been lost" and that the game is "strictly for the birds."

On a more positive (and more recent) note, The Video Game Critic (videogamecritic.com) said *Phoenix* "boasts some of the sharpest graphics and varied shooting action you'll find on the 2600." Further, Earl Green, via thelogbook.com, called it "an extremely playable, addictive slice of the arcade right in your living room." Finally, Keita Iida, writing for Atari Gaming Headquarters (atarihq.com), said, "Compared to other 2600 games of the genre (*Galaxian*, *Demon Attack*, *Threshold*, etc.), *Phoenix* is the best of the bunch."

While *Phoenix* is indeed a must-own title for 2600 fans, it would benefit from a couple of features seen in numerous other games for the system. Unlike such shooters as *Asteroids*, which offers 66 game variations, and *Space Invaders*, which has a whopping 112 options (including invisible invaders, moving shields, and zigzagging bombs), *Phoenix* is entirely lacking in variations—there's only one gameplay mode.

Also, the difficulty switches don't have any effect on the game in terms of skill level. Setting the left difficulty switch to "A" eliminates the background sounds of the bird cries, but that's it. Therefore, an experienced player can get past the mother ship several times before any real sense of challenge sets in.

Regardless, *Phoenix* does what an Atari 2600 port needs to do—it preserves the essence, spirit, and basic gameplay of the arcade original.

In 1981, Centuri released the oddly titled *Pleiades* (developed by Tehkan), the first and only sequel to *Phoenix*. According to Greek myth, Pleiades are the seven daughters of Atlas and Pleione. *Pleiades* was ported to the Atari 2600 in 1982, but wasn't released until AtariAge produced the game in cartridge form in 2003, complete with manual and box.

In 1982, Emerson released *Space Vultures* for the Arcadia 2001. It is similar to *Phoenix*, but lacks a mother ship. Imagic's *Demon Attack* (Atari 2600, Intellivision, various), also released in 1982, evoked *Phoenix* as well. In fact, Atari sued Imagic over the similarities between *Demon Attack* and *Phoenix*. As I mention in the *Demon Attack* chapter in this book, Imagic settled out of court and went on to produce the game for a variety of consoles and computers.

An arcade-perfect port of *Phoenix* was released for the Xbox, PlayStation 2, and PSP in 2005 as part the *Taito Legends* collection. The previous year, the coin-op classic was included as one of the titles in Radica TV's *Space Invaders* plug 'n' play unit, an item I bought to tide me over until *Taito Legends* was released.

FUN FACT:

The arcade version of *Phoenix* was developed by Amstar Electronics, which was located in Phoenix, Arizona.

WHY IT MADE THE LIST:

Like many of the better Atari 2600 coin-op ports, *Phoenix* captures the essence of the arcade original.

CHAPTER 72

PICK AXE PETE!

ODYSSEY2
GENRE: CLIMBING/NON-SCROLLING PLATFORMER
PUBLISHER: NAP
DEVELOPER: NAP
1 PLAYER
1982

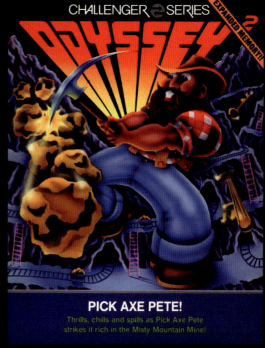

Pick Axe Pete! for the Odyssey2, complete in box. $10.

"ONE OF THOSE CLASSIC TITLES THAT WILL KEEP YOU PLAYING AGAIN AND AGAIN."

Although clearly inspired by *Donkey Kong*, *Pick Axe Pete!*, one of the more arcade-like titles in the Odyssey2 library, is a much different game. Players guide the titular stick figure as he works his way around the Misty Mountain Mine, which amounts to running across horizontal platforms, climbing up and down ladders (which appear and disappear randomly), jumping over gaps and boulders, and using a pickaxe to destroy said boulders.

Although ordinary in appearance, Pick Axe Pete himself is very nicely animated and surprisingly agile—he can duck, crawl, jump in place, and make long leaps. Destroying boulders nets three points, but the way to rack up big numbers is to grab a key (10 points) and head for a doorway to the next mine (20 points). There are three doors, stacked vertically; boulders, which bounce and roll and work their way down screen, enter the playfield through the doors.

The aforementioned keys appear randomly after boulders crash into one another. Crashing boulders can also emit a pickaxe (or nothing at all). The reason extra pickaxes appear is because Pete's pickaxe only lasts about 20 seconds or so. When he's unarmed, he must dodge boulders while waiting to grab another pickaxe or, better yet, a key to the next mine.

It's tough for beginners to last a long time in *Pick Axe Pete!* (a mere 200 points is considered a decent game for newbies), but it's one of those classic titles that will keep you playing again and again to try and better your high score. Going without an axe for an extended period can be excruciating, but it's exciting to grab a key, jump over a bouncing boulder, and dive head first into a doorway. Entering a doorway causes a nifty graphical effect in which Pete, shown in close-up and surrounded by a solid color that wavers back and forth, excitedly waves his arms and legs.

Overall, *Pick Axe Pete!* has fairly simplistic visuals, but, at least in terms of Odyssey2 games, it has a nice look as it doesn't use the typical character graphics found in so many other titles for the system (the trees in *War of Nerves!* look exactly like the ones in *Showdown in 2100 A.D.*, for example).

Gameplay is where it truly counts, and in this respect, *Pick Axe Pete!* delivers the goods. I agree with reviewer William Cassidy (classicgaming.gamespy.com) who said the game "excels at every level," that it "improves upon the basic action of *Donkey Kong*," and that it "is one of the best O2 games around."

In *Classic Gamer Magazine* #5 (fall, 2000), noted Odyssey2 fan Earl Green called *Pick Axe Pete!* "the best game ever created" for the system and "one of the few Odyssey games that can lead to a single round lasting into the wee hours."

When *Pick Axe Pete!* was fresh on the market, it was highly touted by critics as well. In the reviews column in *Electronic Games* magazine #9 (Nov., 1982), Bill Kunkel and Arnie Katz said it "combines several elements of several of today's hottest coin-ops while managing to be totally unique and captivating—even to players who don't dote on typical 'climb and jump' games…a truly enjoyable video game experience."

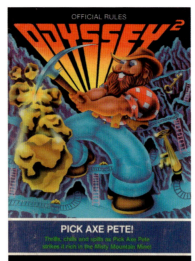

Pick Axe Pete! game cartridge. $4.

Pick Axe Pete! instruction manual. $2.

Confessions Of the Game Doctor (2005, Rolenta Press) by the late, great Bill Kunkel tells the amusing tale of the "*Pick Axe Pete* Pick-Off" competition at the 1982 World's Fair.

Speaking of the late, great Bill Kunkel, in his must-read book, *Confessions of the Game Doctor* (2005, Rolenta Press), he told the humorous tale of the official "Pick Axe Pete Pick-Off" competition held at the disastrous 1982 World's Fair in Knoxville, Tennessee. Kunkel claimed in the book that he didn't remember much about the game itself—despite the aforementioned glowing remarks in *EG* (perhaps Katz wrote that review)—but he certainly remembered the contest, which he and Katz provided commentary for. After praising some of his favorite Odyssey2 titles (*UFO!*, *War of Nerves!*, *K.C. Munchkin!*) to assure readers he was a fan of the console, Kunkel wrote this about the game and contest:

> *Pick Axe Pete!*, as best as I can recall, was not quite in that lofty company. I dunno, maybe it's a forgotten classic, but make sure the emphasis is on "forgotten" because I don't remember a damned thing about it except for the fact that it was all but impossible to do anything like a "play-by-play" or even sensible commentary while watching it. But we had microphones in our hands, so we were obviously supposed to say something. These were the best Pick Axers in the country, but making this lifeless contest seem interesting while standing in the middle of an exhibit hall that was already being given the eye by the demolition crew, was far from my most gratifying gaming moment.

Kunkel's amusing memories notwithstanding, *Pick Axe Pete!* is a quality cartridge that has withstood the test of time in terms of challenge and fun factor.

As I mentioned earlier, *Pick Axe Pete!* is somewhat similar to *Donkey Kong*. According to William Cassidy, "North American Philips took notice of *Donkey Kong*'s tremendous success and wanted to jump on the bandwagon. So, they instructed their chief programmer, Ed Averett, to create a horizontal platform-type game with a 'jumpman' character running around. At the same time, they didn't want to directly rip off the almighty *DK*, so they told Averett to make some gameplay adjustments. The result is a semi-original game that really excels at every level."

During the early development stages, *Pick Axe Pete!* was called *Hammerin' Hank*. However, according to Bob Harris, another O2 programmer, "After losing the copyright case over *K.C. Munchkin!* being, er, inspired by *Pac-Man*, the powers that be decided that a hammer would make this game too similar to *Donkey Kong*."

Donkey Kong comparisons and contest anecdotes aside, if you enjoy climbing games, non-scrolling platformers, and hectic, arcade-style action, you should get a kick out of *Pick Axe Pete!*

FUN FACT:

Ten-year-old Tony Scardigno of New Jersey won the "Pick Axe Pete Pick-Off" by beating four other finalists. To qualify, you had to score at least 9,000 points in the game.

WHY IT MADE THE LIST:

With *Pick Axe Pete!*, programmer Ed Averett borrowed from earlier games, came up with a few ideas of his own, and created a terrific cartridge that is still entertaining today.

CHAPTER 73

PITFALL!

ATARI 2600
GENRE: ADVENTURE/SIDE-SCROLLING PLATFORMER
PUBLISHER: ACTIVISION
DEVELOPER: ACTIVISION
1 PLAYER
1982

COLECOVISION
GENRE: ADVENTURE/SIDE-SCROLLING PLATFORMER
PUBLISHER: ACTIVISION
DEVELOPER: ACTION GRAPHICS
1 PLAYER
1983

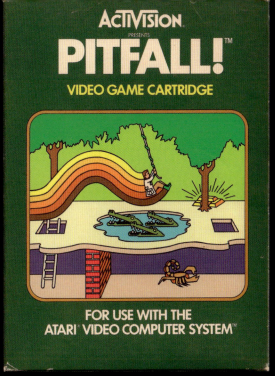

Pitfall! for the Atari 2600, complete in box. $25.

"PITFALL! FOR THE ATARI 2600 DID NOTHING LESS THAN REVOLUTIONIZE THE INDUSTRY IN TERMS OF SIDE-SCROLLING PLATFORM GAMES."

The chief forerunner of and inspiration behind such mega popular titles as *Super Mario Bros.* and *Sonic the Hedgehog*, *Pitfall!* for the Atari 2600 did nothing less than revolutionize the industry in terms of side-scrolling platform games. Technically speaking, it's not a side-scroller—each of its 255 contiguous screens are static (a la *Prince of Persia*)—but its running, jumping, climbing, item-finding sensibilities paved the way for one of the most ubiquitous genres in the history of video games.

Players guide "world famous jungle explorer and fortune hunter extraordinaire" Pitfall Harry as he traverses an expansive jungle, both above and below its surface. His mission is to collect 32 treasures (diamond rings, gold bars, silver bars, and money bags) and return to the starting point within a 20-minute time limit. He begins with three lives and 2,000 points, but running into rolling logs or falling down holes decreases the score. Other obstacles, such as fires, cobra rattlers, crocodiles, and scorpions, are deadly.

As alluded to earlier, Pitfall Harry runs, climbs (up and down ladders), and jumps (over obstacles), but his most memorable ability is swinging on vines (a la *Jungle Hunt*, released the same year), which takes him safely over quicksand and crocodile pits. The crocodile heads open and close their mouths, and Harry can jump on top of closed mouths, but this is a tricky maneuver—timing is everything. Brick walls can impede Harry's progress, and it's up to the player to find his or her way through the non-linear, maze-like jungle.

Pitfall Harry swinging over obstacles in *Pitfall!* for the Atari 2600. *Courtesy of AtariAge.com.*

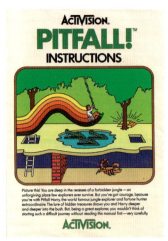

Pitfall! instruction manual (Atari 2600). $5.

Pitfall! for the ColecoVision, complete in box. *Courtesy of Bryan C. Smith.* $25.

A perfect score in *Pitfall!* is 114,000 points, which is achieved by collecting all the treasures without losing any points by falling down holes or tripping on logs. *Pitfall!* designer David Crane offered the following advice (via the instruction manual) for playing the game well: "I'd suggest that you make a map of the terrain each time you play. Knowing the jungle and planning the best route to all the treasures is the only way to insure success time after time."

The winner of the "Player's Choice Award for Most Popular Home Video Game for 1983" (*Video Games* #18, 1984), *Pitfall!* is a beloved cartridge, but there are many fans of the game—including me—that have never actually beaten it. On the other hand, there are gamers who have beaten it many times and are still—to this day— trying to achieve a perfect game and/or improve their finishing time.

Kudos for *Pitfall!* are virtually endless. In the Jan., 1983 issue of *Electronic Games*, *Pitfall!* took home the trophy for "Best Adventure Videogame," with editors Arnie Katz and Bill Kunkel saying: "The fine graphic sense of the Activision design team greatly enriches the *Pitfall!* experience. Watching Harry swing across a quicksand pit on a slender vine while crocodiles snap their jaws frantically in a futile effort to tear off a little leg-of-hero snack is what video game adventures are all about…this is as richly complex a video game as you'll find anywhere."

Here are more accolades for this fine cartridge:

"*Pitfall!* is an extremely colorful game with graphics so good you'll really feel like you're in the jungle… the best game from Activision yet."

—Raymond Dimetrosky
(*Electronic Fun with Computers & Games* #2 Dec., 1982)

[*Pitfall!* is a game that] combines all the necessary ingredients for a sure-fire hit…definitely fun… the graphics are clean, colorful, and innovative…

—Perry Greenberg
(*Video Games* #3, Dec., 1982)

A challenging, graphically entertaining game with wide age group appeal. A 'must-have' cartridge for all VCS owners.

—*JoyStik* magazine #4
(Jan., 1983)

The game was a jewel, a perfect world incised in a mere 4K of code.

—Nick Montfort
(*Supercade: A Visual History of the Videogame Age, 1971-1984*, 2001, The MIT Press)

Pitfall! was very exciting on release and I remember it as one of my favorite Atari VCS games. Hearing the Tarzan yodel when Harry swings on a rope still puts a smile on my face.

—Matt Fox
(*The Video Games Guide*, 2006, Boxtree)

Pitfall! is one of the best games released by Activision, probably the highest praise one can give a VCS game.

—Ben Langberg of Le Geek Retrogaming Reviews
(www.abscape.org/legeek)

Pitfall! demonstrates the full potential of the Atari 2600—that games for it could be complex, challenging, and exciting despite the limitations of the technology. It laid the groundwork for the side-scrolling format of video games, and its replayability factor makes it a true classic.

—Chad Polenz of The Video Game Museum
(www.vgmuseum.com).

Although Atari released a cartridge based on *Raiders of the Lost Ark* themselves, Activision's game is more action-packed and closer in "spirit" to an Indy-like adventure. The only thing missing is a giant boulder to run away from (although I suppose rolling logs will do just fine).

—Scott Alan Marriott of the All Game Guide (allgame.com)

Clearly, *Pitfall!* was (and still is) a critical success. It was commercially viable as well, selling more than four million copies, staying number one on the Billboard charts for 64 consecutive weeks, and helping make David Crane a highly popular industry figure.

In *High Score! The Illustrated History of Electronic Games* (2002, Osborne/McGraw-Hill), Crane spoke about creating his masterpiece. "*Pitfall!* was our 18th game, and the single most amazing fact about it is that it took me 10 minutes to design," he said. "I always wanted to do a game with a little running man, so I took a blank piece of paper and drew a man. 'Where is he?' Put in path. Put in jungle. 'Why is he running?' Put in treasure and obstacles. That was the design. Execution took about 1,000 hours at the keyboard."

The book also states that Crane got the idea to have Pitfall Harry swing on vines to make it over alligators from Paul Terry's classic cartoon, *Heckle and Jeckle*.

Predictably, Activision released *Pitfall!* for other popular systems of the time. The Atari 5200 version is hampered by poor controls while the Intellivision game needlessly employs a second button for letting go of vines. Lacking these setbacks, the ColecoVision port is the better of the three, despite developer Action Graphics not taking advantage of the console's superior graphical prowess (the bushes and trees have slightly more detail, but the treasures actually look better in the 2600 game).

Pitfall! spawned numerous sequels, including the great *Pitfall II: Lost Caverns* (various), the dreadful *Super Pitfall* (1987, NES), the surprisingly good *Pitfall: The Mayan Adventure* (various), *Pitfall: Beyond the Jungle* (1998, Game Boy Color), *Pitfall: The Big Adventure* (2008, Nintendo Wii), and *Pitfall 3D: Beyond the Jungle* (1998, PlayStation), which video game historian Earl Green once called an "engrossing game" and a "worthy sequel."

In 1985, Sega released *Pitfall II: The Lost Caverns* (note the addition of "the" in the title) to the arcades. Spruced up with fancier graphics and additional obstacles (including lightning and volcanic rock), the game incorporates elements of both *Pitfall!* and *Pitfall II: Lost Caverns*. This was a rare occurrence of a console game inspiring a coin-op title (as opposed to the other way around).

After *Combat* and *Pac-Man*, *Pitfall!* is easily one of the more common Atari 2600 cartridges, showing up with alarming frequency in most any stash of 2600 cartridges you may come across. In addition, the game has been translated to numerous modern systems via such collections as *Activision Classics* (1998, PlayStation), *Activision Anthology* (various), and *Activision Hits Remixed* (2006, PSP). In 2010, Microsoft made *Pitfall!* available as a downloadable title for the Xbox 360 Game Room service.

The ColecoVision version of *Pitfall!* is tougher to find than the 2600 cartridge, but it's not exactly rare either, so if you don't already own the game, you should definitely snatch up a copy and start your own 20-minute adventure. Just watch out for those opening crocodile mouths.

FUN FACT:

According to David Crane (via an interview published on www.gooddealgames.com), "One week before *Pitfall!* was to be released, I only gave you one life [as opposed to three] to play the whole game. I was experimenting with that concept as sort of the ultimate challenge. That's right, fall in one pit and start over from the beginning! Well, thankfully my buddies [at Activision] practically tied me to my chair until I put in extra lives and I'm glad they did."

WHY IT MADE THE LIST:

Pitfall! is a highly influential title that remains relevant today.

CHAPTER 74

PITFALL II: LOST CAVERNS

ATARI 2600/ATARI 5200
GENRE: ADVENTURE/SIDE-SCROLLING PLATFORMER
PUBLISHER: ACTIVISION
DEVELOPER: ACTIVISION
1 PLAYER
1984

Pitfall! II: Lost Caverns comic book ad.

"A NEW ADVENTURE AND A VARIETY OF FRESH FEATURES."

A triumphant follow-up to *Pitfall!*, which is nothing less than one of the most critically and commercially successful games ever released for the Atari 2600, *Pitfall II: Lost Caverns* surprised gamers by taking away one of *Pitfall!*'s most popular elements: the ability for Pitfall Harry to swing on vines. Luckily, it's still a great game, offering a new adventure and a variety of fresh features.

Players guide the intrepid explorer as he sets out on an epic quest in an underground Peruvian cave to find his niece, Rhonda. He's also looking for the cowardly cat Quickclaw, a primitive cave rat, and the great Raj Diamond, grabbing as many gold bars as possible along the way. Unlike *Pitfall!*, there is no time limit, and lives are unlimited. If Harry touches an enemy, he will lose points and be transported back to the last checkpoint. As such, *Pitfall II* was one of the first video games to feature checkpoints.

Pitfall II has new enemies to jump over and otherwise avoid, including bats, eels, frogs, and condors (scorpions make a return engagement). In addition, Pitfall Harry can now float across chasms on hot air balloons and swim. Music plays throughout the game, and the areas to explore are more complex, more expansive, and even less linear than those in *Pitfall!*.

In an interview published on Video-Game Ephemera (video-game-ephemera.com), *Pitfall II* designer David Crane offered some insight into the audio/visual excellence of the game. "Whatever you can put in the cartridge that might add functionality is a good thing," he said. "So we designed a couple of chips…I have a patent for the one chip that's in *Pitfall II* [called the Display Processor Chip or DPC for short]. And that one had three different channels of free-running musical accompaniment and a bunch of display capability that could put more things on the screen."

Named number one in the "Best 25 Atari 2600 Games of All Time" feature in issue #46 of *Retro Gamer Magazine*, *Pitfall II: Lost Caverns* is indeed one of the more impressive games in the system's library.

Here's additional praise for the game from a variety of sources:

> A major technological overhaul of the original's somewhat repetitive play mechanic…the most remarkable breadth of any 2600 video game yet produced…simply beyond belief…a must-have for all 2600 owners…a major breakthrough in terms of concept, style, playability, *and* 2600 technology.
> —Bill Kunkel
> (*Electronic Games* #26, July, 1984)

Pitfall II: Lost Caverns game cartridge (Atari 2600). $15.

Pitfall II: Lost Caverns game cartridge (Atari 5200). $25.

Pitfall II: Lost Caverns instruction manual (Atari 5200). $5.

Developer David Crane clearly pulled out all the stops with this one, and the result is an exciting adventure that really pushes the limits of the system.
—The Video Game Critic
(videogamecritic.com)

Pitfall II is my favorite VCS game of all time, and with good reason. Many have called this the greatest VCS game ever made, and frankly, I'd have to agree with them. The scope of the adventure was unheard of at the time, and along with the fantastic controls, gorgeous graphics, and terrific music, it's truly earned its reputation. *Pitfall II* is truly deserving of a place in any VCS fan's library.
—Rob "Dire 51" of Digital Press
(www.digitpress.com)

Pitfall II: Lost Caverns expands on the *Pitfall!* concept to create a robust and complicated adventure that stands as one of the Atari VCS' most accomplished games. The sharp, colorful visuals improve on the original while still retaining their familiar look, and the music is widely considered the best on the console.
—Skyler Miller of the All Game Guide
(allgame.com)

Other versions of *Pitfall II* were released as well. As I wrote in my first book, *Classic Home Video Games, 1972-1984* (2007, McFarland Publishers): "*Pitfall II: Lost Caverns* for the Atari 5200 [adapted by Mike Lorenzen] has only slightly more detail than the Atari 2600 version, but it does include an entirely new cave to explore. This cavern, which is not present in the ColecoVision game [adapted by Robert Rutkowski], offers harder jumps, a crazy flying bat, and other fresh challenges. Best of all, *Pitfall II* for the 5200 doesn't suffer the same control issues that plagued the system's frustrating rendition of *Pitfall!*"

The Atari 5200 version of *Pitfall II* includes "Adventurer's Edition" as part of its onscreen title, which is in reference to the new and vast cave not found in the 2600 game. In issue #34 (Nov/Dec, 1997) of the *Digital Press* fanzine, Al Bakiel reviewed the 5200 cart, calling it a "beautiful game" and a "masterpiece." The Video Game Critic called it "fascinating and fun," but added that "a 'duck' button would have been a really good idea."

Whether you play *Pitfall II: Lost Caverns* on the 2600 or the 5200, you owe it to yourself to go adventuring with Pitfall Harry. Numerous sequels followed, which you can read about in the *Pitfall!* entry in this book.

In 2010, Microsoft made *Pitfall II: Lost Caverns* for the 2600 available as a downloadable title for the Xbox 360 Game Room service. In addition, the game has been translated to numerous modern systems via such collections as *Activision Anthology* (various) and *Activision Hits Remixed* (2006, PSP).

FUN FACT:

Quickclaw and Rhonda were created for the *Pitfall!* cartoon, which was part of *Saturday Supercade* (CBS, 1983-1984).

WHY IT MADE THE LIST:

Pitfall II: Lost Caverns is even better than *Pitfall!*, and that's saying a lot.

CHAPTER **75**

POPEYE

NINTENDO NES
GENRE: CLIMBING
PUBLISHER: NINTENDO
DEVELOPER: NINTENDO
1 OR 2 PLAYERS (ALTERNATING)
1986

Popeye arcade game. $800.

"ENDEARING THEME MUSIC, CUTE GRAPHICS, AND TERRIFIC CLIMBING ACTION."

When Nintendo's arcade classic *Popeye* (1982), which was created by famed video game designer Shigeru Miyamoto (with assistance from Genyo Takeda), was ported to the ColecoVision in 1983, I played the heck out of the cartridge.

Yes, I liked the character Popeye (introduced by Elzie Segar in 1929 for the Thimble Theatre comic strip), whose adventures I had enjoyed in the Saturday morning cartoons, but the real reason I played it so much is because I loved climbing games, and this was a nice example of the genre. Such ladder-ridden games as *Donkey Kong*, *Miner 2049er*, and *Jumpman Junior* kept me busy for hours and hours during my teenage years.

Then, when *Popeye* came to the NES in 1986 (it hit the Japanese Famicom in 1983 as one of the system's three launch titles), I played the game even more, thanks to its improved graphics, controls, and sounds over the ColecoVision port. In a review published on www.8-bitcentral.com, the writer said, "The NES version really stands out with vivid imagery and great sound—including Popeye's theme song when he eats spinach!"

While not quite as cartoon-like as its coin-op cousin (which *Electronic Games* magazine #14 referred to as having "visual magic" and "flat-out cartoon-quality"), *Popeye* for the NES is nevertheless a very fine port, putting players in the title role. The Sailor Man's job is to walk across platforms and go up and down stairs and ladders in order to grab the items Olive Oyle floats downward from the top of the playfield. Said items include hearts (the first screen), musical notes (the second screen, which features a side-view of a four-story building), or letters spelling out HELP (the third screen, which takes place on a boat).

When a floating item reaches the bottom of the screen, the music will change, reminding the player that he or she should hurry down to pick it up before it sinks in the water below and costs the player a life. Once a set number of items has been grabbed (visual indicators show how many items remain), it's on to the next screen. The higher up the item is on the playfield when Popeye grabs it, the more points the player will score.

While working to complete a screen, Popeye gets harassed by such enemies as Brutus, who throws bottles and chases Popeye, the Seahag, who throws skulls, and Bernard the vulture, who flies across the playfield in the third screen. Popeye can punch the bottles and skulls for extra points.

A can of spinach appears once per screen (unless the player dies, making another can appear), and Popeye can grab

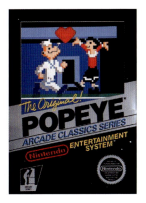

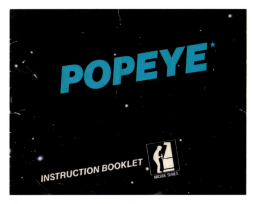

Popeye for the Nintendo NES, complete in box. $130.

Popeye game cartridge. $15.

Popeye instruction manual. $15.

this for temporary extra power, namely the ability to defeat enemies by simply making contact with them (being energized with spinach is the only way to defeat Brutus, though he does reenter the game after a few seconds). When Popeye eats spinach, the famous theme song plays.

Other ways to score extra points include punching a tub to drop it on Brutus's head (screen one), stunning him in the process, and jumping on a springboard to grab a platform holding Swee'Pea (screen two).

Like many of the games in this book, *Popeye*, with its endearing theme music, cute graphics, and terrific climbing action, has the uncanny knack of seducing the gamer into playing it "just one more time" to try and get a better score or reach a higher round (a level counter appears onscreen).

As mentioned earlier, *Popeye* was also available for the ColecoVision. Other consoles with a *Popeye* port include the Atari 2600 (playable, but flat and blocky), Atari 5200 (cute graphics, but poor controls), and Intellivision (flickering, blocky graphics and poor controls). There was also an Odyssey2 version (one screen, terrible graphics, includes two-player simultaneous mode where the other gamer controls Brutus), but it was only available in Europe and South America.

In 1993, Activision released a side-scrolling platformer for the Game Boy called *Popeye 2*. In 2005, Namco released an unrelated side-scrolling racer called *Popeye: Rush for Spinach* for the Game Boy Advance.

When people talk about the NES today, the conversation inevitably turns to such groundbreaking titles as *Super Mario Bros.*, *Metroid*, and *The Legend of Zelda*. That's all well and good (those are indeed great, highly influential games), but players shouldn't forget the system's more retro coin-op classics, such as *Bump 'n' Jump*, *Galaga*, *Joust*, *Xevious*, and, the man of the hour, *Popeye* the Sailor Man.

FUN FACT:

Nintendo's legendary arcade classic, *Donkey Kong* (1980), started life as a Popeye-themed game, but designer Shigeru Miyamoto had to change the characters when the licensing deal fell through.

WHY IT MADE THE LIST:

Popeye for the NES does much more than simply get by on a popular license: it offers cute graphics and good climbing action.

CHAPTER 76

QIX

ATARI 5200
GENRE: MAZE/ACTION PUZZLE
PUBLISHER: ATARI
DEVELOPER: ATARI
1 OR 2 PLAYERS (ALTERNATING)
1982

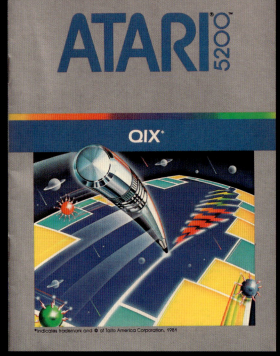

Qix instruction manual. $2.

"THE FIRST GAME OF ITS TYPE."

The oddly titled *Qix* was the first game of its type in which players draw boxes on the playfield to fill in space. Unlike most of the games that it inspired, such as *Amidar* (1982) and *Pepper II* (1982), *Qix* begins with an open playfield, and it is up to the gamer to decide where to draw the lines, which in this case are called Stix.

In the Atari 5200 version of the game, which is an excellent port of Taito's 1981 arcade original, the triangular writing implement players control is called a "chromium electronic marker," which is used to "partition the land, segment by segment." Once the player has filled in a certain percentage of the playfield (50, 65, 75, or 85%, depending on the game variation), the next level will begin.

While gamers guide the marker around the screen, drawing squares, rectangles, and other straight-line shapes, an enemy Qix—a winged-shaped object comprised of wavering lines—roams quickly around space that has yet to be boxed in. Experienced players will learn to box in the Qix to neutralize it, but this is a difficult maneuver for beginners.

Contact with the Qix, either by the marker or an unfinished line, is deadly, but players are safe from the Qix while on the border of the playfield or on lines that have already been drawn. However, fuse-like objects called Sparx patrol the borders as well as the drawn lines, so beware. An additional threat called the Fuse hides and waits until you stop moving and then will travel along your path trying to catch you.

Beginning with the third level, a second Qix will appear onscreen, making the game more difficult. Splitting the two Qix will advance players to the next level, as will the more common method of filling in the requisite percentage of space.

At any given time, players can draw slowly or quickly. The former nets more points while the latter is a safer way to travel since it's easier to keep away from enemies by going fast. Certain strategists will form a bunch of skinny long boxes across or up the screen while going fast and then draw slowly to connect said formation to a wall, enclosing a large portion of the screen for maximum points.

The manual recommends that players "use fast draw to set up a pattern" and "use slow draw to complete the pattern."

Programmed by Eric Manghise, *Qix* is a great and decidedly unusual cartridge, an opinion shared by many gamers.

In issue #49 of the *Digital Press* fanzine (Sept./Oct., 2002), longtime collector Russ Perry Jr. said *Qix* has boring graphics, but that he "liked this game in the arcades, and this

Qix game cartridge. $4.

Qix for the Atari 5200, complete in box. $10. Courtesy of AtariAge.com.

Qix in action. Courtesy of AtariAge.com.

version is pretty well done" and "pretty solid." Perry also said *Qix* has a "decent challenge, some adrenaline moments, and a fair amount of strategy required," but that "I don't think it's for everybody, and even I might have to be in the right mood to play it."

In a review published in *Electronic Games* magazine #20 (March, 1984), Bill Kunkel said *Qix* is "exactly the sort of game that just aches for home translation, where players can learn the tactics and skill necessary to master it." He called the 5200 port a "magnificent coin-op translation, offering a perfectly stylized duplication of the original graphics, right down to the lettering."

In *Electronic Fun with Computers & Games* #8 (June, 1983), William Michael Brown said *Qix* is a "rare treat" and that "Atari has done a masterful job of translating it into the 5200 format…everything's here—from the original playfield, sounds, color, and scoring indicators, right up to the double-Qix/split-Qix bonus scoring."

Perry Greenberg, writing in *Video Games* #11 (Aug., 1983), agreed, calling it "an exciting, challenging, and addicting game that's a must for owners of Atari's 5200. It's not only a challenging game, but it provides a medium that allows a player to express himself artistically."

Raymond Dimetrosky, reviewing the game in *Video Game Players* Vol. 2 #1 (Aug./Sept., 1983), called *Qix* an "excellent adaptation of the arcade hit." He also said that it "requires strategy and is very addicting" and that it's "a fun game simply because it's different than the run-of-the-mill space contests."

The arcade version of *Qix*, unlike most Taito games (such as *Space Invaders*), was created in America and not brought over from Japan. It was designed by the husband and wife team of Randy and Sandy Pfeiffer. According to video game historian Michael Thomasson, Randy "had his automobile decorated with a vanity license plate stating 'JUS4QIX,'" which is where he got the name for the game.

Qix spawned several coin-op sequels, including *Qix II: Tournament* (1981), *Super Qix* (1987), and *Twin Qix* (1995).

Console sequels include *Ultimate Qix* (1991) for the Genesis, *Qix Neo* (2003) for the PlayStation, and *Qix++* for the Xbox 360 (2009, via XBLA).

In addition to the 5200, *Qix* was also ported to the NES (1991), Game Boy (1990), Atari Lynx (1992), PlayStation 2 (2007, via *Taito Legends 2*), and Nintendo 3DS (2011, via the Virtual Console).

Intellivision owners can enjoy a similar game called *Thin Ice*, which you'll find in "The Next 100" appendix at the back of this book.

FUN FACT:

I probably should've mentioned this at the beginning of the essay, but *Qix* is pronounced "kicks."

WHY IT MADE THE LIST:

Qix allows more freedom of movement than most maze games and is more versatile than most puzzlers.

CHAPTER **77**

RAMBO: FIRST BLOOD PART II

SEGA MASTER SYSTEM
GENRE: VERTICAL SCROLLING SHOOTER
PUBLISHER: SEGA
DEVELOPER: SEGA
1 OR 2 PLAYERS (SIMULTANEOUS)
1986

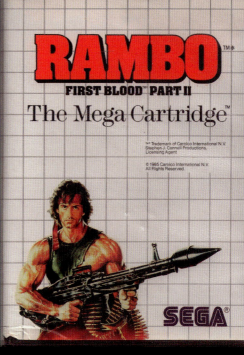

Rambo: First Blood Part II for the Sega Master System, complete in box. $12.

"ONE OF THE BEST MOVIE GAMES OF THE 1980S."

Some of you may be surprised to find a movie-based title other than *Gremlins* for the Atari 5200 in this book, but *Rambo: First Blood Part II* is an exceptional (and exceptionally difficult) entry in the one-man army/vertical scrolling shooter genre established by such coin-op classics as *Front Line* (1982, Taito), *Commando* (1985, Data East), and *Ikari Warriors* (1986, Tradewest).

In one-player mode, you control Rambo, the fictional action hero made famous by Sylvester Stallone in the 1985 feature film (more on that later). Armed with an M-60, which fires unlimited bullets, and five arrow-bombs, which, as the name implies, are more explosive, you must traverse six different types of terrain (meaning the game has six levels): jungle, forest, swamp, desert, mountain, and seacoast.

As you work your way slowly and methodically up the scrolling playfield, which is cluttered with trees, rocks, and other obstructions, such enemies as infantrymen, artillerymen, knife soldiers, policemen, bazooka soldiers, riflemen, snipers, flame throwers, and rocket launchers will try to strike you down. You can shoot up, left, right, up/left diagonally, and up/right diagonally, but you cannot fire downward (even though you can move downward).

The bullets you shoot look like snowballs or large ping pong balls, which is one of the game's only weaknesses, and, confusingly, certain enemies fire this same type of white bullet. Certain bad guys shoot bullets (you'll notice this beginning in the second level) while some enemy bullets explode into four hard-to-avoid projectiles.

Rambo's arrow-bombs are crucial to your success in getting very far in this game. They are used to destroy highway patrolmen, tanks, and concentration camps (flashing buildings), the latter of which frees a POW when destroyed. In addition, the destruction of a concentration camp releases an item that will give you five even more powerful arrow-bombs. (Arrow-bombs are also good for destroying several standard enemies at once.)

After you have killed a certain number of enemy soldiers, power-ups will appear that can upgrade your M-60 with a longer shooting distance and more penetration power for killing multiple attackers with one shot (sounds like there's something Freudian going on here, but I'll hold off on any amateur psychology for now).

Once you make it to the end of a level, you'll need to blow up a barricade blocking your way. This will release more captives from the concentration camp. Don't bother shooting the barricade at first—just keep shooting soldiers as they appear. This can be pretty intense as the screen gets crowded with enemies. After a certain number of enemies are killed, the barricade will begin flashing. To destroy the flashing barricade, shoot it with an arrow-bomb.

As I alluded to earlier, *Rambo: First Blood Part II* is difficult, methodical, and slowly paced, but I prefer it to the faster action of the NES version of *Commando* (1986), which

The back of the *Rambo: First Blood Part II* box.

Rambo: First Blood Part II instruction manual. $2.

Rambo: First Blood Part II game cartridge. $5.

is certainly a good game, just not as much fun as *Rambo*. Not that I don't like fast-paced games of this type—*Guerilla War* (1989), which is even faster and more hectic than *Commando*—is one of my favorite shooters for the NES.

Like *Ikari Warriors* and *Guerilla War*, *Rambo: First Blood Part II* lets a second player (called Zane in this case) join in for some simultaneous fun (unfortunately, *Commando* for the NES can't say the same—it only offers alternating gameplay). This two-player mode does exactly what it should: it puts the odds more in your favor, making the game easier to beat (as opposed to some games, where a second player can actually slow you down). As you progress, your partner, who has the same weaponry as you, can cover you, or you can stay out of each other's way and simply mow down enemies.

One thing you'll notice about *Rambo: First Blood Part II* is that it lacks standard, unhidden continues, something it desperately needs. Luckily, there are cheat codes that let you continue. After running out of lives during a stage, let the title screen appear, enter the corresponding code, and you can return to the beginning of that stage. Codes are as follows:

Return to level 2: down, up, left, right
Return to level 3: right, right, left, up, up
Return to level 4: down, left, right, left, left
Return to level 5: right, right, up, up, down, right
Return to level 6: up, down, right, left, left, down, down

I don't use cheat codes all that often, but for *Rambo: First Blood Part II*, they are absolutely essential if you plan on beating the game (unless, of course, your gaming skills are far greater than mine, which I consider to be above average, at least for older titles such as this).

Rambo: First Blood Part II borrows its name, of course, from the 1985 feature film directed by George P. Cosmatos. The box features a painting of Sylvester Stallone in his John Rambo gear, which includes a huge gun and his patented headband. The art is similar to the movie poster, but with some relatively subtle differences, such as a different tilt angle of the gun. Stallone is shirtless on the movie poster, but is wearing a torn tank top on the game box.

The game was originally released in Japan as *Ashura*, but instead of Rambo and Zane, players control a pair of armed Buddhist monks named Ashura and Bishamon, who must rescue their kidnapped friends. Katsuhiro Hayashi composed the title screen music for the Japanese version, but the Americanized release replaced the tune with an 8-bit take on Jerry Goldsmith's movie theme (the title screen was altered as well with a depiction of Rambo). In addition, despite posing a formidable challenge, the American release is a tad easier (for example, flamethrower soldiers can be killed by standard fire, as opposed to just arrow-bombs).

Rambo: First Blood Part II was released in Australia and Europe under the name of *Secret Command*. Communication got crossed at some point, however, because the title screen refers to it as "Secret Commando." Also, the game is an amalgamation of the American and Japanese releases in that the character names are Ashura and Bishamon, but they look like Rambo and Zane.

Getting back to the movie, *Rambo: First Blood Part II*, which is the sequel to *First Blood* (1982), isn't exactly the *Citizen Kane* of action films (as of this writing, it has an underwhelming, if not disastrous 6.2 IMDB user rating), but it is an entertainingly violent movie. Stallone, giving Arnold Schwarzenegger a run for his money as the ultimate action hero, was born to play veteran John Rambo, who is released from his hard labor prison sentence to search the jungles of Vietnam for POWs.

The Master System game enjoys a slightly higher IMDB rating than the film (7.0), but that's from a much smaller sampling of users. The video game community has generally given the game high marks over the years, but not everyone concurs. In Corey Sandler and Tom Badgett's *Ultimate Unauthorized Sega Game Strategies, For the Master and Genesis Systems* (1990, Bantam Books), the duo give the game a lowly 4 rating out of 10, claiming that the light gun-based *Rambo III* for the Master System (which, to be fair, is also a fine game) has "more exciting action."

Regardless, if you enjoy run-and-gun shooters, I think you should give *Rambo: First Blood Part II* a good play through. Just be sure to use continues and, if possible, enlist Zane to help you out.

FUN FACT:

In 2008, Sylvester Stallone reprised his role as John Rambo in *Rambo*, which was released 20 years after the last film in the original trilogy, which was *Rambo III*. Also in 2008, Sega released an arcade game called *Rambo*, based on the classic films.

WHY IT MADE THE LIST:

One of the best movie-related games of the 1980s, *Rambo: First Blood Part II* is a top-notch entry in the vertical scrolling, ground-based shooter genre.

CHAPTER 78

RIVER RAID

ATARI 2600
GENRE: VERTICAL SCROLLING SHOOTER
PUBLISHER: ACTIVISION
DEVELOPER: ACTIVISION
1 OR 2 PLAYERS (ALTERNATING)
1982

ATARI 5200
GENRE: VERTICAL SCROLLING SHOOTER
PUBLISHER: ACTIVISION
DEVELOPER: ACTIVISION
1 OR 2 PLAYERS (ALTERNATING)
1983

COLECOVISION
GENRE: VERTICAL SCROLLING SHOOTER
PUBLISHER: ACTIVISION
DEVELOPER: SYDNEY DEVELOPMENT
1 OR 2 PLAYERS (ALTERNATING)
1984

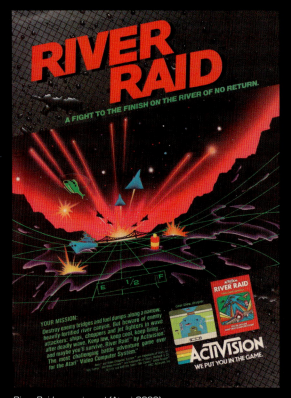

River Raid magazine ad (Atari 2600).

"PRECISE MANEUVERING AND CAREFULLY TIMED SHOTS PLAY KEY ROLES IN THIS SUPER ENTERTAINING GAME."

The first vertical scrolling shooter for a home console, *River Raid* for the Atari 2600 is a manly game that was created by a woman: Carol Shaw, who was the first female to program and design a commercially released video game cartridge—*3D Tic-Tac-Toe* (1980) for the 2600.

Viewed from a top-down perspective, the game has players flying up the River of No Return, shooting tankers, helicopters, jets, and fuel depots, the latter of which are a key strategic element in the game. When your assault jet begins running low on fuel, you should fly over a fuel depot. During the refueling process, seasoned players will destroy the fuel depot for extra points. As the game wears on, fuel depots get scarce, making each one more crucial to your success.

Another challenge is the river itself, with its bays, islands, and narrow channels (crashing into the river bank is deadly). Luckily, the assault jet is highly maneuverable as it can bank left and right and speed up and slow down. When the jet is running low on fuel, it's sometimes necessary to race quickly to the next fuel depot and then slam on the brakes to acquire as much fuel as possible (the slower you fly over the depot, the more fuel you get). Indiscriminate shooting can backfire (so to speak) as it's easy to destroy much-needed fuel depots.

One of the best games in the Atari 2600 library, *River Raid* has sharply defined, non-flickering graphics, smooth difficulty progression, and intense, challenging gameplay—precise maneuvering and carefully timed shots play key roles in this super entertaining game.

Certain modernists claim that *River Raid* hasn't aged well in the light of such razzmatazz vertical scrollers as *Ikaruga* (2003) for the GameCube and *Raiden IV* (2009) for the Xbox 360, but I beg to differ. *River Raid* remains fast, fun, charming, elegant, and, of course, manly.

Many agree with me in this regard. Here are quotes about the game from a variety of sources:

> …one of the best blood and thunder blast-'em-ups ever inserted into a VCS slot…
> —*Electronic Games* magazine #14
> (April, 1983)

> …thrill-a-minute action…
> —*The Electronic Games Software Encyclopedia*
> (1983, The Book Company)

> sharp, colorful graphics…one of the best games going…the ever-changing scenery and the need for a constant shifting of strategy to address the situation at hand gives the game an appeal not found in the ordinary one-scenario video games.
> —*Electronic Fun with Computers & Games*
> (March, 1983)

> *River Raid* is Activision's best action game cartridge to date. The graphics are nicely detailed and the audio effects are convincing, yet not overwhelming. Your jet is easy to control (it even banks realistically), and the game's level of difficulty builds at a sure and steady pace.
> —*JoyStik* #6
> (July, 1983)

> …in all its incarnations, *River Raid* remains an enjoyable, streamlined test of eye-hand coordination.
> —*Electronic Games* magazine #32
> (April, 1985)

> …the execution is near flawless. The graphics are crisp and colorful, the control is spot on, and the game never seems to repeat or end…it's still thrilling to see how far you can go.
> —Ben Langberg of Le Geek Retrogaming Reviews
> (www.abscape.org/legeek)

> With crisp and colorful graphics and great gameplay, Shaw has created a winner. This shooter soars high in my book.
> —Adam King of Atari Gaming Headquarters
> (atarihq.com)

> The sound, graphics, and fluidity are all very impressive for a VCS game.
> —Matt Fox
> (2006, *The Video Games Guide*, Boxtree)

In an interview published on www.vintagecomputing.com, Carol Shaw spoke about the creation of the game. "*River Raid* was actually inspired by a coin-op game called *Scramble*," she said. "It was a space game. So I went to Al Miller and said, 'I'm thinking of doing this space game.' He said, 'There's too many space games. Try to come up with something different.'"

River Raid went through several changes before Shaw hit upon the idea of a jet going up a river.

"I wanted to do a scrolling shooter game," she said, "so I was drawing on the graph paper and saying, 'If I use the playfield for the graphics, that's 4 pixels wide, so scrolling horizontally would not work very well. It'd be very jerky.' So I said, 'I'll scroll vertically,' because you can scroll one line at a time, and the line is about half a pixel, so that's much smoother motion."

Shaw continued: "The other thing was that the playfield, if you don't change it on the fly in the middle of the line, then you can either have the left half of the screen identical to the right half of the screen or you can have the left half be a mirror image of the right half. I was doodling on the graph paper and said, 'Oh, I could make it a mirror image, so it looks like a river with islands in the middle of it.' That's where I came up with the river theme."

One big change during the design process was the drivable vehicle. "At first, your player was a boat," Shaw

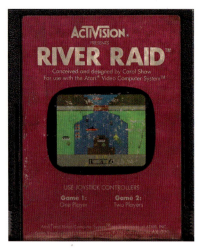
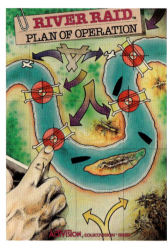

Flying up the River of No Return in *River Raid* for the Atari 5200. *Courtesy of AtariAge.com.*

River Raid game cartridge (Atari 2600). $6.

River Raid instruction manual (ColecoVision). $3.

said. "It wasn't a jet. It was a boat, but my boat did not look very good. So I said, 'How about an airplane or jet? A jet looks good, so I'll make it a jet...[Actually] I think I made an airplane that was not a jet and maybe Dave Crane said a jet would be better."

The Atari 5200 and ColecoVision versions of *River Raid* are very nice adaptations of the 2600 cart. Basic gameplay is similar, but the shoreline is craggy, the river is winding, and new targets were added, including hot air balloons, helicopter gunners (which actually shoot at the player), and tanks that cross the bridges. It's extremely cool to approach a bridge, slow down, wait for the tank to get on the bridge, and then blast said bridge to kingdom come.

The 5200 port's controls are a little loosey goosey, and the ColecoVision port, which is faster than the other renditions, has a slight delay in the controls, but both games are great nevertheless.

The Intellivision port differs from the other versions in that players can fly over land, the fuel depots are round, and there are trees for obstacles. Unfortunately, thanks to poor controls, it's the lesser of the four console versions.

The 2600 rendition of *River Raid* has been re-released on the PlayStation (1998, via *Activision Classics*), PlayStation 2 (2002, via *Activision Anthology*), Game Boy Advance (2003, via *Activision Anthology*), and PlayStation Portable (2006, via *Activision Hits Remixed*). In 2010, Microsoft made the game available as a downloadable title for the Xbox 360 Game Room service.

In 1988, Carol Shaw, working on her final console game, oversaw development of *River Raid II*, an Atari 2600 exclusive. *River Raid II* lacks the pure fun of the original, but it is a solid game, offering a more complex shooting environment, in which players drop bombs, take off and land on aircraft carriers, avoid enemy flak bursts, and destroy buildings, water towers, and other objects not found in *River Raid*.

FUN FACT:
In the original Atari 2600 version of *River Raid*, selecting difficulty switch "A" results in straight missiles while difficulty switch "B" lets players fire guided missiles.

WHY IT MADE THE LIST:
Flying up the River of No Return, dodging obstacles, shooting enemies, and slowing down to fuel up, remains a distinct, testosterone-fueled pleasure, despite significant advances in the genre.

CHAPTER 79

ROBOTRON: 2084

ATARI 5200
GENRE: NON-SCROLLING SHOOTER
PUBLISHER: ATARI
DEVELOPER: ATARI
1 OR 2 PLAYERS (ALTERNATING)
1983

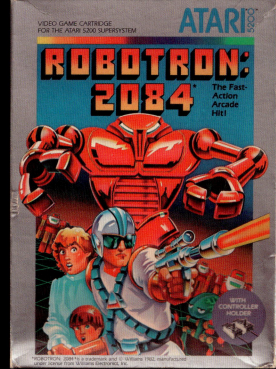

Robotron: 2084 for the Atari 5200, complete in box. $40.

"THE GAME PLAYS ABOUT AS SIMILAR TO ITS COIN-OP COUNTERPART AS POSSIBLE."

Featuring a familiar plot that violates Isaac Asimov's Three Laws of Robotics, in which robots aren't supposed to bring harm to others or themselves, the panic-inducing *Robotron: 2084* taps into mankind's seemingly innate fear of machinery and technology.

As most old-school gamers know, the fast, frantic, fatalistic, super fun action has players guiding a solitary human through one horizontal, rectangular, non-scrolling room after another, firing away at hoards of Robotrons, including grunts, hulks (laser gunfire slows them, but they cannot die), brains, spheroids (which can spawn embryos), enforcer embryos, enforcer sparks, electrodes, quarks, and tanks.

For extra points, players can rescue (by a mere touch) a man, a woman, and a child. These people purportedly comprise the last surviving human family, though they repeatedly appear onscreen.

Like the similar playing *Space Dungeon* for the 5200, *Robotron: 2084* is packaged in a large box with a dual controller holder. This nifty device helps players use the left joystick to move the human and the right joystick to aim and shoot (the laser gun will shoot in the direction the player pushes the joystick), making for an arcade-like experience. Firing is near constant, as is player movement, and the constant sense of being overwhelmed—mitigated somewhat by the powerful, fast-firing laser gun—is palpable.

In *Electronic Games* magazine #29 (Nov., 1984), Tracie Forman said that its "control scheme takes a lot of getting used to," but that *Robotron: 2084* for the Atari 5200 is "all a fast-action fan could want in a game" and that it "has the colorful graphics and shoot-from-the-hip action that first attracted fans at the arcades."

Often described as "*Berzerk* on steroids" (or something similar, like "*Berzerk* gone berserk"), the original arcade version of *Robotron: 2084* was designed by Eugene Jarvis (with Larry DeMar), who also created another intense shooter in *Defender* (1980). Jarvis pioneered the two-joystick controller, first seen in arcade *Robotron: 2084* (1982) and later found on such titles as *Smash T.V.* (1990) and *Total Carnage* (1991).

According to an interview published on www.dadgum.com, Jarvis credits 1980's *Berzerk* (along with *Chase* for the Commodore PET) with inspiring the creation of *Robotron*. "The basic magic of *Robotron* is the independent movement and firing controls," he said. "I was a great fan of the game *Berzerk*, and the frustration of that and all other single joystick games, was that you have to move toward an enemy in order to fire in that direction. *Berzerk* had a mode that alleviated that somewhat in that if you held the fire button down, the character would stand still and then a bullet could be fired with the joystick in any direction. So, essentially, in that mode the joystick fired the bullet. I just put on a separate joystick to fire bullets."

When compared to the arcade original, *Robotron: 2084* for the Atari 5200 has less vibrant coloring. Also, the thumping, pumping sound effects are a bit scratchy. However, the game looks and sounds good overall, and, thanks in large part to the dual controller holder capabilities, the game plays about as similar to its coin-op counterpart as possible. And, as *Robotron* veterans will undoubtedly tell you, that's certainly a good thing.

As Van Burnham's *Supercade: A Visual History of the Videogame Game Age, 1971-1984* (2001, The MIT Press) concisely states, *Robotron* is "one of the most exciting and challenging [arcade] games of its time."

Robotron was also ported to the Atari 7800, but that version lacks a controller holder, meaning gamers are supposed to juggle both joysticks, perhaps holding them in place with tape or a rubber band.

My favorite console version of the game can be found on the *Williams Arcade's Greatest Hits* (1996) collection for the PlayStation, which supports the dual sticks on the PSX controller for a terrific, arcade-like experience (though I still crank up the 5200 game from time to time).

Williams Arcade's Greatest Hits was also produced for the Sega Genesis, Super Nintendo, and Sega Saturn, but, obviously, those systems don't have dual sticks. In 2006, *Robotron* hit the Xbox 360 via Xbox Live Arcade.

In the handheld arena, *Robotron* was produced for the Atari Lynx (1991) and game.com (1997), the latter version found on the *Williams Arcade Classics* collection.

Robotron: 2084 was followed by a pair of 3D console sequels: *Robotron X* (1996, PlayStation) and *Robotron 64* (1998, Nintendo 64). Both games are playable, but highly inferior to the arcade original and Atari 5200 port in all their 2D glory.

FUN FACT:

The arcade version of *Robotron: 2084* was developed by Vid Kidz, the company Eugene Jarvis (with Larry DeMar) formed after leaving Williams.

WHY IT MADE THE LIST:

Robotron: 2084 is one of the most intense arcade games ever made, and the Atari 5200 represents the play action extremely well, thanks in part to the dual controller holder originally packaged with the game.

Robotron: 2084 for the Atari 5200 in action. Courtesy of AtariAge.com.

Robotron: 2084 game cartridge. $6.

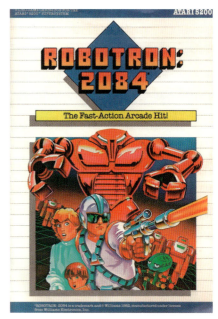

Robotron: 2084 instruction manual. $4.

CHAPTER 80

SCRAMBLE

VECTREX
GENRE: SIDE-SCROLLING SHOOTER
PUBLISHER: GCE
DEVELOPER: GCE
1 OR 2 PLAYERS (ALTERNATING)
1982

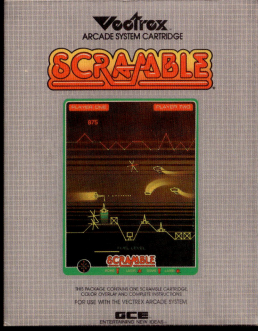

Scramble for the Vectrex, complete in box. $32.

"GAMEPLAY IS SO GOOD AND SO FAITHFUL TO THE ORIGINAL."

Developed by Konami for the arcades, *Scramble*, which is a progenitor of sorts of the *Gradius* series (*Gradius* was called "Scramble 2" during the production process), has a curiously brief history in terms of vintage ports. While its sequel, *Super Cobra* (released in 1981, the same year as *Scramble*), was ported to no less than six Golden Age systems—Adventure Vision, Atari 2600, Atari 5200, ColecoVision, Intellivision, and Odyssey2—*Scramble* had but a single classic console adaptation: this one for the Vectrex.

The original arcade *Scramble* is one of the best side-scrolling shooters ever created (it was #28 in the "Top 100 Arcade Games" feature in the 2008 *Guinness World Records Gamer's Edition*), dazzling players with intense gameplay, the challenge of precise maneuvering and carefully aimed shots, and an ultra-colorful (especially for a shooter) graphical palette: bright blue, deep purple, dazzling pink, rich red, brilliant green, and sunny yellow. In addition, *Scramble* was the first side-scrolling shooter with multiple distinct levels and forced (automatic) scrolling, predating *Cosmic Avenger* (1981) by four months.

At first glance, *Scramble* is an odd choice for the Vectrex, a system that, with its gray, vector-based graphics, excels at such *Asteroids*-style shooters as *Rip Off* and *Solar Quest*. The overlay that comes with the *Scramble* game cartridge gives the visuals a green, yellow, and red tinting, but this hardly compensates for the arcade game's colorful raster display. Luckily, the gameplay is so good and so faithful to the original that you'll find yourself not caring all that much.

As with most side-scrollers, the action moves from left to right. Pushing up and down on the joystick controls your ship's vertical movement while pushing left and right adjusts the speed. Diagonal movement is also allowed. Players guide said ship over mountainous terrain, over buildings, through a cavern, and through a maze, shooting lasers at and bombing airborne and land-based enemies, including missiles (which are on the ground, but frequently take off into the air as you approach them), fuel tanks, mystery bases, and UFOs. Certain airborne enemies move in zigzagging patterns, making them tough to destroy or dodge. There are also waves of "flamoids" (in level three) that you must dodge, but that can't be destroyed.

Scramble for the Vectrex is fairly short at six brief levels of play, with the last level containing but a single objective: to bomb the enemy base (the game starts over after this at level one, but gets harder). However, it's a tough game that is hard to beat, despite unlimited continues. Not only do you have to dodge the enemies, but colliding with the landscape is also lethal. This latter aspect of play is unlike *Defender* (1980), which lets players fly harmlessly through mountains, but is similar to *R-Type* (1987), which has deadly scenery.

One of the coolest things about *Scramble* is the ever-present need for the player to replenish fuel. At the bottom of the screen is a fuel gauge that empties as you fly. Remember those fuel tanks I mentioned earlier? To keep from running out of fuel, you must frequently destroy the fuel tanks, which is ironic if you think about it for a second—how does

Scramble screen overlay. $6.   *Scramble* instruction manual. $4.   *Scramble* game cartridge. $15.

destroying a fuel tank you are flying over fill up your ship's fuel tank? Regardless, this adds tension and urgency to an already exciting game. Also noteworthy is the fact that players are awarded 10 points for every second in flight.

Prior to firing up a game of *Scramble*, players can select from three difficulty levels that vary according to rate of fuel consumption (low, medium, or fast), straight or curved missiles, and average or tight maze width. Gamers begin with five ships and are awarded a bonus ship at 10,000 points.

In 2008, video game historian Scott Stilphen (www.2600connection.com) interviewed Paul Allen Newell, who programmed Vectrex *Scramble*. Newell told Stilphen that his task "was rather straightforward as the goal was to make a faithful copy of the original arcade game."

Newell spent a lot of time playing the arcade version until he had a feel for it, as did others working on the game. "Kim Martin went through the entire game with collision off so he could map the terrain into a hex database, which allowed me to write a driver to display it on the Vectrex," he said. "At that point, I was just doing version after version as I tried to make my version match the original arcade. Lots of folks in the office would try it to see if it had the right 'feel' (speed of motion, responsiveness of joystick and buttons, etc.)."

For Newell, the limited hardware posed a challenge. "The biggest task was trying to get my code to fit into 4K without losing too much of the game," he said. "I think I got done about a half-day before the final ship date and know that no changes were made after."

The end product was surprisingly good.

In *TV Gamer* #1 (summer, 1983), the reviewer extolled the virtues of the port, saying, "*Scramble* is a faithful reproduction of the popular arcade game of the same name…This is by far the best game in this category around at the moment and it is the first cartridge you should buy if you're getting or already have a Vectrex."

The Dec. 4-10, 1982 edition of *TV Guide* has a feature called "The Best Video Games of 1982," in which writer Len Albin called *Scramble* one of the best cartridges for the Vectrex and a "perfect vector-display version of the old arcade warhorse."

In *Electronic Fun with Computers & Games* #10 (Aug., 1983), William Michael Brown described the attributes of the home rendition of *Scramble* well, praising the game's sharp play-action and "quick-reaction-time" while calling the visuals a "sketchy impression of its arcade progenitor."

In the interview referenced earlier, Stilphen told Newell that flyers exist for a proposed Atari 2600 version of *Scramble*, but Newell hadn't heard about it. "I never knew that GCE (Milton Bradley) was considering the VCS format, and nobody ever talked to me about doing a VCS version of *Scramble*," he said. "I would have thought it would have been impossible to be true to the arcade version, since scrolling is vertical in the Atari and *Scramble* is so heavily invested in the visual and design of horizontal scrolling."

Horizontal scrolling games were, of course, made for the Atari 2600 (*Defender*, for example), but *Scramble* is not one of them. Luckily, Vectrex owners can play a fantastic version of the game anytime, and without using a television set (since the Vectrex console is a standalone unit with a built-in screen).

In terms of more modern systems, gamers can play arcade ports of *Scramble* on the PlayStation (1999, via *Konami Arcade Classics*), the Game Boy Advance (2002, via *Konami Collector's Series: Arcade Advanced*), and the Nintendo DS (2007, via *Konami Classics Series: Arcade Hits*). In 2006, *Scramble* was ported to the Xbox 360 via Xbox Live Arcade.

FUN FACT:
In 1982, Tomy released *TomyTronic Scramble*, a small tabletop version of the game.

WHY IT MADE THE LIST:
Scramble, an excellent early side-scroller, is reproduced surprisingly well on the Vectrex.

CHAPTER 81

SHARK! SHARK!

INTELLIVISION
GENRE: ACTION
PUBLISHER: MATTEL
DEVELOPER: MATTEL
1 OR 2 PLAYERS (SIMULTANEOUS)
1982

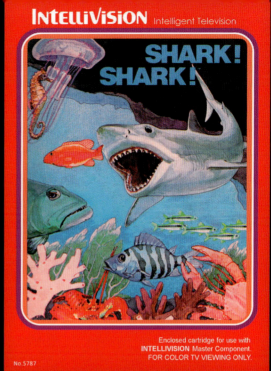

Shark! Shark! for the Intellivision, complete in box. $18.

> "FOR A GAME WITH A SIMPLE ACTION CONCEPT, SHARK! SHARK! IS FAIRLY STRATEGIC IN NATURE."

Long before power-ups were ubiquitous, Mattel released *Shark! Shark!*, a game that has everything to do with powering up your character. Players guide a fish around what is essentially a virtual aquarium, eating smaller fish. You can also nibble at a black shark's tail, but this is very dangerous as it can turn around quickly and get you.

Your character begins as a small, size-one fish, and for every 1,000 points you score, you grow a size, with size five being the largest. After you've maxed out at size five, you earn a bonus fish for every 1,000 points scored. As you grow, you can eat larger and larger fish. At certain sizes, you can eat seahorses and falling crabs and lobsters. However, you can never eat a jellyfish because they are size six (only sharks can kill jellyfish).

In short, *Shark! Shark!* is a fish-eat-fish kind of game, and it's a heck of a lot of fun. I'm not sure if the cartridge taps into some kind of primal, evolutionary, survival-of-the-fittest type of instinct, but what I do know is that it's one of my all-time favorite Intellivision games.

Shark! Shark! looks fantastic, from the blinking (in a good way) seaweed to the rising bubbles to the white coral to the nicely drawn, nicely animated sea creatures. Other than an ominous tone that plays when the shark appears, the sound effects are sparse, but aquariums aren't particularly noisy, so this is no knock on the game. If you want, fire up some music in the background while you play, preferably the soundtrack to *Jaws* (1975) or, for a lighter mood, *The Little Mermaid* (1989).

For a game with a simple action concept, *Shark! Shark!* is fairly strategic in nature. There's risk/reward in nibbling at the shark's tail, which is good for the scoreboard, but takes some practice to get good at. Better players will learn to anticipate the shark's moves and dart in and out before he can turn around. The smaller your fish, the more nibbles it will take to kill the shark.

According to intellivisionlives.com, designer/programmer Ji-Wen Tsao got the ingenious idea for *Shark! Shark!* from the Chinese proverb, "Big fish eat little fish." Unfortunately, the marketing department at the time of the game's release dismissed it as "an inconsequential kiddie game," and the initial shipment was only 5,600 cartridges, which is miniscule, especially when compared to the heavily advertised *Star Strike*, which shipped nearly 800,000 copies.

The site also says that "everyone thought it would be a great gag" to use "Mack the Knife" as the game-over music.

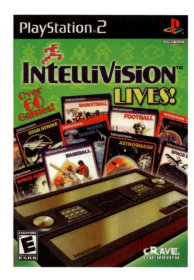

The back of the *Shark! Shark!* box.

Shark! Shark! instruction manual. $3.

In 2003, *Shark! Shark!* was re-released on the PlayStation 2 via Intellivision Lives! $8.

However, Warner Communications, the parent company of Atari, owned the rights to the song, so Andy Sells composed an original tune instead.

Despite the low initial print run, more copies of *Shark! Shark!* were produced, and the game is pretty easy to find in today's collector's market. The box art is gorgeous, so if you can find a complete copy for a decent price (not a terribly hard thing to do), I recommend getting it.

Named one of the "50 Best Games" in the March, 1984 issue of *Electronic Fun with Computers and Games*, *Shark! Shark!* is one of the more critically acclaimed games for the Intellivision.

According to the June, 1983 issue of *Videogaming Illustrated*, it's "an original…a must-own…positively delightful…one of the finest cartridges for the system." In *Electronic Fun with Computers & Games* #7 (May, 1983), Mark Brownstein said the game has "clean and colorful" graphics and that it "forces you into playing 'just one more game' to beat your high score."

In *Video Games* #11 (Aug, 1983), Perry Greenberg said *Shark! Shark!* is a "delightful" game that is both "colorful and challenging." Raymond Dimetrosky, writing for *Video Game Players* Vol. 2 #1 (Aug./Sept., 1983), called the game "enjoyable because of the colorful graphics and great sound effects. The whole thing looks more like a cartoon than a video game." He also said the action is slow, but "a lot of fun."

In issue #6 (July/Aug., 1992) of the *Digital Press* fanzine, the staff called it "a great little game" with a "dynamite end-game theme song."

The Video Game Critic (videogamecritic.com) called the game "enormously fun and addicting" while Matt Paprocki (digitpress.com) said it is "great" and "fun as hell."

In my humble opinion, *Shark! Shark!* is one of the best, most entertaining sea-life games ever created for any console.

If you want to play it on a more modern system, you can do so through *Intellivision Classics* (1999) for the PlayStation or *Intellivision Lives!* for the PlayStation 2 (2003), Xbox (2004), GameCube (2004), or Nintendo DS (2010).

In 2010, Microsoft made *Shark! Shark!* available as a downloadable title for the Xbox 360 Game Room service. In 2012, Intellivision Lives, in conjunction with Sony, remade *Shark! Shark!* for the PlayStation 3 and PlayStation Vita, updating the action with bonus rounds, new graphics and sounds, and different fish patterns.

FUN FACT:

According to intellivisionlives.com: "In animating the sea creatures, Ji-Wen was unsure how a crab moved. After she was unable to find a real or videotaped one, cubicle neighbor Steve Sents (*TRON Deadly Discs*) brought his pet tarantula into the office for her to use as a model. We aren't sure if it was any help as a crab model, but it sure creeped out the other programmers."

WHY IT MADE THE LIST:

Cute, but deadly, *Shark! Shark!* features a protagonist you can power-up and a ruthlessly playable aquarium on your television set.

CHAPTER 82

SLITHER

COLECOVISION
GENRE: NON-SCROLLING SHOOTER
PUBLISHER: COLECO
DEVELOPER: COLECO
1 OR 2 PLAYERS (ALTERNATING)
1983

Slither was originally packaged with Coleco's Roller Controller trackball peripheral, pictured complete in box.
Courtesy of Bryan C. Smith. $90.

"SLITHER IS A MASTERPIECE IN THE 'PANIC GAME' SUBGENRE."

A marvelous port of the GDI/Century II coin-op semi-classic (1982), *Slither* is the perfectly prototypical ColecoVision game in that it takes an obscure, but great arcade game and brings it home to a larger, more enthusiastic audience. One of only five titles specifically designed for Coleco's Roller Controller trackball (*Centipede*, *Omega Race*, *Victory*, and *War Games* are the others), *Slither* is an amalgamation of sorts of *Asteroids* and *Centipede*, but is set in the Southwestern region of the United States (as opposed to outer space or a magical mushroom field).

Players use the Roller Controller to guide a ship in all directions around a non-scrolling desert playfield, firing lasers—upward and downward only—at long and short snakes, the latter of which disappear with one hit. Long snakes, on the other hand, are a bit trickier: hitting their head or tail makes them shorter and faster while hitting their body makes them split into multiple snakes. The latter makes the screen super busy, which I don't recommend.

Each time a new screen starts, a bonus timer begins ticking down. If you manage to kill all the snakes prior to the time running out, you'll get the remaining bonus points on display. If there are snakes remaining, the snakes from the next phase will join in on the fun, resetting the bonus timer and making life in the desert that much more crowded (and difficult).

In addition to snakes, there's a pterodactyl, which bounces, hovers, and dives toward your ship (similar to the spider in *Centipede*), and a tyrannosaur, who gallops across the desert, sometimes leaving a trail of brush (which some players mistakenly call cacti). Like the mushrooms in *Centipede*, the brush can be cleared away by shooting it—one strategy is to leave brush barriers to direct the snakes away from you as they enter the screen. A pair of large, indestructible rocks also clutters the playfield.

Slither is a masterpiece in the "panic game" subgenre. To make it very far, you've got to have a steady hand, quick reflexes, and the ability to follow lots of onscreen action at once. The fact that you can only shoot up and down makes the precise positioning of the ship a frequent necessity.

After extended play, snakes begin disappearing—you can see the "invisible" snakes' beady eyes wriggling toward you—which ups the challenge and is a neat graphical effect. Speaking of graphics, this is a gorgeous game, with mountains, clouds, a colorful horizon, and a setting sun pictured near the top of the screen (which acts as a background of sorts). The day-to-night sequences are impressive as well.

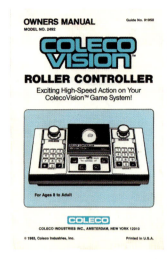

Roller Controller instruction manual. $5.   *Slither* instruction manual. $4.   *Slither* game cartridge. $10.

There's little to no flickering in *Slither*, despite the prodigious quantity of independently moving enemies. Moreover, it's a blast to shoot your way out of trouble and into relatively (not to mention temporarily) safe territory (only *Robotron: 2084* matches the game in this regard). The rapid-fire sound effects and triumphant music match the game's fast, frantic pace.

Ranked as one of "Our Favorite 99 Classics" by the Digital Press staff (www.digitpress.com), *Slither* is a jewel in the crown of the almighty ColecoVision. In a Digital Press review, Bruce Consolazio praised the game's "splendid graphics," referencing the "multi-colored and sharply detailed" ship, the "nicely animated" Tyrannosaur, the "beautifully done" rock formations, and the "stunning" way the "colors change to evening."

Consolazio, calling the gameplay a "dream come true, especially with the arcade quality controls," also appreciates the game's first class audio. "Your laser has a good, solid sound to it, the Tyrannosaur has a suitable stomping footstep, and the music used for the Pterodactyls is arcade-quality, helping prove Coleco's claim of this system's superior sound," he said. "Even the music that plays when you pause the game is worth listening to, as is the tune when you are destroyed, and when the game is over."

When *Slither* was new in stores, Noel Steer reviewed it for the March, 1984 issue of *Electronic Fun with Computers & Games*, saying, "You have to like *Slither*. There's nothing here not to like. Coleco has captured every detail of the arcade parent and done it so well that even the toughest critic will find no fault." He also called *Slither* "one of the best home video games this inveterate player has ever seen, heard, or played."

I agree with these sentiments wholeheartedly.

FUN FACT:

Slither was the pack-in game with Coleco's Roller Controller trackball peripheral. When I bought my Roller Controller at Service Merchandise back in 1983, it was a major hit to the wallet ($69.99), but *Slither* alone made it well worth the price.

WHY IT MADE THE LIST:

A cross of sorts between *Centipede* and *Robotron*, *Slither* is one of the fastest, most intense games in the ColecoVision library.

CHAPTER 83

SOLAR FOX

ATARI 2600
GENRE: MAZE
PUBLISHER: CBS ELECTRONICS
DEVELOPER: CBS ELECTRONICS
1 OR 2 PLAYERS (ALTERNATING)
1983

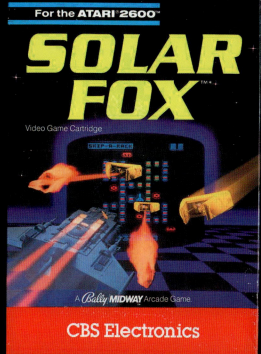

Solar Fox for the Atari 2600, complete in box. Courtesy of AtariAge.com. $25.

"AN OBSCURE MAZE SHOOTER HAS BEEN STRIPPED OF ITS FIREPOWER AND STILL RANKS AS ONE OF THE 100 GREATEST CONSOLE GAMES OF THE ERA."

Solar Fox for the Atari 2600 was a tough call for inclusion in this book. I love the game and still play it, but it has some of the most simplistic graphics of any cartridge produced in 1983—a grid of squares, some enemy projectiles, and a trio of ordinary looking ships—and, more importantly, the play action lacks a key component found in Bally/Midway's largely ignored coin-op game from 1981: shooting.

That's right, an obscure maze shooter has been stripped of its firepower and still ranks as one of the 100 greatest console games of the era. The reason lies in a simple, but all-important three-letter word: F-U-N.

Even though you can't blast the enemies, *Solar Fox* for the 2600 remains a blast to play. As the Video Game Critic (videogamecritic.com) said in his review, it's an "interesting space game [that] combines elements of *Pac-Man*, *Q*bert*, and *Galaga*."

Programmed by Bob Curtiss, *Solar Fox* is set during a time when a depleted Earth, ravaged by centuries of waste and resource mismanagement, is on the verge of global warfare as nations vie with one another to control the planet's remaining energy sources. To help prevent this conflict, you, piloting a starship that looks like an airplane, must gather up solar energy cells that are located in the far corner of the galaxy.

The "grid of squares" I mentioned earlier is actually a series of "solar cell matrixes." There are 26 such matrixes, each with a different layout of small square cells. You must fly over these rows of cells—up, down, left, and right—in order to gather them up. While capturing the cells, Sentinels, one flying along the top of the screen, and one maneuvering along the bottom, guard them. They do this by shooting fireballs that you must dodge.

Your starship can only move in four directions. Depending on the difficulty mode selected, it will fly fast or slow. When fast is chosen, pressing the fire button on the joystick will slow down the ship. Conversely, when you are flying slowly, pressing the button speeds you up. The faster you clear a matrix, the more points you'll score.

Six of the 26 solar cell matrixes are challenge screens that appear after every fifth matrix. As with *Galaga*, enemies don't shoot during the challenge stages, but here you only score points if you clear the entire screen before the timer runs out. After you complete a challenge rack, a letter will be revealed. If you manage to clear all six racks, a mystery word will be spelled out.

The mystery word in question is HELIOS, which is the Greek word for "sun." According to 2600connection. atari.org, HELIOS was a "hint to an upcoming 'surprise'

Solar Fox magazine ad.

Solar Fox in action. *Courtesy of AtariAge.com.*

Solar Fox instruction manual. $5.

from CBS," perhaps a future game, but "it's unknown what happened with this contest."

Getting back to the gameplay, in each of the 20 standard matrixes, there's a Skip-A-Rack timer bar. If you can clear the rack before the bar disappears, you will automatically bypass the next matrix, collecting all of those points from that matrix as well. If your starship gets destroyed during a rack, the timer bar is forfeited for that screen.

Beginning with rack seven, the matrixes are comprised of double solar cells, meaning you have to pass over each one twice before it will disappear from the playfield. This adds a nice challenge and evokes the aspect of *Q*bert* that has you hopping on cubes more than once to change their color.

When *Solar Fox* was released, Raymond Dimetrosky of *Video Games Player* (Oct./Nov., 1983) gave it a "B+", saying it "proves you don't have to have good graphics to have a good game." He praised the game's depth and said it is "straightforward, addicting, very much an eye-hand game, and very tough to beat."

To promote *Solar Fox*, CBS Electronics produced a television commercial in which a stereotypical blonde valley girl munched popcorn and said "awesome" and "totally cool" while watching a guy play the game. The valley girl was none other than Jane Krakowski who, decades later, would achieve fame as Jenna Maroney in NBC's hit sitcom, *30 Rock*.

Another interesting thing about the commercial is that it promised *Solar Fox* would soon be available for the Atari 5200, ColecoVision, Intellivision, and Atari 400/800. However, it was only produced for the 2600 and Commodore 64. Those cancelled versions were victims of The Great Video Game Crash of 1983.

FUN FACT:
The Commodore 64 version of *Solar Fox* includes shooting and is in general a more accurate port of the arcade game.

WHY IT MADE THE LIST:
Although it looks ordinary and the shooting has been removed, *Solar Fox* is one of the better third-party games for the 2600 not produced by Activision or Imagic.

CHAPTER 84

SPACE DUNGEON

ATARI 5200
GENRE: NON-SCROLLING SHOOTER
PUBLISHER: ATARI
DEVELOPER: ATARI
1 OR 2 PLAYERS (ALTERNATING, SIMULTANEOUS)
1983

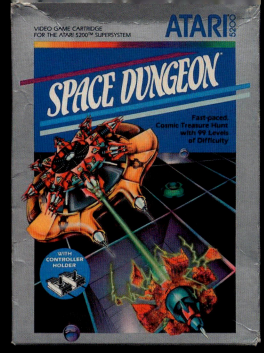

Space Dungeon for the Atari 5200, complete in box. Courtesy of AtariAge.com. $35.

"SPACE DUNGEON IS ONE OF THE MORE ENJOYABLE, MORE INTENSE TITLES IN THE ATARI 5200 LIBRARY."

A cross of sorts between *Berzerk*, *Robotron: 2084*, and *Venture*, *Space Dungeon* for the Atari 5200 is, as the packaging says, a "fast-paced, Cosmic Treasure Hunt with 99 Levels of Difficulty" (meaning there are 99 levels of play, each progressively more difficult—there aren't 99 selectable skill levels).

As the Commander of a space archaeological expedition (a yarn concocted by Atari manual writer John-Michael Battaglia), players guide a laser cannon-equipped ship through a series of connecting, non-scrolling rooms (36 rooms per level), shooting solid, pulsating beams at enemies that are trapped in the titular dungeon. Enemies include deathsquares, guards, enforcers, thieves, executioners, spore cases, and pikers, the latter of which are tough, taking multiple shots to kill.

As in *Venture*, there are treasures to collect (iron cross, copper piece, silver star, golden fleece, and platinum ark), but the hardcore shooter action has more in common with *Robotron*. The contiguous rooms evoke *Berzerk*. As the manual states, "Some rooms are filled with treasure, some with enemies, some with both, and some with nothing but space itself."

To fully complete a level, players must enter every room (rooms are laid out as a 6x6 grid), but it is not necessary to kill all the enemies (since certain enemies regenerate, this is impossible anyway). Completing a level and then entering the Collect Bonus cube (which is located in one of the rooms) awards players 10,000 points. Entering the Collect Bonus cube without fully completing the level will nevertheless send players to the next level. As in *Asteroids*, players earn an extra ship for every 10,000 points scored.

A top-down map helps gamers track their progress through the rooms. It displays locations of the ship, the Collect Bonus cube, the lost treasure room (if a player gets killed, all of his or her accumulated treasures go to one room, which is a nice feature that cuts down on backtracking), and the position of the Thief, who burglarizes treasure. In addition, the radar shows which rooms have been cleared of enemies.

Like 5200 *Robotron*, *Space Dungeon* was originally packaged in an oversized box with a dual controller holder. This nifty device lets players use two controllers simultaneously: the left one to guide the ship (which can move in eight directions) through the rooms, and the right one to aim and fire the laser cannon. For two-player simultaneous action, one gamer controls the ship while the other operates the laser cannon.

Adapted by Allen Merrell and Eric Knopp, *Space Dungeon* is a port of the 1981 Taito arcade obscurity, which was programmed by Rexford Ayers Battenberg. It's not as

Space Dungeon in action. Courtesy of AtariAge.com.

Space Dungeon game cartridge. $6.

Space Dungeon instruction manual. $5.

slick in terms of audio/visual effects, the enemies are less aggressive (though the game is still a formidable challenge), and the intro screens illustrating the enemies, treasures, and points for those items are missing.

However, like some of the better ColecoVision ports, it's a popular and highly entertaining home version of a largely ignored arcade title, a point that Keita Iida, writing for Atari Gaming Headquarters (www.atarihq.com), clearly understands: "*Space Dungeon* is exactly the sort of game that just aches for home translation, where gamers have the chance to sit down and learn the types of tactics and skill necessary to conquer it, without the annoying need to dump token after token into a hungry coin-op machine."

In issue #34 (Nov./Dec., 1997) of the *Digital Press* fanzine, noted collector Al Bakiel said *Space Dungeon* is "one of the best shooters on the system" because it has "lots of depth and hidden surprises."

When the game was new in stores, Bill Kunkel and Arnie Katz, writing in *Electronic Games* magazine #20 (Oct., 1983), said, "In terms of simulating a juggernaut of explosive force, no home video game has ever equaled the vicarious experience attained by *Space Dungeon*."

The legendary duo also put the game into historical perspective in terms of fan complaints over the 5200's notorious non-centering joysticks, saying that Atari began producing "free-flowing, omni-directional" games that "capitalize on the strength of the 5200 controller instead of magnifying its weaknesses."

In *Video Games* #12 (Sept., 1983), Perry Greenberg colorfully nailed the appeal of *Space Dungeon*, calling it "a super-fast, exciting, chaotic game that requires the reflexes of a circus juggler and the strategic mind of a Prussian field general." He also called it a "difficult contest" with "riveting action" that "works beautifully as a two-player cooperative game."

In *Electronic Fun with Computers & Games* #10 (Aug., 1983), Michael Blanchet lamented the arcade version's undeserved obscurity, saying that the "jewel" of a game "combined the best elements of *Venture* and *Robotron*" while adding a "host of other nifty features." In the same review, he called the 5200 port a "must-have" and said that it "offers a degree of intrigue and suspense normally found only in a fantasy/adventure game."

On the other hand, in *JoyStik* Vol. 2 #2 (Nov.,1983), the reviewer gave the game a surprisingly low three out of five stars, calling it a "good game" with "unique appeal," but that "If you don't like it you'll probably hate it." He also stressed that you should try it before you buy it.

A difficult cartridge—though it boasts 99 levels, only skilled players will make it past the fourth or fifth level—*Space Dungeon* is one of the more enjoyable, more intense titles in the Atari 5200 library. In fact, I'd call it an essential cartridge, especially for hardcore shooter fans.

In 2007, *Space Dungeon* was ported to the PSP via the *Taito Legends Power-Up* collection.

FUN FACT:

The coin-op version of *Space Dungeon* contains two messages hidden in the ROM chip: DESIGNED AND PROGRAMMED BY REXFORD AYERS BATTENBERG FOR TAITO AMERICA CORP and STOLEN FROM THE GOOD BUDDY'S AT TAITO BY AN UNAUTHORIZED DO BADDER.

WHY IT MADE THE LIST:

Like *Robotron: 2084*, *Space Dungeon* is intense, dual-joystick action that commands (and deserves) your undivided attention.

CHAPTER 85

SPACE INVADERS

ATARI 2600
GENRE: SLIDE-AND-SHOOT
PUBLISHER: ATARI
DEVELOPER: ATARI
1 OR 2 PLAYERS (ALTERNATING, SIMULTANEOUS)
1980

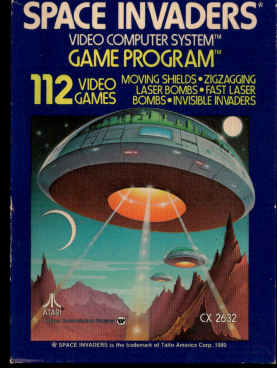

Space Invaders for the Atari 2600, complete in box. $10.

"SPACE INVADERS IS A REMARKABLE, HUGELY ENTERTAINING PORT OF THE COIN-OP CLASSIC."

Released in 1978, the arcade version of *Space Invaders*, designed by Tomohiro Nishikado and manufactured by Taito, ranks up there with *Pong*, *Pac-Man*, *Pitfall!*, *Super Mario Bros.*, and *Super Mario 64* as one of the most important video games ever produced.

The game created a sensation in Japan, causing a shortage of 100-yen coins, and it was the first blockbuster video game in America, grossing $2 billion in quarters by 1982. The game was so popular it prompted entrepreneurs to open arcades on virtually every street corner, helping turn the niche market of video games into a global industry.

Not only was *Space Invaders* a huge commercial success, it was a pioneer in terms of gameplay. It invented the slide-and-shoot genre. It was the first game to save and display a high score (giving players something to shoot for, so to speak). And it was the first game to feature animated alien invaders. In short, it was the first game of its type, paving the way for such similar games as *Galaxian* (1979), *Phoenix* (1980), and *Galaga* (1981), and, ultimately, for such modern shooters as *DOOM* (1993), *Halo* (2003), and *Call of Duty* (2003).

Space Invaders was an important release for the Atari VCS (later the 2600) as well. It was the first time an arcade game was officially licensed for a home video game system (acting on orders from Warner CEO Manny Gerard, Atari president Ray Kassar secured the rights from Taito), and it sent sales of Atari's venerable console soaring, making it the first "killer app" (before the term was coined) for a home console.

According to Leonard Herman, author of *Phoenix: The Fall & Rise of Home Videogames* (1994, Rolenta Press), "Many people bought the VCS just so they could play *Space Invaders* at home. At $415 million, Atari's gross income in 1980 [the year the home version of *Space Invaders* hit stores] was twice as much as it had been in 1979."

Further, *Atari Inc.—Business is Fun*, published by Syzygy Company Press in 2012, reports that 2600 *Space Invaders*, which was the first million-seller video game cartridge, brought in "over $6 million in net profits."

Programmed by Rick Maurer, *Space Invaders* is a remarkable, hugely entertaining port of the coin-op classic. It's not a note-for-note rendition, which in this case is a good thing. Rather, it expands upon the concept by adding true color (as opposed to color overlays) and numerous selectable variations, including moving shields, zigzagging laser bombs, faster laser bombs, two-player simultaneous action (a pleasing variety of cooperative and competitive modes), and, most dauntingly, invisible invaders. In addition, players can toggle

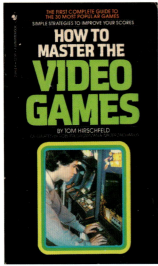 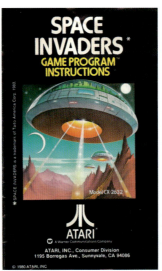 

How to Master the Video Games (1981, Bantam Books) features tips on playing *Space Invaders* and various other arcade games. $10.

Space Invaders instruction manual. $2.

Space Invaders game cartridge. $3.

the difficulty switches to give them a narrow or wide ship, making it possible to handicap two-player games.

A former employee with Fairchild Semiconductor, Maurer had already programmed *Pinball Challenge*, *Hangman*, and *Pro Football* for the Fairchild Channel F system. Remarkably, *Space Invaders* was his first 2600 game. Clearly, he passed this "baptism of fire" with flying colors.

In an interview published on www.dadgum.com, Maurer, who also programmed *Maze Craze* (featured in "The Next 100" appendix near the back of this book), said he was working on a *Space Invaders* clone before it was licensed by Atari.

"Games weren't assigned then," he said. "I knew how the console worked, so I scouted around for a game idea. Visited the arcades. *Space Invaders* just wowed me, especially the sound. So I came back and told people I would do that, they said OK."

Maurer's game was ignored by his coworkers, so he dropped the project for a time. "There was a big discussion about which was better, an original game, or a clone of a successful arcade game," he said. "But nobody was playing my game, and I enjoyed playing several other games in development, so I thought there was something wrong with my game, even though I enjoyed it, besides the amount of flicker which bothered me greatly."

Then, the bigwigs at Atari caught wind of the popularity of *Space Invaders*. "One day, the management was in a tither… Some of them had found out how many quarters were going from customers' pockets into the *Space Invaders* machines… They had a license deal…They wanted someone to work on the game, and found it was already in progress, so I went back to it."

Maurer fixed the flickering, added his variations, "scrunched" 7K of code into 4K, and the rest, as they say, is history.

Most everyone reading this has played *Space Invaders* in some form (the game has found its way to numerous platforms, including the Game Boy and Super Nintendo), but the gameplay essentials bear repeating. Players guide a laser cannon right and left along the bottom of the screen, firing upward at rows of bomb-dropping alien invaders that march in unison across the screen, dropping a level each time they reach either side of the playfield.

Getting shot or letting even a single invader reach the bottom of the playfield is lethal (in fact, the latter ends the game, even if the player has ships in reserve). Offering some help are a quartet (a trio in the Atari 2600 version) of bunkers (a.k.a. shields) positioned in a row just above the laser cannon. The player can hide behind these, but they disappear incrementally each time they get hit by friendly or enemy fire.

Each wave of enemies in the arcade version consists of 55 invaders grouped in 11 columns, five aliens to a column. There are 36 invaders per wave in the Atari 2600 port, grouped in a six-by-six arrangement. Both games feature a command alien ship (also called a UFO or a flying saucer) that periodically flies across the top of the screen and can be shot for extra points (an essential element in racking up high scores).

Both versions are suitably dramatic, giving players a sense of impending doom as they desperately battle to fend off the alien invasion. Expert aiming and timing, along with the ability to maneuver the laser base quickly out of harm's way are essential to staying alive as long as possible.

Space Invaders is "one of Atari's best cartridges" (*Ken Uston's Guide to Buying and Beating the Home Video Games*, 1982, Signet), an opinion shared by many in the industry. In *Playboy's Guide to Rating the Video Games* (1982, PBJ Books), Walter Lowe, JR. gave the port four-and-a-half out of five stars, touting the game's "long-term player interest," "visual attractiveness," and "hand-eye-coordination challenge."

Fending off an alien invasion in *Space Invaders* for the Atari 2600. *Courtesy of AtariAge.com.*

In *The Complete Guide to Conquering Video Games* (1982, Collier Books), Jeff Rovin had this to say about 2600 *Space Invaders*: "The first and still the best of the games based upon a marching aliens theme. The action is furious, the options range from nerve-racking to senses-shattering…the spacing between gun and shields, between shields and aliens is ideal."

Citing the game's timeless nature, a reviewer in issue #1 (summer, 1983) of *TV Gamer*, said, "Of all the video games, this is probably the one that has aged the best, and buffs will regard it as a must for their collections."

More recently, Dave "The Video Game Critic" Mrozek opined thusly: "It's hard to come up with anything negative to say about this classic. In many ways the Atari 2600 version of *Space Invaders* is even better than the arcade, with color graphics and countless options."

Adam King, via Atari Gaming Headquarters (atarihq.com), increased the volume of the rhetoric, stating that "you can't call yourself an Atari fan if you don't have this cartridge."

With its excellent controls, myriad gameplay variations, and daunting challenges, *Space Invaders* is indeed a cornerstone of any reasonably well-stocked Atari 2600 collection, making it an easy choice for inclusion in this book.

Atari also ported *Space Invaders* to the Atari 5200. It has far fewer options, but is an excellent game in its own right. It's fast paced, it has colorfully animated invaders (48 per wave), and it's compatible with the 5200 Trak-Ball controller.

Space Invaders has had countless arcade, console, and handheld offshoots, remakes, and sequels, including *Space Invaders II* (1980, arcade), *Space Invaders '91* (1991, Genesis), *Space Invaders XL* (2001, Nuon), *Space Invaders Revolution* (2005, DS), *Space Invaders Extreme* (2008, DS, PSP), and *Space Invaders Infinity Gene* (2009, iPhone, PS3, Xbox 360).

The game was also the subject of numerous copycats, including *Space Armada* (1981, Intellivision), *Alien Invaders* (1982, Arcadia 2001), and *Space Destroyers* (1979, APF MP1000), the latter of which you'll find in "The Next 100" appendix near the back of this book.

FUN FACT:

While the Atari 2600 and 5200 were the only classic consoles to get a port of *Space Invaders* during the Golden Age, the game finally came to the ColecoVision in 2003 as part of Opcode's homebrew *Space Invaders Collection*, which also includes *Space Invaders Part II*.

WHY IT MADE THE LIST:

Amazingly, thanks to tons of options, *Space Invaders* for the Atari 2600 is even better than the arcade original.

CHAPTER 86

SPY HUNTER

COLECOVISION
GENRE: DEMOLITION/COMBAT RACING
PUBLISHER: COLECO
DEVELOPER: COLECO
1 PLAYER
1984

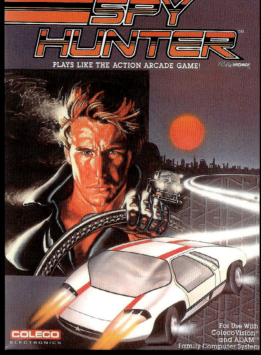

Spy Hunter for the ColecoVision, complete in box. $140.

"CLASSIC ACTION GAME THAT RELIES HEAVILY ON REFLEXES BUT ALSO REWARDS FOR GOOD STRATEGY."

When Bally/Midway's *Spy Hunter* hit the arcades in 1983, gearhead gamers welcomed it as a nice, weapons-charged change of pace from the great but weaponless *Turbo* (1981) and *Pole Position* (1982).

I was struck by the game as well, admiring its speed, rapid-fire bullets, and "Peter Gunn Theme" music. Unfortunately, I was terrible at *Spy Hunter*. I ran into other cars and got bumped off the road a lot, and I don't think I ever truly understood how to play the game. I knew you were supposed to shoot other cars and avoid crashing, but some of the nuances were lost on me, so I pretty much gave up on it after a few tries, even though my friends swore up and down that it was a great game.

Luckily, the ColecoVision version, which was programmed by Michael Price (game adaptation), Jesse Kapili (computer graphics), and Roland Rizzo (audio adaptation), lets you play the game again and again without wasting quarters. This ability to play unfettered by financial constraints (aside from purchasing the game to begin with) is one of the hallmarks of console gaming and one of the reasons I love playing games at home.

After reading the instructions and spending a good deal of time with *Spy Hunter*, a cartridge that is now very hard to find, I got pretty decent at the game and began to thoroughly enjoy it. In fact, it made me feel like an armchair James Bond.

Viewed from overhead, *Spy Hunter* puts you behind the wheel of a specialized sports car armed with a machine gun and unlimited rounds of ammunition. As you race up the roadway, which is lined with such scenery as grass, trees, and rocks, you earn points just for staying alive, and for shooting enemy vehicles. If you shoot a friendly vehicle, the score counter will briefly stop, costing you points. The roadway sometimes curves a little and there are forks in the road.

In addition to the rapid-fire, double-bullet machine gun, which you always have, your car can equip oil slicks, smoke screens, and missiles. These weapons are added by approaching a weapons van from behind and entering said van, which will then drop you off on the side of the road. Oil slicks and smoke screens are used to thwart enemies approaching from the rear while missiles can destroy helicopters that are otherwise impossible to reach.

Helicopters are white, but road-based enemies are dark blue. Enemy vehicles include limousines, bullet-proof sedans, and cars equipped with lethal tire slashers. You should avoid shooting light blue cars and motorcycles.

Spy Hunter game cartridge. *Courtesy of Bryan C. Smith.* $35.

The back of the *Spy Hunter* box.

Spy Hunter keypad overlays for the Super Action Controllers and the standard controllers. *Courtesy of Bryan C. Smith.* $15.

If you stay alive long enough in *Spy Hunter*, you'll come to a narrow road that forks off to the left. This leads to a boathouse, where you'll commandeer a speed boat that must battle and/or avoid barrel dumper boats, explosive barrels, torpedo boats approaching from the rear, and helicopters. When you enter the boat, you'll have the same weapons you had in your car, but you cannot add weapons while boating.

Going to the boathouse is optional in some cases, but at times you must exit to the river because a bridge is out ahead. In both areas, the streets and the river, you can eliminate enemies by bumping them to the side (a la *Bump 'n' Jump*).

Spy Hunter is one of Digital Press founder Joe Santulli's all-time favorite coin-op titles. In a review published on digitpress.com, he said *Spy Hunter* is "aimed squarely at the little boy in all of us who wonders what it would be like to chase down bad guys in our cars." He also called it a "classic action game that relies heavily on reflexes but also rewards for good strategy."

Referring to the stellar cartridge version, Santulli said: "I anxiously awaited the ColecoVision port-over and was not disappointed when it finally arrived. Everything from the arcade game is included here, including compatibility with the ColecoVision's driving module, making *Spy Hunter* one of the most accurate translations in classic gaming history…the driving module really brings the arcade feel home."

Earlier, I mentioned that *Spy Hunter* makes me feel like James Bond (much more so than *James Bond 007* for the ColecoVision). A big reason for this is the dramatic music, which is very nicely reproduced on the ColecoVision. The sound effects are excellent as well, particularly the skidding of the car tires, the "rat-at-tat-tat" of the machine gun, and the whirling blade of the helicopter. The game is an excellent port in general, despite mono-colored cars and less detailed trees.

Less successful is the Nintendo NES port from SunSoft. It was released in 1987, so it could have been included in this book, but it is too darned fast—faster, even, than the arcade game—causing undue frustration. It's way too easy to crash into a motorcycle or get bumped off the road. The game also has spotty collision detection.

The original arcade version of *Spy Hunter*, which is emulated for the home via *Midway's Greatest Arcade Hits: Vol. 1* (2000, Nintendo 64) and *Midway Arcade Treasures* (2003, various), spawned a far less popular arcade sequel, 1987's *Spy Hunter II*. In 1991, Sunsoft released a console sequel, the futuristic *Super Spy Hunter* for the NES.

Spy Hunter, a reimagining of the game, was released for the PlayStation 2 and Xbox in 2001. *Spy Hunter: Nowhere to Run*, based on the Dwayne "The Rock" Johnson film, followed in 2006. In 2012, *Spy Hunter* was reimagined for the Nintendo DS and PlayStation Vita.

None of the sequels or remakes is as good as the original *Spy Hunter*, which, as you've probably gathered by now, has a remarkable ColecoVision port.

FUN FACT:

When the original arcade version of *Spy Hunter* was in production, the developers considered including a helicopter sequence, but scrapped the idea due to lack of memory.

WHY IT MADE THE LIST:

Spy Hunter, a very demanding coin-op game in terms of action and audio/visuals, made a smooth transition to the ColecoVision. The result is a phenomenal cartridge that all James Bond wannabes should own.

CHAPTER 87

STAMPEDE

ATARI 2600
GENRE: ACTION
PUBLISHER: ACTIVISION
DEVELOPER: ACTIVISION
1 PLAYER
1981

INTELLIVISION
GENRE: ACTION
PUBLISHER: ACTIVISION
DEVELOPER: ACTIVISION
1 PLAYER
1982

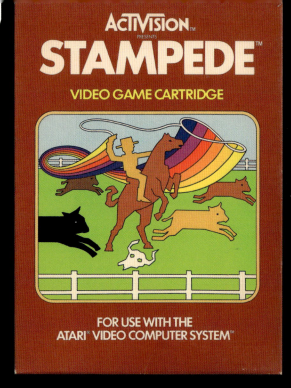

Stampede for the Atari 2600, complete in box. $12.

"STAMPEDE IS HIGHLY ORIGINAL, AS THERE'S NOT ANOTHER GAME QUITE LIKE IT."

One of the more underrated games for the Atari 2600, especially in terms of Activision releases, *Stampede* is often overlooked by the average gamer.

For example, as of this writing, if you look up the Wikipedia entry for "List of Western video games," *Stampede* doesn't even appear. In a 2010 article on the AskMen website (www.askmen.com) entitled "Top 10: Western-Themed Video Games," *Stampede* doesn't make the cut. One has to wonder if it was even considered. (For those of you who are curious, one Atari 2600 game, *Outlaw*, is featured, weighing in at number five.)

In addition to being underrated, *Stampede* is highly original, as there's not another game quite like it. You, as a cowboy astride a horse that makes a nifty galloping sound, maneuver up and down along the left side of the screen, "roping dogies" or, in laymen's terms, lassoing cattle. As the action scrolls to the right, you will catch up with the dogies, some of which appear in horizontal rows of two or three.

As you approach each dogie, you should position your horse directly behind said animal and lasso it, unless strategy dictates that you should "herd" the dogie. Frequently, there will be several dogies on the screen, and if you lasso one, another could get past you. To help prevent this, you can herd (i.e., get very close to) the cow to get it to run forward well ahead of you. This technique is crucial and especially comes in handy when numerous dogies are on the screen.

If you lasso a dogie that's in a row, only that dogie will disappear from the screen, meaning each animal must individually be lassoed. However, herding is different. If you herd a dogie at the back of a row, the entire row will move forward, giving you some much-needed breathing room. Each time a dogie gets past you, a point is deducted from a "stray count" at the top of the screen. For every 1,000 points you score, the stray count increases by one (the maximum count is nine). If the count gets to zero, it's game over.

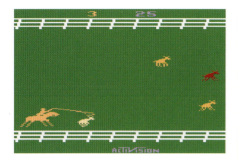

Roping a dogie in *Stampede* for the Atari 2600. Courtesy of AtariAge.com.

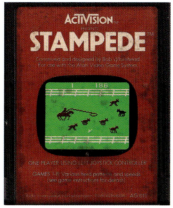

Stampede game cartridge (Atari 2600). $5.

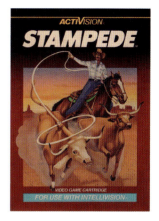

Stampede for the Intellivision, complete in box. $10.

There are four types of cattle you'll encounter in *Stampede*: dark red Herefords (worth 3 points), medium brown Guernseyes (15 points), light brown Jerseys (25 points), and Black Anguses (100 points). Black Anguses only appear periodically and they behave differently than the other cattle. They sit still (as opposed to running to the right) and face you, meaning you must be ready to quickly lasso them. You can't herd Black Anguses, making them a priority to remove from the playfield.

As alluded to above, the mix of lassoing and herding gives this simple, action-oriented game an ample dose of strategy as you must quickly decide which dogies to lasso right away and which to push forward (once the screen gets busy, it's impossible to lasso every dogie as it appears). Also key is the fact that, as the manual states, "each game of *Stampede* offers a different pattern, speed, and movement of the dogies, providing new challenges every time you play."

Beginning players should set the left difficulty switch to "B", which lengthens your rope ("A" shortens it). The select switch lets you choose from eight difficulty levels: Sidekick (dogies run straight ahead in a set pattern); Pilgrim (dogies move up and down to avoid lasso); Cowpoke (same as Sidekick, but no set pattern); Wrangler (same as Cowpoke, but all dogies move up and down); Top Hand, Trail Boss, Rancher, and Cattle Baron (these latter four are similar to the first four, but "all dogies start out at a full gallop"). When I play *Stampede*, I prefer the Wrangler level.

Stampede looks as good as it plays. The cows are recognizable as such and are very nicely animated, especially when they are herded and run quickly ahead. The mounted horse with extending lasso looks fantastic, as do the white fencerows positioned at the top and bottom of the screen. Occasionally, a skull will appear, which is a nice graphical touch as well as a fitting obstacle to avoid.

As with many Activision games, the Intellivision version of *Stampede* is similar in appearance to the 2600 original. Bob Whitehead, who co-founded Activision, programmed both versions of *Stampede*, and he deserves kudos for coming up with such an original title. However, it's a shame he didn't take advantage of the superior processing power of the Intellivision to add a few graphical flourishes. Also, the screen tends to get busier in the 2600 rendition, and the lasso can extend farther.

In the *Stampede* manual, Whitehead offered the following gameplay advice: "First of all, keep in mind the particular sequences in which the dogies appear…one strategy is to lasso the high-point dogies first, while keeping the darker (low-point) ones herded in front of you. Herding is the most important part of the game. But remember, a dogie that is repeatedly herded will get tired and become more difficult to herd, because he won't run as far ahead on the screen."

While the general public sometimes overlooks *Stampede*, it's a critical darling with most reviewers. The Video Game Critic (videogamecritic.com) cited the 2600 version's "clean graphics, smooth animation, responsive controls, and madly addictive gameplay," while Keita Iida, writing for Atari Gaming Headquarters (www.atarihq.com), said the "whole package is full of fun and guaranteed to provide hours of entertainment [and] many amusing moments for the spectator."

Bob Whitehead is a fan of the game as well. In an interview conducted by Scott Stilphen for Digital Press (www.digitpress.com), Whitehead, who also programmed such 2600 titles as *Star Ship*, *Video Chess*, *Boxing*, *Sky Jinks*, and *Chopper Command*, said, "I'm most proud of *Stampede* and *Hardball* [for the Commodore 64]."

Whitehead explained how he got such a sophisticated look for the Atari 2600 version of the game by using a special process named after a type of window covering: "The Venetian blind technique is a very simple visual implementation of the general technique of repositioning the sprites (or high resolution graphic stamps) and displaying them on the next line or later on in the screen, giving the appearance that the hardware has more than two sprites."

When *Stampede* was fresh out of the starting gate, it was well-received by journalists, including Bill Kunkel and Frank Lane, Jr., who, in *Electronic Games* magazine #2 (March, 1982), said: "*Stampede* is one of the sternest tests of hand-eye coordination yet devised by the human mind" and "The visuals are excellent," so "Put on your spurs and chaps, slap that 10-gallon hat on your head and ride 'em cowboy."

The Atari 2600 version of *Stampede* was ported to modern systems via *Activision Classics* (1998) for the PlayStation, *Activision Anthology* for the PlayStation 2 (2002) and Game Boy Advance (2003), and *Activision Hits: Remixed* (2006) for the PSP. In 2010, Microsoft made *Stampede* available as a downloadable title for the Xbox 360 Game Room service.

FUN FACT:

According to the Stilphen interview, Whitehead doesn't think much of modern video games, saying they are: "Too dark and derivative for my taste. The console and computer gaming business is too narrowly-defined by the 14-year-old male mentality and all his not-so-honorable fantasies. It's being driven by what has worked and afraid of what a 10 million dollar development bust will entail. It has lost its moral compass."

WHY IT MADE THE LIST:

Stampede is a highly original, hugely enjoyable game with an unusual setting: the Old West.

CHAPTER 88

STAR CASTLE

VECTREX
GENRE: NON-SCROLLING SHOOTER
PUBLISHER: GCE
DEVELOPER: GCE
1 OR 2 PLAYERS (ALTERNATING, SIMULTANEOUS)
1983

Star Castle arcade flyer.

"OFFERS TWO-PLAYER COOPERATIVE/SIMULTANEOUS ACTION."

In 1980, when the original version of *Star Castle* was new in the arcades, my brother and I were in the habit of going to Malibu Grand Prix in Hurst, Texas (near Fort Worth) almost every Sunday night. At that point, I had mastered *Asteroids* by using the old trick of leaving one small space rock on the playfield while flying up the screen repeatedly, picking off each flying saucer as it would appear. I would rack up tons of points and extra ships this way and sometimes sell a game in progress for 25 cents to someone looking on.

I would then use that extra quarter to play *Star Castle*, a much more difficult game than *Asteroids*. Ship movement was similar—rotate, thrust, fire—and the game had vector

Star Castle for the Vectrex, complete in box. $85.   The back of the Star Castle box.   Star Castle game cartridge. $40.

graphics, but instead of firing at space rocks, your job was to destroy an energy cannon located at the center of the screen. The cannon was surrounded by three oppositely rotating energy rings comprised of 12 segments each. To destroy the cannon, you had to shoot segments of the walls and then aim shots through the newly formed gaps. If you destroyed the entire outer ring, however, the inner walls would expand and a new wall would form around the cannon.

I loved *Star Castle* and the challenges it presented, and I could even destroy the energy cannon (resulting in a great explosion) two or three times before losing all my ships.

Designed by Tim Skelly (with Scott Boden), *Star Castle* is an intimidating game. It has a colorful monitor overlay and sharp vector graphics, but it also has a sinister, siren-like wail, accompanied by sounds that can only be called "booming" and "electrifying." Further, as I mentioned earlier, the game is very difficult. When you clear a line of fire to the cannon, the cannon fires fast shots at your ship. There are also sparks to avoid, which release when you hit certain shield segments.

In *Supercade: A Visual History of the Videogame Age, 1971-1984* (2001, The MIT Press), Skelly discussed a key aspect of *Star Castle*: "The game was made much more interesting by the fact that the enemy's shots—very accurate and deadly—could not pass through the existing ring segments. This meant that by shooting out the shield, the player was eliminating the one thing that was protecting him from that nasty gun in the center."

When the Vectrex console came out in November of 1982, I was still a month away from obtaining the first system I actually owned, a ColecoVision, which I got for Christmas that year (read my first book, *Classic Home Video Games, 1972-1984* for the full story). I couldn't afford a Vectrex, but later in the decade I managed to trade a heavily used VCR to a pawnshop for a Vectrex in excellent working condition, which I considered a great exchange. I was excited to play *Star Castle* at home, and, despite some minor differences, I wasn't disappointed with CGE's excellent take on the arcade classic.

The Vectrex version of *Star Castle*, programmed by William Hawkins (*Rip Off*), has less imposing sound effects than its coin-op counterpart, and each energy ring has eight segments (making them octagons) instead of 12. Gameplay is largely similar, however, and even includes a bonus. In the arcade game, the two-player option is alternating only. However, the Vectrex version also offers two-player cooperative/simultaneous action. And, of course, I could play the game again and again without going broke.

You can play *Star Castle* cartridge-only, of course, or through a multi-cart, but it's best when played using the original screen overlay that came packaged with the cartridge. This gives the playfield the yellow center, red ring, and blue space field, just like in the arcade game.

Star Castle was only ported to one system during the Golden Age of home video games: the Vectrex. However, Atari employee Howard Scott Warshaw, programmer of *Raiders of the Lost Ark* and *E.T. The Extra-Terrestrial*, was assigned to port *Star Castle* to the Atari 2600 back in 1981. Unfortunately, Warsaw discovered that he couldn't do it on the memory-deprived console, so he took the basic concept of *Star Castle* and created *Yars' Revenge*.

"*Yars*' was originally assigned to me as a conversion of the coin-op game *Star Castle*," Warshaw told Game Career Guide (gamecareerguide.com) back in 2007. "After investigating this for a little while I came to the conclusion that this conversion would suck on the VCS system. So I did something no one else had ever done, I went to my boss and said that I had an idea for an original game that would use the same basic play principles of *Star Castle*, but was designed to fit the VCS hardware so it wouldn't suck."

Surprisingly, Atari agreed with their budding young programmer. "And to their credit, they let me go with it," Warshaw said. "Think about that. They blew off a license to let me pursue an original concept with the promise of making a better game for the system. That would never happen today."

Atari's faith in their employee rewarded the company with the best-selling original first-party game for the 2600, not to mention a fondly remembered classic that holds up to this day as one of the best titles for the system.

When D. Scott Williamson, who worked for Atari several years after Warshaw, read about the creation of *Yars' Revenge* in *Racing the Beam* (2009, The MIT Press), he suddenly had a new goal in life: to program a good, playable port of *Star Castle* for the 2600, using an 8K cart.

"Every engineer, no matter the discipline, is drawn to some particular project," Williamson said on his Kickstarter page. "This project becomes the nagging pull that draws an engineer ever-onward. For me, that project was *Star Castle*. I'm an Atari fanatic; I always have been. I'm also a *Star Castle* fan. I used to pump quarters into that machine at the local bowling alley every day after school."

Williamson finished the project in 2011 and, thanks to a successful Kickstarter campaign, offered the game for sale in 2012, complete with cartridge, box, and manual. "This is one of the coolest things I have ever done," Williamson said. "It's a technical accomplishment, and it's really, really fun! I was inspired by one of the greatest and most influential game programmers of all time to make something that he said was impossible. I don't consider this a game development project, rather an alternative history art piece, a demonstration that it could indeed be done."

Getting back to *Star Castle* for the Vectrex, it goes without saying that it's a must-own cartridge for the system, especially for shooter fans who don't mind an intimidating challenge. In a review published in *Electronic Fun with Computers & Games* Vol. 2 #1 (Nov., 1983), Marc Berman said it's "a fabulous game" that "calls for strategy, quick thinking, fast action and precision."

In issue #6 (July/Aug., 1992) of the *Digital Press* fanzine, Joe Santulli said, "The look, the sound, and especially the gameplay made it seem like the arcade experience…there really are no shortcomings…the pace is perfect…this one you gotta have if you're a Vectrex owner."

Further, *Star Castle* was listed as one of the "99 Favorite Classics" by Digital Press (digitpress.com) in 1997, a position it clearly deserves.

In 1997, John Dodzilla produced a homebrew clone of *Star Castle* for the ColecoVision called *Star Fortress*. As a huge ColecoVision fan, this was the first homebrew that I ever bought.

FUN FACT:
As *Star Castle* powers up, you can hold 1 + 2 + 4 until the music stops to view the following onscreen message: "Programmed by William Hawkins."

WHY IT MADE THE LIST:
With its vector graphics and *Asteroids*-style ship controls, *Star Castle* is the ideal port for the Vectrex, which specializes in these types of games.

CHAPTER **89**

SUPER BREAKOUT

ATARI 2600
GENRE: BALL-AND-PADDLE
PUBLISHER: ATARI
DEVELOPER: ATARI
1 OR 2 PLAYERS (ALTERNATING)
1981

Super Breakout arcade flyer.

"INCLUDES ALL THREE MODES OF PLAY FROM ATARI'S 1978 SUPER BREAKOUT ARCADE GAME."

Atari's *Super Breakout* hit the arcades in 1978, the same year *Breakout* was released in cartridge form for the Atari 2600. Two years prior, the *Breakout* coin-op game revolutionized the ball-and-paddle genre. When *Super Breakout* came to the 2600 in 1981, *Breakout* was included as a selectable title, so a little background on that game is in order before I get to *Super Breakout*.

During the mid-1970s, I was a huge pinball buff, playing the game whenever and wherever I could: in malls, convenience stores, bowling alleys, skating rinks, and, of course, arcades. I also thoroughly enjoyed such video games as *Gun Fight* (Midway, 1975) and *Night Driver* (Atari, 1976), but pinball was my favorite way to blow a quarter.

One day, probably in 1977, I was hanging out at one of my favorite haunts, The Land of Oz arcade in the North East Mall in Hurst, Texas (a suburb of Fort Worth), and was struck speechless by a monolith of *2001: A Space Odyssey* proportions: the original *Breakout*, which Atari released to the arcades in 1976, a year before the 1977 debut of the Atari 2600 (then called the Atari VCS).

Breakout was a revelation. It had smooth controls, compelling gameplay, and, years before *Space Invaders* (1978), *Asteroids* (1979), and *Tetris* (1985), it placated that apparent need gamers have to make things disappear from the screen. In terms of the rotary knob-controlled, ball-and-paddle genre, I was already a *Pong* fan, but *Breakout* added color (or at least color overlays) and a deviously addicting solo premise: breaking through rows of bricks positioned across the top of the screen.

In short, *Breakout* made me a video game fan for life.

For an historical analysis of *Breakout*, consider the following, quoted from video game journalist Earl Green's website, www.thelogbook.com:

The year was 1976, and Atari's founder, Nolan Bushnell, had an idea to revive the over-mined "ball and paddle" genre: turn *Pong* into a single-player game, almost like racquetball, in which players must smash their way through a wall of bricks with a ball without missing that ball on the rebound. Bushnell was sure the idea would be a hit.

At Atari, despite being the visionary leader who'd kept the company afloat by sheer force of will, he was alone in that assessment. At the time, engineers could pick assignments from an "idea board" in the Atari offices, and nobody was springing into action to put together Bushnell's baby, so he finally assigned it to someone himself. The job landed in the lap of a young employee who hadn't exactly made a lot of friends at the usually open Atari due to his sometimes awkward social behavior—one Steve Jobs.

Jobs was offered a bonus for every chip he could eliminate from the elaborate circuit board that would be required to implement the game. He wasn't exactly cut out for that sort of design, however, and called his best friend to come in after hours and help, a young Hewlett-Packard employee named Steve Wozniak.

Wozniak pulled an all-nighter redesigning the game's circuitry, and would up eliminating at least 50 chips from the 100-chip original design. The Atari engineers who saw his work were stunned—and some could already tell that Jobs wasn't the one who had pulled this feat off. But there was a new problem now—Wozniak's redesign of *Breakout* was so radical that it couldn't be duplicated. This *Breakout* as we saw it in arcades was a slightly revamped 75-chip design—but Jobs still pocketed a $7,000 bonus…only $350 of which was shared with Wozniak, who was happy simply to hang around the Atari labs playing games, and genuinely thought that $350 was half of the bonus check that had been made out to Jobs. He didn't find out until many years later, when Bushnell inquired about what he did with his "half of the seven grand" at an industry function.

In an interview published in *Game Informer* #241 (May, 2013), Wozniak revealed that he and Jobs were given four days to design *Breakout*. "I went four days with no sleep," he said. "Steven and I both got mononucleosis, the sleeping sickness, and we delivered a working *Breakout* game. That was obviously a big classic. Supposedly, the Atari engineers couldn't understand my design. It was just so beautiful and advanced, but they couldn't get it."

With its wonderful paddle controllers, the Atari 2600 was the perfect system for a *Breakout* port, and the 1978 conversion succeeds brilliantly. In addition to the standard game, it includes a variety of options: timed games, team play, steerable balls, catchable balls, and invisible walls. The game also features a variation called Breakthru, in which the ball can crash through walls, eliminating every brick it touches.

As mentioned earlier, *Super Breakout* for the Atari 2600, which was programmed by Nick Turner (*Demons to Diamonds*), includes *Breakout*, but it also includes all three modes of play from Atari's 1978 *Super Breakout* arcade game (programmed by Ed Logg): Double Breakout, in which players control two vertically stacked paddles; Cavity Breakout, in which the walls have two holes, each hole containing a ball; and Progressive Breakout, which has walls that travel down the screen as the game progresses.

There's a children's version as well, which is similar to the standard game, but the ball doesn't speed up after hitting bricks in the last four rows, and the paddle doesn't reduce to half its original size when the ball reaches the top boundary of the playfield.

As is the case with many 2600 ports, Atari added a back story to *Super Breakout* via the manual: you are supposedly an astronaut in a one-man space shuttle, traveling through space and encountering a force field that you must break through or be forced to turn back.

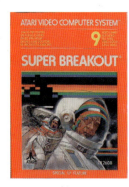
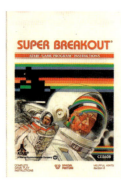
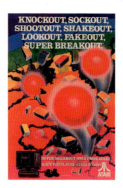

Super Breakout for the Atari 2600, complete in box. *Courtesy of AtariAge.com.* $10.

Super Breakout instruction manual. $2.

Super Breakout magazine ad. *Courtesy of Digital Press (digitpress.com).*

Super Breakout in action. *Courtesy of AtariAge.com.*

One big difference between the arcade versions of *Breakout* and *Super Breakout* and their Atari 2600 counterparts is the graphics. The coin-op games have individually outlined bricks, while the walls in the cartridges appear as solid lines. This is a small gripe in an otherwise stellar pair of games.

Regarding *Super Breakout*, the 2600 game is superior to the arcade cab in one significant aspect, the sound effects, as Arnie Katz and Bill Kunkel explained in *Electronic Games* magazine # 4 (June, 1982): "Instead of muted, exploding punch that signaled the bursting of a brick in prior versions [the review also references the Atari 8-bit computer port], the VCS version features a wide array of accompanying sounds…bricks disappear with the tinkling of fine crystal… bricks break up to a series of musical notes…there's a metallic twang, and an ominous, synthetic fuzz…it's these totally enchanting sounds that turn a well-respected, but slightly dated program into a wildly contemporary hit."

According to episode six (March 31, 2013) of the *2600 Game by Game Podcast* (2600gamebygamepodcast.blogspot.com), Nick Turner said "he couldn't decide which sound to use" when programming the 2600 port, "so he used them all."

Robert Ferguson, who hosts the *2600 Game By Game Podcast*, was a big fan of *Super Breakout* when he was a kid, but doesn't think it has aged particularly well. "I loved this game back then," he said. "It was definitely my favorite for a while. It's still a lot of fun to play now, but the ball physics really bother me. *Super Breakout*'s descendant, *Arkanoid*, fixed this problem with the physics and greatly expands the gameplay."

Super Breakout was also produced for the Atari 5200. In fact, it was the original pack-in game with the console (before *Pac-Man* replaced it in 1983). Unfortunately, the lack of paddle controls makes this a forgettable version and a poor choice for a pack-in title.

Super Breakout has been ported to a number of other gaming devices as well, including the PlayStation (1996, *Arcade's Greatest Hits: The Atari Collection 1*), Sega Saturn (1997, *Arcade's Greatest Hits: The Atari Collection 1*), Game Boy Color (1999), and iPhone (2008), among others. Those versions also suffer from the absence of paddle control.

FUN FACT:

In order to handicap a player in *Super Breakout* for the 2600, gamers should put that player's difficulty switch in the "A" position, which makes their paddle half the size of the paddle when it's in the "B" position.

WHY IT MADE THE LIST:

With its weaponry and different brick arrangements, *Arkanoid* may have passed up *Super Breakout*, but the 2600 game is still a lot of fun to play, at least in my opinion.

CHAPTER 90

SUPER MARIO BROS.

NINTENDO NES
GENRE: SIDE-SCROLLING PLATFORMER
PUBLISHER: NINTENDO
DEVELOPER: NINTENDO
1 OR 2 PLAYERS (ALTERNATING)
1985

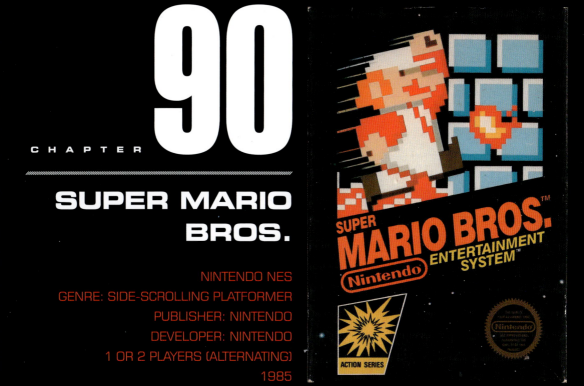

Super Mario Bros. for the Nintendo NES, complete in box. $90.

"SUPER MARIO BROS. MADE ALL PREVIOUS GAMES SEEM ANTIQUATED IN COMPARISON."

When I received my Nintendo NES during the summer of 1986 as a birthday present from my brother, I didn't really "need" it. After all, I already had an Atari 2600, a ColecoVision, and an Intellivision hooked up to the 19-inch television set in my bedroom, and I still played all three systems on a regular basis (numerous consoles would follow, but that's a story for another day).

Regardless, despite my lack of actual need, I really *wanted* an NES. As the system grew in popularity, I kept hearing more and more about a little mind-blower called *Super Mario Bros.*, and I was thrilled when I "finally" (the NES debuted in America in 1985) got an NES of my very own.

From the moment I powered up my newly acquired gray box and plugged in *Super Mario Bros.*, my perception of what a video game was and what it could do forever changed. Like *The Exorcist* (1973) did for horror films and Nirvana and Pearl Jam did to hair metal, *Super Mario Bros.* made all previous games seem antiquated in comparison. I still liked older video games, of course (along with classic monster movies and hair metal), but there was no doubting the fact that a new sheriff was in town in the form of an Italian plumber.

Not only was *Super Mario Bros.* revolutionary, it helped resurrect the home video game industry from the post-mortem doldrums of The Great Video Game Crash, in which such consoles as the Atari 5200 and ColecoVision were discontinued, and such systems as the Atari 2600 and Intellivision barely hung on for their dear lives.

Numerous attributes made *Super Mario Bros.* stand out from all previous games, including gorgeous graphics, unparalleled freedom of movement (the NES D-pad was a nice upgrade over previous controllers), vast side-scrolling worlds filled with secrets and surprises, and a colorful assortment of quirky enemies, including the now-iconic Bullet Bill, Little Goomba (a mushroom), Koopa Troopa (a soldier of the Turtle Empire), The Hammer Brothers (twin turtles who throw hammers), Pirana plants, Lakitu (a turtle who controls the clouds), Cheep-Cheep (who swims and can sprout wings and flies), and, of course, Mario's fire-spitting arch-nemesis Bowser, who is the King of the Koopa.

As most of you reading this well know, players control Nintendo mascot Mario as he runs, jumps, swims, and otherwise makes his way through eight cartoon-like worlds of the Mushroom Kingdom. His goal, of course, is to rescue the daughter of the Mushroom King, Princess Toadstool (later known by her original Japanese name, Princess Peach).

The action in *Super Mario Bros.* is remarkably varied as Mario collects coins, grabs 1UP mushrooms for extra lives, hops on enemies to defeat them, shatters bricks with his fist

 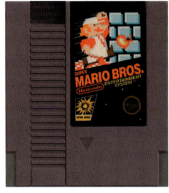 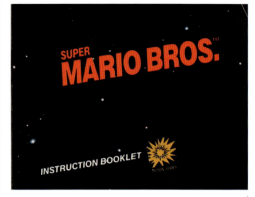

The back of the *Super Mario Bros.* box.　　Super Mario Bros. game cartridge. $12.　　*Super Mario Bros.* instruction manual. $6.

to uncover secrets, goes down pipes to discover hidden areas, kicks turtle shells to knock down enemies, jumps higher via jumping boards, warps to other worlds, and powers up into special characters by grabbing one of three different items: magic mushroom (Super Mario, who can duck, shatter bricks, and take a hit from an enemy); fire flower (Fiery Mario, who can throw fireballs and take a hit from an enemy); and Starman (Invincible Mario, who can destroy enemies by simply touching them). In two-player (alternating) mode, the second gamer controls Mario's brother, Luigi.

The sequel to the non-scrolling *Mario Bros.*, *Super Mario Bros.* was designed by the legendary Shigeru Miyamoto (*Donkey Kong*), with assistance from Takashi Tezuka, Gunpei Yokoi, and Koji Kondo, who wrote the memorable theme music. For the 25th anniversary of *Super Mario Bros.* (2010), Miyamoto spoke with *Famitsu* magazine about the genesis of the game. "I wanted to build upon our tradition of what we called 'athletic games' at the time—games where you controlled a guy and had to jump a lot to overcome obstacles," he said. "We felt strongly about how we were the first to come up with that genre, and it was a goal of ours to keep pushing it."

Speaking to the *Daily News* about the 25th anniversary, Miyamoto discussed the importance of the game to the Nintendo brand. "*Super Mario Bros.* was really our first original title that was built for and epitomized what the NES was supposed to be," he said. "That was what made us say, 'Now we are going to launch this in America.' We thought this game would help people understand the system."

Regarding the design of *Super Mario Bros.*, size mattered to Miyamoto. "When we were making *Super Mario Bros.*, I wanted players to control a Mario character who was bigger than ever," he said in an interview published in *High Score! The Illustrated History of Electronic Games* (2003, McGraw-Hill Osborne Media). "When we made the prototype of the big Mario, we did not feel he was big enough. So, we came up with the idea of showing the smaller Mario first, who could be bigger later in the game ('super'); then players could see and feel that he was bigger."

It's hard to find a retro gamer who hasn't played *Super Mario Bros.*, and it's almost as hard to find a retro gamer who doesn't love it.

Consider the following accolades:

…the crown jewel of platform games, and Mario is King.
—*Game Informer* #100 (Aug., 2001), in which *Super Mario Bros.* is ranked second on the list of "Top 100 Games of All Time"

I have very little doubt that in 100 years this game will be looked at by the video game community as Picasso is now looked at by art lovers.
—Dustin Galley (digitpress.com)

To gain a true sense of 'gamer legitimacy,' you must own this game and you must play it. If there were a class in college on video games, this would be a major part of the curriculum.
—nintendojo.com

Super Mario Bros. is the game that all others will be judged by. Its superb combination of challenges, features, graphics, and music makes it a game to be played over and over.
—*Compute!'s Guide to Nintendo Games* (1989, Compute! Books)

Super Mario Bros. features an enthralling combination of rock-solid gameplay, ingeniously designed levels, vibrant, colorful graphics, and well-written music. The sense of excitement, wonder, and most of all—enjoyment—felt upon first playing this masterpiece of a video game can barely be put into words.
—Geoffrey Douglas Smith (allgame.com)

Playing *Super Mario Bros.* when it was new was an exhilarating experience for me, and it holds up extremely well today. With its expansive worlds, coins to collect, secrets to uncover, and enemies to hop on, it set the stage for all subsequent platformers, including two NES sequels: *Super Mario Bros. 2* (1988), which altered the formula (players throw items at enemies and use potions to create doorways and blocks to reach high places); and *Super Mario Bros. 3* (1990), one of the best (and best-selling) video games of all time.

A cartridge that has "defined so much of what we've been doing in games since its arrival" (*Time Magazine*, Nov. 15, 2012), *Super Mario Bros.*, which influenced Sega's *Sonic the Hedgehog* series, Sony's *Crash Bandicoot* series, and numerous other franchises, also spawned such stunningly awesome sequels as *Super Mario World* (1991, SNES), *Super Mario 64* (1996, N64), *Super Mario Galaxy* (2007, Wii), and *New Super Mario Bros. U* (2012, Wii U), among many others.

If you want to play the original *Super Mario Bros.* on something other than an NES, you can do so on a number of platforms, including the Super Nintendo (1993, via *Super Mario All-Stars*, which has enhanced graphics and sounds), Game Boy Advance (2004, via the "Classic NES Series"), and Nintendo Wii (2006, via the Virtual Console).

FUN FACT:

In 1986, Nintendo released *Super Mario Bros.* in the arcades as part of their PlayChoice series. The arcade version is almost identical to the console game, but has a different ending (which you can view on YouTube).

WHY IT MADE THE LIST:

With the possible exception of *The Legend of Zelda*, *Super Mario Bros.* belongs in this book more than any other game. Not only did it alter the course of the entire industry, it holds up as a charming and inventive platformer.

CHAPTER 91

TURBO

COLECOVISION
GENRE: FORMULA-1/INDY RACING
PUBLISHER: COLECO
DEVELOPER: COLECO
1 PLAYER
1982

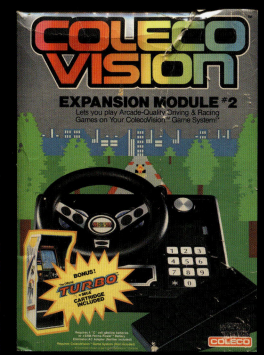

Expansion Module #2 for the ColecoVision, complete in box.

"HOLDS UP WELL IN TERMS OF BOTH GAMEPLAY AND VISUAL APPEAL."

When the ColecoVision arrived on the scene in 1982, it blew the Atari 2600, Intellivision, and other previous consoles out of the water with its colorful, detailed, arcade-like graphics. Nowhere is this more evident than with the eye-popping *Turbo*, based on Sega's popular driving game from 1981. The cartridge was packaged with Expansion Module #2, a.k.a. the steering wheel and gas pedal driving controller.

Before further describing the ColecoVision port, which "looks good, sounds good, and plays good" (*Electronic Games* magazine #14, 1983), a little historical perspective on the arcade classic is in order.

"*Turbo* marked the first real progression in racing games since Sega introduced the hit, *Monaco GP*, in 1979," wrote Van Burnham in her seminal *Supercade: A Visual History of the Videogame Age 1971-1984* (2001, MIT Press). "For *Turbo*, Sega took the gameplay of *Monaco GP*, the first to introduce color along with an aerial perspective, one step further—adding a three-dimensional perspective along with realistic scrolling scenery graphics as you speed along; a vast improvement over *Speed Freak*'s [1978] glowing phosphorescent cows."

Turbo, designed by Steve Hanawa, was released as an upright cabinet, a sit-down cabaret, and in a deluxe cocktail model, complete with gear shift, steering wheel, gas pedal, and red LED instrument panel.

According to Sega8bit (www.smstributes.co.uk), creating *Turbo* was a nightmare. "Steve actually considers it his worst experience working with Sega, because he was hospitalized for over a month after spending hours upon hours coding and debugging the title," the website states. "In addition, though he didn't know it at the time, he suffers from what he later discovered to be spontaneous pneumothorax, which is essentially a spontaneously collapsing lung. His condition was heightened by the stress, and he had to take some time off from work."

Now, back to the ColecoVision cartridge, which, hopefully, was less stressful to program than its coin-op cousin.

Turbo lets console gamers know they are in for a treat from the starting line, which shows your formula-1 racer and several other cars positioned on a city street lined with green, yellow, red, and gray buildings (an odd color scheme to be sure—the arcade game's buildings were mostly blue, black, and light blue—but still impressively designed). The pseudo-3D view also depicts starting lights that count down, preparing you for the race.

You begin in low gear and should shift into high gear shortly after the action begins. The standard ColecoVision controller fits comfortably in a slot beside the steering wheel, and you use the joystick to shift gears—up for low gear and down for high gear. Unfortunately, there is no onscreen indicator of the high and low gear. Also, there's no speedometer, but these are small gripes as the arcade game lacked these amenities as well.

You watch the race from an elevated view from behind your car. After a short time of racing, tall trees take the place of buildings lining the roadway. The arcade game's trees have more detail (multi-colored leaves as opposed to flat green), and you can see a city skyline in the distance, but the Coleco game nevertheless looks fantastic.

Subsequent areas along the *Turbo* raceway offer open roads that twist and turn (but not as often and usually not as sharply as in *Pole Position* or *Night Driver*), straightaways that take place during the dark of night, and snowy roads that make steering slippery and more difficult. One particularly harrowing section of the game has you driving alongside the ocean with a large wall on the opposing side of the road. The transitions from scene to scene are abrupt, but you get used to this after a few rounds of play.

In issue #1 (summer, 1983) of the British publication, *TV Gamer*, the reviewer wrote, "The great thing about this game is the constant change of settings…visually it is the most exciting racing game around." In *Video Games* #7 (April, 1983), David Smith called *Turbo* "a good game with great graphics."

The arcade version of *Turbo* depicts snowcapped mountains in the distance during the winter scenes, an artistic touch not duplicated on the Coleco version. However, when *Turbo* first entered the living rooms of ColecoVision fans everywhere, gamers were stunned by its gorgeous graphics, and by its (relatively) realistic control scheme.

The Expansion Module #2 steering wheel is rather small—about the size of a deck tennis ring—but it's responsive and is fun to use in steering your car. (By the way, you can't play *Turbo* for the ColecoVision without using Expansion Module #2.)

The gas pedal is a nice touch as well, providing a heightened sense of verisimilitude, and I like that you must switch between high and low gears, though I'm glad you don't have to trudge through five or six gears. (I tend to enjoy two-gear games like *Pole Position* and *Out Run*, and I usually select "automatic" for racing games that give you the choice between that and "manual.")

The goal in *Turbo*, as in many racing games, is to pass the other cars. As the manual states, "each car you pass increases your point total and gets you closer to extended play." Conversely, each car that passes you takes away points.

At the top of the screen is a CARS PASSED indicator and a TIME indicator. If you manage to pass 30 cars (either during regular or extended play), the time gets reset to 99.

Turbo offers four skill levels, but no two-player option. Skill level 1 lets you crash an unlimited number of times. In skill levels 2-4, however, the game ends if you crash twice (in all four modes, the game ends if you run out of time). Luckily, passing 30 cars gives you two more crashes (along with an extended play period). In other words, if you keep passing lots of cars and don't crash much, you get to keep playing.

During extended play, passing cars scores extra points, and this total keeps going up with each extended play period: regular play is 50 points; first extended play is 60 points; second extended play is 70 points; and so on. Oil slicks, the occasional ambulance (coming up from behind), and cars that are frequently easier to crash into than to pass can make significant progression difficult in the harder skill levels.

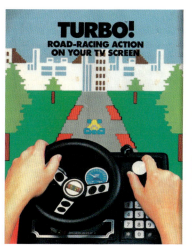

Turbo instruction manual. $2.

Turbo advertisement in ColecoVision Experience magazine.

Turbo game cartridge. $7.

Turbo's closest competitor in terms of similar racing games produced around the same time is *Pole Position* for the Atari 5200, which is fun, but less versatile (it lacks nighttime and snowy roads). The 5200 doesn't have a steering wheel peripheral, but *Pole Position*, which is listed in "The Next 100" appendix near the back of this book, is compatible with the system's Trak-Ball Controller for smooth handling. Both *Turbo* and *Pole Position* showcase the graphical power of their respective systems nicely.

Another racer of the era to consider is *Pitstop* for the ColecoVision, which, as the title suggests, has interactive pit stops, which *Turbo* and *Pole Position* lack. Even so, *Pitstop* falls a little short of its more famous rivals in terms of sheer racing action (though it's also listed in "The Next 100" appendix).

Turbo was also ported by Coleco to the Intellivision. That version has blocky graphics, and, of course, there's no steering wheel for the system. In terms of collectability, the Intellivision cart is a lot harder to find than the ColecoVision game.

According to AtariAge (atariage.com), *Turbo* was also ported to the Atari 2600, but wasn't released back in the day. "Turbo was demonstrated at the 1983 Consumer Electronics Show (and was even featured in Coleco's Atari 2600 catalogs) but was never to be seen again, even though it was roughly 80% complete at the time," the website reports. "Only when former Atari 2600 programmer Anthony Henderson discovered a copy of Turbo in his attic many years later did *Turbo* finally see the light of day."

At the 2010 Classic Gaming Expo, AtariAge released *Turbo* for the 2600, complete with Coleco-style box, box insert, cartridge, and full-color, 12-page manual. The developers included the original prototype in the program, plus a new, arcade-like (relatively speaking) enhanced version with improved audio/visuals. The enhanced version also includes roadside detection, skidding on ice, the extended play system, and more.

Some will argue that I should've featured *Rad Racer* for the NES, with its bigger cars, faster speeds, and more spectacular crashes, in this book instead of *Turbo*. However, I prefer *Turbo*'s elevated view, steering wheel, and more forgiving turns. If it's any consolation, I included *Rad Racer* in "The Next 100" appendix.

Today, despite the proliferation of such feature-rich, photorealistic games as the *Gran Turismo* and *Burnout* series, *Turbo*, adapted for the ColecoVision by Rick Lay (*Venture*), holds up well in terms of both gameplay and visual appeal.

FUN FACT:

Expansion Module #2 is also compatible with *Bump 'n' Jump*, *Destructor*, *The Dukes of Hazzard*, and *Pitstop*.

WHY IT MADE THE LIST:

Turbo is one of the best looking games of the era. More importantly, the driving action holds up well, despite ample competition from other racing titles.

CHAPTER 92

TURMOIL

ATARI 2600
GENRE: NON-SCROLLING SHOOTER
PUBLISHER: 20TH CENTURY FOX
DEVELOPER: SIRIUS SOFTWARE
1 PLAYER
1982

Turmoil for the Atari 2600, complete in box. Courtesy of AtariAge.com. $25.

"FAIRLY WELL KNOWN AMONG HARDCORE ATARI 2600 FANS AS A MUST-OWN TITLE."

I'm a big fan of so-called "twitch" games that test the player's eye-hand coordination, and I also like 2D shooters a whole heck of a lot, so *Turmoil* is definitely my cup of Earl Grey. It's one of the lesser known games among the general public in this book, but it's also one of the fastest and most frantic (not to mention frenetic).

In this game, players quickly guide a ship up and down the center of the screen, firing left and right at colorful alien ships that enter from the sides and move along seven horizontal rows. It's essential to keep shooting and moving, but, of course, care should be taken not to collide with an enemy. Each enemy ship moves at its own pace (faster enemies are worth more points), and players can hold down the joystick button for rapid fire.

In addition to enemy ships moving back and forth, the rows have arrows and tanks. If you allow an arrow to cross the screen, it will turn into a tank, which can only be destroyed from behind. If shot head-on, the tank will be pushed back a bit, but not removed.

There are also prizes and supersonic cannonballs. Prizes appear at the left or right edge of the screen and don't move. When a prize appears, players should zip over and grab it before it turns into a deadly supersonic cannonball, which moves quickly across the screen. All enemies must be shot while your ship is in the center alley.

After grabbing a prize, players should scurry back to the center alley to avoid getting hit by an indestructible ghost ship that always appears in the wake of a grabbed prize. For high scores, prizes are absolutely essential, so as you go about your business, shooting all the other items, make sure to get as many prizes as possible. This requires you to constantly monitor the edges of the screen, keeping your eyes on the prizes (pun intended).

Enemies in *Turmoil* are colorful, well drawn, and nicely animated, and prizes appear as undulating circles. Despite the many objects appearing onscreen at once, there is no flickering, a rarity for a 2600 cartridge of this type. The ghost ships are an odd design—purple cymbals, perhaps?—but this is a mere hiccup in an otherwise fine looking game. Level progress is marked by a wall of colorful rectangles that move vertically in rows, adding to the game's visual appeal.

Prior to playing *Turmoil*, you can select from levels 1-9. The further you progress in the game, the faster and more plentiful the enemies become. Beginning with level four, certain alien traffic lanes become invisible (similar to the maze walls disappearing in the 2600 version of *Mouse Trap*), ramping up the challenge.

Turmoil was created by Mark Turmell, who would go on to develop such highly popular arcade titles as *Smash T.V.* (1990), *NBA Jam* (1993), and *NFL Blitz* (1997).

Turmoil in action. *Courtesy of AtariAge.com.* *Turmoil* instruction manual. $3. *Turmoil* game cartridge. $10.

In the first issue of *Electronic Fun with Computers & Games* (Nov., 1982), Turmell talked about the genesis of *Turmoil*. "Well, my last name is Turmell and all along I thought 'Turmoil' would be a good name for a game," he said. "Very frequently, the name comes before anything else."

Turmell revealed that he doesn't like adventure titles, but he enjoys "working with fast-action games," which are ideally suited to the 2600 console. "There are very strict limitations on what you can design on the Atari VCS, but with *Turmoil*, everything fit perfectly," he said. "It's amazing that nobody thought of the game earlier, because if ever there was a game designed for the Atari, this is it."

In issue #6 of *I Am Entertainment Magazine* (Aug./Sept., 2010), Turmell informed readers about his start making games for the Atari 2600: "I did this game called *Sneakers* on the Apple II computer, which was the first game I created, and the company I was working with [Sirius Software] wanted to get into the Atari VCS (Video Computer System) cartridge business. So they invited me out to Sacramento to develop Atari VCS games…I dropped everything in Michigan and went to California."

Speaking about the development process itself, Turmell said, "Games like *Turmoil*, which was my first Atari VCS game, and *Fast Eddie* [a game that almost made it into this book] took about six weeks with me doing art, programming, and sound by myself. Whereas, eight or nine years later, a game like *NBA Jam* took a team of like seven people nearly 10 months."

Despite its relative obscurity, *Turmoil* is fairly well known among hardcore Atari 2600 fans as a must-own title. The Video Game Critic (videogamecritic.com) called it "well-designed" and "one of the best games for the system." Tom Zjaba of Tomorrow's Heroes (tomheroes.com) said it's his "all-time favorite Atari game and one of my favorite games on any platform." Adam King, writing for Atari Headquarters (atarihq.com), called the game fast-paced, exciting, and 20th Century Fox's "diamond in the rough."

Back in my days working for the All Game Guide (allgame.com), I said that *Turmoil* rivals *Frogger* as "one of the best non-Activision, non-Imagic third-party games for the system."

In *Electronic Games* magazine #21 (Nov., 1983), reviewer Steve Davidson said the game's "visuals are only slightly better than serviceable, but certainly good enough to do the job." However, he also said, "*Turmoil*'s play action…is first-rate, making the cartridge a solid bet to hold up through hours of intense gaming."

In *Electronic Fun with Computers & Games* #6 (April, 1983), Randi Hacker summed up the game thusly: "The graphics are bright and lovely, the action fast-paced and furious…captivating…In all, the game is a lot of fun."

Jim Gorzelany, writing in *JoyStik* #6 (July, 1983), only gave *Turmoil* three out of five stars, but he did call it "a fast moving, highly challenging game, particularly in later attack waves where the lane barriers periodically disappear." He also said it will "certainly give you sore thumbs and wrists and provide you with your money's worth of action long before you're tired of it."

In *Video Games* #9 (June, 1983), Perry Greenberg, clearly no fan of the game, called *Turmoil* "monotonous and fatiguing" and said that players should "expect more from a cart than dodge-and-shoot." However, he did admit that the game has "good, colorful graphics and lively sound effects."

When *Turmoil* was released, 20th Century Fox produced an amusing commercial in which a bespectacled gamer, amidst flashing lights and smoke, dodges items coming out of the screen and from behind him. At one point the game gets so fast and frenzied that he wears his jacket backwards and then proceeds to spin like a top.

Even if you agree with Greenberg that the game is lame—which you probably won't—hop on over to YouTube and take a look at the commercial, if, that is, you could use a good laugh.

FUN FACT:

Turmoil hit the Commodore 64 in 1983, but the 2600 version actually has better, more detailed graphics.

WHY IT MADE THE LIST:

As one of the more finely programmed obscurities of the early 1980s, *Turmoil* is a closet classic that deserves a place in any 2600 owner's library, especially for gamers who enjoy fast-paced action.

CHAPTER 93

TURTLES!

ODYSSEY2
GENRE: MAZE
PUBLISHER: NAP
DEVELOPER: NAP
1 PLAYER
1983

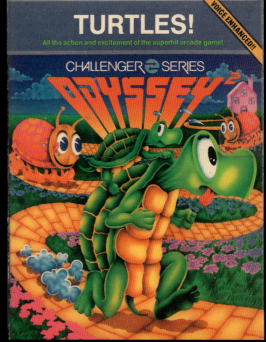

Turtles! for the Odyssey2, complete in box. $30.

"AN EXCELLENT GAME THAT MIMICS ITS COIN-OP COUNTERPART SURPRISINGLY WELL."

The only arcade port for the Odyssey2 to hit the U.S. (*Q*bert*, *Popeye*, and *Super Cobra* were European releases), *Turtles!* is an excellent game that mimics its coin-op counterpart surprisingly well.

It is based on *Turtles* (notice the absence of an exclamation point), the 1981 arcade game developed by Konami and licensed to Stern and Sega, with the latter company calling their release *Turpin*. Oddly enough, Konami manufactured the game as well, calling it *600*.

The action in *Turtles!* takes place in Turtle Towers Hotel, which consists of a series of non-scrolling mazes. Each maze contains several little rooms, each of which is a three-sided box containing a question mark. When you guide your turtle over a question mark, said question mark will turn into a baby turtle or a beetle, the latter of which will chase after you, joining the other maze-roaming beetles. The beetles are similar to the ghosts in *Pac-Man*, but there are no dots to eat in this game.

When the question mark turns into a baby turtle, it will climb onto your turtle's back, and a house will appear in a random location somewhere around the edge of the maze. You must carry the baby turtle to the house, avoiding beetles along the way. The beetles start off blue and "blind," moving randomly around the screen. However, when they turn yellow, they can "see" your turtle along straight pathways. When they turn red, they can see around corners—pretty sophisticated A.I. for the O2.

Unlike *Pac-Man* and so many other maze games, you can't gobble an energizer pill (or other item) to make the enemies vulnerable. However, your turtle begins each game with three bug bombs, which you can drop behind the turtle in the pathway of a beetle, stunning it in the process. The turtle can walk right through a stunned beetle, and when a powerful beetle recovers after a few seconds, it will go back to being blue and blind. By walking over "x" marks that appear in the center of the screen, players can grab extra bug bombs (turtles can carry up to 99 bug bombs).

When you have rescued all the baby turtles on one floor, your turtle will automatically climb to the next floor, which will be tougher to beat thanks to more beetles and fewer bug bombs. The climbing segment is a between-level intermission, which is taken from the arcade original.

Another flourish is the game's introductory attract mode (instead of the traditional SELECT GAME startup screen), also taken from the arcade game. Last but not least, *Turtles!* gives you three lives (as opposed to one), further separating it from the average Odyssey2 title. If you have The Voice speech and sound effects module, you'll hear two songs from the arcade game: an original number and "The Old Gray Mare," which is a classic folk tune.

The back of the *Turtles!* box.

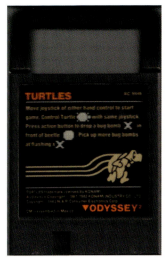
Turtles! game cartridge. $12.

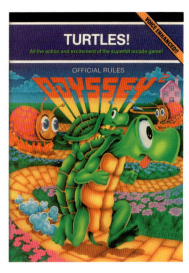
Turtles! instruction manual. $5.

With its slick production values, pinpoint controls, and arcade-like gameplay, *Turtles!* is easily one of the three or four best games in the Odyssey2 library. Naturally, the graphics have been simplified, but the game looks nice nevertheless. I enjoy dot-munching contests, but I like the fact that *Turtles!* sidesteps that formula in favor of taking baby turtles to randomly placed houses. This gameplay element reminds me a little of *Clean Sweep* (1982) for the Vectrex, in which you must deliver money to a vault.

I also like the bug bombs, which are a key strategy in the game, and which were probably inspired by the smoke screens in *Rally-X* (1980). Players can acquire many bug bombs, but it's still important to use them judiciously—in harder levels, they can get scarce. If you get trapped in a corner without a bug bomb, you can say sayonara.

Adapted for the O2 by Jim Butler (*P.T. Barnum's Acrobats!*), *Turtles!* was ranked one of the "Best New Games" by *Games* magazine (Oct., 1983) and awarded an honorable mention for "Best Arcade to Home Translation of 1983" by *Electronic Games* magazine. *EG*'s review in the "Programmable Parade" section of issue #19 (Sept., 1983) was positive, but not entirely so. The editors, comparing it to "the standard of recently published home video games," called it "pleasant" and "moderately entertaining," a "well-done game that is somewhat hampered by a low excitement level combined with overly abstract visuals."

In *Video Games* #11 (Aug., 1983), Perry Greenberg called *Turtles!* "an excellent translation of the moderately successful arcade game…a very challenging game that requires a necessary degree of concentration, and split-second decision making for any appreciable success… possibly [the Odyssey2's] best maze game."

In *Classic Gamer Magazine* #5 (fall, 2000), Earl Green's "Challenger Series" article referred to *Turtles!* as "one of the better cartridges for the console, reproducing everything down to the intermission screens between levels and even a tiny chunk of the arcade game's attract mode, and revealing a new use for The Voice (playing strangely disjointed but amusing music throughout the game)."

On the other end of the spectrum, the reviewer in *JoyStik* magazine Vol. 2 #1 (Sept., 1983), giving the game a measly two out of five stars, said, "There is not much… to this slow-moving game. Even the background music is disappointing and joystick control is awkward. Its title is an apt one."

The *JoyStik* pummeling notwithstanding, for you Odyssey2 naysayers, who have only played such turkeys as *Alpine Skiing!* and *Bowling!/Basketball!*, you'd do well to give *Turtles!* a whirl, though it is one of the tougher to find games for the system.

The fact that it is a relatively scarce game brings me to an interesting (at least to me) point. The rarer games for the Odyssey2—*Turtles!*, *Killer Bees!*, *Power Lords*—tend to be some of the better games for the system while many of the rarer games for the Atari 2600 tend to be pretty bad (*Chase the Chuck Wagon* comes to mind).

Speaking of rare, *Turtles* was also ported to the Adventure Vision, the super scarce tabletop system from Entex. That version, like the other games for the console, was released in 1982 and has red dot matrix graphics.

FUN FACT:

Entex produced a handheld rendition of *Turtles* the same year that Magnavox released the Odyssey2 port.

WHY IT MADE THE LIST:

Turtles! is the closest you can get to playing an arcade game on the Odyssey2.

CHAPTER 94

TUTANKHAM

COLECOVISION
GENRE: MAZE SHOOTER
PUBLISHER: PARKER BROTHERS
DEVELOPER: PARKER BROTHERS
1 OR 2 PLAYERS (ALTERNATING)
1984

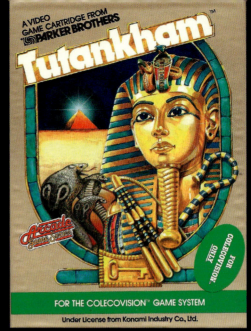

Tutankham for the ColecoVision, complete in box. $100.

"COLECOVISION PORT STILL LOOKS FANTASTIC AND MAINTAINS MOST OF THE FUN."

Before describing the gameplay and extolling the virtues of *Tutankham*, an excellent cartridge that combines adventure gaming with maze shooting action, I'll point out its one overriding flaw. It has some of the choppiest scrolling you'll ever see in a game. The playfield scrolls horizontally, and it's far from smooth. Luckily, this defect doesn't really hamper gameplay all that much. In fact, it's a testament to the greatness of the game that it overcomes this liability to make it into this book.

King Tut's tomb, which is comprised of four burial chambers (each of which includes four mazes), contains "treasures beyond your wildest dreams" tucked behind alcoves, including diamond rings belonging to Queen Nefrititi and sacred boxes containing incense. The door to the treasure room at the end of each burial chamber contains one of the following treasures: a map, an urn, a treasure chest, or the Death Mask of Tutankham. Once you reach the latter, the game starts over, but gets more difficult.

You control a hat-wearing explorer named Archie the archeologist, who is outfitted with a fast-shooting laser gun and a limited amount of flash bombs. As you explore the side-scrolling mazes, killer bats, flying cats, royal cobra snakes, giant-beaked crows, and death dragons of varying speeds emerge from creature nests (a sound will warn you of each creature's arrival), and you should shoot these pests for points (and to keep them from touching you).

You can only shoot left and right, so creatures above and below must be avoided at all costs. If the playfield gets crowded or a pathway is blocked, you may want to fire off a flash bomb to zap all the creatures at once, but you should do so only when absolutely necessary as flash bombs are limited in number.

To complete a stage, you must reach the exit at the end of the maze—it is not necessary to pick up all the treasures (though you will want to in order to boost your score). Prior to exiting, however, you must pick up one or more keys positioned at various points in the maze. You can only hold one key at a time, so backtracking is required, though not annoyingly extensive backtracking as in certain role-playing games—just minor, running-back-to-get-another-key backtracking. Passageways along certain maze walls let you "zip from one part of a chamber to another" (a la the escape tunnel in *Pac-Man*).

Archie moves quickly, which is a good thing. Not only does this help make the game breezy good fun, it lets him complete each maze within the time allotted. You don't die after the timer runs out, but you do run out of ammo (your ammo replenishes itself when you enter a new chamber). I usually play skill level one (of three—six if you count two-player alternating), and I never run out of time in this relatively easy mode, but the game does get pretty challenging for me after I've completed all 16 stages (the creatures get faster and are more plentiful).

Tutankham is somewhat similar to *Venture* (listed in "The Next 100" appendix near the back of this book). Both have fun, creature-shooting, treasure-grabbing action, but *Tutankham* doesn't suffer from the problematic controls

The back of the *Tutankham* box.

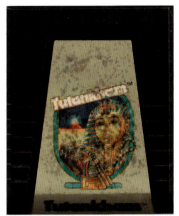

Tutankham game cartridge. $25.

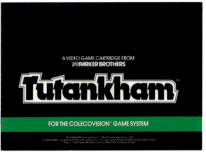

Tutankham instruction manual. $8.

found in *Venture*. *Tutankham* has the same up/down/right/left movement of such titles as *Pac-Man* and *Frogger*, but *Venture*, which has many rooms without maze walls, also lets you move diagonally. Unfortunately, moving diagonally is tough to pull off as the protagonist simply doesn't respond very well to diagonal joystick control.

Another advantage *Tutankham* enjoys over *Venture* (and over *Berzerk*, which no doubt inspired both titles) is its graphics. *Venture* is a cute game, but the chamber walls are simple lines, which is in stark contrast to the craggy, detailed walls found in *Tutankham*. Also, there are more creatures onscreen at once in *Tutankham*, and they move more unpredictably and are more visually interesting. The treasures in *Tutankham* look nicer as well.

Tutankham is based on the arcade game of the same name, which Sega introduced in 1982 and Konami licensed later that same year. Designed by H. Tanigaki, the game was originally going to be called "Tutankhamen" (after the Egyptian pharaoh of the 18th dynasty), but the full name wouldn't fit on the arcade cabinet, so the title was shortened.

In an interview published in Van Burnham's *Supercade: A Visual History of the Videogame Age 1971-1984* (2001, MIT Press), video game scorekeeper and ambassador to the industry, Walter Day, revealed that *Tutankham* is one of his three favorite arcade games of all time (*Make Trax*, for which he once held the world record, and *Centipede* are the others).

I recently emailed Walter to ask him why *Tutankham* appealed to him so much. His response was, "I liked the mysterious theme: exploring a forbidden temple and facing supernatural dangers. Essentially, the game casts the player in the role of Indiana Jones. I loved it." (*Raiders of the Lost Ark*, which was the first Indiana Jones movie, debuted in theaters the year before *Tutankham* hit the arcades.)

In *Electronic Games* magazine #8 (Oct., 1982), Bill Kunkel, in the "Insert Coin" column, espoused his appreciation for the arcade version of *Tutankham*, pointing out the game's "exotic setting, eye-pleasing graphics, and perfectly complementary audio." He also said, "For a game with a different look and lots of familiar play elements, this is as good as they come."

Of course, the original *Tutankham* has some relatively minor features that the ColecoVision port lacks, including a nifty title screen with creature/point identifiers and a *Defender*-like radar at the top of the screen showing the whole maze. In addition, the scrolling is smooth, and Archie, the creatures, and the maze walls are more colorful. Luckily, the ColecoVision port still looks fantastic and maintains most of the fun.

Parker Brothers also ported *Tutankham* to the Intellivision. That version lacks some of the fine graphical detail of the ColecoVision game, and I don't like the color scheme—the dark blue background with the light blue walls is a distraction, as is the green in the second level. In addition, the action moves at a slower pace. However, the game scrolls smoothly and is fairly enjoyable.

The Atari 2600 port, on the other hand, is a wreck. It's not entirely unplayable, but you can only shoot when pushing the joystick, the sound effects are annoying, and the control scheme makes it easy to waste flash bombs.

FUN FACT:
The coin-op version of *Tutankham* appeared on the *Konami Classics Series: Arcade Hits* (2007) collection for the Nintendo DS, but the name of the game was changed to *Horror Maze*.

WHY IT MADE THE LIST:
Like *Lady Bug*, *Pepper II*, and *Mr. Do!*, *Tutankham* is a marvelous ColecoVision maze game (a maze shooter with adventure elements in this case) that has held up remarkably well. It remains fun, and it still presents a challenge after all these years.

CHAPTER 95

VIDEO OLYMPICS

ATARI 2600
GENRE: BALL-AND-PADDLE
PUBLISHER: ATARI
DEVELOPER: ATARI
1-4 PLAYERS (SIMULTANEOUS)
1977

Video Olympics for the Atari 2600, complete in box. Courtesy of AtariAge.com. $12.

"VIDEO OLYMPICS FEATURES SIX TYPES OF SIMPLISTIC BALL-AND-PADDLE CONTESTS."

With the lofty title of *Video Olympics*, you may think that this cartridge is similar to *Summer Games* or *Winter Games*, giving players an assortment of running, jumping, skiing, and skating simulations. Or, judging by the box art, you might assume the game consists of simulations of such sports as basketball, hockey, soccer, and tennis.

You'd be wrong. The Sears release of *Video Olympics* is called *Pong Sports*, which is a better descriptor of the game. *Video Olympics* features six types of simplistic ball-and-paddle contests: *Pong*, Soccer, Foozpong, Hockey, *Quadrapong*, Handball, Volleyball, and Basketball, each of which features several variations.

As most everyone on the planet knows, *Pong* is essentially an early version of video tennis, with each player maneuvering a paddle up and down their side of the horizontal playfield, rebounding a bouncing ball off the paddle, trying to "avoid missing ball for high score" (to quote the original 1972 arcade version of *Pong*'s simple instructions).

Robot Pong lets players challenge the computer (the only one-player variation in the cartridge) while Pong 4 and Pong 4-1 offer four-player action similar to doubles tennis. In Super Pong, each player controls two paddles.

In Soccer, instead of blank space behind your paddle, there's a goal in the middle of a wall. Of course, the ball must go in the goal for the opposite player to score a point. Foozpong is similar to Soccer, but has more paddles (think foosball). Hockey is similar to Soccer and Foozpong, but each goal is moved away from the wall, meaning the ball can bounce behind the goal.

Quadrapong, based on the 1974 Atari arcade game, is recommended for four players and features four Soccer-type goals: one on each end and one at the top and bottom of the screen. *Warlords* fans will enjoy this variation.

In Handball, each player's paddle moves along the same side of the screen. As the manual states, "If you hit the ball out of turn (when your paddle is blinking), your opponent scores one point."

Volleyball has each player guiding a paddle along the bottom of the playfield, one on either side of a net. The net is viewed from the side, and players must return the ball over the net. During doubles play, "the second player on each team will cover the upper portion of the playfield with a smaller paddle."

In Basketball, each player controls a paddle that maneuvers along one half of the bottom of the screen, one player on the left, one on the right. As the ball bounces around the playfield, players try to rebound the ball off their

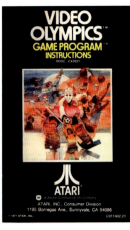
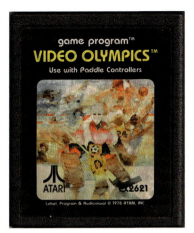

Atari 2600 paddle controllers. $15.

Video Olympics instruction manual. $2.

Video Olympics game cartridge. $5.

paddle and into the opponent's goal, which is a line near the top of the screen. The player on the right shoots for goal on the left while the player on the left aims for the goal on the right. Along with Volleyball, Basketball is easily the weakest game in the bunch, deviating from the formula too much and making luck too important of a factor.

Depending on the game and variation selected in *Video Olympics*, the red fire button on the paddle controller adds speed to the ball (Speed), puts sharper angles on return hits (Whammy), makes the ball stick to the paddle (Catch), or makes the paddle jump to hit or spike the ball (Jump).

So, you may be wondering, how can a game that is nothing more than *Pong* variations be listed among the 100 greatest games, alongside such revolutionary titles as *Pitfall!* and *Super Mario Bros.*? The answer is as simple as the game itself. Thanks to Atari's rotary controllers, which provide smooth, quick, precise paddle movement, and to the timeless nature of *Pong*, which, like *Combat* and *Warlords*, provides pure, competitive simultaneous action, *Video Olympics* simply had to make the cut.

When *Ken Uston's Guide to Buying and Beating the Home Video Games* was published by Signet in 1982, *Pong* was already a decade old, and many considered the game to be an outdated relic that was too primitive to still be fun (trust me, I was there when people were saying that). However, Uston still enjoyed the game, calling *Video Olympics* "a colorful, fast-moving *Pong* game with nice sound effects" and a must-own cartridge that "can provide hours of video game enjoyment, for the solitary player or for groups alike."

In Craig Kubey's *The Winners' Book of Video Games* (1982, Warner Books), however, the author is unforgiving of *Video Olympics*' hyperbolic title, saying: "The games in this cartridge are about as similar to the true diversity, athletic excellence, and thrills of the Olympics as the Des Moines City Council is like the United Nations." Kubey also compared playing the game's many variations to completing "a slow reading of the Budapest phone directory."

Joe Decuir programmed *Video Olympics*, which was a launch title with the 2600 console, but he hesitates in taking too much credit for the game. In an interview published on www.digitpress.com, he told Atari 2600 historian Scott Stilphen that he "took *Pong* as someone else's game, implemented it on Stella [an early working name for the 2600] as a test case, and then went off and invented a lot of variations to complete the cartridge. [Head engineer] Bob Brown allowed me to stop at 50 variations."

As I implied earlier, *Video Olympics* will strike some readers as an odd choice for inclusion in this book. It's primitive, it doesn't do much more than the old dedicated *Pong* consoles (and *Pong* clones), and it lacks the graphical sophistication of some of the games that were relegated to "The Next 100" honorable mentions section at the back of this book, such as *Alex Kidd in Miracle World*, *Missile Defense 3-D*, *Phaser Patrol*, and *Venture*.

However, the pure, unadulterated, highly competitive nature of *Pong*'s various two-player modes is strong enough to make *Video Olympics* one of *The 100 Greatest Console Video Games: 1977-1987*.

FUN FACT:

Video Olympics was one of nine original launch titles released concurrently with the Atari VCS (later called the Atari 2600).

WHY IT MADE THE LIST:

Although it contains nothing more than *Pong* variations, *Video Olympics* is a standout title in the Atari 2600 library, thanks to the timeless nature of trying to "avoid missing ball for high score."

CHAPTER 96

WARLORDS

ATARI 2600
GENRE: BALL-AND-PADDLE
PUBLISHER: ATARI
DEVELOPER: ATARI
1-4 PLAYERS (SIMULTANEOUS)
1981

Warlords for the Atari 2600, complete in box. $12.

"SOME OF THE BEST PARTY-STYLE, FOUR-PLAYER GAMING EVER CREATED, REGARDLESS OF THE ERA."

Like many Atari 2600 games with a coin-op cousin, *Warlords* invents a backstory and features painted box art that bears little (make that no) resemblance to the actual game. In this case, a king named Frederick has quarrelsome quadruplets, each of whom establishes a kingdom in a faraway land. Said kingdoms are engaged in constant battle. The cover art shows a knight wielding a sword, with a catapult in action transposed over his torso.

In reality, the game is a top-down hybrid of *Quadrapong* (a four-player *Pong* sequel released in 1974) and *Breakout* (1976). While this concoction isn't as romantic conceptually as the deceptive story and art combo, it makes for a potent, engaging, thoroughly entertaining game.

Each player controls a paddle-like shield that protects one of the warlords positioned in the four corners of the screen. Surrounding each warlord is a brick castle. By using a paddle controller, each player maneuvers his or her shield around their castle perimeter, protecting it from a ricocheting fireball (slow) or lightning ball (fast).

If the player misses the ball, it can destroy castle bricks. If the ball makes it past the paddle and the depleted brick wall and hits the player's warlord contained within the castle, that player is defeated. The last warlord standing wins the round. The first person or computer player to win five rounds wins the game.

As with *Breakout*, *Super Breakout*, and *Kaboom!*, *Warlords* is an excellent fit for the Atari 2600. The system's paddle controllers operate the shields quickly and smoothly, giving players the arcade experience at home. Since two paddles plug into one control port, four-player action is possible (not to mention highly recommended).

The arcade version of *Warlords*, which Atari released in 1980, has better graphics (textured castle walls, a lighted/mirrored background, warlords represented by a crown or a death mask) than the simple looking 2600 cartridge (which isn't much more sophisticated in appearance than *Breakout*), but both versions represent some of the best party-style, four-player gaming ever created, regardless of the era.

At the 2007 Classic Gaming Expo, a sit-down cocktail version of the *Warlords* arcade game was set on free play, and one of the highlights of the convention was playing that game against other convention attendees.

Medieval Mayhem (2006), an expertly programmed Atari 2600 homebrew updating of *Warlords*, was a tournament game at the 2010 Classic Gaming Expo; I didn't win the tournament, but I had a blast trying. One cool aspect of *Medieval Mayhem* and *Warlords* is the tendency for players to team up against the gamer who is winning, meaning alliances are formed and broken in decidedly dynamic fashion.

Warlords in action. *Courtesy of AtariAge.com.*

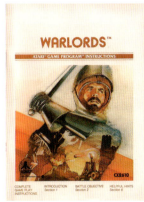
Warlords instruction manual. $2.

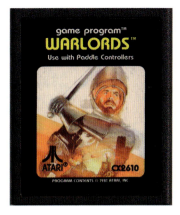
Warlords game cartridge. $5.

In issue #1 (summer, 1983) of the British publication, *TV Gamer*, the writer warned readers not to dismiss 2600 *Warlords* before sitting down to actually play it: "At first glance this game looks a bit crude and simple, but it's worth pursuing. It's a fast-moving, all action cartridge with some nice graphic touches."

In *Playboy's Guide to Rating the Video Games* (1982, PBJ Books), author Walter Lowe, Jr. gave the game four (out of five) stars, saying: "Four-person games are particularly fun because of the total unpredictability on all sides. Quick reflexes are required, and the game responds well to you." He also complimented the game's visuals. "The castles are colored in various russet hues ranging from orange to deep red," he said. "Each shield is a different color, and the color of the warlords corresponds to the color of the shields (yellow, blue, green, and brown)."

In *Ken Uston's Guide to Buying and Beating the Home Video Games* (1982, Signet), the author wrote: "This game is an imaginative combination of *Breakout* and *Pong*. The screen is colorful, the game has a fun-to-play 'catch' option…players may well find this game somewhat addicting."

An engineer named Carla Meninsky, who was one of precious few females programming video games during the early 1980s, designed the Atari 2600 version of *Warlords*. In an interview conducted by Will Nicholes (willnicholes.com), Ms. Meninsky made the following claim: "I would like to set the record straight here—I did the 2600 game before the coin-op game even existed! I think that was the first time a coin-op game derived from the console game."

Meninsky's cartridge-based creation has three main variations: number of players—one, two, three four, or doubles (two players each control two shields); ball speed (fireball slow or lightning ball fast); and ricochet or catch, in which the player's shield either automatically ricochets the ball when hit, or catches the ball when the fire button is being held down—releasing the button sends the ball back into play at a high speed.

In *Game Informer* #100 (Aug., 2001), *Warlords* was voted the 25th greatest game of all time. Here's the *Warlords* entry from that issue:

It isn't pretty, even by Atari 2600 standards, but *Warlords* was the original trash-talking four-player combat game, and it's still the best. The goal of the game is simple: maneuver your shield so the ball destroys other players' walls while protecting your own. With a paddle in everyone's hand, however, *Warlords* quickly transforms from a simple *Pong/Breakout* hybrid into a nerve-wracking fight to the finish. Fast and visceral, *Warlords* is as addicting now as it was 20 years ago.

And it's still addicting and fun here in 2014.

Warlords for the arcade and Atari 2600 are available on various compilation discs for modern systems, including *Atari Anthology* (2004) for the PlayStation 2 and Xbox.

Atari Anniversary Edition (2001) for the Dreamcast and *Atari Anniversary Edition Redux* (2001) for the PlayStation contain the arcade game.

In 2008 and 2012, different updated/remade versions of *Warlords* were released for the Xbox 360 via Xbox Live Arcade. The 2012 version also hit the PlayStation 3 via the PlayStation Network.

In 2010, Microsoft made arcade *Warlords* and 2600 *Warlords* available for the Xbox 360 Game Room service.

FUN FACT:

In 2004, a homebrew clone of *Warlords* called *Castle Crisis* was produced for the Atari 5200 and Atari 8-bit computers.

WHY IT MADE THE LIST:

Whether played in the arcades or at home, *Warlords* is one of the best four-player party games of all time.

CHAPTER 97

WEB WARS

VECTREX
GENRE: VERTICAL SCROLLING SHOOTER
PUBLISHER: GCE
DEVELOPER: GCE
1 OR 2 PLAYERS (ALTERNATING)
1982

Web Wars for the Vectrex, complete in box. $70.

"IT PRESENTS A FORMIDABLE CHALLENGE, BUT IT'S ALSO FUN TO PLAY."

A cartridge that *Electronic Games* magazine co-founder Joyce Worley once called a "virtuoso piece of programming" and a "habit-forming game that shows off the Vectrex video game system to best advantages" (May, 1984 issue), *Web Wars* borrows from *Tempest* (the web looks something like levels eight and nine of *Tempest*), but adds a nifty, ahead-of-its-time feature of its very own: the ability to collect creatures.

Players control the Hawk King, who, viewed from behind, flies down a 3D-esque tunnel called the Web of Fantasy. Pressing left and right on the joystick maneuvers the Hawk King in those directions while pushing forward accelerates and pulling back slows him down.

As you maneuver the Hawk King through the tunnel, squadrons of guardian Drones will appear, and they should be shot or, at the very least, avoided. Several Drones can appear within the web at once, and the shooting is rapid fire (holding down the button shoots continual bullets), so the action gets pretty intense at times.

If you avoid a Drone, it will return to follow you at a greater speed than when it passed you by. You have the option of slowing down to let it get in front of you again, or you can speed past it. The faster you are flying when you destroy a Drone, the more points you will score.

Also populating the Web of Fantasy, which Worley called "a masterful piece of design work, twisting and turning like it's alive," are creatures that appear one at a time. Utilizing an unusual device called a "capture rod," players should grab (stab?) the creatures when they get close. Doing so makes a square portal appear a short time later. Flying through the portal leads to the Trophy Room, where you will deposit the creature, and where you will hear the first seven notes of Norwegian composer Edvard Grieg's "In the Hall of the Mountain King."

There are 20 creatures in all, each with a different design.

If you miss the portal twice in a row or fail to capture a particular type of creature twice, a dangerous, nicely rendered Cosmic Dragon will appear in the distance. As it draws near, it will shoot fireballs directly toward you. You can't destroy this deadly enemy, but, if you move quickly, you can avoid the fireballs. Each time the Cosmic Dragon appears, it will shoot a greater number of fireballs more accurately.

Programmed by William Hawkins, Duncan Muirhead, and Patrick King, *Web Wars* sounds fairly complex on paper, but after you play it a few times, you should get the hang of it. It presents a formidable challenge, but it's also fun to play.

In a Vectrex history article featured on the GameFaqs website (www.gamefaqs.com), a writer with the user name of "Wyrdwad" said *Web Wars* was "a lot of fun" and "definitely the coolest looking Vectrex game," referring in part to the "camera angle that's constantly shifting in very subtle ways."

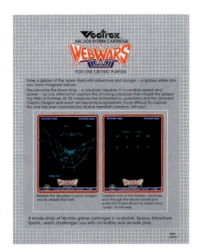 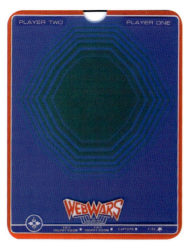 

The back of the *Web Wars* box.   *Web Wars* screen overlay: $15   Catalogue ad for various Vectrex titles, including *Web Wars*.

He also called the game "a great, fast-paced shooter with a really stylish look to it that only the Vectrex could pull off."

In a review published on digitpress.com, noted collector Al Backiel said *Web Wars* "was for many years the closest you could get to the arcade game T*empes*t on a home system" and that it "didn't get the promotion it deserved." Discussing the trophy room, he said, "This was the hook for me. I wanted to see what all of the different bug trophies looked like."

Regrettably, Backiel only saw half of the creatures. "This game gets so fast that it becomes an incredible challenge to get all of the trophies," he said. "I got as far as 10 out of 20 and 23,369 points. It is possible to get more points by staying on the early screens longer and dodging the flying dragon, but I'd rather be an entomologist than a miser."

The Video Game Critic (videogamecritic.com) called *Web Wars* a "*Tempest* lookalike [that] won me over on the strength of its arresting visuals and formidable challenge." He also said the game has a nice "one more time quality" and that the "collection element is a neat idea." However, he did point out that "the collision detection becomes erratic as the pace picks up," which is definitely something I noticed.

In fact, it's my only complaint about the game.

FUN FACT:

The European release of *Web Wars* is called *Web Warp*.

WHY IT MADE THE LIST:

An intense, good looking shooter, *Web Wars* combines creature-collecting with *Tempest*-like gameplay, making it one of the top titles in the Vectrex library.

CHAPTER 98

WORM WHOMPER

INTELLIVISION
GENRE: NON-SCROLLING SHOOTER
PUBLISHER: ACTIVISION
DEVELOPER: CHESHIRE ENGINEERING
1 OR 2 PLAYERS (ALTERNATING)
1983

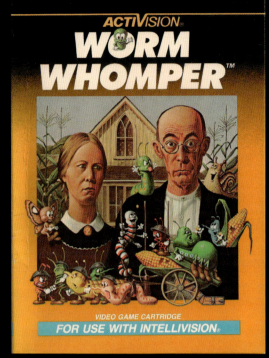

Worm Whomper for the Intellivision, complete in box. $125.

"A GREAT "PANIC GAME," FORCING PLAYERS TO PUT OUT METAPHORICAL FIRES ALL OVER THE SCREEN."

Designed by Tom Loughery, who also created *The Dreadnaught Factor* (found in "The Next 100" appendix near the back of this book), *Worm Whomper* is like *Centipede* turned on its side, with some *Missile Command* elements thrown in for good measure.

Players guide Farmer Felton Pinkerton as he runs around his farm, spraying pesticide (shooting, in other words) to the right at 12 types of pesky pests that enter the screen from the right edge of the playfield and make their way to the left. Said varmints include inchworms, horned caterpillars, snails, millipedes, banana slugs, green moths, white moths, slithering cornsnakes, big brown moths, ravenous red slugs, big black snails, and giant purple moths. Each enemy type has a specific look, point value, and number of sprays—ranging from one to seven—needed to kill it.

Pinkerton's job is to protect two rows of golden corn (five corn plants per row) positioned along the left side of the screen. When touched by any pest other than a moth or an inchworm, a corn plant will shrink, wither, and die. When an inchworm reaches a corn plant, the plant will change color from yellow to brown. A second touch by an inchworm will result in the plant's demise. Once all the corn plants are gone, the game will end (similar to the cities in *Missile Command*).

If an enemy other than an inchworm touches Pinkerton's spray gun, the weapon will disintegrate. Luckily, there's a tool shed at the bottom of the screen that, when touched, will rearm Pinkerton with a new gun. Standard pesticide spray has unlimited firing, but plough balls, which will eliminate every pest in their path (including otherwise unbeatable snail shells and slime trails), are limited in nature (though more plentiful than special weapons in most other video games).

Worm Whomper, which requires a pleasing mix of short, incremental movements and long, faster movements (to reach encroaching bugs farther away from the farmer), is a great "panic game," forcing players to put out metaphorical fires all over the screen. After the first few rounds, the enemies come in droves, and it's a blast (literally and figuratively) to try to keep them from reaching the corn.

It's cool that Pinkerton is armed with lots of powerful plough balls to help keep the field clear, and that he must occasionally (or frequently, depending on the player and the level) run like crazy to the shed to grab another spray can. It's also cool (and strategically important) that the larger, tougher pests move faster and more erratically than the weaker, smaller ones (which are more ubiquitous). It gets

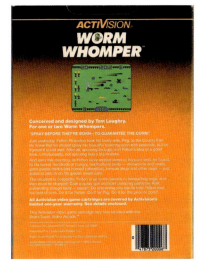  

The back of the *Worm Whomper* box.   *Worm Whomper* keypad overlay. $5.   *Worm Whomper* game cartridge. $25.

especially exciting when there are only one or two corn plants left to protect.

One of the biggest *Worm Whomper* fans appears to be Digital Press (digitpress.com) owner Joe Santulli, who, in issue #19 (May/June, 1994) of his fanzine, called it a "must-play." Three years before that, in the "Closet Classics" column of issue #1 (Sept./Oct. 1991), Santulli and former DP partner Kevin Oleniacz (may he rest in peace) called it "intense," "a real classic," and "one of the best games ever produced for the system."

Another noteworthy fan of the game is *Dragster* (1980, Atari 2600) world record holder Todd Rogers, who once played *Worm Whomper* 72 hours straight. "It got to the point that I had to change the TV screen to black-and-white because of that 'pukey' green color," he said, laughing. "At 26 million points, right after I took a Polaroid of the screen, my friend David Salazar bumped the TV/computer box and my game was lost…what a story!"

In terms of contemporary reviews, Craig Holyoak, writing in the March, 1984 issue of *Electronic Fun with Computers and Games*, nailed the greatness of the game, calling it "fresh, entertaining, and tailor made for the Intellivision's style of graphics and disk controller."

In *Electronic Games* magazine #26 (July, 1984), the late, great Bill Kunkel called *Worm Whomper* "the sort of high-speed action-arcade game they said could never be programed on the highly eccentric Intellivision…whimsically conceived, visually adorable, and a genuine delight to play."

In *Video Games* #17 (Feb., 1984), Mark Brownstein said *Worm Whomper* is "good, cute fun" and a "good addition" to the Intellivision library. He also said it is "nice to see that there are still companies making games for the Intellivision."

Indeed, thanks to its frantic pace, rapid-fire shooting action, sharp look, and console-fitting gameplay mechanics, *Worm Whomper* for the Intellivision is the best shooter for the system and one of the best shooters of the era. Plus, it's got cool box art—an amusing, bug-ridden riff on Grant Wood's classic painting, *American Gothic* (1930).

I didn't own *Worm Whomper* until sometime in the mid-to-late 2000s, when I bought a copy at a Classic Gaming Expo in Las Vegas from co-organizer Sean Hardy, who was selling a variety of games, along with copies of his Vectrex multi-cart (which I also bought). *Worm Whomper*, one of the less common Intellivision titles, was factory sealed and only $7—a real bargain, especially considering the fact that I still play the game on occasion.

FUN FACT:

When Tom Loughery, who Dave Rolfe once called "the best game designer I've ever worked with" (www.gooddealgames.com/interviews/int_rolfe.html), programmed *Worm Whomper*, he was working for Cheshire Engineering, a company contracted by Activision to develop *Beamrider*, *The Dreadnaught Factor*, and, of course, *Worm Whomper*.

WHY IT MADE THE LIST:

Although it borrows from *Centipede* and *Missile Command*, *Worm Whomper* has enough differences to make it stand out. Plus, it's the best shooter for the Intellivision.

CHAPTER 99

YARS' REVENGE

ATARI 2600
GENRE: NON-SCROLLING SHOOTER
PUBLISHER: ATARI
DEVELOPER: ATARI
1 OR 2 PLAYERS (ALTERNATING)
1981

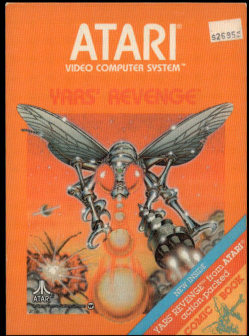

Yars' Revenge for the Atari 2600, complete in box. Courtesy of AtariAge.com. $10.

"REQUIRES MORE STRATEGY AND PLANNING THAN IS FOUND IN MOST SHOOTERS OF THE ERA."

Yars' Revenge is an odd game that is difficult to describe. However, it's one of the best, most fondly remembered titles for the Atari 2600, so it's worth examining in some detail.

Players control a Yar, which is a "fly simulator" that can maneuver and shoot energy missiles up, down, left, right, and diagonally, all around the screen. On the right side of the playfield is a stationary Qotile base that must be destroyed. The Qotile is protected by a vertical shield in the shape of an arch or a shifting rectangle. To clear a path to the Qotile, players must shoot and/or nibble through the shield, which disappears incrementally with each hit absorbed.

Once a pathway to the Qotile has been cleared, a standard shot to the Qotile will not destroy it. Rather, players must call upon the Zorlon Cannon (a fireball) by nibbling a portion of the shield or by making direct contact with the Qotile. The Zorlon Cannon, when it appears, will be on the left side of the screen and will, prior to being fired, move up and down in direct line with the Yar.

A simple press of the joystick button fires the Zorlon Cannon (which shoots in a straight line to the right), but players should get out of the way to avoid getting hit. If the Zorlon Cannon hits the Qotile, the screen erupts with a dazzlingly colorful explosion. Then it's time to repeat the process.

To make the game a challenge, the Qotile shoots two types of weapons: destroyer missiles, which appear constantly (one at a time) and move slowly; and swirls, which appear infrequently, wind up, and rush quickly toward the Yar. Both should be avoided at all costs.

Another key element of the game is the Neutral Zone, which is a wide, colorful, glittering vertical stripe near the center of the screen. While in the visually stunning Neutral Zone, the Yar cannot shoot, nor can it be harmed by a destroyer missile. However, it can be eliminated by a swirl.

The best-selling original first-party Atari 2600 game of all time ("original" meaning not based on an arcade game), *Yars' Revenge* was developed by Howard Scott Warshaw, the man responsible for the largely derided *E.T. The Extra-Terrestrial* and the adventurous *Raiders of the Lost Ark*. The name "Yar" is Ray spelled backwards, referring to Ray Kassar, who was president and CEO of Atari at the time.

According to an Atari Times (www.ataritimes.com) interview, Warshaw was the next Atari programmer in line to get an assignment, and management wanted a *Star Castle* clone (*Star Castle* was Cinematronics '1980 arcade semi-classic). "I analyzed the game [*Star Castle*] and found what I thought was fun about it," Warshaw said. "I reconfigured it and made a few modifications in a way that would work on the 2600. And they [management] were cool about it because there weren't too many arcade hits at the time and *Star Castle* wasn't all that."

According to *Atari Inc.—Business is Fun* (2012, Syzygy Press Company Press), *Yars' Revenge* "almost didn't make it out of Atari" because Director of Game Development Steve Wright "hated it, insisting there was something wrong with it… Steve tried to kill off *Yars'* by pitting it against the forthcoming home version of *Missile Command*. The plan backfired, and *Yars'* ended up testing with an average of 4.5, rating it as one of the highest play-tests Atari ever did and ensuring its release."

Yars' Revenge instruction manual. $2.

Yars' Revenge comic book. $2.

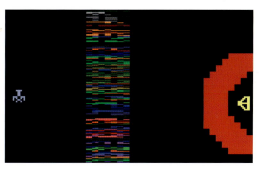
Yars' Revenge in action. Courtesy of AtariAge.com.

The book also points out some of the game's unusual (for the time) features, including its "pause between game levels" and its "full-screen death sequence explosion."

Yars' Revenge, which was originally packaged with a comic book (a first for the industry) produced by DC Comics, is one of the Atari 2600 titles I still play on a regular basis, thanks to its originality and fun factor. The fly simulator moves quickly and efficiently, making for a fast and enjoyable game to control. There's no real reason to shoot to the left, but destroying the Qotile requires more strategy and planning than is found in most shooters of the era.

Clearly, I'm far from the only video game journalist/reviewer who feels that *Yars' Revenge* is a key title in the Atari 2600 library.

In *Ken Uston's Guide to Buying and Beating the Home Video Games* (1982, Signet), the author cited the game's "superior graphics" and addictive nature. Walter Lowe Jr., in *Playboy's Guide to Rating the Video Games* (1982, PBJ Books), gave the game four-and-a-half out of five stars, praising its intellectual challenge (relatively speaking), long-term entertainment value, hand-eye-coordination challenge, and visual attractiveness.

Bill Kunkel and Arnie Katz, in their "Programmable Parade" column in *Electronic Games* #8 (Oct., 1982), said that *Yars' Revenge* "misses greatness by an eyelash" and that it "isn't quite as exciting as it could be," but that "many gamers are sure to greatly enjoy it."

In *Video Games* #2 (Oct., 1982), the opinion on the game is mixed as well. The writer said the action is repetitious, but that the game has "fine graphics and sound effects."

In issue #1 (Summer, 1983) of the British publication, *TV Gamer*, the reviewer commented on the fact that *Yars' Revenge* was one of the few sci-fi titles from Atari that was not previously an arcade game: "It's a pleasant change to discover an original space game, and even better to find one as good as this."

More recently, The Video Game Critic (www.videogamecritic.com) called *Yars' Revenge* a "real gem" and said that it "provides a level of strategy and challenge you don't see in many Atari 2600 games." Earl Green, via www.thelogbook.com, referred to *Yars' Revenge* as "a brilliant arcade-style game" and "one of the coolest gamers ever conceived of for the Atari 2600."

Joe Santulli, who runs www.digitpress.com, appreciates the timeless appeal of *Yars' Revenge*. "No matter how complex games get today," Santulli said, "very few reach the level of pure entertainment *Yars' Revenge* or others in its era achieved. With only one screen, seven objects, and solid programming, Howard Scott Warsaw created what I believe to be his masterpiece."

In an interview conducted by Darrin Powell for *Classic Gamer Magazine* #2 (winter, 1999-2000), Warshaw revealed why he believes the game looks and plays as well as it does: "The reason everything came together in *Yars' Revenge* is because it has an up-down, left-right thing. You have a vertical axis and a horizontal axis going simultaneously in the game, which I think makes things visually compelling…and I put in the full-screen explosion because I wanted there to be a big payoff."

In terms of audio effects, the near-constant buzzing sound in *Yars' Revenge* may prove annoying to some (including me), but many fans of the game feel differently. The Video Game Critic, for example, said, "The ominous pulsating background 'music' is simply brilliant."

If you don't have an Atari 2600 (or even if you do have one), you can play *Yars' Revenge* on the PS2 or Xbox (2004, *Atari Anthology*), the PSP (2007, *Atari Classics Evolved*), or the Xbox 360 (via XBLA). In 2010, Microsoft made *Yars' Revenge* available as a downloadable title for the Xbox 360 Game Room service.

In 1999, Telegames released a Game Boy Color remake of *Yars' Revenge*, complete with enhanced graphics, 250 levels of play, passwords for saving progress, and a scrolling, high-speed chase through a dangerous asteroid field.

FUN FACT:

Matt Fox, author of *The Video Games Guide* (2006, Boxtree), gave the game only one star, saying: "*Yars' Revenge* is surprisingly well remembered and I can only assume that's down to the excellent box art, rather than the actual gameplay."

WHY IT MADE THE LIST:

Yars' Revenge is one of the most important and most enjoyable first-party games for the Atari 2600 not based on a coin-op title.

CHAPTER 100

ZAXXON

COLECOVISION
GENRE: VERTICAL SCROLLING SHOOTER
PUBLISHER: COLECO
DEVELOPER: COLECO
1 PLAYER
1983

Zaxxon for the ColecoVision, complete in box. Courtesy of Bryan C. Smith. $15.

"IT'S A GORGEOUS GAME THAT COMES ABOUT AS CLOSE AS YOU COULD POSSIBLY HOPE FOR FROM A CONSOLE OF THE ERA."

Like *Miner 2049er*, *Zaxxon* retailed for $50 when it first hit retail shelves. Most of the rest of the games in the ColecoVision library were $30. My funds were limited when those two games were released, so I didn't pick them up right away. Luckily, I had a friend who bought both of them, quickly became tired of them, and sold them to me used for $30 each.

Unlike my friend, I never grew tired of either title and still play them from time to time to this day. *Miner 2049er*'s high price was due in part to its length—11 levels of play. *Zaxxon*, on the other hand, commanded big bucks because of its breathtaking visuals. It doesn't perfectly mimic Sega's 1982 coin-op classic (it's slower and is missing a lot of the background detail, such as planets and floor markings), but it's a gorgeous game that comes about as close as you could possibly hope for from a console of the era.

The action in *Zaxxon* for the ColecoVision, which was programmed by Lawrence Schick, takes place across alien asteroid fortresses that you fly over while at the helm of a futuristic fighter. The manual calls the cartridge a "stunning 3D space game." It's not actually in three dimensions, but Schick did a nice job of recreating the isometric (three-quarters) perspective of the arcade original, which simulated 3D. (Historically, *Zaxxon* was the first coin-op game to boast isometric projection, and it was the first to be advertised on television—Paramount Pictures produced the ad at a cost of $150,000.)

As you pilot the fighter across each fortress, you'll fly through gaps in walls, dive down to shoot gun turrets, mobots, and base missiles, and climb and bank to avoid walls, turret blasts, and base missile explosions. Piloting along the floor is dangerous, but if you fly too high for too long (a scant few seconds), a missile that is tough to dodge or destroy will home in on your fighter. Plus, you need to shoot fuel tanks to keep the Fuel Remaining Indicator from becoming empty.

As your fighter climbs and dives, an altitude indicator will help you determine where the ship is in relation to your surroundings. Even so, as you approach a wall, it's a good idea to volley off a stream of shots to let you know if you are at the right altitude to pass through the oncoming gap in said wall.

After the second asteroid fortress, it's time to face the Robot Warrior, which has a missile cradled at its side. To destroy this boss-type character (a rarity for the era), players must shoot the missile "with two more shots than the number of the skill level (1, 2, 3, or 4) at which you are playing." You must work quickly to kill the Robot Warrior. As with most shooters of the time, *Zaxxon* ends only after all your ships have been eliminated. (For the record, I prefer playing skill level 3.)

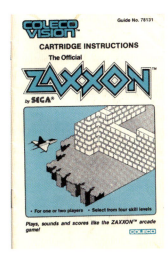
Zaxxon instruction manual. $2.

The back of the Zaxxon box. Courtesy of Bryan C. Smith.

Zaxxon game cartridge. $5.

Coleco also released *Zaxxon* for the Atari 2600 (1982) and the Intellivision (1983), but those versions are virtually unrecognizable as they scroll directly forward, with players viewing their fighter from behind. Altitude remains a factor, but the games are hopelessly un-*Zaxxon*-like, and they aren't particularly good entries in the vertical scrolling shooter genre either.

In 1984, Sega entered the home video game market and produced games for various consoles, including four titles for the Atari 5200: *Buck Rogers: Planet Of Zoom*, *Congo Bongo* (also sporting an isometric perspective), *Star Trek: Strategic Operations Simulator*, and *Zaxxon* (Sega got the rights back from Coleco to produce a home version).

The 5200 port, programmed by Ron J. Fortier, looks good and is highly collectible (it's hard to find and has beautiful box art), but it's missing ground-based rocket fire (despite box art that prominently shows just that). The action scrolls more smoothly than the Coleco game, but the controls aren't as good. Further, the 5200 version of the Robot Warrior is laughably small (but is still tough to destroy). Both games are quality shooters, but the ColecoVision version gets the nod and is the one I have played and enjoyed the most.

The coin-op version of *Zaxxon* was followed by a sequel, *Super Zaxxon*, which hit the arcades in 1982. *Super Zaxxon*, though nowhere near as popular as its progenitor, had superior graphics, and it replaced the outer space battle, where it was tough to judge your altitude, with a tunnel sequence. In addition, the Robot Warrior was supplanted by a fireball-breathing dragon.

Super Zaxxon was never ported to a classic console, though it was available for a variety of home computers. *Super Zaxxon* is playable on the go via the *Sega Genesis Collection* (2006) for the PSP, while regular *Zaxxon* is included in the PlayStation 2 version of the compilation. In 2010, *Zaxxon* was made available to Nintendo Wii owners via the Virtual Console.

Console sequels include the great *Zaxxon 3-D* (1988) for the Sega Master System, which would have been included in this book if it had come out a year earlier, and *Zaxxon's Motherbase 2000* (1995) for the 32X, an execrable, highly disappointing game plagued by sluggish controls, slowdown, blocky polygonal graphics, and annoyingly large bosses.

Getting back to *Zaxxon* for the ColecoVision, opinions are sometimes divided (a review on ultimateconsoledatabase.com calls it "crap," citing its choppy scrolling and slow gameplay), but most retroists can appreciate the quality of the game. For example, Jeff Irwin, writing for the All Game Guide (allgame.com), called it "arguably the best game ever released for the ColecoVision," referring to its "crisp, clear, and colorful visuals" and its "skillfully executed and innovative design."

When *Zaxxon* was new in stores, Arnie Katz and Bill Kunkel reviewed it in *Electronic Games* magazine #13 (March, 1983), calling the game's graphics "pretty incredible" and the game itself "the best home video game cartridge in the land."

A review published in *TV Gamer* #1 (summer, 1983) said, "This is the only game on the market that scrolls diagonally and Coleco has made a convincing job of it. The graphics and sound are superb. All in all, this is about the best video game translation from arcade to home so far produced."

FUN FACT:

The ColecoVision version of *Zaxxon* has a feature not found in the arcade classic: hemispherical robots that glide along the ground and fire at your ship.

WHY IT MADE THE LIST:

Visually, *Zaxxon* is one of the most sophisticated console games of its era. It's also a lot of fun to play.

APPENDIX

THE NEXT 100: HONORABLE MENTIONS

There were well over 200 legitimately great games published from 1977 through 1987, so I had to make some tough decisions regarding what to include in this book and what to leave out. To recognize some of the games that didn't quite make the cut (and to keep fans of these games from hating me too much), I decided to add a list of honorable mentions:

Alex Kidd in Miracle World (1986, Sega Master System): Although it has rock/paper/scissors for boss fights (a terrible idea), this side-scrolling platformer is a solid answer to Nintendo's *Super Mario Bros.* Before Sonic came along in 1989, Alex was the closest thing Sega had to a company Mascot.

Astroblast (1982, Atari 2600): This M Network version of the ubiquitous *Astrosmash* for the Intellivision benefits from paddle control, helping make it a better game than its more popular progenitor. *Astroblast* is a terrific slide-and-shoot game, but it's not as versatile as *Space Invaders* or *Communist Mutants from Space*.

Ballblazer (1985, Atari 5200; 1987, Atari 7800): Essentially split-screen soccer of the future, *Ballblazer* looks and sounds great. Not only is it futuristic thematically, it was ahead of its time in terms of gameplay and audio/visuals.

Battlezone (1983, Atari 2600): Based on the 1980 Atari arcade classic, *Battlezone* lacks the vector graphics and periscope viewer of the original game, of course, but it maintains the basic gameplay (despite the lack of barriers to hide behind). *Battlezone* was a huge influence on Activision's *Robot Tank*.

Beamrider (1984, ColecoVision): I'm not as fond of *Beamrider* as I am of such similar titles as *Phoenix* or *Space Invaders*, but it's a highly polished game that I still play from time to time. You move your ship along the bottom of a grid, firing at enemies with such names as green blockers, orange trackers, and red zig bombs. The action can be described as simplified *Tempest* turned into a slide-and-shoot game.

Bedlam (1982, Vectrex): A great reason to own a Vectrex, *Bedlam* is essentially *Tempest* turned inside out. The ship players control rotates on an invisible axis in the center of a star-shaped playfield and shoots outward at alien escort ships, astral defenders, destroyer droids, and colonist transports.

B-17 Bomber (1982, Intellivision): "Beeeeeseveeenteeeen Booommmberrrrr." As Intellivision apologists know, this is what the Intellivoice speech module sounds like when saying the title of this game, which has players flying a USAAF B-17 over World War II-era Europe, shooting and bombing enemies. A nostalgic favorite among longtime Intellivision fans.

Chopper Command (1982, Atari 2600): *Chopper Command* has sharp graphics, rock solid gameplay, and rapid-fire shooting, but it's not as deep as *Choplifter* or *Defender*. Some fans call the game "*Defender* in the Desert."

Commando (1986, NES): *Commando* is a solid port of the *Front Line*–influenced Data East arcade game (1985), despite flickering enemies and less detailed graphics. Interestingly, the protagonist, Super Joe, is seen eating food instead of smoking cigarettes while resting at the end of the first level (a concession to the family-friendly nature of the NES).

Double Dribble (1987, NES): A less colorful version of Konami's 1986 arcade cab, *Double Dribble* is a fun basketball game that I spent hours and hours playing back in the day. However, in the wake of such titles as *NBA Jam*, *NBA Street*, and *NBA 2K9*, it hasn't aged well enough to make it into the top 100 list.

Dragonfire (1982, Atari 2600; 1984, ColecoVision): *Dragonfire* is a gorgeous game with some good, twitchy action, with players running across a bridge and then around a room filled with treasures, but it doesn't quite rank among my favorites. The treasures look better in the 2600 game, but the ColecoVision version has better graphics overall, plus an exclusive treasure room troll in later levels.

The Dreadnaught Factor (1983, Atari 5200; 1983, Intellivision): The 5200 version of *The Dreadnaught Factor* scrolls vertically while the Intellivision game scrolls horizontally. Both are strategic, nicely programmed shooters with players aiming for specific targets on a huge dreadnaught ship.

Enduro (1983, Atari 2600): One of many quality titles from Activision, *Enduro* is a game that barely missed the main section of this book. Players race through rain, darkness, snow, and fog, trying to maintain high speeds while at the same time using precision controls to handle the car.

Entombed (1982, Atari 2600): Despite simplistic graphics and sounds, *Entombed* is an inventive maze game with forced scrolling, two-player cooperation, and the ability for players, as archeologists, to tear down and create walls. Getting trapped in "the catacombs of the zombies" can seem unfair at times, though.

Excitebike (1985, NES): A nice port of Nintendo's 1984 arcade game (sans the bonus rounds), *Excitebike* is a game I played many, many times when I first got my NES back in 1986. Players ride a motorcycle on a track that includes hills, obstacles, mud pits, and ramps, the latter of which are a blast to jump.

Fathom (1983, Atari 2600; 1983, ColecoVision): A highly original creation from Imagic, *Fathom* has players guiding Proteus, a member of Neptune's court, as he searches the skies and the sea for pieces of Neptune's broken trident. To achieve this, Neptune, who must also rescue Neptina, can turn into a seagull and a dolphin.

Fireball (1982, Atari 2600): Produced as a cassette for the Starpath Supercharger, *Fireball* borrows heavily from *Super Breakout* and *Circus Atari*, but instead of a paddle or a teeter totter, players control a juggler who can catch and hold several balls at once. A great ball-and-paddle game that almost made the top 100.

Fishing Derby (1980, Atari 2600): Designed by David "*Pitfall!*" Crane, this early fishing title is great fun, especially in two-player (simultaneous) mode. Each fisherman sits on an opposing dock, releasing their lines, hooking fish, and reeling them in.

Fortune Builder (1984, ColecoVision): A precursor to *SimCity*, *Fortune Builder* was ahead of its time, giving you control of undeveloped land where you can raise capital to build condos, malls, bridges, marinas, gas stations, and other businesses. Bad weather, workers going on strike, consumer trends, and other such factors are key elements in the game, which can be played solo or against a friend.

Frankenstein's Monster (1983, Atari 2600): One of the better horror-themed games of the Golden Age, *Frankenstein's Monster* is almost as much fun to lose as it is to play. If you fail at the climbing, jumping, platforming action, the Frankenstein monster will get loose and charge toward the screen, an extremely impressive visual effect.

Frogger II: Threeedeep! (1984, Atari 2600, Atari 5200, ColecoVision): *Frogger II* is a great game that expands upon the original in challenging and interesting ways. However, I wouldn't go as far as Ted Salamone, who, writing for *Electronic Games* magazine (March, 1985 issue), said it was more fun than *Frogger*.

Frogs and Flies (1982, Atari 2600): The M Network version of the Intellivision's *Frog Bog* (which was featured in the 2006 comedy film, *Grandma's Boy*), *Frogs and Flies* doesn't look quite as nice as *Frog Bog*, but it has better controls. Simplicity personified, the game has each player guiding a frog as it hops back and forth across a pair of giant lily pads, trying to catch flies with its tongue.

Frostbite (1983, Atari 2600): One of several Activision titles I hated to leave out of the main section of this book, *Frostbite* combines elements of *Frogger* and *Q*bert*. The game is less colorful than the average Activision cartridge, but it's a lot of fun.

Gauntlet (1987, NES): Although missing the famous (infamous?) voice effects ("Elf needs food badly"), *Gauntlet* for the NES keeps the four-player action of Atari's 1985 coin-op classic intact, but adds moving walls and 100 all-new levels. An excellent translation of a highly memorable arcade game.

Gorf (1983, ColecoVision): You won't find the voice effects or the Galaxians level from the 1981 Bally/Midway arcade original, but *Gorf* for the ColecoVison is nevertheless a fine port, clearly superior to the Atari 5200 version. (For an even better and more complete version of *Gorf*, check out the spectacular Game Boy Advance homebrew release from gooddealgames.com.)

Gunfight (1978, Astrocade): A colorized take on Midway's *Gun Fight* (1975), *Gunfight*, which is built into the *Astrocade* console, is similar to *Outlaw* for the Atari 2600, with each player guiding a cowboy around the screen, trying to shoot the other gunslinger. Like *Combat* and *Pong*, *Gunfight* is an early game that has held up incredibly well over time, giving players pure, competitive, two-player simultaneous action.

Happy Trails (1983, Intellivision): Designed by Carol "*River Raid*" Shaw, *Happy Trails* "made a lot of people at Mattel Electronics angry since they felt it was a rip-off of the Konami arcade game *Loco-Motion*, which Mattel had licensed for Intellivision; to add insult to injury, Activision released *Happy Trails* before Intellivision *Loco-Motion* came out. *Happy Trails* received reviews lauding its originality; *Loco-Motion* looked like an also-ran." (Quoted from www.intellivisionlives.com.)

Haunted House (1981, Atari 2600): A cartridge that many consider to be the first game in the survival horror genre, *Haunted House* is recommended for *Adventure* fans hankering for something creepier. Players guide a pair of eyes through a multi-screen mansion, avoiding creatures and using matches to light the way while searching for three pieces of a magical urn.

The Heist (1983, ColecoVision): Recommended for fans of such carts as *Keystone Kapers*, *Miner 2049er*, and *Pitfall!*, *The Heist* puts players in the role of Graham Crackers, jumping over alarms, gaps, and other obstacles while grabbing paintings in a 90-room museum. The game isn't as polished as the aforementioned titles, but its epic length and strategy-intensive action are impressive.

Ice Climber (1985, NES): A system launch title, *Ice Climber* was programmed by Kazuaki Morita, who would go on to work on various *Super Mario Bros.* and *Legend of Zelda* titles. The vertical scrolling action, which oozes old-school charm and challenges, has each player guiding an Eskimo up 32 platform-based mountains by jumping into ice block floors to create holes, avoiding creatures or bonking them with an ice hammer along the way.

Ice Hockey (1981, Atari 2600): A game that The Video Game Critic calls "quite possibly the best sports game ever produced for the Atari 2600," *Ice Hockey* is another winner from Activision. It has solid graphics, fast-paced gameplay, good passing (each gamer fields a team of two players), and angled shots (determined by where the puck hits the stick). Very good when played alone, but great when you are challenging another gamer.

Jumpman Junior (1984, ColecoVision): The sequel to *Jumpman*, a widely praised computer classic, *Jumpman Junior* is a great climbing game, barely missing the main section of this book. There are 12 screens (one more than the ColecoVision version of *Miner 2049er*) and eight selectable game speeds (I recommend #2).

Jungle Hunt (1983, ColecoVision): Taito's 1982 arcade classic, which has players controlling a jungle explorer who swims, runs up hills, and swings on vines, is represented extremely well on the ColecoVision. One disappointment, however, is the fact that the hero kissing the girl after rescuing her has been left out of this otherwise terrific port.

Kangaroo (1983, Atari 5200): All four screens are intact (unlike the 2600 game, which leaves out the third level), as is much of the fun and charm of Sun Electronics' 1982 arcade classic in this 5200 port of *Kangaroo*. It doesn't quite rank up there with *Donkey Kong*, *Miner 2049er*, or *Pick Axe Pete!*, but it's in the same league.

Keystone Kapers (1983, Atari 2600; 1984, ColecoVision): Using Matt Sennett's *Keystone Cops* series of silent films as inspiration, Garry Kitchen created *Keystone Kapers*, a great platformer with excellent graphics and tricky jumps. Players guide Keystone Kelly as he works his way up the floors of a department store, riding elevators and escalators, ducking under and jumping over obstacles, and trying to catch Harry Hooligan before he escapes via the building's roof.

Kid Niki: Radical Ninja (1987, NES): Ranked #49 on IGN's (ign.com) "Top 100 NES Games" list, *Kid Niki* is a short, but sweet port of Irem's 1986 arcade game. Players guide the spike-haired title character, clearly a "rad dude," through seven cute, cartoonish worlds, battling enemies with a spinning sword.

Lock 'N' Chase (1982, Intellivision): When *Lock 'N' Chase*, a terrific maze game, hit the Intellivision in 1982, I thought it was a welcome change of pace from all the sports and outer space titles. Lately, I've been playing an even better version of *Lock 'N' Chase* via *Data East Arcade Classics* (2010) for the Nintendo Wii (Data East released the arcade original in 1981).

Loco-Motion (1983, Intellivision): A slick port of the Konami arcade game (1981), which apparently inspired Carol Shaw to create *Happy Trails*, *Loco-Motion* is a deviously addicting puzzler in which gamers arrange square puzzle pieces sporting railroad track designs. The objective is to arrange the pieces to form complete tracks.

Lode Runner (1987, NES): The NES version of *Lode Runner* is a step down from the original computer version (1983), offering just 50 levels of play (as opposed to 150), but the climbing action remains solid. One disappointment is that you can't save the levels you edit.

Looping (1983, ColecoVision): An excellent port of Venture Line's 1981 arcade obscurity, *Looping* has you flying an airplane over a city and through a pipe maze, shooting such enemies and obstacles as balloons, bouncing balls, green droplets, and twinkle monsters. As the title suggests, the looping flight method makes the game highly unusual.

Maze Craze: A Game of Cops'n Robbers: (1978, Atari 2600): One of those great early two-player simultaneous games for the Atari 2600, *Maze Craze* is loaded with options, another hallmark of older 2600 titles. Thanks to a maze-generating algorithm, a new maze is in place each time you play.

MegaMania (1983, Atari 5200): This slide-and-shoot title from Activision doesn't quite rank up there with such greats as *Space Invaders* and *Communist Mutants from Space*, but it is an entertaining entry in the genre. The Atari 5200 version is a step up over the original 2600 game, thanks to graphics that actually let you know you are shooting at cookies, hamburgers, tires, and other seemingly random items.

Mike Tyson's Punch-Out!! (1987, NES): Re-released as *Punch-Out!!* after the licensing agreement with Tyson had expired, *Mike Tyson's Punch-Out!!* is based on Nintendo's *Punch-Out!* (1984) and *Super Punch-Out!!* (1985) arcade games. However, instead of the green wireframe look of the player's boxer (so you can see your opponent), the home game, a favorite among armchair pugilists, simply reduces the size of the boxer, whose nickname is "Little Mac."

Millipede (1984, Atari 2600): If trackball control for 2600 *Millipede* were as quick and responsive as the Atari arcade classic (1982), this game, which was the sequel to *Centipede* (1980), would have made the main section of this book. Regardless, it's still fun, fast-paced, and challenging, capturing the spirit of the original.

Missile Defense 3-D (1987, Sega Master System): A game volume seven of the *Digital Press Collector's Guide* (2002) calls "a marketing nightmare" because it requires two peripherals, the Sega Light Phaser gun and the SegaScope 3-D Glasses, *Missile Defense 3-D* boasts fun gameplay and excellent three-dimensional graphics. As nuclear missiles head for The Arctic, Space, The Eastern and Western Missile Bases, and The Eastern and Western Capitals, players shoot said missiles out of the air.

Montezuma's Revenge (1984, Atari 2600): This ahead-of-its time adventure platformer is a monumental feat on the Atari 2600, putting players in the Indiana Jones-like role of Panama Joe, who solves puzzles, rides conveyor belts, climbs ladders, jumps over fire pits, and much more. The 2600 game has better controls than the Atari 5200 and ColecoVision versions.

Moonsweeper (1983, ColecoVision): A gorgeous game and a nice upgrade over the Atari 2600 rendition, *Moonsweeper* for the ColecoVision will appeal to fans of such games as *Solaris* for the 2600 and *Buck Rogers* and *Star Wars: The Arcade Game* for the Atari 5200 and ColecoVision. Players land on the moon, fly along the surface and through accelerator rings, and shoot and avoid contact with comets, meteors, satellites, and the like.

Mountain King (1983, Atari 2600): A terrific action/adventure game, *Mountain King* is tailor-made for players who enjoy exploring virtual areas, in this case a large mountain. Gamers climb ladders, leap over gaps, walk across platforms, search for treasure, use a flashlight, avoid creatures, and listen for audio clues (a nice touch) hinting that items are nearby.

Ms. Candyman (1983, Astrocade): Called "one of the best independent cartridge games we've seen" in the Oct. 24, 1983 issue of the *Arcadian* newsletter (Vol. 5, No. 2), *Ms. Candyman* is a delightful maze game played on a grid, with arcaders guiding the title character around the screen, gobbling lifesavers while avoiding ghosts and goblins that roam the maze. Published by L&M Software and developed by Bit Fiddlers, *Ms. Candyman* is the sequel to the cassette-based *Candyman*.

Muncher (1983, Astrocade): A very nicely programmed *Pac-Man* clone, *Muncher* has a rather convoluted history that is covered nicely in volume seven of the *Digital Press Collector's Guide* (2002). The game was subject to litigation by Atari, which is why it was called *Muncher* instead of *Pac-Man* (though it was sold under the label name of "TEST PROGRAMME" through the Arcadian newsletter and as "DEMO" through another source).

Night Driver (1978, Atari 2600): Programmed by Rob Fulop (*Demon Attack*, *Space Invaders*), *Night Driver* is a nice, upgraded port of the 1976 coin-op game of the same name, which was the first arcade racer to offer a first-person perspective (not including electromechanical machines). The Atari 2600 cart, which is paddle controller compatible, adds color, oncoming cars, roadside trees and houses, and a crudely drawn player's car (as opposed to a blank box representing the car's width).

Oil's Well (1984, ColecoVision): I've spent many hours with this sensational maze title, which is based on the Commodore 64 game (which itself was patterned after a 1982 coin-op game called *Anteater*), and which barely missed the main section of this book. What makes the game stand out from the many character-based maze titles is that you guide a retractable drill tethered to a well by a pipe, although eating dots (oil pellets in this case) remains the objective.

Phaser Patrol (1982, Atari 2600): The pack in game with the Starpath Supercharger, *Phaser Patrol* is a first-person space combat simulator in which players select a space sector from a 36-sector grid and then guide a targeting sight around the screen, shooting alien ships. Keita Iida with Atari Gaming Headquarters and Dave "The Video Game Critic" Mrozek call *Phaser Patrol* the best 2600 game of its type (an opinion I share), ahead of *Star Raiders*, *Star Voyager*, and *Starmaster*.

Pitstop (1983, ColecoVision): Called "the driving game for purists" and "an exhilarating experience" (for those who own the driving module) by Will Richardson of *Electronic Games* magazine (Nov., 1984 issue), *Pitstop* is one of my favorite racing titles, barely missing the main section of this book. A nice mix of strategy and gearhead action.

Plaque Attack (1983, Atari 2600): *Plaque Attack* is one of those quirky, oddly themed 2600 carts that is so much fun to play (at least in short doses). Programmed by Steve Cartwright (*MegaMania*, *Seaquest*), the fast-paced action has players maneuvering a tube of toothpaste inside an open mouth, shooting at junk food to keep it from decaying (i.e. making contact with) the teeth.

Pole Position (1983, Atari 5200): The twisting, turning, racing action of *Pole Position* gives *Turbo* for the ColecoVision a run for its money, but it comes up just short of the main section of this book. It's a fine port of the 1982 Atari/Namco arcade classic, despite the expected concessions to the console format (in this case muted colors and explosions and seemingly slower car speeds).

Pressure Cooker (1983, Atari 2600): Another winner from Activision, this one programmed by Gary Kitchen of *Keystone Kapers* fame. The quick, pressure-packed (pun intended) action has cute, nicely detailed graphics, but demanding gameplay. Arcaders guide a chef as he assembles burgers on a conveyor belt, juggling up to three orders at once.

Q*bert (1983, ColecoVision): This excellent port of the 1982 Gottlieb arcade game may have made the main section of this book if I didn't spend more time these days playing *Q*bert* (1999) for the PlayStation and *Q*bert 3* (1992) for the Super Nintendo, both of which expand on the original concept, but keep the basic cube-hopping action intact. ColecoVision *Q*bert* is missing Sam and Wrong Way, but the game controls surprisingly well, even though it's recommended that you hold the controller diagonally.

Quick Step (1983, Atari 2600): *Quick Step* evokes *Q*bert* to some degree, but the fast, hugely entertaining two-player simultaneous action sets it apart. Instead of hopping on a pyramid of cubes, gamers jump on rectangular trampolines that scroll down the screen.

Rad Racer (1987, NES): Developed by Nasir Gebelli (programming), Hironobu Sakaguchi (design, supervision), and Nobuo Uematsu (music) of Square, each of whom would go on to work on *Final Fantasy*, *Rad Racer* is an excellent game that evokes Sega's *Out Run*. The cartridge originally came packaged with 3D glasses, and it spawned an NES sequel, *Rad Racer II* (1990).

Raid on Bungling Bay (1987, NES): This overhead view free-roaming shooter, based on Will "*SimCity*" Wright's first game (1984, Commodore 64), has players guiding a helicopter over a playfield comprised of 100 contiguous screens, shooting and bombing bombers, fighters, battleships, and tanks. Gamers must also protect aircraft carriers, land for repairs, and locate and destroy six secret weapons factories. Two-player simultaneous action lets a friend control enemy gun turrets.

RealSports Baseball (1983, Atari 5200): Far superior to the Atari 2600 game of the same name, *RealSports Baseball* for the 5200 is one of the better sports titles of the era, wowing gamers with detailed graphics and excellent controls. Whether it's your turn to pitch or bat, you'll have a great time playing the game, even if you are only a casual baseball fan.

Rescue on Fractalus (1985, Atari 5200): This first-person space shooter, which includes flight sim features and mission-based objectives, was ahead of its time, impressing gamers with randomly generated mountains to fly over. Developed by LucasFilm, the game has players shooting aliens and flying saucers and landing on the surface to rescue stranded pilots.

Rip Off (1982, Vectrex): A favorite among Vectrex owners, *Rip Off* is a quality title, but I don't like it as much as *Scramble*, *MineStorm*, *Web Wars*, or *Fortress of Narzod*, hence its relegation to honorable mention status instead of the main body of the book. It's a port of the first two-player coop arcade game, which Cinematronics released in 1980.

Robot Tank (1983, Atari 2600): Inspired by (but less complex than) Atari's *Battlezone*, *Robot Tank* was programmed by Alan Miller, who is known for such 2600 sports titles as *Basketball* and *Ice Hockey*. Viewing the action from inside a tank, players shoot other tanks while dealing with various weather conditions, including fog, rain, and snow.

Roc 'N Rope (1984, ColecoVision): Like the ColecoVision rendition of *Donkey Kong*, *Roc 'N Rope* only has three out of the four arcade screens. The port doesn't control as well as the arcade obscurity it is based on (1983, Konami), but it's nevertheless a solid climbing cart that I spent quite a bit of time with during the mid-late 1980s (these days, I usually play the coin-op version via *Konami Arcade Classics* for the PlayStation).

Rush'n Attack (1987, NES): Based on the 1985 Konami Arcade game, which was called *Green Beret* in Japan and Europe, *Rush'n Attack* is one of those tough titles that gives the NES the reputation of a hardcore console. Players guide a knife-wielding soldier through six brutal stages (Iron Bridge and Missile Base, Airport, Harbor, Forest and Airshed, Warehouse, and Enemy Base), picking up extra weapons, rescuing POWs, and battling such enemies as artillerymen and machine gunners.

Rygar (1987, NES): When I first bought *Rygar* in 1987, I was disappointed that it wasn't a straightforward action title, but instead featured non-linear gameplay and RPG elements not found in Tecmo's 1986 arcade classic. However, after spending a little more time with the cart, I grew to enjoy it quite a bit.

Seaquest (1983, Atari 2600): A cartridge that many call "*Defender* under water," *Seaquest* is pure arcade-style action that is typical of the quality output from Activision. Programmed by Steve Cartwright (*Barnstorming*, *MegaMania*), the game has players guiding a submarine as it shoots sharks and other subs, along with rescuing divers and surfacing for air.

SkyKid (1987, NES): During all my years of attending video game conventions and going to retro gaming stores, I've never heard anyone talk about *SkyKid*, a terrific, but apparently underrated side-scrolling shooter for the NES. It is based on the relatively obscure Namco arcade game from 1985, adding two features to the formula: a target practice bonus round and girlfriends blowing kisses.

Smithereens! (1982, Odyssey2): I absolutely LOVE this medieval shooter, which has each player using a catapult to hurl boulders across a lake toward an opposing castle. The game is similar to *Artillery Duel*, but is not turn-based and is more simplistic (certain gamers will prefer the fast pace to the relatively slow action of *Artillery Duel*). Great fun, but it barely missed the top 100, primarily because *Artillery Duel* did it first and best.

Solar Quest (1982, Vectrex): Rotate, thrust, fire, repeat. Based on the 1981 Cinematronics arcade game, *Solar Quest* features *Asteroids*-style controls, but alters the formula by having players shoot geometrically shaped aliens while avoiding a centrally located sun (which evokes the sun in *Space Wars*).

Space Battle (1980, Intellivision): A title gaming and gambling guru Ken Uston once called a "must-own" cartridge for those who "like strategy-type games," *Space Battle* is a first-person space shooter later released under the M Network banner as *Space Attack* for the Atari 2600. The complex Intellivision controller is ideally suited for the game, featuring different buttons for Squadron, Return to Base, Go to Battle, Radar, Alien, Aim Lasers, and Fire.

Space Destroyers (1979, APF MP1000): *Space Destroyers* is an excellent *Space Invaders* clone that was the last and by far the best game released for the obscure APF MP1000 console. Although it lacks the many options of Atari 2600 *Space Invaders*, it boasts the full 55-alien regiment from the coin-op classic, plus all four bunkers.

Space Panic (1983, ColecoVision): A cartridge that barely missed the main section of this book, *Space Panic* is based on Universal's early climbing/platform arcade game (1980), which inspired such classics as *Lode Runner* and *Mr. Do!'s Castle*. The game is severely underrated in some circles (The Video Game Critic gives it a "D-", citing its "flaky controls" and "boring graphics"), but I enjoy its strategic challenges, such as dropping a row of vertically aligned monsters through several floors at once.

Spiders (1982, Arcadia 2001): A slide-and-shoot title with unusual gameplay—players fire at spiders, webbing that grows, and cocoons that randomly fall—*Spiders* is based on Sigma's 1981 arcade game and is one of the three or four best titles in the Arcadia 2001 library, barely missing the main section of this book. Those disappointed by Activision's *Spider Fighter* should hunt down this challenging and enjoyable game.

Spike (1983, Vectrex): A significant departure from the many space shooters in the Vectrex library, *Spike* is a character-based platformer with an angled perspective and voice effects: "Eek! Help, Spike!" and "Oh, no! Molly!" As I wrote in *Classic Home Video Games, 1972-1984*, players climb "a moveable ladder up and down to reach three tiers of moving catwalks, running across those catwalks, jumping across gaps, grabbing a randomly appearing key, and taking said key to the top of the screen," all the while avoiding bouncers and birds.

Squish'em featuring Sam (1984, ColecoVision): The sequel to *Sewer Sam*, this is a great climbing title upgraded from the original computer version with voice effects. Called "a fast-paced, fairly straightforward cartridge that holds up well under replay" by Arnie Katz of *Electronic Games* magazine (Sept., 1984 issue), the game, which will appeal to fans of such classics as *Beauty & the Beast* for the Intellivision and *Crazy Climber*, is one of my favorite third-party ColecoVision titles.

Star Wars: The Arcade Game (1984, Atari 5200; 1984, ColecoVision): Neither the Atari 5200 nor the ColecoVision version of this game is perfect (the controls could use some polishing), but both are impressive ports of *Star Wars*, the popular vector-based arcade game produced by Atari in 1983. The ColecoVision rendition has more spectacular explosions than the 5200 game, but both are finely programmed.

Star Wars: The Empire Strikes Back (1982, Atari 2600): Called a "gripping, challenging game that literally leaves your palms sweating" by Dan Gutman, who was managing editor of *Electronic Fun with Computers & Games* magazine (circa early 1980s), *Star Wars: The Empire Strikes Back* recreates a portion of the Hoth scene from the feature film of the same name. The side-scrolling action puts you at the helm of a snowspeeder, firing at Imperial Walkers that are making their way toward the Rebel power generator. It takes 48 hits to bring one down.

Stargate (1984, Atari 2600): A first-rate arcade adaptation (of the 1981 Williams classic) that barely missed the main section of this book, *Stargate*, re-released in 1988 as *Defender II*, fixes all the things that *Defender* for the Atari 2600 got wrong. The game takes both joysticks to control: the left controller maneuvers the ship and fires, while the right controller activates smart bombs, inviso, and hyperspace.

Starmaster (1982, Atari 2600): Similar to Atari's *Star Raiders*, but upgraded with better graphics and gameplay, Activision's *Starmaster*, created by Alan Miller (*Robot Tank*), is a space combat simulator taking you through 36 sectors. Your mission is to defend starbases while using a targeting sight to blast meteors and enemy starfighters.

Super Pro Football (1986, Intellivision): It's a shame the vast majority of Intellivision owners have never played *Super Pro Football*, an upgrading over the far more common *NFL Football* with such features as audibles, players stats, more elaborate play-calling, a view of the stadium (complete with blimp), and a one-player mode. The game was the first in the line of "Super Pro" sports titles produced by INTV Corporation.

Tapper (1984, Atari 2600; 1984, ColecoVision): Although *Tapper* for the Atari 2600 and ColecoVision are noticeable downgrades of Bally/

Midway's *Root Beer Tapper* (1984) arcade cab, the original is so strong that it nevertheless shines through. Both versions feature all four screens, as well as the bonus round.

Tarzan (1984, ColecoVision): One of the most graphically gorgeous console games released in America prior to 1985, *Tarzan* is a lush jungle adventure with solid running, jumping, climbing, punching, swinging, and swimming action. It's also one of the better original (meaning not based on an arcade or computer game) titles for the ColecoVision.

Thin Ice (1986, Intellivision): *Thin Ice* is essentially a cartoonish take on *Qix*, with players guiding a skates-wearing penguin named Duncan around the screen, creating lines as he skates. This weakens the ice, dropping other penguins (along with a seal and polar bears) into the frozen pond. *Thin Ice* was inspired by *Disco No. 1* (1982), the Data East arcade game.

Thunder Castle (1986, Intellivision): I agree with Jonathan Sutyak of the All Game Guide when he says *Thunder Castle* has "some of the best visuals ever seen on the Intellivision" and that it "has nicely drawn characters, detailed backgrounds, and creatures that move fluidly." Gamers guide a knight through three fantasy mazes (forest, castle, and dungeon), battling demons, dragons, and sorcerers.

Tower of Doom (1987, Intellivision): Called *Advanced Dungeons & Dragons Tower of Mystery* in the Mattel catalogs of 1984, the year Mattel Electronics shut down, this game remained unfinished and unreleased until INTV completed the job (the company changed the name to *Tower of Doom* to avoid licensing fees). It's a relatively complex, action-oriented RPG with 32 maze-like levels containing weapons, food, monsters, magic items, and/or traps.

Treasure Cove (1983, Astrocade): A quality third-party release for the Astrocade, *Treasure Cove* looks and sounds fantastic. Players, cast in the role of a diver, avoid turtles, fish, and other sea creatures while collecting treasure from the ocean floor and swimming to the surface to deposit it into a ship.

Tron Deadly Discs (1982, Atari 2600; 1982, Intellivision): My third favorite *Tron* game after the arcade classics *Tron* (1982) and *Discs of Tron* (1983), *Tron Deadly Discs* lets players reenact a key scene from Disney's 1982 feature film. The player, immersed in arena-based combat, hurls discs at a trio of computer-controlled warriors. The 2600 version is missing the Recognizer enemy, but both games are a lot of fun.

UFO! (1981, Odyssey2): Playing to the strengths of the Odyssey2, *UFO!* features numerous moving objects onscreen at once with no flickering. Gameplay is stellar, with arcaders piloting a battle cruiser while avoiding and shooting at simplistic, but deadly ships and flying saucers (each enemy looks like a spinning letter X). I especially like that you can fly across the screen in one direction while firing in another.

Up'n Down (1984, ColecoVision): A strong port of the 1983 Sega/Bally Midway arcade game, *Up'n Down* has players driving a Volkswagen Bug up zigzagging roads, avoiding oncoming cars and trucks while grabbing flags. Your car can also jump on top of enemy vehicles, an enjoyably destructive method previously seen in *Bump 'n' Jump*.

Vanguard (1982, Atari 2600): The Atari 5200 version of *Vanguard* is a more accurate port of the 1981 Centuri arcade game in some respects, such as graphics and sounds, but the 2600 rendition plays better thanks to superior controls. Gamers guide a spaceship through horizontal and vertical scrolling tunnels, firing up, down, right, and left at enemies while avoiding tunnel walls and other obstacles.

Venture (1982, ColecoVision): If it weren't for its dodgy diagonal controls, *Venture* would've made it into the main section of this book. It's a dazzling port of Exidy's 1981 coin-op game, in which arcaders guide a smiley-faced character named Winky through 12 dungeons, grabbing treasure and firing arrows at creatures.

Videocart-20: Video Whizball (1978, Fairchild Channel F): Obviously inspired by *Pong* (1972), but with a decidedly unique twist, *Video Whizball* is clearly the best game in the Fairchild Channel F library. Each player mans a small square in front of a goal on opposing sides of the horizontal screen, shooting at large blocks to push them across the playfield and into the opposite goal.

WarGames (1984, ColecoVision): One of the better movie-based video games of the 1980s, *WarGames* is essentially a slow, complex version of *Missile Command*, with players using ABMs, interceptor jets, satellites, and submarines to protect the U.S. from enemy missiles, planes, and subs. The action takes place across six screens representing the United States.

Winter Games (1987, Atari 2600): This eight-player game features seven fun Olympic events: Slalom (skiing), Bobsledding, the Luge, Ski Jumping, the Biathlon, Speed Skating, and Hot Dog (skating tricks). Figure Skating from the Commodore 64 version of the game is missing, but this is a tour de force for the 2600, especially in terms of colorfully detailed visuals.

Wizards & Warriors (1987, NES): A side-scrolling platformer with adventure and combat to spare, *Wizards & Warriors* weighed in at #56 on IGN's list of 100 best NES games (www.ign.com/top-100-nes-games). Players guide a Brightsword-wielding knight as he battles ghosts, goblins, werewolves, and the like and collects such items as keys, axes, cloaks, and potions. As with *Mega Man* and *Kid Icarus*, there's lots of vertical scrolling.

World Championship Baseball (1986, Intellivision): Other than a bug in the program that can occasionally crash the game (an admittedly large flaw), *World Championship Baseball* is a nice simulation of America's Pastime. It looks a lot like *Major League Baseball* and in fact uses code from that game, but it improves upon its progenitor by adding such features as a one-player mode, fly balls, and the ability to overrun bases.

Xevious (1987, Atari 7800): Programmed by Masanobu Endō, the original arcade version of *Xevious* (1982) was "the first vertical scrolling shooter to have background graphics that weren't a simple starfield" (www.hardcoregaming101.net). The Atari 7800 port is an excellent rendition, despite the expected playfield formatting to fit the television screen.

BIBLIOGRAPHY

Bissell, Tom. *Extra Lives: Why Video Games Matter.* (New York, NY: Pantheon Books, 2010).

Burnham, Van. *Supercade: A Visual History of the Videogame Age 1971-1984.* (Cambridge, MA: The MIT Press, 2001).

DeKeles, Jon C.A. *Video Game Quest.* (Northridge, CA: DMS, 1990).

Demaria, Rusel, and Johnny L. Wilson. *High Score! The Illustrated History of Electronic Games.* (Berkeley, CA: McGraw-Hill/Osborne, 2002).

Forster, Winnie. *Game Machines 1972-2012—The Encyclopedia of Consoles, Handhelds and Home Computers.* (Utting, Germany: GAMEplan Books, 2012).

Fox, Matt. *The Video Games Guide: 1,000+ Arcade, Console and Computer Games, 1962-2012, 2d ed.* (Jefferson, NC: McFarland, 2012).

Galaxy, Bill. *Collecting Classic Video Games.* (Atglen, PA: Schiffer Publishing, 2002).

Goldberg, Marti and Curt Vendel. *Atari Inc.—Business is Fun.* (Carmel, NY: Syzygy Company Press, 2012).

Herman, Leonard. *ABC to the VCS (A Directory of Software for the Atari 2600).* Second Edition. (Springfield, N.J.: Rolenta Press, 2005).

Herman, Leonard. *Phoenix: The Fall & Rise of Videogames.* Third Edition. (Springfield, NJ: Rolenta Press, 2001).

Kent, Steven L. *The Ultimate History of Video Games.* (New York: Three Rivers Press, 2001).

Kunkel, Bill. *Confessions of the Game Doctor.* (Springfield, NJ: Rolenta Press, 2005).

Loguidice, Bill, and Matt Barton. *Vintage Games: An Insider Look at the History of Grand Theft Auto, Super Mario, and the Most Influential Games of All Time.* (Burlington, MA: Focal Press, 2009).

Melissinos, Chris, and Patrick O'Rourke. *The Art of Video Games: From Pac-Man to Mass Effect.* (New York, NY: Welcome Books, 2012).

Palicia, Deborah. *Pac-Man Collectibles: An Unauthorized Guide.* (Atglen, PA: Schiffer Publishing, 2002).

Mott, Tony. *1001 Video Games You Must Play Before You Die.* (New York, NY: Universe Publishing, 2010).

Santulli, Joe (editor in chief). *Digital Press Classic Video Games Collector's Guide.* Advance Edition. (Pompton Lakes, NJ: Digital Press, 2004).

Sheff, David. *Game Over.* (New York, NY: Random House, 1993).

Weiss, Brett. *Classic Home Video Games, 1972-1984: A Complete Reference Guide.* (Jefferson, NC: McFarland, 2007).

Weiss, Brett. *Classic Home Video Games, 1985-1988: A Complete Reference Guide.* (Jefferson, NC: McFarland, 2009).

Weiss, Brett. *Classic Home Video Games, 1989-1990: A Complete Guide to Sega Genesis, Neo Geo and TurboGrafx-16 Games.* (Jefferson, NC: McFarland, 2011).

Wicker, Robert P., and Jason W. Brassard. *Classic 80s Home Video Games.* (Paducah, KY.: Collector Books, 2008).

WEBSITES:

AtariAge (www.atariage.com)
Brett Weiss: Words of Wonder (www.brettweisswords.com)
Digital Press (www.digitpress.com)
GameFAQS (www.gamefaqs.com)
GameSpot (www.gamespot.com)
Intellivision Lives (www.intellivisionlives.com)
International Arcade Museum, The (www.arcade-museum.com)
J2 Games (www.j2games.com)
Nintendo Age (www.nintendoage.com)
replacementdocs (www.replacementdocs.com)
2600 Connection (www.2600connection.com)
Video Game Critic, The (videogamecritic.com)

INDEX

Activision Anthology, 89, 109, 124, 171, 173, 182, 202
Activision Classics, 89, 109, 124, 171, 182, 202
Activision Hits: Remixed, 171, 173, 182, 202
Advanced Dungeons & Dragons Tower of Mystery, 234
Adventure, 8-10, 78, 130, 140, 231
Adventure II, 10
Air-Sea Battle, 11, 12, 89, 124
Alex Kidd in Miracle World, 219, 230
Alien, 6, 119
Alien Invaders, 197
Alpine Skiing! 215
Amidar, 163, 176
Angry Birds, 18
Animal Crossing, 133
Antarctic Adventure, 13
Anteater, 232
Anti-Aircraft, 12
Arcade Classic No. 1: Asteroids/Missile Command, 144
Arcade Classic No. 3: Galaga/Galaxian, 99
Arcade Classics, 144
Arcade's Greatest Hits: The Atari Collection 1, 144, 206
Arcade's Greatest Hits: The Midway Collection 2, 146
Arkanoid, 15-16, 206
Arkanoid: Doh it Again, 16
Arkanoid DS, 16
Arkanoid Live! 16
Arkanoid Plus, 16
Arkanoid Returns, 16
Arkanoid: Revenge of Doh, 16
Armor Ambush, 56
Armor Battle, 56
Artillery, 18
Artillery Duel, 17, 18, 233
Ashura, 179
Asteroids, 6, 15, 19-21, 55, 60, 140-141, 154, 164, 185, 189, 193, 202
Asteroids Deluxe, 19-20, 59
Asteroids Hyper 64, 19
Astroblast, 230
Astrosmash, 230
Atari Anniversary Edition, 221
Atari Anniversary Edition Redux, 221
Atari Anthology, 10, 12, 21, 54, 56, 69, 221, 227
Atari Classics: Evolved, 10, 12, 54, 56, 69, 227
Atlantis, 22-24, 29, 63
Atlantis II, 24
Attack of the Timelord!, 25-26
Attack of the Zolgear, 96
Avalanche, 123-124
Baby Pac-Man, 157
Ballblazer, 230
Balloon Fight, 27-28, 117
Balloon Fight-e, 28
Balloon Kid, 28
Barnstorming, 233
Baseball! 26
Baseball Stars, 160
Basketball, 233
Battlezone, 230, 233
Beamrider, 225, 230
Beauty & the Beast, 29-30, 66, 233
Bedlam, 230
Beef Drop, 41
Beef Drop VE, 41
Berzerk, 31-32, 84, 90-91, 110-111, 183, 193, 217
Blasteroids, 19-20
Blockout!/Breakdown! 16
Blue Lightning, 58
Bomberman, 33

Boulder Dash, 33-34
Boulder Dash EX, 34
Boulder Dash-XL, 34
Boulder Dash-XL 3D, 34
Bounty Bob Strikes Back, 35-36, 66, 139
Bowling, 159-160
Bowling!/Basketball!, 25, 159, 215
Boxing, 6, 160, 201
Breakaway, 16
Breakout, 15-16, 53, 205-206, 220-221
Bridge, 124
B-17 Bomber, 230
Buck Rogers: Planet of Zoom, 229, 232
Bump 'n' Jump, 14, 37-38, 175, 211, 234
BurgerTime, 37, 39, 40-41, 65-67, 84, 150
BurgerTime Deluxe, 41
BurgerTime World Tour, 41
Burnin' Rubber, 38
Burnout, 14, 211
Call of Duty, 195
Candyman, 232
Car Wars, 69
Carnival, 22, 42-43
Castle Crisis, 221
Castlevania, 44-45, 100, 102, 157
Castlevania II: Simon's Quest, 45
Castlevania III: Dracula's Curse, 45
Castlevania: Bloodlines, 45
Castlevania: Lords of Shadow—Mirror of Fate, 45
Castlevania: Symphony of the Night, 45
Cat N Mouse, 47
Cat Trax, 46, 47
Centipede, 19, 20, 48-50, 59, 75, 84, 87, 121, 126, 154, 189-190, 217, 224-225, 232
Centipede: Infestation, 50
Championship Bowling, 159
Championship Sprint, 113
Chase, 183
Chase the Chuck Wagon, 215
Choplifter!, 51-52, 230
Choplifter II, 52
Choplifter III, 52
Choplifter HD, 52
Chopper Command, 61, 201, 230
Chuck Norris Superkicks, 18
Circus, 54
Circus Atari, 53-54, 230
Clean Sweep, 215
Clowns, 54
Clowns/Brickyard, 16, 54
Combat, 11, 12, 55-56, 87, 89, 171, 219, 231
Combat 2, 56
Combat Two, 56
Commando, 178-179, 230
Communist Mutants from Space, 57-58, 78, 230-231
Computer Gin, 67
Congo Bongo, 66, 229
Contra, 104, 134
Cosmic Ark, 23, 63
Cosmic Avenger, 82, 102, 185
Cosmic Commuter, 109
Crash Bandicoot, 209
Crazy Climber, 29, 233
Crazy Gobbler, 46
Crystal Castles, 84
Crystal Mines, 34
Crystal Mines II, 34
Cubicolor, 63

Daleks, 32
Data East Arcade Classics, 231
Deadly Dogs, 65
Defender, 32, 52, 59-61, 81-82, 110, 183, 185-186, 217, 230, 233
Defender II, 61
Defender 2000, 61
Demon Attack, 58, 62-63, 86-87, 140, 165-166, 232
Demon's Crest, 101
Demons to Diamonds, 205
Destructor, 211
Devil May Cry, 102
Dig Dug, 27, 34, 63-65, 149-150, 152
Dig Dug II, 65
Dig Dug II: Trouble in Paradise, 65
Dig Dug Arrangement, 65
Dig Dug Deeper, 65
Dig Dug: Digging Strike, 65
Diner, 41, 66-67
Disco No. 1, 234
Discs of Tron, 234
DK Jungle Climber, 76
DK King of Swing, 76
Do! Run Run, 151, 153
Dodge 'Em, 68-69, 88, 157
Donkey Kong, 21, 28, 29-30, 32, 70-76, 91, 130, 132-133, 138-139, 141, 147, 152-153, 161, 167-168, 174-175, 208, 231, 233
Donkey Kong 3, 6, 74-76, 132
Donkey Kong 3-e, 76
Donkey Kong 64, 76
Donkey Kong Classics, 71, 74
Donkey Kong Country, 76
Donkey Kong Country 2: Diddy Kong's Quest, 76
Donkey Kong Country 3: Dixie Kong's Double Trouble!, 76
Donkey Kong Country Returns, 76
Donkey Kong Country Returns 3D, 76
Donkey Kong Country: Tropical Freeze, 76
Donkey Kong Jr., 71, 73, 74
Donkey Kong Jr. Math, 74-75
Donkey Kong Jungle Beat, 76
Donkey Kong Junior, 73-75, 132, 150
Donkey Kong Land, 76
Donkey Kong Land 2, 76
Donkey Kong Land III, 76
DOOM, 32, 195
Double Dribble, 102, 160, 230
Dragonfire, 230
DragonStomper, 57, 77-78
Dragster, 88
The Dreadnaught Factor, 224-225, 230
Duck Hunt, 101
The Dukes of Hazzard, 211
Eagle, 58
Enduro, 23, 230
Entombed, 230
Epic Adventure, 10
Escape from the MindMaster, 79-80
E.T. The Extra-Terrestrial, 107, 118, 203, 226
Excitebike, 230
Fantasy Zone, 52, 81-83
Fantasy Zone II, 52, 81-83
Fantasy Zone Gear, 83
Fantasy Zone: The Maze, 83
Fast Eddie, 213
Fast Food, 84
Fatal Fury, 145
Fathom, 29, 63, 230
F-18 Hornet, 109
Final Fantasy, 8, 232
Fireball, 230
Fishing Derby, 88, 230

Flicky, 83
The Flintstones: BurgerTime in Bedrock, 41
Flipper Slipper, 16
Food Fight, 84, 85
Fortress of Narzod, 86-87, 233
Fortune Builder, 230
Forza Motorsport 4, 112
Frankenstein's Monster, 230
Freedom Fighters!, 26
Freeway, 88-89
Frenzy, 6, 32, 84, 87, 90-91
Frog Bog, 231
Frogger, 18, 88-89, 92-94, 213, 217, 230-231
Frogger II: Threeedeep!, 94, 230
Frogger 3D, 94
Frogger: Ancient Shadow, 94
Frogger Beyond, 94
Frogger Returns, 94
Frogs and Flies, 231
Front Line, 178, 230
Frostbite, 231
Funky Fish, 47
Gaiares, 104
Galactic Invasion, 98-99
Galactic Protector, 83
Galaga, 26, 58, 75, 86, 95-96, 98-99, 150, 175, 191, 195
Galaga 3, 96, 99
Galaga '88, 96, 99
Galaga '90, 96
Galaga: Demons of Death, 95
Galaga: Destination Earth, 96
Galaga Legions, 96
Galaxian, 58, 63, 96-99, 164-165, 195
Galaxian 3, 99
Gaplus, 96, 99
Gargoyle's Quest, 101
Gargoyle's Quest II, 101
Gauntlet, 19, 231
Ghosts 'n Goblins, 100-101
Ghouls 'n Ghosts, 101
Gorf, 71, 75, 87, 91, 231
Gotcha, 68
Gradius, 102-104, 185
Gradius III, 104
Gradius III and IV, 104
Gradius V, 104
Gradius Collection, 104
Gradius Gaiden, 104
Gran Turismo, 14, 211
Gran Turismo 6, 112
Green Beret, 233
Greenhouse, 76
Gremlins, 105, 178
Gremlins Gizmo, 107
Guerilla War, 179
Gun Fight, 15, 205, 231
Gunfight, 231
Gyruss, 98, 150
Halo, 195
Hangman, 196
Happy Trails, 231
Hardball, 201
Haunted House, 44, 231
Head On, 2, 68-69, 157
The Heist, 231
H.E.R.O., 108-109
Hogan's Alley, 101
Horror Maze, 217
Ice Climber, 231
Ice Hockey, 231, 233

237

Ikari Warriors, 178
Ikaruga, 181
The Incredible Wizard, 110-111
Indy 4, 113
Indy 500, 112-113
Indy 800, 113
Invaders from Hyperspace!, 26
Intellivision Classics, 188
Intellivision Lives!, 188
It's Only Rock 'n' Roll, 17
James Bond 007, 146, 199
Jawbreaker, 84, 114-115, 119
Jawbreaker II, 115
Joust, 27, 28, 54, 116-117, 133, 150, 175
Joust Pinball, 117
Joust 2: Survival of the Fittest, 117
Jr. Pac-Man, 47, 118-119, 157
Jump Bug, 145
Jumpman, 231
Jumpman Junior, 174, 231
Jungle Hunt, 169, 231
Kaboom!, 12, 53, 109, 123-124, 220
Kangaroo, 161, 231
K.C. Munchkin!, 6, 27, 46, 120-122, 162, 168
K.C.'s Krazy Chase!, 6, 26, 120-122, 140
Keystone Kapers, 231-232
Kid Icarus, 136, 234
Kid Niki: Radical Ninja, 231
Killer Bees!, 6, 27, 125-126, 215
King of Fighters, 145
Konami Arcade Classics, 186, 233
Konami Classics Series: Arcade Hits, 186, 217
Konami Collector's Series: Arcade Advanced, 186
Lady Bug, 42, 46, 47, 97, 119-120, 127-129, 148-150, 156, 161-163, 217
The Legend of Zelda, 8, 64, 74, 100, 106, 119, 129-131, 136, 157, 175, 209, 231
The Legend of Zelda: A Link Between Two Worlds, 131
The Legend of Zelda: A Link to the Past, 131
The Legend of Zelda: Ocarina of Time, 131
The Legend of Zelda: Skyward Sword, 131
The Legend of Zelda: Twilight Princess, 131
Life Force, 104
Link: The Faces of Evil, 131
Lock 'N' Chase, 119-120, 127, 148, 231
Loco-Motion, 231
Lode Runner, 139, 231, 233
Looping, 231
Lunar Lander, 20
Major League Baseball, 234
Make Trax, 217
Mario & Luigi: Superstar Saga, 133
Mario Bros., 28, 54, 74, 132-133, 208
Mario Clash, 133
Masters of the Universe: The Power of He-Man, 67
Maximo: Ghosts to Glory, 101
Maximo vs. Army of Zin, 101
Maze Craze: A Game of Cops'n Robbers, 9, 196, 231
Medieval Mayhem, 220
Mega Man, 134-135, 157, 234
Mega Man 2, 135
Mega Man Anniversary Collection, 134
MegaMania, 109, 231-233
Metal Gear, 14
Metal Gear Solid, 14
Metroid, 27, 64, 74, 100, 119, 136-137, 157, 175
Metroid II: Return of Samus, 137
Metroid Fusion, 137
Metroid: Other M, 137
Metroid Prime, 136-137
Metroid Prime Pinball, 137

Metroid: Zero Mission, 137
Midway Arcade Treasures, 199
Midway Arcade Treasures 2, 111
Midway's Greatest Arcade Hits: Vol. 1, 199
Mike Tyson's Punch-Out!!, 231
Millipede, 50, 232
Miner 2049er, 29, 35-36, 138-139, 153, 174, 228, 231
Miner 2049er II, 139
MineStorm, 140-141, 233
MineStorm II, 140-141
Missile Command, 22, 62, 142-144, 155, 224-226, 234
Missile Command II, 144
Missile Command 3D, 144
Missile Defense 3-D, 219, 232
Monaco GP, 210
Montezuma's Revenge, 232
Moon Cresta, 62
Moon Patrol, 145-146, 150
Moonsweeper, 232
Mountain King, 232
Mouse Trap, 42, 46-47, 70-71, 119-121, 127, 147-149, 156, 163, 212
Mr. Do!, 27, 34, 128-129, 149-151, 153, 217
Mr. Do! Vs. Unicorns, 152
Mr. Do!'s Castle, 40, 139, 151-153, 233
Mr. Do's Wild Ride, 151, 153
Ms. Candyman, 232
Ms. Pac-Man, 47, 84, 95, 118-119, 121, 150, 154-158, 161
Ms. Pac-Man: Maze Madness, 155
Ms. Pac-Man/Galaga: Class of 1981, 155
Muncher, 232
Namco Classic Collection Vol. 2, 65
Namco Museum 64, 96
Namco Museum: Virtual Arcade, 96
NBA Jam, 212-213, 230
NBA Street, 230
NBA 2K9, 230
Nemesis, 104
Neo Mr. Do!, 151
New Dig Dug, 65
New Super Mario Bros. U, 209
NFL Blitz, 212
NFL Football, 233
Night Driver, 53, 62, 205, 210, 232
Nightmare, 85
Nimble Numbers Ned!, 126
Nova Blast, 30, 61
The Official Frogger, 57, 78, 92-93, 94
Oil's Well, 232
Oink, 53
Omega Race, 87, 189
One-on-One, 34
Out Run, 210, 232
Outlaw, 200, 231
Pac & Pal, 157
Pac-Land, 157
Pac-Man, 27, 36, 46-47, 55, 68, 74, 84, 92, 99, 110-111, 114-115, 118-122, 127, 129, 138-139, 147, 149, 152, 154-159, 161-165, 168, 171, 191, 195, 214, 216-217, 228
Pac-Man Battle Royale, 157
Pac-Man Championship Edition, 96
Pac-Man Championship Edition DX, 157
Pac-Man Plus, 157
Pac-Man VR, 157
Pac-Man World Rally, 157
Pac-Man World 20th Anniversary, 157
Pac-Mania, 157
Pakkuman, 157
Parodius, 104
PBA Bowling, 158-159
Pengo, 160-162

Penguin Adventure, 14
Pepper II, 161-163, 176, 217
Peter Pepper's Ice Cream Factory, 41, 66
Phaser Patrol, 219, 232
Phoenix, 58, 62, 86, 98, 164-166, 195, 230
Pick Axe Pete!, 167-168, 231
Pinball Challenge, 196
The Pit, 34
Pitfall!, 97, 109, 118, 140, 169-172, 195, 219, 230-231
Pitfall II: Lost Caverns, 53, 171-173
Pitfall 3D: Beyond the Jungle, 171
Pitfall: Beyond the Jungle, 171
Pitfall: The Big Adventure, 171
Pitfall: The Mayan Adventure, 171
Pitstop, 211, 232
Plaque Attack, 232
Pleiades, 47, 166
Pole Position, 14, 38, 150, 210-211, 232
Pong, 11, 15, 84, 195, 218-221, 231, 234
Pong Sports, 218
Popeye, 28-29, 74, 93, 150, 174-175, 214
Popeye 2, 175
Popeye: Rush for Spinach, 175
Power Lords, 215
Power Racer, 69
Pressure Cooker, 232
Prince of Persia, 169
Pro Football, 196
Professor Pac-Man, 157
P.T. Barnum's Acrobats, 54, 215
Puck Man, 157
Punch-Out!!, 231
Q*bert, 93, 150, 191-192, 214, 231-232
Q*bert 3, 232
Qix, 163, 176-177, 234
Qix II: Tournament, 177
Qix Neo, 177
Qix++, 177
Quadrapong, 218, 220
Quantum, 85
Quest: Fantasy Challenge, 151
Quick Step, 232
Racing Pak, 113
Rad Racer, 211, 232
Rad Racer II, 232
Radarscope, 98
Rage Racer, 14
Raid on Bungling Bay, 232
Raiden IV, 181
Raiders of the Lost Ark, 171, 203, 226
Rally-X, 215
Rambo, 180
Rambo: First Blood Part II, 178-180
Rambo III, 179
RealSports Baseball, 232
Rescue on Fractalus, 232
Resident Evil 2, 102
Ribbit, 94
Rip Off, 185, 203, 233
River Raid, 180-182, 231
River Raid II, 182
Robot Tank, 230, 233
Robotron 64, 184
Robotron: 2084, 59, 183-184, 190, 193-194
Robotron X, 184
Robots, 32
Roc 'N Rope, 233
Rockman, 135
Root Beer Tapper, 234
R-Type, 52, 102, 185

Rush'n Attack, 102, 233
Rygar, 233
Samurai Shodown, 145
Satan's Hollow, 86
Scramble, 82, 102, 104, 181, 185-186, 233
Seaquest, 232-233
Secret Command, 179
Sega Classics Collection, 82
Sega Genesis Collection, 229
Sewer Sam, 91, 233
Shark Attack, 119
Shark! Shark!, 187-188
Showdown in 2100 A.D., 167
SimCity, 230, 232
Sir Lancelot, 117
Sir Lancelot/Robin Hood, 18
Sky Jinks, 201
SkyKid, 233
Slither, 189-190
Slot Racers, 8, 9
Smash T.V., 183, 212
Smithereens!, 18, 233
Sneakers, 213
Solar Fox, 191-192
Solar Quest, 185, 233
Sonic the Hedgehog, 169, 209
Sonic's Ultimate Genesis Collection, 83
Space Armada, 197
Space Attack, 233
Space Battle, 233
Space Destroyers, 197, 233
Space Duel, 19
Space Dungeon, 183, 193-194
Space Fantasy Zone, 83
Space Fury, 91
Space Harrier, 83
Space Invaders, 6, 15, 19-20, 22, 55, 58, 60, 63, 84, 86-87, 96-98, 117, 164-166, 195-197, 230-233
Space Invaders II, 197
Space Invaders Collection, 197
Space Invaders Extreme, 197
Space Invaders Infinity Gene, 197
Space Invaders '91, 197
Space Invaders Part II, 197
Space Invaders Revolution, 197
Space Invaders XL, 197
Space Panic, 40, 139, 152-153, 233
Space Patrol, 146
Space Race, 89
Space Vultures, 166
Space War, 60
Space Wars, 233
Spacewar, 20
Speed Freak, 210
Speedway!/Spin-Out!/Crypto-Logic!, 26
Spider Fighter, 233
Spiders, 233
Spike, 233
Sprint One, 113
Sprint 2, 113
Sprint 4, 113
Sprint 8, 113
Sprintmaster, 113
Spy Hunter, 198-199
Spy Hunter II, 199
Spy Hunter: Nowhere to Run, 199
Squish'em featuring Sam, 91, 233
Stampede, 200-202
Star Castle, 202-204
Star Fortress, 204

Star Raiders, 69, 232-233
Star Ship, 201
Star Strike, 187
Star Trek, 150
Star Trek: Strategic Operations Simulator, 229
Star Voyager, 232
Star Wars, 233
Star Wars: The Arcade Game, 232-233
Star Wars: The Empire Strikes Back, 233
Stargate, 61
Starmaster, 232-233
Stella Gets a New Brain, 57, 78, 94
Stellar Track, 77
Street Fighter, 134, 145
Street Racer, 124
Subroc, 23
Summer Games, 218
Super Asteroids, 144
Super Asteroids and Missile Command, 144
Super Breakout, 12, 16, 53, 204-206, 220, 230
Super BurgerTime, 41, 66
Super Castlevania IV, 45
Super Centipede, 144
Super Cobra, 82, 102, 214
Super Demon Attack, 63
Super Fantasy Zone, 83
Super Ghouls 'n Ghosts, 101
Super Mario Advance, 133
Super Mario All-Stars, 133, 209
Super Mario Bros., 6, 44, 97, 101, 119, 130, 132-133, 154, 169, 175, 195, 207-209, 219, 230-231
Super Mario Bros. 2, 209
Super Mario Bros. 3, 133, 209
Super Mario Galaxy, 209
Super Mario Kart, 157
Super Mario 64, 195, 209
Super Mario World, 209
Super Metroid, 136-137
Super Missile Attack, 155
Super Missile Command, 144
Super Pac-Man, 150, 157
Super Pitfall, 171
Super Pro Football, 67, 233
Super Punch-Out!!, 231
Super Qix, 177
Super Smash Bros. Melee, 76
Super Sprint, 113
Super Spy Hunter, 199
Super Zaxxon, 229
Superman, 6
Swordquest, 10
Taito Legends, 166
Taito Legends 2, 177
Taito Legends Power-Up Collection, 194
Tank, 56
Tank Plus, 56
Tapper, 84, 234
Target Fun, 12
Tarzan, 234
Tecmo Bowl, 160
Tempest, 53, 69, 222-223, 230
Tetris, 15
Thin Ice, 177, 234
3D Bowling, 159
3D MineStorm, 141
3D Missile Command, 144
3D Tic-Tac-Toe, 181
Threshold, 165
Thunder Castle, 234

Thunderball!, 25
ThunderForce II, 104
Time Pilot, 150
Tomarc the Barbarian, 17-18
Tomarc the Barbarian/Motocross Racer, 18
Tomb Raider, 8
TomyTronic Scramble, 186
Total Carnage, 183
Tournament Arkanoid, 16
Tower of Doom, 67, 234
Track & Field, 102
Treasure Cove, 234
Tron, 234
Tron Deadly Discs, 65, 188, 234
Tropical Trouble, 30
Turbo, 14, 161, 209-211, 232
Turmoil, 212-213
Turpin, 214
Turtles, 214-215
Turtles!, 25, 214-215
Tutankham, 34, 93, 216-217
Twin Qix, 177
TwinBee, 81
Type & Tell!, 126
UFO!, 168, 234
Ultimate Ghosts 'n Goblins, 101
Ultimate Qix, 177
UniWar S, 146
Up'n Down, 234
Utopia, 6
Vanguard, 234
Venture, 91, 193-194, 211, 216-217, 219, 234
Victory, 189
Video Chess, 201
Video Olympics, 12, 218-219
Videocart-20: Video Whizball, 9, 234
Viewtiful Joe, 102
Virtual Missile Command, 144
War of Nerves!, 167-168
War Room, 126
WarGames, 189, 234
Warlords, 69, 218-221
Web Warp, 223
Web Wars, 222-223, 233
Wii Sports, 159
Williams Arcade Classics, 184
Williams Arcade's Greatest Hits, 117, 184
Winter Games, 218, 234
Wizard of Wor, 110-111
Wizards & Warriors, 234
Wolfenstein 3D, 32
World Championship Baseball, 234
World Championship Football, 67
Worm War I, 6
Worm Whomper, 66, 224-225
Xevious, 102, 175, 234
Yars' Revenge, 203, 226-227
Zaxxon, 86, 98, 138, 161, 228-229
Zaxxon 3-D, 52, 229
Zaxxon's Motherbase 2000, 229
Zelda: The Wand of Gamelon, 131
Zelda II: The Adventure of Link, 130-131
Zelda's Adventure, 131